P9-DXD-419

After Occupy

After Occupy

Economic Democracy for the 21st Century

Tom Malleson

OXFORD
UNIVERSITY PRESS

Oxford University Press is a department of the University of Oxford.
It furthers the University's objective of excellence in research, scholarship,
and education by publishing worldwide.

Oxford   New York
Auckland   Cape Town   Dar es Salaam   Hong Kong   Karachi
Kuala Lumpur   Madrid   Melbourne   Mexico City   Nairobi
New Delhi   Shanghai   Taipei   Toronto

With offices in
Argentina   Austria   Brazil   Chile   Czech Republic   France   Greece
Guatemala   Hungary   Italy   Japan   Poland   Portugal   Singapore
South Korea   Switzerland   Thailand   Turkey   Ukraine   Vietnam

Oxford is a registered trademark of Oxford University Press
in the UK and certain other countries.

Published in the United States of America by
Oxford University Press
198 Madison Avenue, New York, NY 10016

© Oxford University Press 2014

Library of Congress Cataloging-in-Publication Data
Malleson, Tom.
After Occupy : economic democracy for the 21st century / Tom Malleson.
    pages cm
Includes bibliographical references and index.
ISBN 978–0–19–933010–2 (hardcover : alk. paper)   1. Democracy—Economic aspects.
2. Equality—Economic aspects.   3. Socialism—Economic aspects.   I. Title.
JC423.M296 2014
330—dc23

9 8 7 6 5 4 3 2 1
Printed in the United States of America
on acid-free paper

This book is dedicated to my grandfather, Maurice Millner (1912–2005)
AMANDLA NGAWETHU!

Power to the People!

Protest slogan

The task for a modern industrial society is to achieve what is now technically realizable, namely, a society which is really based on free voluntary participation of people who produce and create, live their lives freely within institutions they control, and with limited hierarchical structures, possibly none at all.

Noam Chomsky
(quoted in Albert & Hahnel, 1991, p. 13)

Contents

Acknowledgments   *ix*

Introduction   *xi*

1. Economic Democracy: Beginning Orientations   1

Part One Workplaces

2. Should Workplaces be Democratized?   27
3. Worker Cooperatives in Practice   54

Part Two The Market System

4. Democracy and the Market System   93
5. Democratizing the Market System   112

Part Three Finance and Investment

6. Should Finance and Investment be Democratized?   137
7. Finance and Investment Democracy in Practice: Capital Controls, Public Banks, and Participatory Budgeting   169

Conclusion: Toward a Feasible Socialism for the 21st Century   198

Notes   *219*

Bibliography   *241*

Index   *267*

Acknowledgments

No person is an island and no project has a sole author. This book would not have existed were it not for the confluence of friends, family, and colleagues who supported and guided me along the way. I share Montesquieu's sentiment that in completing this work I have simply tried to make a bouquet of other people's flowers and have provided little myself but the string with which to bind them. I would like to acknowledge parts of that bouquet here.

I am grateful to Bruce Baum as well as Richard Sandbrook and Gustavo Indart who first encouraged my interest in this area of study. I have benefited enormously from endless hours of discussion and debate with my friends, including Jeff Carolin, Daniel Cohen, Juliette Daigre, Martin Danyluk, Gary Dunion, Nassim Elbardouh, Emma Hughes, David Lizoain (my most reliable critic), Devon Lougheed, Jess Neligan, Jonah Peranson, Seth Prins, Adam Ramsay, Robert Tarantino, David Wachsmuth, and Alex Wood.

I would also like to thank my dissertation committee: J. J. McMurtry, Margaret (Peggy) Kohn, Simone Chambers, and Joe Carens for their wonderful support and guidance. In particular, my supervisor, Joe Carens, has been a constant source of sympathetic critique as well as an intellectual mentor. The influence of his thought is visible on every page.

Thanks to David Schweickart, Thad Williamson, and particularly Erik Olin Wright, who have not only provided the intellectual inspiration for my work, but who have been incredibly generous with their time and feedback; this work would undoubtedly have been much the worse without their aid and enthusiasm.

Many thanks to the staff at OUP and especially Angela Chnapko for guiding me through the publication process and her kind enthusiasm for this project.

Thanks as well to my family—Roey, Sarah, and Pete—for their unwavering encouragement. I would also like to acknowledge my grandparents, Maurice and Pat Millner, whose influence is constantly with me.

My debts to you all are enormous.

This work, and indeed my life, has been molded, shaped, and inspired by the women and men who constitute the struggles for social justice. The anti-authoritarian activists and organizers of every sort—the writers, thinkers, protesters, agitators, and community builders—thank you!

T.M.

Introduction

These days it is easy to be cynical about democracy. Skeptics point to low levels of turnout in national elections, the degree to which money corrupts the process, the difficulties of mass participation in large and complex systems, the lack of opportunities for participation at local levels, as well as the informal hierarchies that emerge in even the most democratic of organizations. But despite this skepticism, one fact emerges as practically indisputable: almost all people, in every corner of the globe, prefer democracy to the lack of it. Since 1900, the number of political democracies (i.e., countries with multiple competing parties and universal suffrage) has exploded: from 0 to 22 by mid-century to 119 by the year 2002 (Warren, 2002). The recent wave of protest for democratization in the Arab Spring reminds us that it is likely that this trend will continue.

Facts like this should remind us that for all its limitations, democracy is hugely important. In 1994, millions of black people in South Africa formed huge lines waiting in the rain and shine for up to three days to cast their votes for the first time in their lives. It was the culmination of a struggle that the African National Congress and others had been fighting for over 80 years.[1] In 2010, millions of Egyptians took to the streets, occupying Tahrir square, risking jail, mistreatment, and even torture, in a defiant call for democracy that finally brought down a dictatorship of 30 years. Of course, these people had heard all the reasons why some are skeptical about democracy; they were as familiar as could be with anti-democratic attitudes and arguments. But their actions spoke louder than words that, notwithstanding its limitations, democracy is worth fighting for.

Why is it exactly that over the last 150 years so many people, from England to Egypt, have risked life and limb struggling for democracy? On the one hand, a central motivation is that democracy provides basic formal equality. It gives all adults, regardless of status or stature, poor as much as rich, blacks as much as whites, a formally equal say in the structuring of their laws, which is why it is incompatible with systems like apartheid. Additionally, people fight for democracy because of the basic civil liberties that it provides. For democracy to work, citizens must be able to talk freely, to meet and form groups, to criticize the government, and so on—so political democracy and basic rights (free speech, free assembly, freedom of conscience, etc.) go hand-in-hand (Bobbio, 1987). In a more general sense, and one that we will refer back to frequently, democracy provides two essential kinds of freedom: accountability and self-determination. Accountability is what prevents the government from acting in secret or throwing dissenters in jail. It forces the government to pay attention to the needs of the people—which is why democratic states never have famines (Sen, 1999). Moreover, democracy provides the freedom of self-determination, allowing the population to collectively map out their basic priorities for the future. This is why the democratic drive to decide one's future oneself goes hand-in-hand with struggles to overthrow outside or elite interference, be it colonialism, racial domination, military dictatorship, aristocratic privilege, or any other force that prevents popular self-determination.

In other words, one of the main reasons that people in the West are skeptical about democracy is simply that they have forgotten how terrible the alternative is. But there is a second, more justifiable, reason for skepticism, which is that democracy in practice has to a large extent betrayed its promise of real equality. A large part of the appeal of a democratic society is the promise of equality, the idea that all will be able to equally partake and participate in social life. Aristotle articulated the hope in the power of democracy like this: "For if indeed freedom and equality are most of all present in a democracy, as some people suppose, this would be most true in the constitution in which everyone participates in the most similar way" (trans. 1998, 1291b34). However, Western states have now had political democracy for a hundred years, yet the expectation that this would lead to deep, substantive equality has nowhere been realized. Not even close. To take one example, the United States has had universal suffrage (at least among whites) for over 90 years, yet Bill Gates has sufficient wealth to employ 2.2 million of his fellow citizens.[2] To update Tocqueville ([1835] 1945, Vol. 1, chap. 2), it might be said that although the surface of American society is covered with a layer of democratic paint, one can still see, particularly in the economy, the old oligarchic colors breaking through.

So as democratic societies have evolved it is not surprising that feelings of skepticism and disillusion have accompanied this disjuncture between democracy in theory and inequality in fact—resulting in widespread political apathy. With this in mind I want to suggest one intriguing possibility: it is not quite right to say that democracy has failed in its egalitarian objectives, *since it has not yet been comprehensively tried*. A genuinely democratic society cannot quarantine democracy in its political structures; democracy must spread beyond formal political structures into the economy itself, since it is the economy that is the root of much social inequality.[3] As I argue in this book, only when political democracy evolves to include economic democracy will our societies have any chance of establishing meaningful equality for all.

While struggles for political democracy were a central issue for much of the 19th and 20th centuries, I suspect that the 21st century will witness similar struggles, but this time for *economic* democracy. This is not to say that economic democracy is any kind of utopian vision—as we will see, democratizing the economy contains many of the same limitations and constraints as political democracy. Yet for all that, it is still much better to have it than to not have it. At the end of the day it likewise offers the promise of real concrete improvements for the population at large.

The Democratic Paradox

Societies in the West are fervent about their democratic credentials. Our politicians give speeches extolling the virtues of democracy; our self-conception of being citizens in a democratic state is deeply ingrained in our identity. And yet, despite this, a central part of society, the economy, has very little democracy in it at all. Workers do not elect the managers of their firms. Bankers do not allocate finance with any accountability to the communities in which they operate. Investment decisions are not made with any participation of the citizenry. It is like we have erected a wall down the middle of society, and said that in this half, the economy, there is no need for democracy, while at the same time insisting on calling society as a whole "democratic." So we must ask ourselves: is this acceptable?

Another way to see this paradox is to recall that a fundamental democratic principle is that public power should be accountable to those who are affected by it (i.e., the public). This is a basic safeguard against tyranny and one of the most fundamental rationales for having democracy at all. Yet in a variety of ways, managers, employers, investors, and financiers clearly exercise power too. Their decisions have massive social and public consequences—from a manager's decision to lay off a thousand workers, to a corporate decision to invest in dangerous deep sea oil extraction, to bankers' decisions to provide risky subprime mortgages and resell them as complex debt instruments—these decisions have undeniable public consequences. Yet in stark contrast to our political system we do not demand that these people be accountable to those affected in any standard democratic way. How is this justifiable?

These are thus the central questions that motivate this study: Does a commitment to democracy in the political realm, which we all share, imply that we should be open to expanding it into the economy? Can we truthfully call ourselves democrats while at the same time maintaining an economy along standard capitalist lines?

The Argument

The central goal of this book is to place the economy under a democratic microscope. In other words, the task is to ask whether an expansion of democracy into the economy is indeed desirable. In doing so, we will investigate both the theory and practice of economic democracy. The book will look at the economy in three parts—workplaces, the market, and finance/investment—because these areas constitute the cornerstones of the economy. Workplaces, as well as finance and investment institutions, are the main loci of economic influence and power, and the market ties them all together. For each of these three parts, one chapter investigates the normative and theoretical side of the question: Should this aspect of the economy be democratized? Would the pros of doing so outweigh the cons? And one chapter investigates the practical and empirical side of the question: Do the democratic alternatives work well in practice? Do their benefits outweigh their costs? How could transition plausibly occur from the institutions that exist today to more democratic institutions that might exist tomorrow?

In a nutshell the basic argument is the following: Within capitalist societies in the West today, there are extremely unequal amounts of wealth. This unequal wealth is translated through several main mechanisms into unequal access to decision-making power. Those with substantial wealth have influence in many ways, but their wealth is translated into socially relevant power (i.e., sustained relationships of power over other people) in three main areas.

(i) Workplaces—in these associations, the power of owners and managers to organize work directly affects the freedom of the internal workers.
(ii) Finance—the power of financiers to provide/restrict credit makes the economy grow or falter in ways that directly affect the freedom of the nation's citizens.
(iii) Investment—the power of businesses to invest/divest likewise causes the economy to grow or falter in ways that directly affect the freedom of the nation's citizens.

The power that is exercised over workplaces, finance, and investment is, I claim, for all intents and purposes political power, since it involves public, sustained relationships of authority and subordination, resulting in fundamentally different levels of freedom for different people. Unaccountable, unequal political power in a democratic society is unjustifiable, and so new economic arrangements should be experimented with in order to allow these sources of power to be accountable to the citizenry on a formally equal basis (cf. Pierson, 1992).

Developing these arguments means challenging some common taken-for-granted beliefs in modern society: obviously it challenges the belief in a fundamental separation between the political and the economic, as well as the belief that contemporary complex economies necessarily require formal hierarchy (in the sense of having unaccountable top-down power).[4] This, I will argue, is wrong. A non-hierarchical economy is entirely possible and indeed much preferable. Of course, that does not mean that authority structures are unnecessary, that everyone can participate in every decision, or that there can be complete equality between decision-makers and decision-takers, but it does mean that there is nothing inevitable about having powerful decision-makers who are unaccountable to those significantly affected by their decisions. The existence of public power without accountability is, in essence, a throwback to a feudal era; it has no place in a genuinely democratic society.

Chapter 1 situates economic democracy within the main political traditions. In chapters 2 and 3 I analyze workplaces and suggest, with several important caveats, that they should be democratized and transformed into worker cooperatives. Chapters 4 and 5 examine the democratic strengths and weaknesses of the market, specifically in terms of the ability to "vote" with one's dollars, and the possibility of shaping the market system to better foster democratic businesses, such as co-ops. In chapters 6 and 7 I argue that the present systems of finance and investment are deeply and problematically undemocratic. I contend that finance should be democratized through the use of capital controls and the creation of Public Community Banks, and investment should be democratized through mechanisms of public investment, particularly at the local level, for example, through participatory budgeting. The conclusion ties together the strands of the previous chapters to illustrate what a society with real economic democracy might look like. It is a vision of market socialism, which is bottom-up, thoroughly democratic, and fundamentally different from the state socialisms of the 20th century. The conclusion describes how the different democratic components described throughout—the worker co-ops, the community banks, the capital controls, the participatory investment structures, and the regulated cooperative market system—could fit together and sustain each other.

While I think that economic democracy does have significant potential to improve society, no reforms are ever costless. Making changes in social life always involves trade-offs and the introduction of new costs alongside the new benefits. So a central goal of this book is to illustrate the relative costs and benefits of democratizing the economy in a clear and balanced manner so that the reader can judge for herself whether the benefits outweigh the costs. In general, the main benefits that flow from increased economic democracy, at least when the democratic institutions work well, are those of increased freedom (in terms of accountability as well as self-determination), increased equality (in terms of formal rights and status, as well as wages and wealth), and less hierarchy, alienation, and powerlessness. Economic democracy also potentially brings an important range of corollary benefits from environmental protection to increased happiness (that flow from the greater equality, cooperation, and trust which democracy usually brings).

The general costs include the risk of bad outcomes from decisions that uninformed participants may make, the substantial amount of tax dollars required for facilitating the spread of democracy in workplaces and financial institutions, and the administrative costs of monitoring public institutions and combating corruption. Additionally, there are important constraints on democracy which are not costs as much as they are recurring limitations that show up again and again in the actual practice of democracy. The most important of these are size, complexity, and unequal participation. Robert Michels ([1911] 1962) in his classic work on democracy argued that size and complexity inevitably turn democratic organizations into oligarchic ones. While Michels thought this was an "iron law," it is more accurately seen as a tendency that always exists, but which, as we will see, can be mitigated with appropriate awareness and institutional safeguards. Furthermore, scholars such as Jane Mansbridge (1980) have illustrated the ubiquity of unequal participation (what I call the "tyranny of the eloquent") that so often undermines the ideal of egalitarian democratic participation. This defect too can be mitigated, even though it remains a constant danger. Being aware of these constraints is important because it sensitizes us to the fact that structures of democracy can all too easily be undermined by informal hierarchies that arise from size, complexity, and unequal participation. In the real world creating democracy is never completed once and for all; it is a constantly evolving process.

For all of these reasons democracy is both a constant hope and a continual disappointment. Yet it seems to me that in most cases, the benefits of expanding democracy into the economy outweigh the costs of doing so. But, of course, each of us must ultimately make this calculation for ourselves.

It is also perhaps useful to say a word about what this book is not about. Economic democracy is not by any means the solution to all economic problems or a panacea for all economic injustices.

One way to think about the economy, along the lines suggested by Tawney (1931), is to recognize two major areas of concern. On the one hand, the economy has a social dimension, usually associated with production, where collectivities of people (such as workers in firms or citizens in the state) are involved in various economic associations. On the other hand, the economy has an individual dimension, usually associated with personal consumption. Now, economic democracy is largely focused on the former social dimension of the economy, which is not at all to say that issues of individual economic freedom are unimportant. Indeed, it may well be that the single most urgent need for economic justice today is to provide poor individuals with more consumption power by giving them more money and better public services. Such arguments are undeniably important, but they will not be made here. I sidestep issues of individual economic freedom and unfreedom, not because they are unimportant, but because others have talked about them at length. A discussion of some of the problems of the social relationships within the economy, and a potential remedy through economic democracy, is more than enough material for one book.

Why Does Economic Democracy Matter?

On September 17, 2011, a small group of protesters occupied Zuccotti Park on Wall Street. This tiny gathering sparked a mass movement. Within two months the protests had spread from New York to 951 cities in 82 countries across the world, clearly demonstrating a broad interest and popular concern with issues of economic justice and inequality (Rogers, 2011). However, it is undeniable that the overall direction of the protests remained vague, the goals remained unclear, and the underlying vision opaque. I am not the first to suggest that economic democracy has the potential to be one of the unifying and orienting ideas of broad new social movements of this type (Arsdale et al., 2012). What should social movements after Occupy be aiming for? What is the underlying vision and what are the ultimate economic goals? These pages represent an attempt to provide at least a partial answer to these questions.

There is no standard usage of the term "economic democracy." While the main themes that fall under it—ranging from cooperatives to public invest-ment to regulations of the market—have long been familiar points of discus-sion in political economy, the term itself has only become commonly used since the 1980s, and still today it is not particularly widespread. Probably the most common use of the term is simply as a synonym for workplace democ-racy or worker participation; indeed some of the most prominent books on the subject have focused almost entirely on the question of workplaces (Archer,

1995; Dahl, 1985; Ellerman, 1992). That said, other authors have used the term "economic democracy" as a label for very different issues: from pension funds in Sweden, to co-determination in Germany, to Employee Stock Ownership Plans in the United States. There is now a sizable, though disconnected, literature on many different aspects of economic democracy, with some authors focusing on workplaces, some on investment and finance, and some on the market itself. Yet the fact is that many of the issues in one of these areas have important implications for other areas. For example, a common theme of worker cooperatives is that they struggle to acquire external finance. So the question of expanding workplace democracy is necessarily linked to a question of financial systems. For another example, it is sometimes argued that the market would be more democratic if the population had more equal amounts of wealth (so that people had similar numbers of dollar "votes"), yet trying to reduce inequality is very difficult so long as private investors can threaten capital strike. This means that democratizing the market is inherently tied up with democratizing investment. However, to date there has been an unfortunate lack of work that attempts to bring together these disparate strands into a coherent and cohesive whole. Such is a central purpose of this book. It is an attempt to provide a synthesis of the main strands of economic democracy in order to integrate the parts into a whole.

There are several reasons why a project like this is important. First, looking at economic democracy as a whole allows for a comprehensive perspective that is too often lost from a narrower focus. It allows us to appreciate the interconnections and interdependencies of the parts and recognize how the pieces fit together, like the sides of an arch that are fused together by the weight of each on each. Second, a synthetic project like this allows us to bring together theory and practice in an interdisciplinary way—the ideas of how democratic institutions should function, with the empirical records of how they actually do function. This is useful since pure theory by itself can often lack the compelling force and messy texture of real-world example, whereas pure reliance on current evidence can prevent us from seeing beyond the actual to the desirable. Moreover, bringing together theory and practice is particularly useful for considering the question of transition. The most elegant theory in the world will convince no one if there is no understandable explanation of how to get there. This is why every empirical chapter of this book explicitly takes up the question of how we might transition from the institutions that exist today toward democratized ones that might exist tomorrow.

Of course, the question of transition has a sociological as well as a political-economic component. The former (which is beyond the scope of this work) asks important questions about the specific political alignments, social movements, party politics, and so on that make social change likely or unlikely in particular contexts. The latter, which is our focus, asks how the institutions of the present might evolve into the institutions of the future. So the questions about transition that concern us are the following: If the political will existed to make such reforms possible, then would the reformed institutions actually work? Would they be sustainable? And would they deliver on their promises? From this kind of institutional perspective, one can think about transition at three different levels of abstraction. The first is the level of immediate reforms (i.e., things that are possible now). The second level is that of longer-term reforms—things that significantly change the balance of power or deeply shift the way institutions function. The third level is that of revolutionary changes—thinking about what a fundamentally different society might look like and how it might function. This work is situated mainly on the second level. The proposals advocated here are things that a variety of social movements could incorporate into their long-term visions as a way of orienting their struggles. In particular I am interested in exploring the continuities that exist from the first to the second level, in other words, the immediate reforms that have the potential to lay the groundwork for deeper seismic changes. The task is to try to illustrate how a significantly different society (even a democratic socialist society) might evolve, slowly and incrementally, out of the present society—without needing to wave the magic wand of revolution, which allows one to imagine that any kind of new institution is possible "after the revolution." Concretely, I want to show that economic democracy can be incrementally and institutionally realized by slowly democratizing workplaces, alongside increasingly democratized financial institutions, in the conducive framework of a cooperative market system—as well as demonstrating how these features interlock in a coherent fashion. Of course in the real world any processes of democratization will likely proceed by parts, unevenly, and with substantial experimentation, but the point is not to predict how changes would actually happen in specific countries, but to try to clarify the institutional requirements that would make reforms robust and stable wherever they occur.

The third and final reason for studying economic democracy as a whole is that it offers a compelling vision of societal change. Many on the Left today feel easily demoralized and pessimistic about the future because they do not possess a serious model of a better alternative. In the 1960s Milton Friedman ([1962] 2002) famously declared that there are only two possible ways of organizing complex economies: free market capitalism (along the lines of the United States) or state socialism (along the lines of the Soviet Union). With the decline of state socialism, Margaret Thatcher was happy to draw the conclusion that only one possibility remains, declaring triumphantly that "there is no alternative" (TINA). Of course, many progressives are rightly skeptical of the idea that history is over, or that American-style capitalism is the only option. But nevertheless it is true that large sections of the Left today, from trade unionists to Occupy protestors to community organizers, are much better at articulating what they are against than what they are for.[5] The rhetorical trump card of conservatives condescendingly demanding, "what is the alternative?" is still a devastating question, all too often met with unease, confusion, and silence.

Part of the problem is that left theorists have long been skeptical about model building, following Marx's (1873) warning against writing recipes for the kitchens of the future. While there is wisdom in the warning that the complexity of society is so great that we can never accurately predict what will occur in a complete way, there are nevertheless several good reasons why model building is a useful endeavor. First, there is a difference between a model as a blueprint for a future order, and a model as a *compass* providing orientation and direction. While it is probably impossible (not to mention hubristic) to think that one can offer complete blueprints of social phenomena as hugely complex as economies, there is still value in having a model that serves as a compass: it provides a fixed point toward which people can orient their struggles. Having a goal to aim toward is crucial for thinking strategically about what kind of reforms we should engage in now in order to move in the direction we want to go. Second, as mentioned before, visions of an alternative help combat the cynicism and hopelessness that comes in the wake of a dominant cultural belief in TINA. At least for some people, having a model to strive toward is empowering and invigorating. Third and finally, as Erik Wright (2010) points out, the loss of belief in fundamental change has also weakened the achievability of more modest reforms. So even for people whose goals are more short-term, by helping to reconstruct comprehensive visions of feasible change we also augment possibilities of immediate improvement.

Central Objections

A project of this type tends to face doubts from every corner. Liberal readers may see it as utopian. Socialist readers may see it as compromised by compromise, or as dirty reformism. There is a sense in which both charges are accurate, yet there is a deeper sense in which the aim of this work is to extend the common ground of a variety of readers. That said, clearly no work can address itself to everyone. The bulk of this book is aimed at the progressive mainstream—liberals and social democrats—who feel the pull of the ideals of equality and freedom, and so cannot help but feel some discomfort toward the reigning inequality of our societies. My strategy here is to try to leverage this discomfort by showing how the basic ethical commitments that many of us share (about freedom, equality, and democracy) should, when taken to their logical conclusion, lead to support for very different institutions than those which presently exist.

There are three predominant objections to economic democracy that recur frequently enough that it is worth mentioning them up front. First, it is important to ask why economic democracy is worth pursuing over and above social democracy (i.e., a system that makes extensive use of markets, but regulates them heavily and uses the state to partially redistribute market outcomes for reasons of social justice). The second objection is the worry that economic democracy invariably risks economic inefficiency and therefore undermines prosperity. The third is the worry that more democracy may in fact be antithetical to freedom (by suppressing minority rights, by encouraging capricious decision-making, or by silencing those who are less good or able at participating, etc.).

These objections are legitimate and serious, yet throughout this work I hope to convince the skeptical reader that they are not at all fatal. Here we can just point to the bare bones of the rebuttals that will be fleshed out later. First of all, there are good reasons to expect that economic democracy would allow significantly more freedom than social democracy. Workplace democracy allows, for the first time in history, ordinary workers to participate in the management of their firms with others who are peers and of equal status. Democratizing finance and investment allows for increased accountability and self-determination in the economic development of people's communities. In addition, economic democracy allows for a much more egalitarian society than social democracy. Not only do co-ops compress incomes but democratizing investment allows for higher levels of redistributive taxation than social democracy can achieve. We will see that this greater equality of income and status has the potential to lead to a host of additional benefits, such as better health and increased happiness.

Neither is it the case that democratizing the economy inevitably brings severe inefficiencies. On the contrary, the evidence is compelling that in many instances democratized institutions operate with just as much economic efficiency as capitalist institutions—even though they tend to produce superior social outcomes. In terms of workplaces, what democratic firms lose in terms of motivation from fear of the boss and the single-minded obsession with profits, they gain from the reduced demoralization, increased trust, and improved motivation of being one's own boss. Similarly, at the economy-wide level, societies which have more market regulation, higher taxes, and more generous welfare systems (such as the Nordic countries) turn out to be no less efficient than the more capitalistic market systems (like the United States). This is largely because what is lost in terms of incentives (from high taxes and generous welfare) is balanced out by increased opportunities and capabilities that are acquired from heavy public investment.

Lastly, it is true that the relationship between democracy and freedom is a complex one. When it works well, democracy is deeply conducive to freedom. Indeed, in its essence democracy *is* the basic institutional form of social freedom. Moreover, when it works well and when conditions are right, democratic institutions can foster self-determination, which is a fundamentally important aspect of freedom that is all too often lacking in contemporary societies. But, of course, things often do not work well. We should have no illusions about the inevitability of democratic structures leading to greater freedoms. As we shall see, all too often democratic structures get undermined by a host of informal hierarchies, corruptions, and internal constraints. But recognizing such problems is the first step in dealing with them. The bottom line is that democratizing the economy can indeed offer profound improvements in the amount of freedom that most individuals enjoy, but only by being vigilant about monitoring for potential corruption, and being attentive to the defects and informal hierarchies that inevitably arise, in order to engage in an ongoing process of experimentation to fix such problems. For democracy, the goal is the process and the process is the goal.

Radical Realism

The methodological approach used here is one that I call radical realism. It is inspired by works in political science and sociology that are concerned with feasible socialism, such as Robert Dahl and Charles Lindblom's *Politics, Economics, and Welfare* ([1953] 1976), Alec Nove's *The Economics of Feasible Socialism* (1991), and Erik Olin Wright's *Envisioning Real Utopias* (2010). The essence of radical realism is the conviction that we should be radical with our goals, but realistic about our means. Radical realism is radical in the conviction that our political-economic institutions should foster freedom, equality, and solidarity as much as possible. Unfortunately, in the social sciences, radicalism is often denigrated as utopian. While it is important to avoid utopianism in the sense of unrealistic, ahistorical analysis, we should not avoid utopianism in the good sense of the word: having conviction that the world can be a fundamentally better place that it is now. As Oscar Wilde (1891) reminds us, "a map of the world that does not include Utopia is not worth even glancing at, for it leaves out the one country at which Humanity is always landing. And when Humanity lands there, it looks out, and, seeing a better country, sets sail. Progress is the realisation of Utopias."

Radical realism is realistic in three main senses. First, it starts from the premise that there are intractable tensions and conflicts in social life that cannot be wished away. These tensions come partly from the inevitable messiness of real-life institutions and partly from the happy fact of human plurality—that different people have irreducibly different projects, priorities, and values about what constitutes a good life. This means that all feasible politics is, ultimately, a politics of compromise. Those who seek purity by way of the abolition of tension and contradiction are doing something—theology perhaps—but whatever it is, it is not politics. Second, radical realism assumes that while some institutions may be better than others, all institutions have costs, and so there must always be a central focus on weighing the costs versus the benefits of different political-economic possibilities. In general, political scientists and sociologists tend to focus on the four most common kinds of political-economic mechanisms: markets, democracy, state/bureaucracy, and associations (such as unions). These can provide freedom in different ways (via exit and dollar "votes," via voice, via regulation, and via a combination of regulation and voice), and they all come with different kinds of costs; so a central goal of this book is to point out the specific areas in which democracy is the preferable institution. Third, radical realism is essentially reformist. It assumes that in a democratic society, legitimate changes can only occur with the support of the majority of the population. This means that changes are likely to be incremental and piecemeal. But that does not mean that fundamental change is impossible. On the contrary, small changes can, over time, add up to major changes. Seen from up close a hundred incremental changes over the years look like a hundred reforms, but take a step back and it looks like a revolution.

After Occupy

1 Economic Democracy
Beginning Orientations

Introduction

One of the peculiarities of economic democracy is that it has very rarely been subject to direct attention by the main political traditions. No tradition directly focuses on it, yet every tradition implicitly argues for or against it in some way. Although the main traditions are dominated by great debates about private ownership versus public, market versus plan, capitalism versus socialism, just under the surface, yet rarely articulated, is another debate about economic democracy. So the central purpose of this chapter is to set the scene by orienting the reader as to how economic democracy relates to these traditions.

Today practically everyone claims to support the values of freedom and equality. This is as true for social democrats as it is for neoliberals, Marxists as well as anarchists. Yet "freedom" is an elastic and essentially contested concept (Gallie, 1955), meaning dramatically different things to different people. It is therefore crucially important to ask what kind of freedoms one hopes to equalize. Classical liberals argued for an equal right to *protection from arbitrary interference* from government, particularly in terms of their private property and religious views. Modern liberals usually argue for equal *civil and political freedoms*, as well as equal *opportunities* to compete in the marketplace, whereas socialists have tended to push for much greater social equality, arguing that liberal freedoms are empty without the necessary *resources and material means* for their enactment.

From the perspective of economic democracy, then, what kind of freedoms should we strive to equalize? The overarching normative argument of this book is that people ought to have equal *formal decision-making power* in their core economic associations: workplaces, finance, and investment institutions.[1] Of course, the attempt to increase the equality of people's decision-making power should also be sensitive to the risks of homogenization, such as losing the benefits of specialization. The overarching practical argument is that the best way to institutionalize this kind of equal freedom is through economic democracy: democratization of firms, finance and investment structures, and the market system. While the bulk of the book is dedicated to developing these arguments, this chapter lays the preparatory groundwork by orienting economic democracy vis-à-vis the major political traditions.

Although economic democracy as I conceive it borrows much from these traditions, it also diverges in some significant respects. It differs fundamentally from classical liberalism (or contemporary "neoliberalism") in its emphasis on equality, as well as the focus on people's freedom in a social setting. It differs from left liberalism not so much in terms of values as in doubts about whether such values are better institutionalized through capitalism or economic democracy. Similarly, it differs from Marxism in seeing the appropriate means for institutionalizing ideals of social equality not in state ownership and planning but in economic democracy. Economic democracy shares the greatest affinity with certain strands of anarchism. Its main difference is in terms of realism: wishing to provide more specifics about possible institutional arrangements and more balance about the costs of radical egalitarianism.

Beyond simple orientation, I hope to describe a number of reasons why readers attached to one of the dominant traditions ought to pay attention to the issues of economic democracy. These traditions contain certain latent sympathies for economic democracy that lie half-hidden and which can be unearthed to show why, if not neoliberals, then at least left liberals, Marxists, and anarchists should be open to considering an expansion of democracy into the economy on the basis of their own ethical commitments. Of course, it is not possible to develop a comprehensive historical survey of all of these traditions. But we can point to a few key areas where these traditions resonate with ideas of economic democracy more strongly than their protagonists might explicitly say.

Classical Liberalism

As liberalism has evolved from the 17th century, it has tossed and turned over the kind of "freedom" it seeks to promote and about what kind of institutions—the market, private property, state regulation, unions, and so on—might be best suited for maintaining it. While its evolution has been complex and convoluted (Eccleshall, 1986), it is possible today to discern two main branches of liberalism: a neoliberal branch, which continues most directly from the classical tradition, and a social democratic branch, which we look at in turn.[2]

Classical liberalism includes such figures as John Locke ([1689] 1980), Adam Smith ([1776] 2006), Jeremy Bentham ([1802] 1894), James Mill (1821), Friedrich Hayek (1960), Milton Friedman ([1962] 2002), and Robert Nozick (1974). Friedman's liberalism—which is usually called *neoliberalism*—is probably the most influential version of these ideas today. The main tenets are shared to a large degree by the heads of the IMF, OECD, Wall Street, the City, and the bulk of Conservatives in Europe and Republicans in the United States. Neoliberalism, with Friedman as one of its fountainheads, is perhaps the dominant ideology of the world today.

Without question, the core value of Friedman's liberalism is individual freedom: "As liberals, we take freedom of the individual, or perhaps the family, as our ultimate goal in judging social arrangements" ([1962] 2002, p. 12). What exactly does Friedman mean by "freedom"? He recognizes three kinds of freedoms—political, civil, and economic. Political and civil freedoms include the usual rights of electing representatives, freedom of assembly, expression, and so on. His book *Capitalism and Freedom* ([1962] 2002), however, focuses mainly on economic freedom, by which he means chiefly two things: freedom to use and dispose of one's property as one sees fit, and the freedom to enter into voluntary business agreements with others.

Although freedom is his paramount value, he also believes in formal equality of rights and opportunity, but not equality of outcome. Unequal outcomes are just according to Friedman as long as they are formally or procedurally fair (such as might occur when a group of friends visit a casino; the rules apply equally to all, but some win and some lose). Everyone has the right to participate in the market, and no one should be discriminated against, but whatever inequality results is just; wealth should not be forcibly redistributed in the name of equality of outcome, for to do so directly conflicts with individual freedom (Friedman [1962] 2002, p. 174). Equality, in other words, is a kind of subsidiary value for Friedman. If it threatens individual freedom, the latter takes priority.[3]

How does Friedman believe these values are best institutionalized? He thinks that economic freedom requires a pervasive market and a minimal state. Friedman's writing is clear and powerful, in part because he finds such a tight fit between values and institutions. Indeed, competitive capitalism is defined as a free system of "voluntary exchange" ([1962] 2002, p. 13). Who could possibly be opposed to that?

According to Friedman, there are two great virtues of competitive capitalism. First, it provides economic freedom directly. One can detect a basic syllogism in his reasoning that markets = voluntary exchange; voluntary = free; therefore markets = freedom. Second, it promotes political freedom indirectly by reducing the size and scope of government. Just as markets are seen as inherently conducive to freedom, government is seen as inherently detrimental to it: "Every act of government intervention limits the area of individual freedom directly and threatens the preservation of freedom indirectly" ([1962] 2002, p. 32). So less government is a central, probably the central aim of Friedman's liberalism.

Friedman's conceptual scheme is remarkably straightforward: markets = freedom, while the state = unfreedom. But this does not mean there should be no government—"The consistent liberal is not an anarchist," Friedman tells us ([1962] 2002, p. 34). He supports the existence of a democratic state, just a minimal one—hemmed in by a constitution, on one side, and the market, on the other. Government is required to be rule-maker and legal umpire (maintaining law and order, enforcing contracts, etc.); it is also necessary to provide services that the market is unable to adequately provide because of monopoly or neighborhood effects (i.e., externalities); and it is necessary to provide the minimal degree of necessary paternalism (e.g., looking after "madmen" ([1962] 2002, p. 33)).[4] So although government should not be totally done away with, many of its current functions should be drastically curtailed in order to enlarge the scope of individual freedom. There should be reductions of tariffs and price regulations, including the abolition of rent control and minimum wages, government (and what he sees as union) monopolies; there should be much less regulation of the market, including banking, radio, and TV, and less enforced licensing, including for medical practitioners. Finally there should be far less social services: no public housing, and much reduced welfare and social security, along with substantial privatization—of national parks, mail delivery, highways, and so on ([1962] 2002, pp. 35–36).

So how does this vision relate to economic democracy? In order to see the differences clearly, it is useful to have a picture in our minds of what Friedman's ideal society might look like in practice—a kind of Reaganite revolution, taken even further, with minimal restrictions on the market and workplaces and much less public and social services. The first thing to notice is that there is little scope for democracy in such a society. The market is the main institution, while the state, the only place where democracy is seen as relevant, is kept as small as possible. Clearly such a society would lead to an explosive gap between rich and poor. The wealthy would pay little tax, encounter little interference with their businesses, and be free to donate as much as they choose to their friendly tax-cutting politician; the poor would have no security and be forced to take any job for peanuts, as the lack of welfare leaves no alternative. The jobs themselves would become riskier and more dangerous—without union protection or state regulation—allowing employers to increasingly cut corners.

Such a society would likely resemble a Dickensian one where a poor person walks to work (since there would be no public buses and the street owners would have raised their tolls), where she is paid $1/hr to clean a building with toxic chemicals, with no mask provided, unable to earn nearly enough to pay for her children to go to the private universities. She would eventually fall sick and go to a doctor who, unlicensed and offering a spring time "sale," prescribes the wrong drugs by accident, which leaves her sicker than before. With no pension or subsidized housing, the private security forces evict her onto the street. Such a description may be colorful, but it is clearly within the realms of what Friedman sees as legitimate. Yet it stretches regular language as well as credulity to call this a "free" society.

Friedman's conception of "freedom" is problematic on two basic levels.

(i) On the individual level, which is his focus, the poor have very little freedom. This is a critique that has been made amply elsewhere (Cohen, 1995; Van Parijs, 1995), so here we will simply mention the central ideas. The first problem is that individual economic freedom is empty without the material conditions for its enactment—that is, a basic amount of money and a decent level of human capital. The "freedoms" of a poor or homeless person are surely very limited. This is particularly true in a society where everything from the roads to the parks has a price tag. The second problem is that the massive inequality in this kind of society significantly undermines the freedom of the weaker party. The "voluntary" bargaining that Friedman sees as characteristic of a market economy may well be unfree when it occurs between vastly unequal parties, such as when a young unskilled woman applies for a job at a massive company like Walmart. In cases like this, talking of the "freedom" of the market participants can obscure the fact that, as Tawney (1931) famously said, "Freedom for the pike is death for the minnow" (p. 164). The lack of equality makes Friedman's commitment to freedom somewhat hollow, since how can one value "freedom" so highly while being content with only a minority of people having it in a meaningful sense? Why should we value the freedom of the rich to avoid taxation over the freedom of the poor to have free schools and hospitals? Moreover, it is important to note that remedying either of these issues—providing actual freedom by ensuring material conditions for real choice and protecting weaker parties from economic domination—both require the action of the state, particularly in terms of redistribution, welfare provision, and accessible education. So Friedman's notion that the state is inherently antithetical to freedom is, in many cases, simply wrong (Sen, 1999). Of course, the state can undermine freedom—as his favorite example of the USSR clearly shows—but it can also augment it. Nordic countries have much higher levels of state involvement than the United States—and yet this results in better healthcare, more accessible education, longer life expectancy, less poverty, fewer jails, and so on (Pontusson, 2005), meaning that the great bulk of the citizens are in many respects substantially freer than their American counterparts in their ability to implement and act out their own plan of life (surely a more meaningful sense of the word freedom than Friedman's "right to exchange property").

(ii) More relevant for us, and less commonly recognized, is the social dimension of freedom, in other words, the relationships between individuals in their associations. A major contention of economic democracy is that control over economic resources can give certain members of associations power over other members, while those at the bottom of economic hierarchies find themselves powerless and potentially dominated. In other words, a major point of divergence from Friedman is the belief that in a capitalist economy, property can translate into power over others: structural inequality can lead to systematic unfreedom.[5] Friedman, and neoliberals more generally, tend to be insensitive to the importance of social freedom. This is likely because they imagine the economy as composed of private individual bargains. They see the economy in idyllic terms, like a Walrasian auction, where there is a multitude of buyers and sellers, all small, and unable to affect prices. In such a model each individual is free to bargain or, if she does not like one deal or the offer of employment at one firm, she is free to move on to the next. In such an idealized setting the ability to exit is all the freedom one needs. If I do not want to sell my product to person A, no problem, I can simply go on to person B.

In the chapters that follow, I present a very different (but I hope more realistic) picture of the economy by examining three main areas—workplaces, finance, and investment—where issues of social freedom are pressing.

For instance, Friedman ([1962] 2002, p. 13) sees the economy as operating through individual market exchanges between small producers, where firms are simply "intermediaries" for voluntary exchanges between individuals. Such a prosaic image is, however, deeply misleading since large firms today are not like large meeting rooms where individuals come to bargain and exchange. They are concentrated loci of power and authority, typically hierarchically organized, where top managers have substantial discretionary power over lower ranks of employees. The reality today is that a large number of working people now work for corporations, some of which are richer than nations, employing thousands of people, and of massive consequence for society at large. Corporate capitalism still involves the market, but the chief actors are no longer individuals, but large firms and massive banks. The main locus of contemporary capitalism is not the individual, but the large hierarchical firm. Here we see an example of values clashing with institutions. Friedman ([1962] 2002) says that "a liberal is fundamentally fearful of concentrated power" (p. 39). I share this fear, but I also think that if this conviction is to be applied consistently, one must be critical of concentrated power wherever one finds it, such as in many contemporary workplaces. Consistency requires that one be concerned with the power of large corporations and the liberty of their workers, just as Friedman worries about the power of the state vis-à-vis the liberty of its citizens. Of course, Friedman shies away from this kind of analysis because he refuses to see property—for him the embodiment of freedom—as a potential source of unfreedom.

Additionally, instead of seeing finance and investment as the simple interplay of individual bargains, it is important to recognize, for instance, how the power of capital flight and capital strike can place powerful limits on government policies, thus deeply restricting the social freedom of the populace to decide their own future.

Economic democrats are skeptical of the idea that the economy can be adequately conceived as a purely private realm of individual transactions. Instead, a more accurate picture of the economy is that it is composed of overlapping associations where the decisions of certain individuals in their associations—particularly those who wield economic power because of their control of economic resources—produce waves of consequences rippling out and affecting society at large.

So although Friedman, like much of classical liberalism before him, formally embraces the value of economic freedom, it is a vision of freedom which is starkly individualistic, overly tied up with private property ownership, and largely indifferent to social inequality, particularly in terms of power relations within economic associations. It is, broadly speaking, hollow on an individual level, and nonexistent on a social level. My vision differs from that of neoliberalism in the conviction that a genuinely free society would require institutionalizing freedom on the social level (i.e., in the associations in which economic power is most relevant) as well as finding a way to ensure that such freedom is distributed in an egalitarian fashion. Equality in terms of equal formal decision-making power is of central importance; this is perhaps the point more than anywhere else where the paths of economic democracy and neoliberalism diverge.

Left Liberalism

The general perspective of left liberalism is that of social democracy. The essence of this position is that people's political and civil freedoms should be guaranteed in equal fashion by a democratic state, while economic freedoms (for individuals to acquire property and meet their basic needs) should be protected by a combination of the market and a welfare state that regulates the economy and protects the citizens from excessive deprivations. Prominent figures in this tradition are Keynes (1936), Beveridge ([1942] 1969), Dahl and Lindblom ([1953] 1976), and, more controversially, Rawls (1971). Social democracy was the dominant perspective from World War II until the 1970s, instituted by socialist parties throughout Europe and the New Deal in the United States (Sassoon, 1996).

John Rawls is commonly seen as a major intellectual defender of social democracy and the welfare state (Freeman, 2007; Sandel, 1998).[6] For instance, Paul Krugman, perhaps the most famous social-democratic economist alive today, defines his own position thus: "I believe in a more or less Rawlsian vision of society—treat others as if you could have been them—which implies a strong social safety net. I also believe that a mostly market economy, with public ownership and provision of services only in some limited areas, works best" (Krugman, 2011). In what follows I describe Rawls's basic position, and then describe several ways in which economic democracy diverges from it.

Rawls's theory of justice is guided by the question of "which principles are most appropriate for a democratic society that not only professes but wants to take seriously the idea that citizens are free and equal, and tries to realize that idea in its main institutions?" (2001, p. 39). His answer is that all citizens should be entitled to equal basic freedoms (his first principle of justice). These basic liberties include: freedom of thought and conscience, political liberties (e.g., the right to vote), freedom to associate, rights of integrity of the person, and rights and liberties covered by rule of law. Importantly, Rawls (2001) insists that citizens should also be guaranteed the "fair value" of political freedoms, meaning that all citizens must have "roughly an equal chance of influencing the government's policy and of attaining positions of authority irrespective of their economic and social class" (p. 46). Beyond this, all citizens should have equal opportunities (his second principle of justice). And economic and social inequalities should only be permitted if they are to the benefit of the least advantaged (the so-called "difference principle"). It is important to recognize that the "least advantaged" are not simply those with the least money, but are those with the least "primary goods,"[7] which are things that every individual will want regardless of his or her conception of the good life. Rawls says that the first principle should take priority over the second in order to provide some guidance about what to do when freedoms clash (Freeman, 2007). Without a doubt, freedom and equality are core values for Rawls, and the kind of freedom that he cares about equalizing—the ability of individuals to pursue their own conception of the good life—is attractive and powerful.

How are these values to be institutionalized? Rawls's writing is incredibly rich and detailed, but in a nutshell we can say that he requires that basic civil and political rights be protected, equally, in a constitution, while in social and economic life, equality of opportunity should be provided for by widespread education and training as well as inheritance taxes to reduce class distinctions. In the economy, the difference principle should be institutionalized through a market system that is regulated by a democratic legislature. Rawls sees the market as useful for efficient economic allocation, but thinks that it must be regulated by a democratic state which ensures that the outcomes are justly redistributed (through taxes, transfers, and subsidies), with an eye to ensuring that the primary goods are distributed to benefit the least advantaged. So it is clear why this vision is often seen as a defense of the welfare state: Rawlsian justice calls for a state to protect equal political rights, a market to coordinate the economy, and state regulation and redistribution to mitigate the worst deprivations.

How does economic democracy differ from this vision? For the most part, I have no quarrel with Rawlsian values. Left liberals have a deep commitment to both freedom and equality that is commendable. The major difference is that Rawls (at least as he was conventionally read after the publication of *A Theory of Justice* (1971)) is optimistic that these values can be adequately institutionalized in capitalist structures. I am more skeptical. There are three main points of divergence.

(i) Reading Rawls, one is often struck by a stark divide between politics and economics. While some have critiqued Rawls on the grounds that this division is largely arbitrary (Clark & Gintis, 1978; Young, 1979), I want to make the more modest point that this division tends to underemphasize the importance of freedom in the economy, specifically at work. It is undeniable that Rawls is deeply concerned with people's freedom. He argues that political and civil freedoms are in fact so important that they should be constitutionally protected: they may not be revoked for the sake of economic efficiency or even by majority decree. Yet it is jarring that in the economy, his concern shifts from freedom to welfare. Freedom is central to the first principle pertaining to politics, but not the second principle pertaining to economics. This is not to say that he has no concern for freedom in the economy—the principle of equal opportunity is clearly important in this regard—but it is to say that he is insufficiently attentive to the issue of freedom at work. Other critics have pointed out the problem that Rawls discusses the economy in terms of allocation and distribution, but he largely ignores production (Gould, 1988). In other words, he largely ignores the extent to which capitalist workplaces can undermine workers' freedom—the degree to which employers have power over their employees and the ways in which this can lead to subordination and even domination. Given the importance and centrality of work to our societies this is a problematic oversight for anyone who values freedom highly.

Nowhere in *A Theory of Justice* does Rawls explicitly discuss the issue of workplace freedom. He seems to assume, with the mainstream of the liberal tradition, that the right to exit, combined with state regulation for things like health and safety, and the right to join unions to collectively bargain over wages and work conditions, are generally sufficient to protect freedom at work. (In the following chapter I argue that such things are not sufficient, and so workplace democracy is necessary for real freedom at work.) However, it is important to note that although the idea of increasing workers' freedom through increased democracy is largely outside of the liberal tradition, there is actually support for this idea from within Rawls's principles themselves. In other words, there are good reasons for Rawlsian liberals to take workplace democracy seriously on the basis of their own ethical commitments (Hsieh, 2005; O'Neill, 2008).

To see this, consider the difference principle more closely: "Social and economic inequalities are to be arranged so that they are ... to the greatest benefit of the least advantaged" (Rawls, 1971, p. 302). Recall as well that the "least advantaged" are defined in terms of their access to primary goods. The third and fifth are particularly relevant here. The third primary good is "powers and prerogatives of offices and positions of authority and responsibility," and the fifth is "the social bases of self-respect, understood as those aspects of basic institutions normally essential if citizens are to have a lively sense of their worth as persons and to be able to advance their ends with self-confidence" (2001, pp. 58–59).

It seems to me that there is a solid case for thinking that workplace democracy (or at least increased worker participation in management) is actually implied by the difference principle. This is because it seems implausible to argue that the current hierarchical system of workplace management is better for the "least advantaged," either in terms of providing them with increased powers of office, positions of authority and responsibility, or providing them with the "social bases of self-respect," than would occur from increased workplace democracy. For instance, compare two schemes: one in which people work for a large cooperative like that of Mondragon (to be discussed in detail in chapter 3), and one in which they work for a similar capitalist firm. Even though Mondragon is in many respects far from an ideal worker co-op, its members are still considerably better off than comparable workers in a capitalist firm. Mondragon members elect their management, and so enjoy democratic freedoms completely absent in the conventional firm; they have greater opportunities for participating in decision-making; Mondragon members have much greater equality in wages, with the highest paid getting less but the lowest paid getting more (which Rawlsians can hardly see as undesirable);

and their jobs are much more secure. Furthermore Mondragon is just as efficient (if not more so) than comparable capitalist firms, and it has closer connections with the community (so the least advantaged outsiders benefit more from this scheme as well).[8] It is clear, I think, that at least from the perspective of the "least advantaged," workplace democracy would be superior to the current system of workplace hierarchy. It may be worse from the perspective of the top managers and owners—but they, Rawls tells us, should not be our ethical focus. According to the difference principle, therefore, Rawlsian liberals should, at the very least, be open to the possibility of expanding worker participation in management.

(ii) A central value for Rawls, which I share, is that people should have basically equal political freedom. They should have "roughly an equal chance" as he says, of influencing their political system. Rawls recognizes (as neoliberals usually do not) that this equality can be undermined by capitalism to the extent that massive differences in wealth corrupt the political process. To ensure equal political freedoms, therefore, Rawls (2001, p. 149) sensibly advocates public funding of elections, restrictions on campaign contributions, and assurance of a more even access to public media. I agree that these reforms are useful, but, and this is where we diverge, equal political freedoms are undermined by deeper mechanisms than simple corruption by wealthy people. Equal political freedoms can also be undermined by the very structures of capitalism themselves, in particular by private control of finance and investment (Lindblom, 1977; Przeworski, 1985; Wolff, 1977).

This argument will be developed systematically in chapter 6, but the basic point is that in capitalist market systems the underlying health of the economy is to a large degree determined by the functioning of finance and investment. If private financiers stop providing credit to firms, or if managers and owners stop investing, the economy falters and eventually starts to crack. Unemployment rises, GDP falls, and the government comes under mounting pressure for something to be done. This means that a basic priority of the government, any government, of the Left or the Right, is to ensure that financiers and investors are happy and confident enough to continue their activities—thereby ensuring relative stability. After all, basic economic stability is the necessary prerequisite for any kind of politics that the government may wish to pursue. But since finance and investment are largely controlled by an unaccountable minority of the population, their control over such basic levers of the economy means that there cannot be equal political liberties for all citizens. Business people are in a "privileged position" as Lindblom (1977) says. Government must pay attention to this minority above and beyond anyone else. In chapter 6 we explore the full extent to which this economic arrange-ment undermines democratic sovereignty, but here we must suffice with reit-erating the conclusion that we reach there: private control over finance and investment fundamentally undermines the values of equal political liberties for all.

This means that Rawls's value of equal political liberties is unable to be sustained within current capitalist structures. Since political freedoms are arguably systemically unequal due to the fact that a minority has unac-countable control over finance and investment, it follows that what is needed is a way to ensure that basic decisions about such things are more widely dispersed and systemically accountable, hence the need for eco-nomic democracy. Of course, this does not mean that everyone needs to have a say over every investment decision in the economy, but it does mean that the people who are making those decisions are accountable in a demo-cratic manner to the people principally affected by such decisions, perhaps by having finance allocated by Public Community Banks, and local invest-ment decided through participatory budgeting (see chapters 6 and 7 for more detail on this).

Since the important liberal value of equal political freedom cannot be sus-tained in capitalism, liberals and social democrats should be open to consider-ing economic democracy as a means to making their values concrete.

(iii) The final difference from Rawls is less an institutional issue as it is a conceptual one. Rawls (2001) sees the main purpose of democracy as protec-tion: "the political liberties...are only essential institutional means to pro-tect and preserve other basic liberties" (p. 143). In this respect, Rawls is very much within the mainstream of the liberal tradition, stretching back to Locke ([1689] 1980) and including classical liberals such as James Mill (1821) and Jeremy Bentham (1817) who developed their defense of democratic principles primarily on the grounds of protection (Macpherson, 1977). The idea is that democracy is useful in providing *freedom from* powerful people, or "tyrants" in the state. This understanding sees democracy as valuable because it is a mechanism providing protection from tyranny, or, alternatively, accountabil-ity. When one lacks this kind of democratic freedom, one is in a position of subservience.

I agree that this is an important dimension of democracy. But I want to emphasize a second dimension of democratic freedom that Rawls down-plays: the *freedom to self-determine*.[9] This is the notion of individuals collec-tively deciding their future together. It is the aspect of democracy associated with popular sovereignty. This is the aspect of freedom—sovereignty and self-rule—that indigenous and anticolonial movements often articulate. For instance, this is the ethos captured by the slogan of the independence move-ment in Quebec, "maîtres chez nous," masters of our own house.

In Western thought, this idea is central to republicanism.[10] Rousseau is probably the most well-known exponent of such an ideal, arguing that peo-ple are only free if they rule themselves in the sense of being the authors of their own laws (Rousseau, [1762] 1987). Though central to republicanism, this idea clearly has much broader appeal. The attractiveness of the concept of self-determination comes from the idea of collective autonomy, of being in control of our own lives. There is something very powerful in the idea of people coming together to cooperatively build the society they want to live in because it reflects the notion that our fate is not predetermined; we can be active actors in our lives, captains of our own ship. Indeed the attractiveness of this concept is obvious by noticing the distaste which we typically feel toward its absence—dependence, impotence, and helplessness.

While "freedom from" is about protection and defense, "freedom to" self-determine is a more active conception of freedom. It requires doing, act-ing, and cooperating with others, which is why this kind of freedom is more potent at small scales that allow for direct participation. On a national scale, it may be possible to feel the first kind of freedom, that, for instance, the Prime Minister, for all her power is still accountable to me; it is much more difficult, however, to feel the second kind of freedom, that she is acting out my will, or that I am in any meaningful sense directing the ship of state.

The self-determination that comes from active participation is important because participation allows one to actively take a role in managing one's own affairs. To be not just a passenger, but to exert some control over one's associations. Participation can be exhilarating even if it is also exhausting and time-consuming, which is why the Students for a Democratic Society (SDS), used to say, with a kind of rueful gravitas, that "freedom is an endless meet-ing" (Polletta, 2002).

One of the central reasons for advancing economic democracy is that it fur-thers both dimensions of democratic freedom, yet Rawls focuses only on the first. Rawls (2001) downplays the importance of self-determination because he is nervous about a tradition in republicanism (that he calls "civic humanism") which argues that participation is "the privileged locus of our (complete) good" (p. 142). In other words, he is, rightly, nervous of the claim that people must participate, they must engage in politics, they must come together to self-determine in order to be free, regardless of their personal conception of the good life. They must, as Rousseau ([1762] 1987) ominously said, "be forced to be free" (Sec. 1.7). If self-determination means self-mastery by a "higher" or "truer" portion of oneself, then, as Isaiah Berlin (1969) famously noted, this kind of freedom may be no better than a disguise for tyranny, allowing the state to "ignore the actual wishes of men or societies, to bully, oppress, torture them in the name, and on behalf, of their 'real' selves" (p. 133).

We can wholeheartedly agree with Rawls that self-determination and participation should not be forced on anyone, yet we should still insist that having the opportunity to self-determine is incredibly important. It is not necessary to agree with Pericles and Rousseau that humans should want nothing more than to address their fellow citizens from the agora, while still believing that most of us do want, in our meetings at our workplaces and elsewhere, to be listened to as equals, to be empowered to articulate, devise, and implement a plan of action, and not be constantly overruled, shushed, or sidelined.

We can still be neutral with respect to the good life while going further than Rawls does in ensuring that those who do want it have the opportunity to self-determine through participation in collective decision-making in their important economic associations. For instance, in the following chapters it will be argued that self-determination is an important freedom not only at work, but vis-à-vis finance and investment. Extending democracy to finance and investment is in large part about expanding what it means to be an equal citizen of a democratic state. The democratization of finance and investment provides citizens with the actual tools necessary for them to have a say in collectively determining the direction of the development of their own communities, which I think Rawlsians would agree is a good thing.

In summary, I diverge from Rawls in three respects. First, I hold that the liberal concern with freedom should extend to the workplace. Rawlsians should be more open to thinking about ways to democratize workplaces because the difference principle provides solid grounds for doing so. Second, I believe that equal political freedoms are unlikely to be maintained within capitalist structures because they can be undermined by private control of finance and investment. For this reason, Rawlsians should be more open to democratizing finance and investment in order to substantiate their own goal of equal political freedoms. Third, self-determination is an important aspect of democracy, and though it should not be forced on anyone, it is a vitally important kind of freedom for those who desire it.

In fact these differences may not be so large as they first appear. In later life, Rawls came to accept much of this kind of criticism and moved substantially closer to embracing economic democracy. Indeed, in the preface to the revised version of *A Theory of Justice* (1999) and, most explicitly, in *Justice as Fairness* (2001), Rawls aligned himself closer to left liberals like Walzer (1983) and Dahl (1985) who were already calling for economic democracy. In these works, and to the surprise of many, he announced his rejection of the prevailing system of welfare capitalism, of which he was (and often still is) seen as the most prominent defender. He began to explicitly argue that welfare capitalism could not in fact fulfill his principles of justice because it allows for very large inequalities in the ownership of property "so that the control of the economy and much of political life are in few hands" (2001, p. 138).[11] This is very similar to the argument I made above; it appears to open the door to democratizing investment and finance as an institutional means for preventing political and economic life from falling into a few hands. Indeed, Rawls clearly desires a transition away from welfare capitalism to a society that would place (in his words) control of political and economic life in the hands of citizens more broadly. And yet since such a transition is hard to imagine without some sort of democratization of the enormous, concentrated power of financiers and investors, it appears unavoidable that Rawls would endorse some sort of economic democracy.

Moreover, in terms of workplace democracy, though he says "I shall not pursue these questions" in any detail, it is clear that his later work was sympathetic to it. Having disregarded welfare capitalism, he argues that there are two kinds of societies that fulfill his principles of justice: a Liberal Socialism and a Property-Owning Democracy.[12] He firmly supports a Liberal Socialist system, wherein "a firm's direction and management is elected by, if not directly in the hands of, its own workforce" (2001, p. 138). Likewise he supports a Property-Owning Democracy, in which Freeman (2007, p. 220) believes there would likely be substantial amounts of workplace democracy too, evidenced by Rawls's statement that "Mill's idea of worker-managed cooperative firms is fully compatible with property-owning democracy" (2001, p. 176).

There are thus good reasons why Rawlsians, and left liberals more generally, should be open to economic democracy. A genuine commitment to freedom and equality which left liberals have naturally leads, as it did over Rawls's career, to a greater support for the extension of democracy into the economy.

Marxism

Classical Marxism (in the tradition of Marx, Engels, Kautsky, Lenin, etc.) had an ambiguous and paradoxical relationship to ethical values, such as freedom and equality. On the one hand, they tended to deride such values as mere bourgeois prattle, ideological, and designed to obfuscate actual social reality, while on the other hand, as Lukes (1985) remarks, "Open practically any Marxist text, however aseptically scientific or academic, and you will find condemnation, exhortation, and the vision of a better world" (p. 3). So even though these Marxists were sometimes critical of the idea of morality, they tended to be devoted, indeed passionately devoted, to the enlightenment principles of the French Revolution: freedom, social equality, solidarity, progress. In Engels's words: modern socialism "originally appears as a more developed and allegedly more consistent extension of the principles laid down by the French philosophers of the Enlightenment in the eighteenth century" (quoted in Archer, 1995, p. 1).

In most respects Marxists have shared with others progressives the values of freedom and equality.[13] Where they differ, primarily, was in regards to institutions. Marxists thought that there could be no real equality, freedom, or democracy so long as capitalism existed. They believed that actualizing their normative values would require a material basis and institutional structure that was incompatible with capitalism. As long as a small class owned the means of production, democracy would basically be a smoke screen behind which the bourgeoisie would rule. Probably the most important contribution the Marxists made to economic democracy is their astute analysis about the ways in which capitalist structures could operate to undermine people's social freedoms. While left liberals recognized that disparities in wealth could lead to the corruption of political democracy, the Marxists saw the deeper structural impediments that capitalism imposed on democracy. They pointed out the structural constraints on equal political freedom, discussed above, that flow from private control of investment and finance (Block, 1977; Przeworski, 1985).[14] Additionally, they pointed out how capitalist workplaces can lead to alienation and hierarchy, thus undermining freedom and equality at work (at least for those below the highest echelons) (Braverman, 1974; Marx, [1844] 1978).

On an abstract level I share much of the values of equality and freedom professed by Marxists. But the crux of the issue and the source of major disagreements is in the institutionalization of these values. While the Marxists have often been insightful in pointing out the ways that capitalist structures can undermine equal freedoms, their own institutional proposals have often been severely problematic.

How have Marxists thought that their values should be institutionalized? This is a difficult question because of the breadth of Marxism as a tradition. Marx himself can be read in many different ways. He definitely had an authoritarian undemocratic side. In the *Manifesto of the Communist Party* ([1848] 1968) and elsewhere he clearly calls for centralization and state control.[15] He expelled Bakunin and other anarchists from the First International, silencing their democratic call for bottom-up federations of workers' associations. However, it is also possible to read Marx as a kind of radical democrat, concerned above all else with overcoming alienation.[16]

Although there is not a single reading of Marx, nor a single tradition of Marxism, there is, historically speaking, a dominant tradition, usually called classical or orthodox Marxism, which sees a line of continuity from Marx to Engels to Kautsky and Lenin. This tradition tended to be severely undemocratic in its institutional proposals—and so it is here that economic democracy diverges most sharply from Marxism.

By the beginning of the 20th century, orthodox Marxism was quite clear that the solution to the problems of capitalism did not involve economic democracy, but rather nationalization and state control of production in a planned manner. Kautsky, who at the turn of the century was read much more widely than Marx himself (Sassoon, 1996), described the coming socialist society as being "nothing more than a single gigantic industrial concern" (Kautsky, 1888, chap. IV.9). A giant factory, owned by the state, and operated (supposedly) for the benefit of the population at large. Instead of the "anarchy of production" that Marx decried, the state would rationally plan production and distribution. In their more honest moments these Marxists recognized that this economic planning was in clear tension with workers' freedom. "It is true," Kautsky admitted, "that socialist production is irreconcilable with the full freedom of labor, that is, with the freedom of the laborer to work when, where and how he wills" (1888, chap. IV.10). These are words that Trotsky would take to heart with his brutal implementation of the militarization of labor (Brinton, 1975)—organizing industry along military lines, strictly hierarchical and intensely disciplined[17]—continued more viciously by Stalin.

In addition, Engels (1874 [1978]) famously ridiculed the idea of workplace democracy, thus starting a tradition of contempt for workplace democracy that orthodox Marxists would follow consistently, largely on the grounds that it risked undermining state control. Thus Lenin would deride the idea of "a producer's congress! What precisely does that mean? It is difficult to find words to describe this folly. I keep asking myself can they be joking? Can one really take these people seriously? While production is always necessary, democracy is not. Democracy of production engenders a series of radically false ideas" (Lenin, quoted in Albert & Hahnel, 1991, p. 22).[18]

That said, it is important to point out that there has always been an alternative, albeit smaller, tradition of anti-authoritarian Marxism, much more concerned with workers' control and much closer aligned to economic democracy. This is the tradition associated with such figures as Bernstein ([1899] 1993)—who famously equated socialism with the extension of democracy—Pannekoek ([1936] 1970), Castoriadis (1974), Brinton (2004), and Schweickart (1996).

Since 1989 and the fall of the Berlin Wall, many Marxists have engaged in substantial revision of the earlier orthodoxies. This revision has occurred around three main points, all of which have made Marxists more sympathetic to economic democracy. First, contemporary Western Marxists are now universally in favor of democracy, at least in the state. Second, there has been substantial criticism (from within Marxism and without) of the belief that a free and equal society requires state ownership and central planning. It has become widely recognized that state ownership need not result in any important change in the character of the workplace itself. Work in public or nationalized firms often remains top-down, hierarchical, and alienating. This was blatantly the case in the USSR, just as it is in the welfare states of the West, where nationalized firms often made no attempt to alter the hierarchical structures of work. Changing the "boss" from a private businessperson to a state bureaucrat often had very little impact on the actual degree of power that workers had over their workplaces.[19] Third, many critics across the political spectrum, including Marxists, have expressed grave doubts that central planning is a good method for allocating labor, goods, and services, and have therefore become less implacably hostile to the market (Bardhan & Roemer, 1993). Some have pointed to the advantage that markets have in allowing a greater freedom of choice of occupation (Dahl & Lindblom, [1953] 1976; Nove, 1991). Additionally, there is significant consensus across the board that markets are more efficient than comprehensive planning (Roemer, 1994).[20] Many leftists have therefore concluded that it may be desirable to alter the market's overall distributions (e.g., through taxation and subsidy) for the sake of justice, while still endorsing the use of the market for basic issues of allocation. I share this perspective. In chapter 4 I will argue that the market can in fact be a democratic mechanism of allocation, a kind of voting-machine (though this is true if and only if there is a profound reduction in the inequality of the number of dollar-votes each person has, as well as a reduction of distortions from things like externalities and monopolies).

Today, many Marxists no longer support the USSR-style of socialism. Instead their work spans many fields, such as arguing for market socialism (Roemer, 1994) and a universal basic income (Van Parijs, 1995), refining principles of justice (Cohen, 1995), analyzing capitalist globalization (Harvey, 2006; Wallerstein, 1974), and indeed, pursuing questions of economic democracy (Miller, 1989; Schweickart, 1996). Erik Olin Wright's book *Envisioning Real Utopias* (2010) is a masterful attempt by an anti-authoritarian Marxist to outline the prospects for socialism today, and it reaches very similar conclusions to the ones expressed in this book. Indeed, Wright (2010, p. 189) ends up identifying the core of socialism with economic democracy. For Marxists like this, the concerns of this work are very much their own.

So there are several good reasons why contemporary Marxists should be open to ideas of economic democracy. (i) In the short term, building economic democracy allows for the growth of what Marxists often call "dual power,"[21] which is important because it means that the chances of reforming neoliberal capitalism are much more likely (Wright, 2010). For example, Crotty and Epstein (1996) argue that reforms to democratize finance, such as capital controls (discussed in chapters 6 and 7), are vital in order to change the balance of power in society, and enable a working-class movement to push for a new kind of class compromise. (ii) In general, building economic democracy strengthens the so-called "working class" and weakens the "capitalist class." This happens in several ways. Workplace democracy has the potential to empower workers—a consistent Marxist goal—much more substantially than state ownership. Likewise, financial democracy has the potential to increase the freedom of working people vis-à-vis financiers by giving them more say over how finance should be directed. Generally speaking, Marxists have often had a strong analysis of the ways in which capitalism undermines equal freedoms, but more often than not their instinct was to replace capitalism with the state, which is deeply problematic since the state is often a poor substitute for actual popular power. Thinking about ways to concretely democratize work, finance, and investment in viable decentralized institutions, so as to concretely increase the power of regular working people, is closely in line with Marxists' historical ethic. (iii) Ultimately, economic democracy leads to a vision of market socialism that accomplishes many of the traditional goals of Marxism—challenging elite control over the economy, increasing equality in material terms and in terms of economic power, reducing "alienation" at work, and, more generally, aiming for greater freedom for people to control their lives—while avoiding the failures and brutalities of the Soviet model. Economic democracy offers the potential of a non-state socialism, which is feasible and viable for the 21st century. The conclusion of this book illustrates a vision of this kind of democratic socialism that I suspect many Marxists would find attractive.

Anarchism

Of all the major traditions of political thought, the anarchists have probably been the most consistent advocates of an expansion of democracy throughout society and into the economy, and therefore have the most affinity with economic democracy. Unfortunately, much contemporary democratic theory largely ignores this tradition.[22] Today anarchism is less a single cohesive political doctrine as it is a large family of those with similar convictions and aspirations: hostility toward unaccountable authority,[23] distrust of hierarchy and power, and optimistic belief in the capacity of ordinary people to control their own lives and organize social relationships on the basis of freedom, equality, and solidarity. In Chomsky's words, "what attracts me about anarchism personally are the tendencies in it that try to come to grips with the problem of dealing with complex organized industrial societies within a framework of free institutions and structures" (quoted in Marshall, 2010, p. 579).

Within the anarchist family there have been two main traditions: an individualistic and a social tradition. The smaller tradition of individual anarchism focuses on individual freedom conceived of in terms of personal autonomy; this tradition places less emphasis on equality and is less hostile toward capitalism than it is toward the state. Its main proponents are Proudhon (at some points) (Graham, 1989; Proudhon, [1847] 1888), Warren, and Tucker (Marshall, 2010). This tradition bears some affinity with that of the new right libertarians (Nozick, 1974; Rothbard, 1982). Its central message is that "society must be constructed as to preserve the sovereignty of the individual" (quoted in Marshall, 2010, p. 384). This tradition has little in common with economic democracy.

The dominant anarchist tradition is that of social anarchism, sometimes called anti-authoritarian or libertarian socialism. Its principal exponents include Proudhon (at other points) (Vincent, 1984), Bakunin (1980), Kropotkin ([1912] 1974), Malatesta (Richards, 1965), Rocker ([1938] 1988), Bookchin (1971), and Chomsky (Mitchell & Schoeffel, 2002). Unlike the Marxists, anarchists generally had no hesitation about declaring their ethical commitments: their core values are freedom balanced by a belief in social equality.[24] Social anarchists are passionate defenders of an ideal of freedom as self-determination or self-government in a community of equals. Moreover, they have gone further than most in thinking through the kinds of structures that might institutionalize equal freedom, in the sense of providing everyone with the means to self-govern in political and economic life, both as individuals and in associations with others. They have tended to describe their ideal in contrast to (classical) Marxism.

> Marx is an authoritarian and centralizing communist. He wants what we want, the complete triumph of economic and social equality, but he wants it in the state and through the state power, through the dictatorship of a very strong and, so to say, despotic provisional government, that is, by the negation of liberty. His economic ideal is the state as sole owner of the land and all kinds of capital, cultivating the land under the management of state

engineers, and controlling all industrial and commercial associations with state capital. We want the same triumph of economic and social equality through the abolition of the state and of all that passes by the name of law (which, in our view, is the permanent negation of human rights). We want the reconstruction of society and the unification of mankind to be achieved, not from above downwards by any sort of authority, nor by socialist officials, engineers, and other accredited men of learning—but from below upwards, by the free federation of all kinds of workers' associations liberated from the yoke of the State. (Bakunin quoted in Ward, 2005, pp. 247–48)

So what is the relationship between social anarchism and economic democracy? Reading the social anarchists one gets the impression of a kind of schizophrenic attitude toward democracy. At times severely critical, and at times intensely supportive. Yet this confusion is, I think, mainly an issue of terminology. Rhetorically, the social anarchists often expressed virulent dislike of "democracy." For instance, Proudhon, that "perpetual contradiction,"[25] at one point says that "democratic government is nothing but a monarchy returned," yet practically in the same breath declares "we want the mines, canals, railroads given to workers' associations, organized democratically."[26] Criticism of "democracy" is widespread throughout the history of anarchism, from Malatesta (Richards, 1965, p. 50) to Gelderloos today who declares that "democracy is an authoritarian, elitist system of government designed to craft an effective ruling coalition while creating the illusion that the subjects are in fact equal members of society" (Gelderloos, 2004, p. 18). This criticism of "democracy" is best interpreted as criticism of the social order of contemporary democratic states. Classical anarchists tended to be critical of actually existing democracies because of the widespread exclusions of workers, women, and racialized people (which was standard throughout the 19th century), the lack of meaningful participation in the centralized state structure, and, particularly, what they saw as the meaninglessness of political democracy given the reality of massive social and economic inequality, the massive inequality in wealth as well as the de facto disenfranchisement of the majority of people from economic decision-making. This is why Bakunin ([1866] 1980) says that even in the "democratic" states "self-government of the masses...remains a fiction" (p. 143). In other words, the social anarchists were not opposed to democracy per se; they were opposed to a system that called itself a "democracy" while maintaining the capitalist systems and entrenched social hierarchies which they saw as undermining any possibility of real democracy or equality.

The fact is that although they often lambasted "democracy," it is undeniable that whenever they started to seriously discuss proposals for alternatives, their visions were always deeply imbued with a democratic ethos. Their ideals were fundamentally visions of radical democracy, of people having equal decision-making power in their associations, even if they tended to shy away from using the word "democracy" in favor of words like "bottom-up," "self-management," "autogestion," "workers' control," "self-government," and so on—words which display an unmistakably democratic impulse.

In broad outline the social anarchists envisioned a replacement of the state with a federation of communes—which they saw as deeply democratic bodies, with elected and easily revocable delegates, providing as much direct participation as feasible.[27] More importantly for our purposes, they envisioned the economy being run according to similar principles of democracy and bottom-up control: empowering regular people with decision-making power. The main current of this tradition thought the economy could be run by federations of workers' councils coordinating with federations of consumers' councils (Mikhail Bakunin, [1866] 1980; Berkman, 1929; Bookchin, [1968] 2005). However, the degree to which different industries were to coordinate their activities with each other and with consumers via a market, a plan, or some kind of bargaining, was always very unclear. The clearest example of these ideas in practice is the organization of industry in Spain, particularly in Barcelona, during the Spanish Civil War, when anarchists found themselves in charge of large parts of the country, and proceeded to democratize industry including construction, metal industry, bakeries, slaughter houses, public utilities, transportation, health services, theaters, cinemas, even the regional textile industry employing 250,000 workers. Each newly collectivized factory was reorganized: wages were equalized, formal distinctions between workers were abolished, and the administration of the factory was reorganized on the basis of self-management, with all managers being elected and revocable to the rank and file. Each factory from the same industry was organized into a Local Federation. All the Local Federations then sent delegates to the Local Economic Council which coordinated economic exchange. In order to facilitate exchanges across regions, the Local Economic Councils formed National Economic Federations (Dolgoff, 1990).

In terms of principles, then, the social anarchists have historically been the most consistent supporters of economic democracy, particularly in their committed advocacy of ideas of self-management and workers' control. In practical terms, however, they were often overly vague about the specifics. Since anarchists were rarely in power their theorists felt little need to spell out the details of how their institutions would concretely work. How should economic coordination happen? Should a market and price system be used? If not, what is a better alternative? How should finance be allocated? Who, exactly, should have a say about the direction of societal investment? How should conflicts between different democratic bodies be resolved? What kind of equality is possible and desirable in complex large-scale systems? These vitally important practical questions were too often left unanswered, with far too much confidence that they would simply work themselves out "after the revolution" (for an acute example of this naïveté, see Berkman 1929).

So while economic democracy shares many of the normative aspirations of anarchism, it is more cautious and realistic about institutional possibilities. Economic democracy attempts to be more realistic in its attention to costs (not just benefits) of increased participation and equality. For example, while economic democrats agree that equality is a fundamental value, anarchists often go further than this in implying that more equality is always better—yet this, I think, is wrong. Total equality in decision-making can only be achieved with huge costs. There are costs in terms of size (since equal input in every decision means organizations must remain very small), inefficiency (since total equality makes specialization impossible), and homogeneity (since consensus decision-making over long periods of time is difficult to achieve without similar people). This argument will be spelled out in more detail in chapter 3, but here it is useful just to make the point that one place where economic democracy diverges from the anarchism is in the belief that the goal is not total equality but equality in formal decision-making power, since this offers similar democratic benefits with much fewer costs.

Conclusion

We have seen that economic democracy shares with the major traditions a basic commitment to equality and freedom, even if diverges at various points. It differs fundamentally from neoliberalism in its emphasis on equality, particularly in terms of the desire to expand equal formal power in major economic associations. It shares with both left liberalism and Marxism a broad commitment to freedom and equality but differs from left liberalism in doubting that such values are likely to be sufficiently institutionalized in capitalist structures, and differs from classical Marxism in doubting that they can be well institutionalized through state ownership and central planning. Economic democracy has the closest affinity to anarchist traditions, particularly the parts of those traditions that emphasize the importance of freedom and equality in economic associations, though it differs from the bulk of anarchist theorizing in wishing to provide more specifics about possible institutional arrangements, and more nuance in its evaluation of trade-offs.

I have also tried to point out why left liberals, Marxists, and anarchists should feel some affinity with a project of economic democracy, like the one described in subsequent pages, since in many respects such a project resonates with their own ethical commitments. This is not to say that such people will have no legitimate doubts or concerns about economic democracy. A number of issues are recurring, such as concerns about paternalism and the tyranny of the eloquent. There are also pragmatic worries about efficiency, corruption, and practicality, particularly on a large scale, combined with doubts that economic democracy is really preferable to social democratic alternatives. The analyzing of these issues is a major goal of the following chapters.

So although economic democracy, as I envision it, crisscrosses various traditions, it is not reducible to any of them. One of the main contributions of economic democracy—and in this respect we have much to thank other authors on the subject (Archer, 1995; Carnoy & Shearer, 1980; Dahl, 1985; Ellerman, 1992; George, 1993; Melman, 2001; Schweickart, 1996)—is that it helps to change the focus of political-economic debates away from 20th-century obsessions with questions of public versus private ownership, to new debates about who should have power in various types of economic decision-making. This is a new paradigm, which, as we will see, can illuminate old problems in a new light.

Part One

Workplaces

2   Should Workplaces be Democratized?

The modern corporation may be regarded not simply
as one form of social organization but potentially (if
not yet actually) as the dominant institution of the
modern world.
                    (Berle & Means, [1932] 1962, p. 356)

Introduction

In many ways these words of Berle and Means have now come true. Large
corporations today are vastly influential and massively powerful. They are
among the most powerful organizations in the contemporary world, central
features of liberal-democratic societies, yet they themselves are fundamentally
undemocratic, since the people at the top of the structures are unaccountable
to the people at the bottom. This means that a dominant institution of modern "democratic society" is not democratic itself. Is this justifiable? Although
we are appalled at states that do not allow their citizens to elect their leaders,
we take it for granted that workers should have no ability to elect their bosses.
Why is this so? The present authoritarian structure of workplaces means that
the majority of the population spends the majority of their lives in associations that are severely undemocratic and hierarchical, yet we unhesitatingly
call our societies "democracies." This is a puzzle and a paradox.

But the lack of democracy at work is not simply an academic puzzle. It
is also a fact of life, and an often terrible one at that. Many workplaces in
our society, particularly for working-class jobs, are organized so hierarchically
that they are deeply unpleasant if not outright oppressive. Almost everyone
has experienced at some time or another the degradations of workplace hierarchy—yelling bosses, managers who act like petty tyrants, supervisors who
stonewall and stifle feedback, arbitrariness and inequality, favoritism and
snobbery, privilege and superiority. In such ways hierarchical work can undermine the freedom of large numbers of working people to adequately control
their own lives.

27

Arguments for workplace democracy are not new and tend to reappear every generation or so. The first theoretical defense of cooperatives as "working men's associations" appeared in the writings of Phillipe Buchez in France in the 1830s and 1840s (Estrin, 1989, p. 169). More recently, most countries in the West experienced a wave of substantial enthusiasm for workplace democracy starting in the 1960s, galvanized by the student movements. From that generation, some of the most well-known political theorists—Carole Pateman (1970), Michael Walzer (1983), and Robert Dahl (1985)—came to advance justifications for workplace democracy. In recent years we are perhaps witnessing another wave of interest (e.g., the international Occupy movement) galvanized in part by the global financial crisis and in part by unprecedented levels of economic inequality.

The central argument of this chapter is that the current system of hierarchical work is deeply unjust because the majority of workers are compelled to join workplaces within which they are fundamentally unequal—in their functional role, essentially servants. It is very difficult for the average person to choose an alternative to hierarchical work in the form of a democratic workplace. The argument here is that no one should be compelled to be subservient at work and so everyone should have a meaningful choice of workplace democracy. For such a choice to be real, the state needs to foster and facilitate the expansion of worker cooperatives.

The argument proceeds by first examining the hierarchical nature of most workplaces, and then showing the degree to which people are compelled to join them due to a combination of material pressure, cultural pressure, and lack of alternatives. The following section differentiates workplaces from purely private associations, such as clubs, to clarify why the state should be involved in fostering the expansion of democratic workplaces. The next section examines what this concretely means in terms of spreading worker cooperatives. The final sections consider some common objections to workplace democracy.

Workplace Hierarchy and the Compulsion to Accept Subservience

Perhaps the most common perspective on work in contemporary capitalism is that it is structured on the basis of voluntary contracts so there are no problems of "power" or "hierarchy." Alchian and Demsetz (1972) are among the most influential defenders of this position. They argue that there is no question of authoritarian control at work because work is simply a series of voluntary contracts that the worker can terminate at any point: "the employee 'orders' the owner...to pay him money in the same sense that the employer directs... [the employee] to perform certain tasks. The employee can termi-nate the contract as readily as can the employer" (1972, p. 783). The intuition behind Alchian and Demsetz's argument is that because work involves a vol-untary contract there can be no exercise of power of one over the other. The employer and worker are just exchanging something for something in a deal that both agree to. This is why they do not see any difference between the standard employer-employee relationship and the standard customer-seller relationship.

> [The firm] has no power of fiat, no authority, no disciplinary action any different in the slightest degree from ordinary market contracting between any two people... telling an employee to type this letter rather than to file that document is like my telling a grocer to sell me this brand of tuna rather than that brand of bread. (1972, p. 777)

I find this portrayal of contemporary society highly inaccurate. In general, workplaces in capitalist society are hierarchies: they are based on structural inequality in a way that gives employers significant and unaccountable power over their employees, and are therefore deeply damaging to most workers' freedom. In stark contrast to Alchian and Demsetz, I will argue that the aver-age person in our societies faces intense material and culture pressure to get a job. But due to the large inequality in ownership of productive assets and skill levels, most workers apply for jobs in situations where they have significantly less bargaining power than their employers, and so are compelled to sign con-tracts handing over large discretionary power. This means that the average working person in developed societies is, in his or her functional role at work, essentially a servant.

Most workers are compelled to join hierarchical workplaces because of two essential factors: (i) pressure to get a job, and (ii) lack of alternative democratic options.

(i) Generally speaking, pressure to work comes in two forms: material and cultural. The precise degree of material pressure that individuals face varies from country to country and depends on a number of factors, most impor-tantly, the level of unemployment, one's bargaining power in the labor mar-ket, and the generosity of social security. For our purposes, the simplest way to think about the labor market in developed countries is to recognize that the working population can be divided into three main categories, which we might label, "owners," "professional workers," and "average workers." In the United States, for example, owners represent roughly 8% of the population; they are the richest portion of society, defined by their ability to live off the income generated by their private property. Professionals are highly skilled workers representing about 25% of the population, while what I am calling "average workers" are medium or low-skilled and constitute about 60% (the remaining 7% are self-employed).[1] The point of this distinction is that it gives us some nuance in terms of the degree of material pressure different people face in our societies. While all workers (or non-owners) are compelled to work to make ends meet, professionals clearly face less intense pressure than other workers because they possess scarce skills that put them in a stronger bargaining position. Material pressure is also clearly contingent on the level of social support. While no developed country yet provides their citizens with a guaranteed basic income, material pressure to work is particularly severe in the United States due to the weak welfare supports. The average welfare provision is about $17,000/year for a family of four, whereas a living wage is calculated to be close to $50,000.[2]

In terms of cultural pressure to get a job, it is well known that the lack of work in the form of chronic unemployment often leads to severe psychological suffering. We cannot be flippant about the seriousness of this deprivation when we recall that there is a strong correlation between unemployment and suicide (Lewis & Sloggett, 1998). Work is often an important element of one's social status and is crucially important for many people's sense of dignity and self-worth (Jahoda, 1987). This means that the pressures of finding work can extend far beyond purely financial ones.

(ii) The final important factor is that there are very few alternatives to hierarchical work. (Again, by "hierarchical work" I mean workplaces where managers are structurally unequal and unaccountable to workers.) Most workers are unable to choose to work in a democratic firm for the simple reason that there are basically no options to do so. In most Western countries (Italy is a partial exception), genuinely democratic workplaces (i.e., worker cooperatives) make up only about 1% of firms. In the United States, 99.9% of private workplaces employing more than one person are, strictly speaking, hierarchical firms (Dow, 2003).

That said, over the years there have been occasional waves of interest in trying to soften workplace hierarchy through experiments with worker participation in management (Strauss, 2006). The best overview of the contemporary US economy comes from Blasi and Kruse (2006), who analyzed a large, random sample of survey data from 3,081 firms in 1997. They found that in 11.9% of firms the majority of nonmanagerial employees worked in self-managed teams. Moreover, in 47.2% of firms, a majority of employees regularly participated in meetings covering workplace issues. Although this sounds impressive, it must be recalled that meetings by themselves need not mean very much. The simple fact of having a meeting does not imply any democratic equality or accountability between the participants, as managers in all of these firms are perfectly within their rights (though perhaps unwise) to completely ignore workers' complaints if they wish. Overall, the authors find that only 1.10% of firms in the United States are what they call "high-performance workplaces," meaning they make use of at least half of the following eight participatory and good management practices (self-managed work teams, work-related meetings, training, benchmarking, job rotation, flatness of the organization, advanced practices of recruitment, and pay/benefits). So we can see that the US economic landscape does contain some opportunities for limited participation within the overarching hierarchical management structures (the 11.9% of firms with self-managed teams is not meaningless), but very few opportunities to escape hierarchical, undemocratic work itself.

So other than the minimal number of worker cooperatives, are there any other ways to escape hierarchical work? One potential route is to become self-employed. This is, at present, the most institutionally plausible path for some people to achieve self-determination at work—roughly 10% of the labor force do this—but, of course, it is only available to those who can afford to start their own business, are willing to take the substantial financial risks, and able to dedicate the requisite time and energy. For everyone else, the only way that is currently institutionally possible for workers to acquire democracy at their present workplace is to become co-owners, through buying enough shares from their employers that they acquire equal decision-making power with the other owners. But, of course, for most people this is merely a formal possibility. Many firms are private and will not sell their property rights, and even if they would, most workers could never afford to buy sufficient shares to acquire equal decision-making power. It is estimated that 80% of families have an average net worth of only 50% of the capital stock of their firm per employee; and of this, about half again is tied up in cars and homes (Dow, 2003, p. 189). The bottom line from all of this is that democratic alternatives to workplace hierarchy are, in general, highly inaccessible.

So force of circumstance and lack of alternatives mean that most workers find themselves compelled to join hierarchical workplaces. Due to the large inequality in ownership of productive assets and scarce skills, average workers apply for jobs in situations where they have significantly less bargaining power than the owners, and so are compelled to sign contracts handing over large discretionary power to the employers. It is standard for contracts to give management not only the power to fire and discipline but also to determine the rules and regulations by which employees are expected to abide. Workers who are unionized may have some general level protections, especially around wages, but most union contracts include a so-called "management clause," which reserves essential powers and decision-making ability to management alone.[3] The broad discretionary powers given to managers allow them to compel workers to do things that they would not otherwise do—to do this task, in this way, at that pace, and so on. This is the sense in which contracts typically establish the governing of workers. The most important point about contracts for regular kinds of work is that since all the precise tasks and minutiae that a worker must do can never be fully described in all the specific details, what contracts really establish is the general parameters of authority and obedience (we might say, parameters of government) that are expected to be followed. If workers simply followed the contract to the letter, doing nothing more and nothing less, the workplace would grind to a halt almost immediately—which is precisely the rationale behind work-to-rule strikes. In other words, a fundamental purpose of the standard employment contract for low-skilled work is formalizing inequality by establishing power and authority over the worker in order to extract a variety of particular work from an inevitably general contract (Simon, 1951).

Of course, we should not overgeneralize about the position of workers in their firms. At the very least, we need to recognize a spectrum between highly skilled professionals and low-skilled workers. Professionals (e.g., university professors or programmers at Google) can sometimes bargain for increased levels of decision-making autonomy at work and often have a choice about the kind of job they take. However, the average low-skilled worker typically lacks this bargaining power and so is compelled to accept unequal voice at work. (As a spectrum there is no sharp demarcation between "high" and "low" skill—in the middle they may blur into each other—but for the most part the distinction is clear.) The average worker is, in a functional sense, essentially a servant. Since the collection of work tasks can never be definitively adumbrated, a central duty of every non-professional job in a hierarchical workplace is obedience to whatever the boss or manager wants (within, of course, legally defined boundaries).

This is not to say that all jobs in hierarchical workplaces are terrible or that all employees in such firms are oppressed or powerless. Not at all; professionals are often able to demand an important degree of autonomy at work, and managers sometimes initiate worker participation schemes (usually with the hope that it will increase productivity). The point is rather that as far as formal structures of power are concerned, average workers are fundamentally unequal in decision-making power with respect to their employers. In the rich societies of the West average workers are, in a functional sense, like Alfred—the butler of Bruce Wayne (Batman's alter ego); they are not starving or living terrible lives (indeed, by global standards they are quite rich). And they are definitely not slaves, since there are clearly defined limits to employer power and even the most dependent worker is not usually utterly dependent on her employer for life and limb. But neither are they equals. When Bruce Wayne calls, Alfred comes running.[4]

The reason that it is so important for average workers to have a choice about democratic alternatives is that workplace hierarchy can be terrible. Hierarchical workplaces deprive individuals of freedom in the two senses mentioned in the last chapter—first, they make workers unfree from the (potentially) arbitrary power, coercion, and bullying of those in authority. This is the sense of unfreedom as subservience. It is the result of inequality in terms of formal decision-making power. This kind of unfreedom often manifests itself in hierarchical workplaces through arrogance and caprice, on the one hand, fear and fawning, on the other. Additionally, workplace inequality tends to make workers unfree in the republican sense of lacking self-determination or sovereignty. This is the sense of unfreedom as helplessness and dependence, marked by the inability of workers to collectively manage the direction of the firm themselves. This is unfreedom as impotence, the stultifying of creativity and the stifling of enthusiasm that results from disempowering work.

Overall, it is clear that Alchian and Demsetz's claim that workers can fire their bosses just as easily as the reverse is a strange perspective as it implies that the employee is in general in a position of equal bargaining power vis-à-vis the employer—a perspective that flies in the face of practically all the evidence of recorded capitalist history. They mistake the formal truth that a worker *may* legally terminate a contract just as well as the other way around, with the substantive truth that an average worker is usually far less *able* to do so. The standard situation in the Western world is that inequality of resources (in terms of money and skills) compels the average worker to accept unequal authority relations stipulated by standard employment contracts. So employers' power over workers comes de jure from the employment contract but de facto from unequal bargaining positions. This produces the paradox that the typical worker is largely compelled by force of circumstance to be subservient at work in a society that prides itself on its democratic equality.

Free to Choose?

When Milton and Rose Friedman named their book *Free to Choose* (1980), they were attempting to advance their conservative arguments by appeal to a widely held sentiment that a core goal of liberal societies is that individuals should be free to choose the products, services, and kind of employment that they desire. In an important article, Ian Maitland (1989) argues in a similar vein that there is no need for the state to foster workplace democracy because workers can freely choose to have meaningful work if they so desire. In a competitive market system, he argues, workers are free to bargain for whatever kind of benefits they want; if they desire more meaningful work they can trade it off against lower wages so that firms have an incentive to offer it to them. And the fact that this does not seem to happen very frequently is taken as evidence that in fact workers do not want more meaningful work. The upshot of his argument is that workers are presently free to choose and indeed have chosen en masse to stick with subservience.

Now while Maitland's argument focuses on "meaningful work" we can easily imagine a similar argument about "democratic voice." The argument would go as follows: workers are free to choose the degree of democracy at work that they want by bargaining with employers for more/less democracy in exchange for lower/higher wages. There is no reason that workers cannot bargain for more democracy just like they commonly do for more vacation time or better benefits. A competitive labor market allows for workers to bargain for any particular package of benefits that they may want.

In fact, democracy at work is not something that workers can easily bargain for. There are two basic reasons why. The first is that it is not institutionally available. It is simply not common practice anywhere for firms to offer varying degrees of democratic rights to prospective workers. This does not mean that it would be impossible for them to do so (the current practices of limited worker participation in management could conceivably evolve into more robust forms of democratic equality and power sharing), but it does mean that there is currently no well-functioning market for democratic rights. There is a market failure, in other words, in the sale of democratic rights, and this is precisely one of the reasons why the state should help to expand democratic workplaces—in order to provide a choice for democratic work that the market is failing to provide. The broader point is that choice always happens against a set of background conditions. Think about a cafeteria in a university. If there are ten restaurants all of which are corporate fast food chains, and after a year 99% of the students have eaten at one of the chains at some point, we cannot sensibly conclude that this proves that students overwhelmingly prefer fast food to healthy or fair-trade alternatives. People's choices are inherently constrained by the existing institutional options.

The second, and more profound, issue is that workers have not generally been strong enough to put the issue of firm governance on the bargaining table. The lack of widespread bargaining for democratic voice that we see today does not, I think, reflect a lack of interest in democratizing work (*pace* Maitland) but rather reflects a lack of bargaining power. The reason that the shark and the tuna do not harmoniously share the sea has little to do with the wishes of the tuna. The evidence for this is clear: at the height of workers' bargaining power—in the 1970s in social democratic countries—governance issues and economic democracy were firmly on the bargaining table. Indeed, it was precisely at the height of this union power that major moves toward economic democracy were made in the form of co-determination in countries like Sweden and Germany, the Auroux laws facilitating *autogestion* in France, Tony Benn's call for industrial democracy in the United Kingdom, and so on (Sassoon, 1996).

In other words, I share the liberal sentiment that people should be free to choose. The choice of workplace governance structures, of whether to spend thousands of hours of our lives in associations in which we are formally equals or in which we are formally subservient, is a very important one with profound consequences for our freedom, happiness, and well-being. But I disagree that such a choice is currently open or institutionally accessible for the majority of people. In fact, as we will see below, there is strong evidence that many people do desire more democracy at work; the problem is that there are so few avenues for people to actually choose this option.

Are Workplaces Private Associations?

So far the argument has been that the average person is compelled to join hierarchical workplaces due to force of circumstance and lack of alternative options. Widespread inequality in the possession of skills and ownership of productive assets leads to unequal bargaining positions which in turn lead to inegalitarian contracts that establish hierarchical relationships where most workers are essentially servants. This, I believe, is unjust and so requires that the state foster democratic alternatives to remedy the situation. Implicit in this argument is that workplaces are different kinds of associations than, say, clubs. They are not "private" in quite the same way.

It is a widely accepted liberal notion that private associations such as clubs do not need to be democratically organized. Liberals have long maintained, and rightly so, that people should be free to start or join any kind of association that they choose, and that there is nothing wrong with undemocratic kinds of clubs as long as one can always exit easily. As Mayer (2001) says: "Clubs do not have to be democratic, even in a democratic society. Founders are free to craft the governance structure they deem best, and new members have no moral right to require political equality where it does not exist" (p. 240). Rawls (1971) echoes this sentiment, "Particular associations may be freely organized as their members wish, and they may have their own internal life and discipline subject to the restriction that their members have a real choice of whether to continue their affiliation" (p. 212). Liberals are quick to point out that if the state were to mandate particular kinds of club structures (such as democratic ones)—this would be deeply paternalistic (Rosenblum, 1998). Forcing democracy on private associations (e.g., mosques or churches) would drastically and dramatically undermine the freedom of individuals to associate together through whatever governance structure they prefer. It would limit individuals' choices and require the state abandoning neutrality to impose a particular vision of the good life on the civic lives of its citizens.

Several critics of workplace democracy have made the same kind of argument vis-à-vis workplaces. For example, Arneson (1993) implies, and others are more explicit (Mayer, 2001, p. 240), that workplaces should be seen as analogous to clubs. The implication being that since workplaces are private, workers and employers should simply be left alone to associate however they please, democratically or not; the state should not be involved.

This, I think, is wrong because workplaces are fundamentally different kinds of associations than clubs. First, it is not nearly as easy for workers to exit their workplace as it is for people to exit their clubs. Most people are compelled to join workplaces for a variety of material and cultural reasons that are simply not the same with joining, say, a typical bowling or bird-watching club. That means that the power that is exercised in hierarchical workplaces cannot be easily avoided. This is not to say that people are completely bound to any particular workplace—I accept the general empirical claim that most people can exit their workplace easier than they can exit their state, for example.[5] And so there may well be a deeper inalienable right to democracy in the state that does not exist in the workplace (see Arneson 1993 and Malleson 2013a for this argument). Nevertheless, it is also true that, generally speaking, it is significantly harder to exit workplaces than clubs. While people can exit particular workplaces (one can leave a hierarchical job at McDonalds for an equally hierarchical job at Burger King), it is much more difficult to avoid hierarchical work altogether. The compulsion to join a workplace is of a different order of magnitude than for clubs.

Second, workplaces occupy a position of central importance to people's lives that is largely different from private clubs. On the one hand, people typically spend much more time and energy at work than they do at clubs. The average employed American, for instance, spends about 35 hours per week working, compared to only 2 hours per week involved in religious or other associations (Estlund, 2000, pp. 8–9). Moreover, work plays a crucially important role in determining one's social status. One's position in the workplace has broad implications for one's overall social standing, sense of self-respect and dignity, in ways that are not all comparable to most clubs.[6] For these reasons, the power that is exercised in workplaces and the significance of the internal governance relationships are much more "socially consequential" than in clubs (Bowles & Gintis, 1986). The state cannot be totally "hands off" vis-à-vis workplaces because ignoring long-term inequality in such associations means abandoning people to second-class status. For this reason it is not quite right to characterize workplaces as either straightforwardly "public" or "private" associations. We might more accurately call them "socially consequential private associations" (Malleson, 2013a).

The fact that workplaces have these differences from clubs means that we must be much more concerned and proactive to ensure that, as Rawls puts it, people have "a *real* choice of whether to continue their affiliation" to their workplace (emphasis added). Unfortunately, the current state of affairs is one in which people generally do not have such a choice; the typical working person is compelled to join a hierarchical workplace where she is essentially a servant. Because of the centrality of work to people's lives this is a serious problem. Long-term involuntary subservience at work can be detrimental to one's self-respect, damaging to the full development of one's moral powers, and an affront to one's ability to exercise meaningful control over one's own life. Since work is so socially consequential the state does need to be involved in order to ensure the background conditions are such that an individual's choice to enter such associations is genuinely voluntary: the choice of joining a hierarchical workplace must be "real." There is nothing particularly radical about this. All liberals would agree that it is unjust to compel people to join other kinds of hierarchical associations—such as churches or mosques—since a compulsion to join such organizations would curb one's personal pursuit of the good life. Likewise, we need to ask: Does it not restrict people's pursuit of the good life when so many people are systematically denied the opportunity to be equals at work (in the sense of possessing formally equal governing influence)?

To clarify the underlying argument, consider another important association: that of marriage in the 1930s or 1940s. Recall that the "governance structure" of the family at this time was often intensely patriarchal. The husband was the head of the family—making the important decisions and controlling the family's resources—while the wife was informally but substantively subservient. Women were the second sex. They could be raped by their husbands without legal repercussion; they married young, were expected to have children, and devote themselves to care-giving and life within the home.

The essential fact about marriage in this era is that it was characterized by a limited degree of exitability. Although divorce was legal, there was nevertheless substantial pressure—both material and cultural—for women to get married. In 1940, for example, white married women relied on their husbands to provide an average of 86% of their economic support (Sorensen & McLanahan, 1987, p. 669). Moreover, while marriages were (and still are) intensely private affairs, they were also deeply socially consequential—one's position in family life was often a central locus of one's time and energy and an important determinant of one's social standing, self-respect, and sense of moral worth.

So what does justice require for the internal governance relationship of the marriage? This is a thorny question because the family has characteristics of both private and public associations. On the one hand, marriage is an intensely private affair; we clearly do not want to paternalistically tell families how to organize their internal relationships because it is important that we respect people's choices about organizing their private family life as they see fit. On the other hand, the personal is the political; we cannot in good conscience abandon women to a lifetime of subservience in hierarchical marriages, which they may deeply dislike, but are constrained to remain in due to the lack of viable alternatives. We should neither abandon women to subservience nor mandate democratic equality.

I would argue, and suspect that many liberals would agree, that justice in such cases requires that the state should foster the background conditions so that women are empowered to choose alternatives; they should be free (but not forced) to choose egalitarian relationships if they so desire. Concretely, this requires a range of state policies—facilitating divorce, ensuring child support, alimony, and pension sharing, instituting laws against physical abuse or rape within marriage, facilitating material independence by outlawing discrimination at work, legalizing maternity leave, providing affordable daycare, and so on.

Historically, what has happened in most developed countries is that state policies such as the above helped to increase the bargaining position of women (by reducing women's dependence on a husband and increasing the economic ability to leave). Such policies, combined with a growing culture of gender equality galvanized by second wave feminism, allowed women to leverage their new bargaining power to insist on more democratic equality. So, state policies that fostered women's ability to leave had the indirect effect of simultaneously fostering egalitarian voice.

Moreover, it is worth noting that as the background conditions have changed over the last 70 years (though perhaps not as much as we would want), and as women's choices about marriage have become less constrained, we have concurrently witnessed a corresponding surge in egalitarian relationships. Today the egalitarian marriage is (for the most part) the norm. The more the choice of equality has become a real possibility, the more that such a choice has actually been made.

Now I want to argue that the same argument holds in the case of workplaces. Workplaces today are likewise characterized by a limited degree of exitability. While exit is legal, the average worker is nevertheless largely compelled to join a hierarchical workplace due to force of circumstance and lack of alternative options. Additionally, workplaces, like families, are deeply socially consequential since they constitute a central locus of people's time, energy, and social standing. And just as justice requires that women should not be compelled to be subservient in their marriages, justice requires that workers should not be compelled to be subservient at work. This does not mean that people should be forced to adopt workplace democracy; people should be allowed to sign up for subservience at work if they so choose (just as consenting sexual partners can choose to engage in BDSM). The point is only that the choice needs to be genuine; people must have a real choice about whether to work in a hierarchy or a democracy. And for that to happen there need to be real alternatives. The bottom line is that justice requires the state to foster the background conditions so that just as women are free (but not forced) to choose egalitarian relationships, workers become likewise free (but not forced) to choose democratic workplaces. Concretely this requires that the state foster the expansion of workplace democracy so that this choice becomes readily accessible (in ways that are discussed below).

It is important to realize that while the argument advanced here is not standard among liberals, it is in no way illiberal. It is based on standard liberal convictions that long-term relations of subservience are dangerous (because they risk undermining human autonomy and dignity) and that free choice is important for safeguarding people's freedom. Liberals are right to be wary of forcing a particular form of association (democratic or otherwise) on people because of a respect for individual free choice. But the intuition that says "people should be free to associate however they want—even subserviently" must be balanced by another intuition—just as rich in the liberal tradition— that says with Kant and John Stuart Mill "sapere aude!"[7] Subservience conflicts with human dignity. Free men and women cannot be content and are unlikely to develop their capacities and moral powers to their full potential in long-lasting relationships of subservience. We cannot force people to be free. But we can and should arrange the background conditions so that those people who desire democracy at work are genuinely able to choose it. Granted, this is no strict state neutrality. A state that acts to foster opportunities for people to replace hierarchical relationships with democratic ones is not strictly neutral, but it is nevertheless entirely defensible on a relatively thin account of the good life that many people can endorse—based only on common liberal-egalitarian values of the importance of equal opportunity, self-determination, and individual choice.

Fostering Workplace Democracy

What would it mean for a workplace to be organized democratically? While democratization can take multiple forms, the standard model of a democratic workplace is that of a worker cooperative where ultimate authority resides with the general assembly on a one-person one-vote basis. This means that, although different jobs may have different roles and pay different wages, the management of the firm is decided on a strictly egalitarian basis. In small firms, decisions might be made collectively through direct participation of all members. Many small cooperatives, such as co-op cafes, restaurants, bike shops, and so on work in this way. For instance, the Mondragon Bookstore in Winnipeg (named after the famous Mondragon co-op) has used its democratic structure to implement a system of balanced job complexes (BJCs) (Burrows, 2008). The idea here is that normal capitalist firms tend to have a stark division between workers with more empowering jobs at the top of the hierarchy and those that get stuck with the less empowering "drudgery." The basic idea behind BJCs is that an attempt is made to share out the unpleasant work as well as the more empowering work so that neither falls entirely on one group of people, without meaning that everyone is expected to do everything (Albert, 2003).[8] What is crucial about the democratic structure of the workplace is that it has allowed the Bookstore to experiment with new ways of organizing things in an attempt to improve the quality of people's working lives.

Larger co-ops with high levels of complexity and specialization can clearly not make all their decisions through general participation—they require delegation of authority by electing representatives in the familiar ways of representative democracy. For example, the 40,000 or so worker-members of the Mondragon co-ops meet as a whole in a Cooperative Congress, which acts like a mini-parliament, composed of elected representatives from every co-op (in rough proportion to their size).

Co-ops often hire new workers on a temporary basis who do not have equal democratic rights. Of course, this may not be a problem for those workers who want to be only temporary, but it is important that a significant majority of the workers in a co-op be full members so as to prevent the emergence of an exploited subgroup of disenfranchised workers. I would argue that for co-ops to be genuine they must fulfill two standards: the significant majority of the workers are full members (perhaps 75% or more), and, even more importantly, the nonmembers are able to become members should they wish to do so (after a reasonable probationary period and a not prohibitively high investment stake). It is hard to characterize workplaces with less than 50% members as genuine co-ops; they are more accurately seen as "capitalist partnerships" (Malleson, 2013b).[9]

Large co-ops that meet these specifications will still require specialization and so still have order-givers and order-takers. But those who give orders are now fundamentally accountable to those who take them. This is what makes a co-op a democracy and not a hierarchy. The democratic structure of the firm creates an important basis of formal equality in terms of decision-making power and basic freedoms. The basic parliamentary structures protect workers' freedom in the negative sense, while the avenues that exist for direct participation enable workers' self-determination in the positive sense. Participation is easy in small co-ops but it must be cultivated in large ones (we examine how this can be done in the next chapter). Ideally, a co-op structure means that all people in positions of power and authority are elected, revocable, and accountable to the rank and file. Authority no longer derives from shareholding and property rights, but, ultimately, from the consent of the workers themselves. Whereas capitalist firms are characterized by the fact that capital hires labor and uses it for its benefit, cooperative firms are characterized by what Mondragon workers call the "sovereignty of labour." This explains the fact mentioned above that workers in hierarchical firms are, in a functional sense, "servants"—a word that I use purposefully in order to highlight the heteronomy or subservience of work for the average worker. In most cases, average workers are tools; their hands and brains are directed by others, for projects determined by others, toward goals selected by others. Whereas servants are functional tools of their bosses, co-op members are, at root, self-determining equals who have chosen managers for their purposes (and can remove them should they wish).

However, it must be immediately pointed out that it is entirely possible for structural equality to coexist with informal hierarchy. Most real-world co-ops and democratic organizations are negatively affected to a greater or lesser degree by the informal hierarchies that can stem from expertise, control of information, patriarchy, and so on. But this does not diminish the importance of formal equality. Creating formal equality is an absolutely necessary (if not sufficient) step toward developing genuinely empowering workplaces, which will be discussed further next chapter.

Notice that workplaces have the potential to be substantially more democratic than contemporary states. In particular, workplaces have the potential to be much more deeply democratic than states because they are much smaller and so have much more scope for direct participation and therefore more possibility for meaningful self-determination. In 2007 the American economy had a total of 6.05 million firms (involving more than one person). Of these, 5.41 million had fewer than 20 employees. In other words, 89% of all American businesses (discounting single-person businesses) involved the cooperation of fewer than 20 people (and 99.7% involved fewer than 500 people) (SBA, 2010, p. 121). The economy with its millions of small firms thus provides fertile ground for democratic participation, and therefore meaningful self-governance at a scale and scope that is simply unimaginable in the political arena. Additionally, the fact that there are huge numbers of workplaces means that there is vastly greater opportunity for democratic experimentation—workplaces can experiment with different kinds of governing structures, different organizations of work (such as using BJCs), different patterns of remuneration (such as according to effort instead of productivity), and so on. In this respect workplaces offer much more fertile ground for the flourishing of democracy than the state which has been its historical pasture.

Concretely, what is required to foster the expansion of opportunities for democratic work? There are two broad public policy paths available. The first is to follow the same route as with marriages: increase the bargaining power of workers in relation to hierarchical firms. This could be done by facilitating the growth of the union movement or by facilitating workers' ability to leave undemocratic work. Over the short term this latter possibility could be accomplished by enhancing the welfare system, and over the long term by implementing a guaranteed basic income.[10] The higher a basic income is set, the less compulsion workers face to accept the first job that they are offered, thus providing them increased bargaining power to demand increased democratic say from conventional employers.

The second public policy route is for the state to encourage the formation of democratic workplaces in the form of worker cooperatives. This requires both legal and material support. Legal support ranges from short-term objectives of establishing a robust legal framework within which cooperatives can operate (some American states still lack this); the most important long-term legal objective would be for the state to pass legislation giving a majority of workers the right to transform their workplace into a cooperative if they so wish. What would this require? In the majority of cases, this would require a legal right for workers to buy out their workplace from their employers. Theoretically, workplace democracy can be achieved without direct ownership, for instance, by workers collectively renting the facilities and capital stock of the firm from the bank or from old owners (Ellerman, 1992). This might be possible for small NGOs or service-oriented businesses with little reliance on physical infrastructure. However, in practical terms, it is an empirically robust fact that generally cooperative businesses require collective ownership of the business property to succeed.[11] So in order for workplace democracy to become a meaningful option for large numbers of people, workers require a right to buy out their employers or shareholders in order to transform their workplace into a co-op.

These legal rights require material support for them to be fully meaningful since such buyouts would clearly be expensive. Over the short term, material support could include tax breaks or the establishment of a cooperative bank to provide financing help. Over the long term, an economy-wide profit-sharing program, such as a variant of the Meidner Plan, would have the most potential for greatly increasing workplace democracy. Such proposals are discussed more fully in the next chapter.

While I have been arguing in favor of democratization, I do not mean to imply that such reforms would be costless. Arguably the democratization of families had costs associated with it. For instance, the increased ability of women to leave their husbands has likely led to an increase of single-parent families. Although not ideal, I think most would agree that such costs are clearly outweighed by the benefits of female independence. Similarly, democratizing work is sure to have costs (most obviously the financial costs associated with paying for its expansion). It is important not to sweep these costs under the rug. Indeed, a central goal of this chapter and the next is to provide a full picture of the relative costs and benefits, so that we are in a position to sensibly decide whether expanding workplace democracy is worth it.

A Caveat

At this point we need to introduce an important caveat into the argument. Although I have argued that workers should have the option of transforming their workplace into worker co-ops, there are several sectors of the economy where this is not appropriate (Nove, 1991). The two main areas where worker cooperatives are not an appropriate model are the public sector[12] and areas of very high capital intensity.

Workplaces that are public tend to be so because they are thought to directly fulfill a general public interest that the market would be unlikely to satisfactorily provide (e.g., hospitals, schools, post offices, water, electricity, transportation, etc.). Such workplaces are particular in that they significantly affect two different constituencies—the smaller association of internal workers and the larger association of the community itself. How a school operates, for instance, is obviously of concern to the internal teachers as well as to the broader public. Public workplaces today are partially democratic in that they are supposed to be accountable to the citizenry at large via their elected representatives who ultimately control them, but they are not currently democratic with respect to the internal workers. The denial of democracy to the internal workers seems to me unjust for all the reasons of freedom and equality articulated above. But in cases like this, it does not make sense for such workplaces to be entirely controlled by the workers. We would not want all the electricity in a country to be controlled by the handful of workers who worked the plants, nor the school curriculum decided unilaterally by the school staff, since this would be undemocratic from the perspective of the larger community who genuinely do have a public interest in such things. So, in these cases, some broad type of co-management seems appropriate. This might mean having a board of directors for public firms which splits authority between state and worker representatives,[13] or having certain public sector workplaces (such as schools or hospitals) reorganized as cooperatives, but with their funding remaining contingent on meeting state-specified objectives (Hirst, 1994). Indeed, in northern Italy, many social services are provided by this kind of "social cooperative" (Restakis, 2007).

The final sector that is inappropriate for co-ops consists of firms with large capital intensity (i.e., few workers but very expensive equipment) (Drèze, 1993). These kinds of industries (oil, steel, auto, pharmaceutical, etc.) are inhospitable for cooperative governance because it is basically impossible for a group of average-income workers to acquire ownership of firms like this. Nor would we want the state to help fund a small group of workers to take over multi-million-dollar capital stock, since far from increasing societal equality, this would simply create a handful of new elites. So in this sector too, a better solution is that of co-management: firms like this could be bought by the state, but instead of being run in the usual way, management should be divided between representatives of the internal workers and representatives of the community. This kind of nationalization-with-democratization need not be costly for the state (indeed it can be very profitable) provided such firms are run well.[14] It would give workers some control over their workplaces without requiring the enrichment of a handful of workers to render such control possible.

The Social Democratic Objection

At this point it is important to consider the social democratic objection. Think of Sweden or another social democratic country where workers have heightened bargaining power due to a combination of a strong welfare system, powerful unions, and state regulation of business. In such a context is there still a need for workplace democracy?

While social democratic institutions are an important advance over neoliberal ones in the increased protections they offer to workers, they still do not address the fundamental issue which is that workers do not have a genuine choice of working in democratic workplaces; the option of equality at work remains largely unavailable.[15] It is true that there is less compulsion to take a job in, say, Sweden because the safety net makes it easier to leave. But the average Swedish worker who does not want to be on welfare her whole life (i.e., the vast majority) is still effectively compelled to join a hierarchical firm because there are so few democratic alternatives. The worker cooperative sector accounts for a miniscule amount of the economy (about 0.2%), and given that only about 0.12% of the adult population stay on welfare for long periods of time, the vast majority of the population clearly has little alternative to hierarchical work.[16]

Social democratic institutions do indeed increase workers' freedom in the negative sense of protection. This is a good thing, but it is still inadequate for two basic reasons. First, workplaces within social democracies retain deep-seated structural inequality. Protective regulations do not change the basic fact that business owners have power over workers not because they were elected, but because they own property. Perhaps they acquired their property through inheritance; perhaps they were frugal all their lives and saved it; perhaps they won the lottery. Whatever the case, it is fundamentally unfair for some to have substantial decision-making power over others simply on the basis of their wealth. Walzer (1983) is right to insist that "what democracy requires is that property should have no political currency, that it shouldn't convert into anything like sovereignty, authoritative command, sustained control over men and women" (p. 298). The idea that legitimate decision-making power over other people can stem from property ownership is a feudal anachronism that we need to outgrow. Getting rid of the last remnants of feudalism, which we have not yet fully done even in the progressive social democracies, means recognizing that legitimate authority can only rest on agreement between equal human beings. No matter how strong unions are in social democracies, the workers are never the equals of managers and owners. In a co-op, however, workers and managers are fundamentally equal. Although elected managers have more decision-making power, both managers and workers are subject to the same rules and enjoy the same fundamental rights and status. In other words, social democratic workplaces retain structural inequality in the form of hierarchy. As long as they do so, there is a constant and ubiquitous danger of workers getting abused, mistreated, and oppressed. Unions and regulations may soften the dangers, but they cannot alleviate their source. They are like taking aspirin for cancer: painkillers but not a cure.

Second, unions and state regulations are fundamentally inappropriate institutions for enhancing the freedom of self-determination. Unions (ideally) are defensive organizations.[17] They exist to soften the work hierarchy and make inequality bearable. Although they are responsible for most of the freedoms that citizens in the Western world now enjoy (from public pensions to universal healthcare to the existence of the weekend), they are not designed to transform the management of the workplace or to challenge who is in ultimate control. Fundamentally, G. D. H. Cole (1920, p. 20) is right to say that unions have in their hands only a brake and never a steering wheel. They maintain workers in the passenger seat of history—unable to steer for themselves and able only to pull the handbrake in times of emergency. In contrast, co-ops (ideally) are organizations for workers' self-management and self-determination. They are not designed to soften work hierarchy, but to abolish it (in the sense of removing formally unaccountable power). They are not simply defensive organizations but are active ones, enabling workers increased power to navigate their own path. This is not to say, of course, that co-ops are always successful at doing so. Too often they prove inadequate in their defensive role (as the strike in 1974 at Mondragon famously demonstrated) and equally inadequate in their active role of providing meaningful avenues for widespread participation (as we will see in the next chapter). Nevertheless, co-ops offer a real potential to foster the freedom of self-determination that is lacking in social democracy.

Notwithstanding the welfare system, the unions, and the state regulations, workplaces in the social democracies do not allow for egalitarian self-determination. This is a major problem. Having the power to influence the direction of your workplace, being able to participate as an equal in the evolution of a project, these are things which are currently a privilege in our society, available only to a lucky few. Cooperative workplaces are hardly paradises. But, when they work well, they provide definite improvements by fostering broader avenues for participation than conventional firms, as well as significantly reducing the alienation and powerlessness from which the bulk of workers suffer in a manner of quiet frustration which for too long has simply been accepted as the norm.

Further Objections

The skeptical reader will likely have a number of further objections to the idea of workplace democracy. Three in particular deserve our attention. First, there is the objection that people do not really want democracy at work. Second, one might worry that workplace democracy undermines the freedom of the entrepreneur to direct her business as she sees fit. Third is the Platonic or technocratic objection that employers and/or managers should have superior say because of their expertise in running the business.

The Desire for Workplace Democracy

It is sometimes suggested that talk of workplace democracy is moot since most working people do not actually want it. Indeed, it is true that there are valid reasons why one may well feel hesitant toward the prospect of increased democracy at work. Most obviously, people may not want to risk the money required to buy out their firm or start a new one.[18] But beyond the familiar material restraints, there may be other reasons why people are resistant to democracy itself. They may not want the time commitment that democracy requires—reflecting Oscar Wilde's quip that the chief defect of socialism is that it would take too many evenings; they may not want the responsibility and stress that comes with being "in charge"; all in all, people may feel that self-determination is simply too hard work for it to count as "freedom."

Those who value increased democracy at work do so because they subscribe to the ethic that self-governing through participation in decision-making is an important aspect of freedom (though not the only kind of freedom, since being left alone to engage in one's own pursuits is clearly an important kind of freedom too). Yet if there is one critique that I find most difficult to answer, it is the rejection of the notion that self-determination counts as a type of freedom. For some, this simply cannot be freedom. Freedom cannot be an endless meeting, but must be the opposite, such as collapsing in front of the TV. Life is hard as it is, so freedom must be light and relaxing. Easy, like a tremendous exhale. This is the intuition that many have which runs precisely counter to the ideal of self-determination. Although it is true that life is hard, I think that freedom is hard too. Which is not to say that it is terrible—in fact it can be one of the best things in life—even if it is hard. I do not know how to counter the common intuition that freedom must be easy except by juxtaposing it with another equally powerful intuition: that abandoning self-determination requires relinquishing something very deep about the desire of human beings to not be controlled. A character in Ursula Le Guin's novel *Dispossessed* puts it this way: "It's always easier not to think for oneself. Find a nice safe hierarchy and settle in. Don't make changes, don't risk disapproval, don't upset [others]....It's always easiest to let yourself be governed" (1974, p. 149). It goes without saying that easier is not always better.

What is the empirical evidence concerning workers' desire for increased democracy at work? The answer depends a lot on how you phrase the question. On the one hand, it is clear that most countries in the West have very limited amounts of workplace democracy right now (Dow, 2003). We have seen that some on the Right argue that this shows that workers do not actually want it, for if they did they would be willing to take lower wages for increased democratic voice (Maitland, 1989). However, the empirical fact about the rarity of workplace democracy may simply reflect businesses' intransigence and hostility toward the idea of forfeiting control over the firm,[19] combined with the fact that even if workers really do value workplace democracy they may perfectly reasonably not wish to sacrifice substantial amounts of income for it. That does not mean that workers do not value increased say at work, only that it may not be their primary concern.

On the other hand, when workers are directly asked whether they would like more say at work, they clearly answer yes. In a comprehensive study of social attitudes, Zipp et al. (1984, pp. 406–7) report that although most Americans report job satisfaction, there is also "widespread favorable feelings toward increased democracy in the workplace"—with 79% of respondents stating they would rather work for an employee-owned firm than an investor- or government-owned one. A Federal Commission sponsored by the US Department of Labor found that 84% of workers would like to participate more in workplace decisions (Commission on the Future of Worker–Management Relations, 1995, p. 39). Probably the most comprehensive analysis of American workers' attitudes toward workplace relationships is Freeman and Rogers (1999). Their data show "as conclusively as any survey can that the vast majority of employees want more involvement and greater say in company decisions affecting their workplace," with 63% of workers indicating their desire for more influence over workplace decisions (1999, pp. 40–41).[20] Even this degree of enthusiasm for increased worker influence is somewhat surprising given the dominant cultural norms that take for granted the need for experts and superiors, the naturalness of hierarchy, the idea of work as a drag, and freedom as independence understood as relaxing in front of the TV.

Related evidence for people's desire to control their own lives is the widespread desire to be self-employed. Indeed, the fact that so many people—10% of the labor force in most countries—are willing to face the daunting odds (the high risks, the long hours, the low pay, and the fact that roughly 40% will fail in their first year (Taylor, 1999)), speaks volumes about the widespread desire to escape hierarchical work. Not only is self-employment a dream of many people, but whenever people are asked why they want it, their answers invariably refer to the absence of a boss, the capacity to make decisions oneself, to be in control of one's own working schedule; in short, the ability to self-determine.[21]

The bulk of the evidence thus indicates that while a minority may indeed choose subservience at work the majority has subservience thrust upon them.

One of the most interesting aspects of the evidence on participation is that once workers begin to participate, they tend to want to more and more; in other words, participation breeds participation (Mason, 1982; Sobel, 1993). This trend has been noted in co-ops all over the world, from England to Venezuela (Cornforth et al., 1988; Piñeiro, 2007). Such a trend suggests that, in general, the more people are exposed to workplace democracy, the more they will desire it (other things being equal). I suspect this is generally the case, since freedom is like a muscle of the human spirit; it tends to atrophy and diminish with neglect, but grows and becomes stronger from regular use. It is instructive to recall that throughout the 1950s millions of middle-class women started to work outside the home, even though the work conditions were often unpleasant and the material requirement to do so was often quite limited. Sixty years later, the desire to work outside the home, and the recognition of the kind of freedoms that can come with this, have grown immensely and become normalized. Indeed, today, the denial of the freedom to work outside of the home would strike us as atrocious. The radicalism of the second-wave feminists in demanding opportunities to participate in the workforce has become our common sense. Similarly, I suspect that were the real material opportunities for workplace democracy to increase, we could expect a drastic increase in the number of cooperatives as well as in the number of people who desire increased workplace participation and feel distinctly unfree without it.

Property Rights versus Democratic Rights

Consider the case of an entrepreneur; call her Rana. Most would agree that there is nothing wrong with her renting capital and/or machines in order to start a business. Such a process is often an important source of innovation, and should she produce something that others wish to buy (and assuming they can afford it), her self-interested behavior can serve the public good. Should the business prosper, Rana will likely wish to hire employees in order to expand. But this is where difficulties arise. It is not a problem for Rana to rent the capital or machines and use them however she wishes, but it is a categorically different issue to rent human labor and use it however she wishes.[22] Some have argued that it is never acceptable to rent human beings (Ellerman, 1992)—but I want to sidestep that debate here. The important point is that when a business is a one-person business, then the entrepreneur legitimately has total control over it. However, when Rana starts hiring others, the business becomes less and less a simple extension of her particular vision and more and more an association of work. Time is the crucial factor here. On the day that Rana hires Hanan, it seems clear that we would still want to call the business Rana's. Yet if Hanan were to work there for several years, then so much of the business would be the product of joint labor, joint effort, joint intelligence, joint creativity, and so on that it seems increasingly false to see the business as solely Rana's, and increasingly unfair for Rana to retain supreme control over it, to be able to direct Hanan as she sees fit, order her around, and so on. After a certain time a group of people working together start to constitute a work association, and Hanan should acquire a right to choose whether she wishes to become an equal in the association.

Consider the injustice we would feel at the following (common) situation: Rana decides to give the company to her daughter Ranette. All of a sudden Ranette is in charge. She may have never set foot in the business before and know nothing about it, but she comes in on Monday morning, twenty years younger than all the workers, with the power to hire and fire, to give raises, slash pensions, and much more. She orders Hanan and the others to change the business direction, ordering them to scrap one project that they had been working on for years to take up an entirely different one. She insists on a more formal workplace than her mother did—requiring the workers to dress differently and refer to her as "Ma'am." We feel the injustice of such a situation because it is clear that what is being inherited here is not simply wealth but power.

After a certain time the employer should not lose her right to her property, but she should lose the right to use her control over property as a means for controlling other people. So we see that conventional private enterprises are really a bundle of two distinct things: (i) a set of property and capital (offices, machines, etc.) and (ii) an association of work involving power relations between people. Usually, (i) implies (ii); that is, unequal ownership of property compels those without property—Hanan in our example—to accept the work relations within the association dictated by the owner. Usually, unequal ownership of property is translated through the employment contract into power over people.

It is important to remember that firms are always both of these things (a set of property and an association of workers) because *ownership of things should not translate into power over people*. This should be a basic principle of a democratic post-feudal society. Since work is a particularly important type of association—one that is deeply socially consequential—Hanan and the other workers should have the legal right to choose to democratize the workplace.

But this is difficult as long as Ranette is the sole owner of the property of the firm (because if one person owns the property there cannot be equal decision-making about how to use it). So in most cases what is required is a right for the workers to hold a referendum to decide if they would like to buy out Ranette (so that the workers come to collectively own the firm, and therefore are in a practical position to democratically govern it). The right to do this is conditioned in part by time. Having worked for one week does not seem to be enough time to give an employee a right to equal say, whereas 10 years is more than enough. Deciding the time limit at which point a worker is considered no longer temporary but part of the association is, of course, slightly arbitrary, but the underlying principle should be clear: after sufficient time the right of property owners to direct labor is eclipsed by the right of the associated laborers to choose whether they would like to self-determine. One year seems to me about right. Note that no workers are forced to work in a democratic firm: this remains purely a private choice. What is at stake here is simply the provision of a real opportunity for workers to access workplace democracy should they desire it. The purpose is to foster egalitarian opportunities not dictate democratic outcomes.

Connected to this issue is the worry that giving a voice to employees might seem to require unfair redistribution of property. For instance, if Rana initially invests $10,000 into her business then works hard on it by herself for 10 years, it seems unfair for Hanan, a new employee, to immediately acquire say over the business property now worth $100,000. Indeed, for Hanan to have equal say over this capital is tantamount to expropriation. This kind of expropriation would strike many as unjust.[23] Hanan should not instantly acquire a right to voice, but only after a certain time. And even then, her right should be to buy out Rana (or become co-owners with her) so there is no issue of expropriation of property, only redistribution of voice.

Democracy and Experts

While the legal basis of the authority of management rests on contracts and ownership, the ideological basis for their authority usually involves some claim of expertise. CEOs typically justify their exorbitant salaries with the claim that such is the market value of their managerial expertise.[24] Does expertise justify a lack of democracy in the workplace? The first thing to say about this is to point out that in fact managers (and this is even truer for external shareholders) may have very limited knowledge of much of the complex inner workings of a firm—and often substantially less than the workers who engage in such operations on a daily basis. The mass of workers are likely to have hundreds of ideas for improving the firm's operations; however, they usually have no incentive (or power) to implement them, since whatever benefits result will flow to the employers alone. In Colin Ward's words, "the fantastic inefficiency of any hierarchical organization is the outcome of...[the fact that] the knowledge and wisdom of the people at the bottom of the pyramid finds no place in the decision-making leadership hierarchy of the institution" (1982, p. 41). One of the fundamental arguments in favor of democratization is that it unleashes the creativity and contributions of all those who had been disempowered but now feel a sense of ownership.

This said, it is clear that complex organizations do require specialization and expertise—so the question remains as to whether experts should have authority over rank-and-file workers on the basis of their expertise.

This is a difficult question. On the one hand, we should reject the idea that ordinary people, nonexperts, should be disenfranchised from decision-making. Just as the state should not be controlled by the political science professors or philosopher-kings on the basis that they know the most politics, neither should business be run by "economist-kings." Democrats throughout history have rejected this Platonic justification for elite rule and rightly insisted on the capacities of ordinary citizens to decide for themselves what is best for themselves. Experts need to remain accountable to the workers. On the other hand, there may well be situations where experts require substantial autonomy to do their job well—constant surveillance and monitoring would only serve to undercut their effectiveness.

There is a real tension here—it is an instance where democratic practice is more art than science. Overall I would stress two things: first, the importance of balance. Both accountability and autonomy are important for experts, but since these cut in opposing ways they need to be kept in balance. Ultimately, I think a wise co-op would treat experts as indispensable and respectable tools to be used for the co-ops' purposes. Just as members of parliament will often assemble a group of experts to inform and advise them, so should various departments or work-teams in co-ops use experts to advise them and guide their own decision-making. The important point is that the experts see themselves as equals to the workers, and view their role as that of "advisors" not "bosses." Experts are necessary, but they should serve, not lead—they should be "kept on tap, not on top" (Dahl, 2000, p. 71).

Conclusion

The central argument of this chapter is that the current system of hierarchical work is deeply unjust because the majority of average workers are largely compelled to join workplaces within which they are fundamentally unequal—essentially servants. In both neoliberal and social democratic contexts, it is very difficult for the average person to choose an alternative to hierarchical work in the form of workplace democracy. I have argued that no one should be compelled to be subservient at work, which means that everyone should have the opportunity to choose workplace democracy should they so desire. For such a choice to be real, the state cannot be hands off, but must foster and facilitate the expansion of worker cooperatives.

Although my focus has been on issues of equality and freedom, these are not the only reasons for caring about workplace democracy. There are good reasons to think that a cooperative-based economy would have substantially more income equality and job security. Co-ops are less likely to abandon their town or city to engage in a race-to-the-bottom, and they are less likely to sacrifice employment for profit maximization. And yet they operate with a degree of economic efficiency that is largely comparable to standard firms. It is to these kinds of arguments about the real-world performance of co-ops that we now turn.

3 Worker Cooperatives in Practice

The decision-making process [of cooperatives] as a
whole can be seen as the assertion of economic rationality with a human face.
(Morrison, 1997, p. 188)

Introduction

One of the most striking facts about life in the developed world today is
that the average person is more than twice as rich as 50 years ago, and yet
for all the tremendous increase in wealth, people's overall happiness has not
improved at all (Layard, 2005). No one knows for sure why this contemporary malaise is so pervasive, but one thing is clear: work has not become the
place of creativity and freedom it was often hoped it might be. One sugges-
tive study of 900 women in Texas reported that of normal day-to-day pursuits working was their least enjoyable activity, and overall, the very worst
part of their regular day was interacting with the boss (Kahneman et al.,
2004). Across the economy, even in the richest countries in the world, many
workers continue to suffer from hierarchy at work, feeling powerless and
demoralized. Such is the reality of work at the present time. But is there no
alternative?

Many people can see the strength of the theoretical case for workplace
democracy. That working people should not be compelled to accept subservience at work and so should have a real democratic alternative. However, for
many, the fatal problem with workplace democracy (and economic democracy more generally) is not the theory, but the practice—the fact that there
do not seem to be obvious real-world examples, particularly since the major
attempts to democratize the economy—the USSR in the East and social
democracy in the West—have largely failed in terms of providing genuine
workplace democracy.

This chapter (as well as the other two empirical chapters) thus has two
major goals: first to look at the empirical evidence concerning the kinds of
democratic economic institutions that already exist, and second, to inquire
about how transition to a fuller, more robust form of economic democracy

might be accomplished. In other words, the goal is to explore how the democratic examples that we have here and now might be deepened and expanded.

Here we are concerned with the practical experience and empirical evidence that we have of democratic workplaces in the form of worker cooperatives. We assess this evidence by contrasting co-ops with conventional hierarchical firms, on the one hand, and egalitarian collectives, on the other. The central finding of the chapter is that the evidence shows that cooperatives operate with levels of economic efficiency that are comparable, if not superior, to normal capitalist firms. They are very much viable economic organizations. Moreover, they appear to be socially superior in certain ways. There are, however, a number of key obstacles that keep co-ops rare, which will need to be overcome to enact any transition to an economy with widespread democratic workplaces.

Before turning to the real-world examples it is worth pointing out that there is now a sizable theoretical economic literature attempting to predict and describe cooperative behavior. Unfortunately, the literature is extremely contradictory (see Bonin & Putterman, 1987).

Among the critics, the two most well-known critiques of cooperatives come from Ward (1958) and Furubotn and Pejovich (1970). Ward argued that co-ops will strive to maximize net income per worker. Since co-ops share their profit equally the more members they have means the more slices of the pie there are. So the attempt to maximize personal income will mean that co-ops will react perversely to changes in the market—hiring in bad times, and firing in good times (Domar, 1966; Ward, 1958).[1] Furubotn and Pejovich (1970) theorized that co-ops are doomed to underinvest and so will never be able to compete with capitalist firms. Their critique centered on the idea of the "horizon problem," which is essentially the idea that in co-ops that are collectively owned, the individual worker will not see any benefit from making an investment until that investment pays off down the road (unlike a capitalist firm where investment increases the value of sellable shares today by representing the value of future profitability). And since some of the workers will retire before the investment pays off, their limited time horizon will create a disincentive to invest, thus leading, at least in theory, to substantial underinvestment in comparison to capitalist firms.

Other critics have argued that worker co-ops will be less disciplined (Alchian & Demsetz, 1972; Jensen & Meckling, 1979), less innovative (Roemer, 1994), or suffer from collective decision-making problems (Hansmann, 1996). Still others have argued that co-ops will inevitably degenerate over time due to market pressure (Luxemburg, [1900] 1986; Mandel, 1975; Marx, [1867] 1933; Webb & Webb, 1907) or due to problems of internal structure (Ellerman, 1984).

On the other hand, a number of economists have predicted quite the opposite, that co-ops will react normally to market changes (Vanek, 1970), be sustainable over the long term (Ellerman, 1990; Vanek, 1970), and that they will in fact be more efficient than capitalist firms because co-op workers will be more motivated, more self-disciplined, more trustful, and less conflictual (Ben-Ner & Jones, 1995; Bowles & Gintis, 1993; Bradley & Gelb, 1981; Greenberg, 1981; Horvat, 1986; Stiglitz, 1993). These authors also tend to stress the social advantages that are predicted to flow from the co-op form: greater job stability, greater equality of wages, better workplace conditions, and increased self-management.

Which of these perspectives is better reflected by the evidence? The rest of this chapter reviews the empirical evidence to attempt to answer this question. Indeed, I hope to provide the most up-to-date review of the empirical literature on worker co-ops that presently exists. We will see that the popular stereotype of cooperative inefficiency is better known in theory than it is supported in fact.

We begin by looking briefly at some of the most important and widely studied co-ops in the Western world: Mondragon in northern Spain and La Lega network in northern Italy.[2] These examples have much to teach us about how co-ops should (and should not) be structured, as well as how they might be replicated elsewhere.

Mondragon

Mondragon[3] is seen by many as the world's outstanding example of a cooperative economic system within the global capitalist economy (Gibson-Graham, 2003; Morrison, 1997; Whyte & Whyte, 1988).[4] The Mondragon cooperatives (often referred to simply as Mondragon) started when five young workers graduated from a technical training school run by Catholic priest José María Arizendiarrieta in the small town of Mondragon, in the Basque country of northern Spain. In 1956, with minimal resources, they managed to scrape together enough money from friends and acquaintances to buy a bankrupt factory in order to start producing stoves as a small worker co-op.

After a few years, demand for the products was sufficient for the co-op to expand, though they soon found themselves with limited access to finance as local banks were skeptical about the long-term viability of co-ops and were hostile to worker ownership (Morrison, 1997). A decisive breakthrough came in 1959 when a small handful of co-ops affiliated together to create a co-operative bank—the Caja Laboral (CL)—to pool the co-ops' resources and attract local savings in order to finance their development. The CL was set up as a second-degree cooperative, meaning that it was structured as a co-op of co-ops, managed by a mix of its own workers as well as representatives from the co-ops that were its principal clients. The CL was designed to perform two basic functions: to provide finance at below market rates and, through its Empresarial division, to provide business and managerial advice to help set up new cooperatives and assist those in economic trouble.[5] The CL was (and still is) organized like a credit union, which allows it to attract the savings of the local population, as well as to hold the deposits of the associated co-ops. In this way the CL acts to recycle the community's capital through the democratic workplaces. Its significance can hardly be overstated: as Morrison (1997) points out, it effectively freed Mondragon from dependence on capitalist financiers. With the help of the CL, Mondragon grew enormously—by 2011 it employed 83,000 people, with assets of a tremendous €32 billion (Mondragon, 2011).

The co-ops operate according to ten guiding principles (Morrison, 1997). These are: (i) *Open Admission*—no one can be denied entry based on gender, ethnicity, and so on; (ii) *Democratic Organization*—one-member one-vote;[6] (iii) *Sovereignty of Labor*—meaning that members control the co-op and distribute its surplus; (iv) *Instrumental Character of Capital*—so that the co-ops pay a just but limited return on invested capital and ensure that owning capital does not give any additional rights of governance beyond membership; (v) *Participation in Management*—to ensure member participation and the ongoing development of skills necessary to manage; (vi) *Pay Solidarity*—to limit the differential between highest and lowest paid;[7] (vii) *Intercooperation*—cooperation among the co-ops; (viii) *Social Transformation*; (ix) *Universality*—emphasizing solidarity with all workers; and (x) *Education*—which is ongoing in terms of both cooperative values and technical skills.[8]

New members are required to pay a substantial investment fee (that goes into their personal internal capital account).[9] This fee acts to screen out workers who are not committed to staying, is psychologically important in making workers feel like co-owners, and is important for providing an internal source of financing. In contrast to other co-ops, such as the Plywood co-ops in the northwestern United States, Mondragon is collectively owned (but with individual capital accounts instead of shares), so membership is not for sale.[10] Each year a portion of the firm's profits goes into the individual capital accounts, which receive interest. Workers are permitted to withdraw the interest but not the principal, until they leave the firm. This assures a large and vital source of internal finance. Since new members simply open new internal accounts, membership (with the corresponding governance rights) is importantly distinct from property rights.[11] If a co-op does well, members get more money in their individual accounts, but membership itself (and governance rights) does not become more expensive. In this way the co-ops avoid the structural problems that led many co-ops in the United States and elsewhere to degenerate.

Of a co-op's surplus, 10% is mandated by law toward charities and non-profit organizations, 45% goes into the firm's collective reserve fund, and the remaining 45% goes into members' individual capital accounts (the bulk of which cannot be withdrawn until retirement (Freundlich, Grellier, & Altuna, 2009)). In other words, this structure effectively means that up to 90% of profits are saved internally to help refinance the whole system.

The ultimate authority in each co-op has always been the General Assembly, which meets at least once per year. It elects the Governing Council, which is the highest governing body of the co-op—representing the Assembly between meetings, overseeing the execution of Assembly decisions, and monitoring senior management (Lafuente & Freundlich, 2012). The Governing Council also appoints the CEO and approves his or her choice of senior managers; the CEO and senior managers form the Management Council which runs the day-to-day affairs of the co-op. There is also a Social Council, elected by members in various departments to help with personnel issues (e.g., health benefits, safety). Although it officially has only advisory power, its purpose, while somewhat vague, is generally seen as a kind of internal union. It does not engage in collective bargaining but serves to strengthen communication, represent shop- or office-floor perspectives, and allow rank-and-file members more direct engagement with management. Whyte and Whyte (1988, p. 148) argue that whereas the Governing Council represents the members as owners, the Social Council represents them as workers—playing the essential role of guiding education, discussion, and decision-making. Finally, an Audit Committee audits the books.

Since 1987, the Mondragon co-ops as a whole have been collectively represented in a Cooperative Congress, which acts like a mini-parliament, composed of elected representatives from every co-op (in rough proportion to their size) to consider issues of broad concern to the whole system. It is important to note that while each co-op is independent (i.e., under the direct democratic control of its members), it is also embedded in a larger network of supporting structures that provide financial, business, technical, educational, and social support (Lafuente & Freundlich, 2012; MacLeod & Reed, 2009).

Mondragon underwent massive, some would say fundamental, changes in the 1980s and 1990s, due to substantial pressures from globalization. Members widely believed that they would have to adapt to the global competition if they were to survive. To get a sense of the global pressures they faced consider the dilemma of Irizar—one of the most successful co-ops associated with Mondragon. In the 1990s Irizar was able to manufacture a bus at home at a cost of €180,000, whereas the same vehicle could be produced by competitors in China for only €12,000 (MacLeod & Reed, 2009, p. 137). Pressures like these led Mondragon to undertake significant restructuring in the 1990s so as to be better able to compete internationally. The system changed its name from the "Mondragon Cooperative Group" to the "Mondragon Cooperative Corporation"; since 2007 the corporation has simply been referred to as "Mondragon." The co-ops which had previously been organized into geographical groups were reorganized into four business groups: a financial group, a retail group (dominated by the Eroski supermarket chain), an industrial group (itself divided into several divisions), and a knowledge (research/training) group—thus allowing for greater inter-firm cooperation and synergy, as well as economies of scale (MacLeod & Reed, 2009, p. 120).

Probably the most significant change of this period was the composition of its workforce. Mondragon has witnessed a massive expansion of nonmember workers through two avenues. First, the 1990s saw a sharp increase in the number of temporary nonmember workers in the co-ops (reaching a high of 29.8% in 2000 (Arando et al., 2010, p. 19)). Second, and more significantly, there has been a dramatic increase in the number of nonmember workers working in Mondragon-owned subsidiaries and affiliates that are not co-ops. This happened primarily through the expansion of the large Eroski supermarket chain outside of the Basque region into other parts of Spain and France (Arando et al., 2011). It also happened from Mondragon becoming a multinational and, like others multinationals, establishing foreign subsidiaries in places with low-cost labor, such as China, Brazil, Mexico, Poland, and the Czech Republic. It is important to note that these firms outside of the Basque region, in Spain and overseas, are structured as conventional capitalist firms; the employees are not members of Mondragon.[12] While Smith (2001) points out that there is no evidence that Mondragon has refused any requests for foreign subsidiaries to be transformed into co-ops, it is nevertheless clear that the priority is in maintaining the co-ops "at home" as opposed to democratizing the affiliates (Luzarraga & Irizar, 2012). The official rationale for not having democratized any of the foreign subsidiaries is (i) that legal barriers exist in certain countries to setting up worker co-ops; (ii) the fact that some of the subsidiaries are joint ventures with conventional investors; and (iii) the supposed lack of interest in cooperatives amongst many of the foreign workers (Azevedo & Gitahy, 2010).[13]

This expansion has significantly altered the character of Mondragon (Errasti et al., 2003). While the base of Mondragon in the Basque country has remained staunchly cooperative, Mondragon as a whole has not. The fundamental fact is that, according to José María Ormaechea (a past president of the General Council[14]), by 2006 *only 38%* of workers in Mondragon were co-op members compared to 80% in 1990. In addition, four joint-stock companies were being established for every one co-op (cited in MacLeod & Reed, 2009, p. 134). Today Mondragon encompasses 254 firms—111 of which are co-ops and 143 non-cooperative subsidiaries (of which 94 are abroad) (Mondragon, 2011). The fact that less than 40% of the personnel are actual co-op members means that members now represent only a minority of total workers in the business as a whole.[15] The members have, in effect, become privileged quasi-capitalist employers of a larger body of nonmember workers. As I argued last chapter, firms of this type should not be seen as genuine co-ops, but more accurately as a kind of capitalist partnership.

In order to evaluate the empirical performance of the Mondragon co-ops, it is best to divide the analysis into two periods, corresponding to the original Mondragon Group (from the 1950s to the 1980s) and the global Mondragon Corporation (from the 1990s to the present).

Beginning with the first period, it is clear that, from an economic perspective, Mondragon has been a stunning success. Starting from five workers with basically no assets, by the late 1980s it had grown to 166 co-ops, employing 21,000, with $1.6 billion in sales (Morrison, 1997). In their analysis of Mondragon, Thomas and Logan (1982) found that co-op efficiency actually exceeded that of the largest conventional firms in Spain by 7.5% and medium and small enterprises by 40%. Levin (1983) confirms that Mondragon had higher labor productivity than the largest Spanish firms. Likewise, Bradley and Gelb (1981, p. 224) report that more than half the members considered themselves to be working "significantly harder" than they would for conventional firms. According to Whyte and Whyte (1988), "all economists who have studied Mondragon's financial history report that the cooperatives have far outpaced private Spanish firms" (p. 131). Indeed, I am not aware of a single study finding Mondragon to be consistently less efficient than comparable conventional firms, though it is fair to say that the comparative empirical literature is not large.[16]

Since the publication of Ward's (1958) famous theoretical paper, neoclassical economists have often predicted that co-ops will react perversely to changes in the market—firing when demand increases and expanding during downturns. There is however, no evidence for this here. In fact, although Mondragon reacts to changes in market demand in the normal manner (rising demand leads to growth, slow times lead to declines), the kind of changes are often more humane than in capitalist firms. For instance, during the recession from the mid-1970s to 1984, when the region saw the loss of 100,000 jobs and a 20% unemployment rate, capitalist businesses tended to react to the down-turn by disinvesting, often permanently closing their doors or moving to new sites where unions were weaker or taxes lower. The co-ops, however, reacted quite differently. The co-ops tended to treat labor as a constant cost, achiev-ing flexibility in other ways. Recession was dealt with in the short term by transfers between co-ops, cutting prices, and producing for inventory, while in the long term, wages and hours were cut (in ways that were collectively chosen to be fair across the board), and large-scale reinvestment occurred. Lay-offs, at least of members (nonmembers is a different story which we dis-cuss below), practically never happened, and only as a last resort. Indeed, this pattern of humane response to recession has repeated itself in the 2008 reces-sion (Arando et al., 2010).

In terms of the social characteristics of Mondragon, the most striking social achievement is the virtual elimination of job loss and the minimization of business failure. For instance, Morrison (1997, p. 174) claims that during Mondragon's first 30 years of operation over 160 co-ops were formed yet only 3 closed. Likewise, Moye (1993, p. 253) reports that even during the Basque recession not a single Mondragon member lost his or her job. Such stable employment in a capitalist context is practically unheard of.

Like other co-ops, the wage scale in Mondragon is greatly compressed in the direction of equality. In the early years the largest permissible difference between the highest and lowest paid was 3:1. In the 1980s this was relaxed to 6:1, at which level it has basically remained ever since (Arando et al., 2010).[17] The general picture at Mondragon today is that the lowest earners tend to earn more than in comparable capitalist firms, the middle earners the same, and managers and the highly skilled earning up to 30% less (Arando et al., 2011). Managers stay for a variety of other reasons and moral incentives, such as their ethical commitment to the co-ops; indeed the fact that the co-ops can attract such loyalty (so that managers decline leaving even though it could substantially increase their salary) strongly suggests that the co-ops are socially different kinds of firms, and deeply rewarding in their own way—why else would managers stay?

Furthermore, the level of democracy and participation in firm governance in this period was much greater than in comparable conventional firms. The General Assemblies (through their Governing Councils) can fire the top management and have occasionally done so (Smith, 2001, p. 32). One study found that 13% of co-op members felt that they directly "participated in important decisions," and 20% indirectly through representatives, com-pared to only 4% and 3% respectively in comparable capitalist firms (Bradley & Gelb, 1981, p. 222). Inversely, 30% of co-op members felt that they did not participate in firm governance, compared to 80% in capitalist firms. This points to considerably more participation in the co-ops but clearly not any kind of universal engagement (at least during the time of this study).

A further social strength of Mondragon during this period was the connection with the community. One of its ten principles, of course, is "social transformation." This principle is given some tangibility by the practice (mandated by Basque law) of directing 10% of annual profits toward charities and community projects. Beyond this, the community clearly benefits from the long-term stable employment, and the fact that the revenues of the firms largely stay in the community through the CL. Both of these factors have brought decades of positive externalities to the community. In this light, the deep roots that the Mondragon co-ops have laid in the region belie the traditional Marxist objection that co-ops are simply group-capitalists, interested only in profit maximization.

Moreover, even though in certain respects shop floor conditions have not been noticeably different than in capitalist firms (Dow, 2003), it is nevertheless apparent that members have far preferred working in a co-op to the alternative. Mondragon members have reported being much less likely to be willing to transfer jobs to a capitalist firm (even for monetary increases of up to 50%) than the other way around—27% compared to 54% (Bradley & Gelb, 1981, p. 220).

Overall these facts provide strong evidence for the viability of the cooperative model. Mondragon shows us the possibility of a democratic business model that is just as effective economically and substantially superior socially. Of course, we need to remember that such results were achieved in an era without direct competition from multinationals producing in quasi-sweat shops in the Global South. But given that the bulk of trade competition from countries in the Global North today does not actually come from the Global South (imports to the OECD from the Global South account for only about 20% of imports),[18] and given that there are large parts of the economy (such as the service sector and many localized industries) that are not threatened by such competition,[19] we can be confident that there is a large if not predominant part of the economy where cooperative practices of the type exemplified by the original Mondragon would likely be entirely appropriate and effective.

Turning now to the second period, the period of global Mondragon, we can see that, economically speaking, the internationalization process was very successful. Throughout the 1990s and 2000s Mondragon managed to substantially increase its growth and market share (Errasti et al., 2003). Moreover, Mondragon grew faster than many other firms: from 1996 to 2008, sales grew by 213% compared to 140% for similar firms in the same Basque region (Arando et al., 2010). According to the Economist Intelligence Unit, Irizar is "probably now the most efficient coach builder in the world" (Forcadell, 2005, p. 256). While this growth is impressive, and shows that Mondragon has been successful at sustaining its jobs at home in substantial part through expansion abroad, the fact that this has been achieved by a workforce of whom the majority are conventional, disenfranchised, non-co-op members, means that the success is not entirely different from that of other multinationals.

What have been the social results of global Mondragon? In certain ways it appears that the company has become more corporate. For instance Cheney claims that the democratic participation in the co-ops has become somewhat undermined by the routinization of participatory practices in the General Assemblies, centralization of corporate strategic policymaking, and the decline of the Social Councils—often accused of simply rubber-stamping management decisions; moreover, he argues that education in cooperativism is increasingly taking a back seat to financial and technical training (1999, p. 135). He also reports workers saying things like "this place *feels* a lot more like a corporation and a lot less like a cooperative than it used to" (1999, p. 75).[20] In terms of employment stability, Mondragon has been able to maintain its record of virtual guaranteed employment, although again this fact is less impressive when it is recalled that global Mondragon is able to assure work for its members by firing its nonmembers when necessary. For example, in the midst of the recession of 2008–2009, the number of members rose by 6.1%, whereas the overall numbers of employment fell by 8.3%, meaning that the security of the members was achieved, at least in part, through the disposability of the nonmembers (Flecha & Cruz, 2011, p. 160).

However, even if Mondragon is no longer a true co-op, it is still by most measures a better place to work than most comparable multinationals. The job security, profit-sharing, and democratic opportunities clearly make Mondragon a great place to work for members. Indeed, Mondragon was ranked in 2003 by *Fortune* magazine as one of the ten best firms to work for in Europe (Forcadell, 2005). Additionally, employment in Mondragon may be somewhat better even for nonmembers than the alternatives. For example, Irizar pays the workers in its foreign subsidiaries 20% more than the local competition (MacLeod & Reed, 2009); while this is commendable, it is unclear how general this practice is, as the authors recognize that Irizar represents "best practice" with respect to internationalization (2009, p. 133).

Taking a step back now, what does Mondragon's "degeneration" imply for our broader interest in co-op efficiency?[21] Do we need to reevaluate our positive assessment of the original Mondragon in light of global Mondragon?

Does the recent "degeneration" imply that co-ops are an obsolete form of business, best rejected to the trash bin of history? I do not think so.

First, Mondragon itself may well *re-democratize* in the coming years and emerge as a competitive multinational cooperative. It is clear that the existence of so many nonmember workers in Mondragon has been a source of much soul-searching and debate within the organization and is something that many members wish to change. The bulk of Mondragon's nonmembers emerged from the expansion of the supermarket chain Eroski during the 1990s. To combat this, by the late 1990s a partial employee-ownership structure was established, and starting in 2011, Eroski approved a multi-year initiative to cooperativize its operations, to be completed by 2014–2016; this is expected to bring the ratio of members to workers back up to 70–75% for Mondragon as a whole (Arando et al., 2010, pp. 20–21). If this is successful, it will represent a profound re-democratization of Mondragon. Beyond this, it is not inconceivable that the foreign subsidiaries will be slowly democratized, perhaps by being transformed into full member co-ops where local conditions allow, or at least acquiring increased rights to participation and profit-sharing. Moreover, it is important to remember that a fundamental reason that a re-democratization of Mondragon is possible is that, as many commentators have pointed out, its democratic culture is a key to its competitive advantage (Cheney, 1999; Forcadell, 2005; MacLeod & Reed, 2009). Its economic edge comes, at least in part, from the participation, motivation, loyalty, commitment, and constant training that flow from a democratically empowered workforce. This implies that even in a neoliberal global market environment, Mondragon may well be able to emerge as an exemplary model for democratic multinational business. Time will tell.

Second, it is possible that in the coming years the global marketplace will face little regulation or moderation and so will become increasingly harsh— characterized by a fierce race to the bottom. In such a case it is likely that any firm that cares about anything other than the bottom line (from co-ops to unionized firms to firms with environmental policies) will be forced under. Decent firms may well be unable to survive in such a brutal marketplace. But it must be remembered that this is not evidence of the invalidity of the cooperative form, any more than it is of the invalidity of unions or environmental protection. Indeed, most of us recognize that the fact that pregnant women are not as competitive as men does not justify their being paid less—it means that the market should be regulated (e.g., by mandating pay equity); the fact that green electricity companies cannot compete against coal-burning ones does not mean that we should abandon green firms—it means that the market should be structured differently (e.g., by putting a price on carbon emissions).

If socially decent types of business, like the original Mondragon, cannot survive in a harsh global market environment, this is a condemnation not of the firms, but of the environment itself. The answer is not to abandon co-ops (or other progressive kinds of firms) but to work toward reforming the market environment which is biased against them, for example, by striving to implement regulations and tax incentives to motivate firms to work toward a broader bottom line.[22]

To sum up, it is, I think, fair to say that Mondragon, particularly in its original 30 years, has been a hugely successful enterprise. It many ways it serves as conclusive evidence for the viability of the cooperative form and should give pause to anyone who intuitively doubts the feasibility of workplace democracy. We can learn much by noting several of the key innovations that have been instrumental to Mondragon's success. First and foremost, the CL has been vital for loosening the constraints of finance, as well as providing an Empresarial division for providing business assistance and starting up new co-ops. Next, Mondragon has discovered a lasting structural form. It mandates high levels of internal investment (at least 45% but up to 90% of profits). The innovation of having personalized internal capital accounts allows for divorcing membership rights from property rights (thus avoiding degeneration *à la* Plywood co-ops). The presence of a Social Council importantly complements the Governing Council, providing a mechanism for workers to deliberate as workers as well as owners. Next, Mondragon has shown the importance of ongoing educational training both in terms of cooperativism (teaching the values of solidarity and participation as well as the practical skills of bookkeeping, information sharing, participating in meetings, learning how to manage, etc.) as well as technical training. This is vital because it is only through teaching people themselves how to manage that "self-management" becomes less rhetoric and more reality. Finally, the networking of co-ops together for social and economic support (for instance forming co-op Groups) has been extremely useful.

La Lega

Whereas Mondragon grew out of the Christian vision of one man, La Lega cooperatives emerged out of a vast socialistic political movement. The early cooperative movement in Italy formed itself into various networks, one of which was The Federation of Italian Co-operatives, formed in 1886 with 248 co-ops representing 74,000 members (about 38% of these were worker co-ops, 44% were consumer co-ops (Ammirato, 1996, p. 69)). In 1893 the Federation changed its name to the National League of Cooperatives (commonly called "La Lega").

In 1947, co-ops received formal recognition in the Italian constitution as organs to be promoted by the state. The Basevi Law determined the structure that co-ops were to adopt, reflecting the principles of the International Cooperative Alliance.[23] It stated that co-ops are to be governed according to one-person one-vote (with the General Assembly electing the Governing Council, which in turn is to appoint and oversee the management). Admission must be open to all. Membership shares are not sellable. There are limits on the amount of money that workers can invest in their own firms, as well as limits on the amount of white-collar workers allowed in. Interest on capital is restricted to 5% (though this was later relaxed). The co-ops are to distribute their surplus by keeping 20% in a reserve fund (with reduced rates of taxation), allowing up to 20% for supplementing wages, while the remaining had to be used for social activity or reinvestment—thus guaranteeing substantial levels of reinvestment. In the event of dissolution, the co-ops are not permitted to distribute assets to members, which must instead be devoted to a public fund—the purpose of which is to ensure that co-ops will not degenerate by being sold off to private enterprises for speculative purposes. So although this law constrained the co-ops in certain ways, it also supported them through tax breaks and privileged access to public contracts (Ammirato, 1996, p. 82).

The structure of La Lega as a whole is formed by each individual co-op electing representatives to a National Congress held every four years, which then elects the overarching governing bodies. The main functions of La Lega are to provide general guidance, support, and cohesiveness to the member co-ops. For instance, La Lega lobbies the state for support, it provides legal, business, and accounting services, it provides research and development information, it helps coordinate business evolution, and helps finance the development of new cooperatives. Overall, the structure is broader than that of Mondragon, but less centralized. The main strategic economic direction does not come from above, but from decentralized consortia—which are groups of co-ops that have formed together for economic reasons, to pool resources and obtain economies of scale.

The 1950s was a period of economic stagnation for La Lega, which Ammirato (1996) attributes largely to the difficulty of acquiring finance as well as managerial skills (both of which were often disparaged as part of an alien capitalist culture). By the 1970s, however, these problems started to be overcome. The consortia were developing and became capable of providing managerial skills and business strategy (Menzani & Zamagni, 2010). In addition, La Lega developed its own financial system, around the financial consortium Fincooper. Fincooper provides three main services. First and foremost, it provides finance to the co-ops at below market rates; second, it provides financial services, and third, it acts as a major shareholder in strategic companies useful to La Lega as a whole. Fincooper finances itself by charging each co-op a fee as well as attracting deposits from co-ops. Attracting deposits is facilitated by the state, which allows depositors to pay only 12.5% tax on the interest received, compared to the 25% they would have to pay in regular banks.

These factors combined to help make the last several decades a time of great growth for cooperatives. Even with increased pressure from globalization, as well as attacks from Berlusconi's right-wing government, the co-ops have grown impressively. In 1950 there were about 10,000 Italian co-ops (including but not only worker co-ops) employing about 2% of all workers. By 2001, there were 53,000 co-ops employing 5.8% of workers (Zamagni & Zamagni, 2010, p. 56). During the 1990s, the number of people employed by co-ops rose by 60%, compared to an average of 9% for capitalist firms (Restakis, 2010, p. 70). Worker cooperatives, particularly large ones, are now major players across the Italian economy: accounting for roughly 18% of all workers in large firms in the food processing sector, 23% in construction, 16% in trade, 19% in hotels and restaurants, 17% in financial intermediation, and 17% in facility management services. By 2006, La Lega represented 15,200 firms, with 7,500,000 members and 414,000 direct employees (Zamagni & Zamagni, 2010).

Economically, La Lega co-ops have been remarkably successful. They constitute a vibrant sector of the economy and are now leaders in their fields of construction, agriculture, retail, housing, food catering, transport, health, ceramics, machineries, rubber products, furniture, and hi-tech equipment.

Bartlett et al.'s (1992) robust study summarizes the economic evidence from La Lega: they find that the co-ops have compressed wages compared to capitalist firms, fewer managers as a fraction of the workforce, more hours worked per person, significantly lower assets per person, significantly higher productivity (i.e., value added per worker per hour worked per unit of fixed capital), fewer strikes, absentee days, and quit rates (although interestingly not higher wages). Ammirato (1996, p. 93) concurs that the co-ops tend to outcompete capitalist firms. The co-ops increased their value-added by 42% from 1976 to 1980, whereas the national average was only 18%. Likewise, the co-ops maintained higher levels of employment for firms of similar size, increasing employment by 16% compared to 6% for conventional firms.[24]

So it is clear that notwithstanding certain neoclassical expectations, La Lega co-ops have not underinvested or underemployed (Ammirato, 1996, pp. 236–238; Bartlett et al., 1992). On the contrary, they have proven to be eminently sustainable. Many of the co-ops employ hundreds of people and have survived for decades (Ammirato, 1996, p. 2).

Can this success be attributed to state subsidy? Definitely the Italian state has been significantly involved in the economy, more so than in many parts of the Western world. The Italian state explicitly determined how co-ops were to be structured and how they were supposed to function—sometimes supporting, sometimes hampering. Italian co-ops have historically been much more explicitly political than elsewhere, leading them to prosper under sympathetic governments and be attacked or sidelined under others (Ammirato, 1996). On the one hand, co-ops have in some ways been supported over and above conventional firms, primarily through being allowed to bid for public contracts without competition and receiving tax benefits (Forte & Mantovani, 2009). However, it is also true that in certain ways the co-ops have been restricted vis-à-vis conventional firms: they were long restrained in the amount of interest on capital they could pay (to 5%), which acted as a deterrent to investing in co-ops. Likewise, the number of white-collar workers was long restricted. As well, the co-ops often received much less financial support from the state than capitalist firms.[25] Furthermore, in many ways the state is not particularly focused on co-ops at all but is simply interventionist in general, supporting all kinds of firms.[26] The issue of state support is thus complicated. It is probably fair to say that the Italian market environment has generally been supportive of co-ops, but undoubtedly it is inaccurate to dismiss La Lega's success as simply due to subsidy.

Whereas capitalist firms, generally speaking, find themselves enmeshed in a political-legal system that has been set up with them in mind, co-ops are like freshwater fish in a capitalist sea. What is remarkable about La Lega, and a core ingredient of its success, has been its ability to develop its own system of supporting structures through a large and highly developed cooperative network. This network provides the best glimpse we have of what a cooperative market system might look like—where the market system itself is structured and regulated so as to facilitate the creation of new co-ops, provide credit and training, help problem-solving, and encourage expansion in ways that are specifically relevant for cooperative firms.

What about the social features of La Lega co-ops? Ammirato (1996) argues that the co-ops operate efficiently but with a different kind of business ethic. They have a broader bottom line than simply profit maximization, extending to social concerns of the workers as well as the community (e.g., through donations of a portion of profits and other solidarity initiatives). In many ways, the co-ops strive to balance social and economic considerations.

La Lega co-ops have significantly more internal equality than comparable firms, with wage differentials usually not exceeding 3:1 (Ammirato, 1996,

p. 91). Additionally, most co-ops try to institute a culture of equality, which manifests itself in a variety of ways, such as through common cafeterias that everyone uses and replacing the formal language that is the business norm with the egalitarian "tu" between managers and workers (Holmstrom, 1989).

Moreover, the co-ops have much greater levels of democracy than in conventional firms: the General Assembly has final authority, with day-to-day authority delegated to management who serve at the pleasure of the Assembly. Some co-ops proudly proclaim signs on their walls with slogans such as "40 years of self-management!" (S. Smith, 2001, p. 32). Holmstrom (1989) provides an importantly balanced view, documenting the wide variability of democracy in different co-ops. He shows that, as Smith notes, the co-ops do have quite strong democratic structures, yet it is also true that there is rarely widespread rank-and-file participation in management. Most technical aspects of production are decided by management and simply assented to by the Governing Council. There is often little experimentation with direct democracy, or alternative work practices, and even General Assemblies are in some cases little more than symbolic events.[27]

All in all, La Lega co-ops have shown themselves to operate with levels of economic efficiency at least comparable to capitalist firms, while being socially superior in many ways. What have been the main reasons for La Lega's success? First, the co-ops have adopted a sustainable internal structure—mandating high levels of reinvestment and preventing sell-offs. Next, the league itself has been vital in allowing co-ops to cluster into a shared network which promotes shared values, lobbies the state, provides services, and promotes new co-ops. The consortia have been important in terms of improving market competitiveness by pooling resources, achieving economies of scale, and promoting intersectoral co-op trade, thus providing the basis for national and perhaps even international competitiveness. The financial support and services provided by Finacoop and other financial/banking bodies devoted to cooperative success have been immensely useful. Finally, the self-identification of the co-ops as part of a political movement has allowed them valuable alliances with trade unions and political parties, which in turn has been valuable in galvanizing state support—and this has been consistently helpful in providing tax incentives, financing support, and access to public contracts.

Egalitarian Collectives

While co-ops are characterized by their democratic organization, they do not generally involve complete equality. Co-ops tend to utilize a division of labor with different people performing different tasks: managers and specialists oversee various aspects of the business and possess the authority to direct others. However, at the extreme of the cooperative movement there are organizations that endeavor to organize on completely egalitarian grounds. These can be called "egalitarian collectives" and provide a useful contrast with normal co-ops as they illustrate the trade-offs that different kinds of business structures allow.

Egalitarian collectives are workplaces that aim for more-or-less complete equality between all the members; their goal is not democracy per se, but radical equality. Rothschild and Whitt (1986), in their excellent work on the subject, describe a number of firms of this sort. For example, in the small newspaper *The Community News*, which employed between 14 and 18 people, there were no managers or formal hierarchy of any sort. Decisions were made collectively and by consensus in meetings where everyone was encouraged to participate, usually taking up to four hours per week. Jobs were rotated—the photographer this month might be the writer or the layout designer next month—so that no one acquired expertise over anyone else.

In general, egalitarian collectives are defined by the following characteristics. The locus of authority rests with the whole group on an egalitarian basis and is not delegated. Decisions are made through a collective participatory process, usually by consensus. There tends to be no distinction in status between any members. Jobs are shared or rotated and wages are usually equal for all. Such firms are always small, with low levels of capital intensity and basic technologies, and tend to be quite homogeneous in their personnel. For instance Rotschild and Whitt (1986) describe how practically all of the American collectives that arose in 1970s were formed by middle-class participants of the student movement, well-educated, and ideologically committed (see also Schoening 2010).

Studying firms of this sort is extremely useful because it forces us to see the inevitable trade-offs that exist in social life. Total equality in the workplace, while an admirable goal in certain respects, brings with it at least two major requirements: collective decision-making (or else some will become managers) and shared tasks or job rotation (or else some will become specialists). What are the consequences of these requirements? Collective decision-making is much easier with similar kinds of people—similar cultural background, ideological perspective, and levels of education, which is why these organizations tend to be quite culturally homogeneous. Furthermore, collective decision-making necessarily requires smallness as groups much bigger than 10 or 20 simply cannot make decisions in this manner in any reasonable amount of time. And with smallness comes lack of broader impact. Small may be beautiful, but tiny and culturally homogeneous firms can only be marginal firms and are therefore unlikely to impact conditions of work for the majority of people. Likewise, sharing tasks or rotating jobs means that the firm's operations must remain quite simple with little advanced technology or production processes. Without a division of labor, people cannot specialize in activities in which they are particularly skilled but find themselves performing activities they cannot do particularly well, creating massive inefficiency and low-level productivity (Mansbridge, 1980, pp. 246–247); as Adam Smith ([1776] 2006) pointed out centuries ago, division of labor and efficiency are inextricably linked. With substantial inefficiency comes a lack of competitiveness, which is why firms of this sort are so few and far between.

Another trade-off that exists is between equal wages and motivation. Equal wages means that motivation must rely solely on moral incentives. Egalitarian collectives show that these kinds of incentives often are sufficient for stimulating substantial motivation, at least among particularly devoted people (Mansbridge, 1980; Rothschild & Whitt, 1986). However, the dark side of pure reliance on moral incentives is that it may encourage free riding, since you know you will get paid the same no matter how much you do or how much you shirk. Pure reliance on moral incentives also brings with it a culture of moral expectation and conformism—"why aren't you sacrificing as much for the collective as I am?"—which can be oppressive in its own way. Of course, this is not to say that equality of wages should be totally abandoned as a goal, but that there is probably a sensible balance to aim for between motivating via money, on the one hand, and via coworkers' moral expectations, on the other. Whereas conventional firms tend to be extremely unbalanced in the direction of inequality, egalitarian collectives tend to be unbalanced in the opposite direction of abolishing financial incentives altogether.

In the real world it is, unfortunately, not possible to combine any kind of characteristics one might want. One must choose either equality or large-scale transformative potential, either homogenization or expertise, either equal wages or material incentives. In practice this means that you can have democratic workplaces that are egalitarian, participatory, with no division of labor, that are small and homogeneous, *or*, you can have democratic workplaces, like most co-ops, that allow some inequality, are representative, use specialization, and are potentially large and diverse. The restraints of reality mean that this trade-off is inevitable: we cannot have our cake and eat it too.

In my opinion the weaknesses of egalitarian collectives usually outweigh their strengths. This is because complete equality in all kinds of decision-making requires serious leveling, smallness, homogeneity, and inefficiency, and therefore lacks large-scale transformative potential. It seems to me advisable to relax our insistence on ideological purity in terms of insisting on absolute equality for the sake of building organizations that can grow, include diverse kinds of people, and operate efficiently so as to have real potential for actually improving the lives of broad swathes of the population. Egalitarian collectives do not have this kind of potential. However, as we will now see, worker cooperatives do.

Compiling the Economic Evidence

Historically, co-ops in the West have been almost entirely financed by personal savings. They therefore have tended to be small and confined to areas of low capital intensity, particularly in industries that lack significant scale economies, require few specialized physical assets, and have limited barriers to entry, such as construction and certain branches of manufacturing, printing and publishing, clothing, food production, textiles, glass, ceramics, wood and furniture (Dow, 2003). Traditionally, co-ops have had basically no presence in industries that are highly capital intensive, such as chemical or pharmaceutical industries, iron, steel, transport, or auto. That said, Mondragon and La Lega demonstrate that co-ops with significant capital intensity can be viable provided that financing difficulties can be overcome.

The central empirical question regarding cooperatives is "are they efficient"? This broad question can best be analyzed by breaking it down into the following criteria: productivity, ability to grow and create jobs, appropriate reactions to changes in the market, and sustainability over a sufficiently long term.

In terms of productivity, there is wide-ranging evidence that cooperatives have just as high if not higher productivity than comparable capitalist firms. This is seen in the United States (Berman, 1967; Craig & Pencavel, 1995; Pencavel & Craig, 1994), in West Germany (Cable & FitzRoy, 1980), in Italy (Ammirato, 1996; Bartlett et al., 1992; Maietta & Sena, 2008; Zevi, 1982), in Sweden (Thordarson, 1987), in Denmark (Mygind, 1987), in France (Defourny, 1992; Fakhfakh, Perotin, & Gago, 2009), in Spain (Bayo-Moriones, Galilea-Salvatierra, & De Cerio, 2003; Thomas & Logan, 1982), and in Poland compared to state-owned firms (Jones, 1985). Of particular interest is Doucouliagos's meta-analysis compiling the results of 43 studies comparing the productivity of co-ops to capitalist firms. He concluded that there is a strong association between co-op profit-sharing and productivity and a small but statistically significant association between worker participation in decision-making and productivity thus "rejecting the traditional view that democratic management of the firm is associated with *reduced* efficiency"

(1995, pp. 67–69). Probably the most rigorous and large-scale comparative study is from Fakhfakh et al. (2009), who analyzed 7,000 French firms, about 500 of which are co-ops. They found that "overall these results suggest that…[the co-ops] are as productive as conventional firms or more productive, and use their inputs better" (p. 18).[28]

The evidence is thus robust that being your own boss does seem to improve productivity. This likely comes from two main sources: the *increased motivation* that comes from profit-sharing and the *smoother coordination* that comes from increased trust and reduced alienation. There is now wide-ranging evidence that profit-sharing enhances productivity (Doucouliagos, 1995; Estrin, Jones, & Svejnar, 1987; Kruse, Freeman, & Blasi, 2010). But what about workplace coordination? Co-ops do not appear to have the lack of discipline that authors like Alchian and Demsetz (1972) suspected (Cornforth et al., 1988). On the contrary co-ops tend to have an efficiency advantage in terms of smoother coordination that stems from increased trust. This manifests itself in terms of reduced worker–manager conflict which can be empirically seen from lower levels of absenteeism and quit rates (Bartlett et al., 1992). Increased trust also allows co-ops to substantially reduce monitoring costs (Bartlett et al., 1992; Fakhfakh et al., 2009; Greenberg, 1986).[29] This is important because monitoring costs for capitalist firms typically account for as much as one-fifth of total labor costs (Bowles & Gintis, 1998). Trust is so important because it is like the grease applied to the gears of a machine, lubricating the coordination of the parts; co-ops tend to have more of it, and hence less friction in their operation.

Indeed, we should not find co-op productivity surprising, since even in capitalist firms the coordination that happens is only partially order-giving and order-taking. An enormous amount is achieved by workers solving problems amongst themselves on the basis of mutual aid ("can you show me how to do X?," "send me an email about Y," "remind me to do Z"). Coordination does not generally happen through endless commands among finely grained hierarchy. Indeed it is impossible to imagine any sophisticated coordination whatsoever happening without extensive amount of co-operation even within hierarchical structures. The only reason that the gears of a hierarchical system can turn at all is that they are constantly lubricated by millions of micro-acts of cooperation. The coercion, not the cooperation, is the anomaly.

Next, the evidence demonstrates that co-ops have no trouble in generating jobs and growing. Zevi (1982) shows that Italian co-ops tend to grow *faster* than capitalist firms, as do Arando et al. (2010) in Spain, and Burdín and Dean (2012) in Uruguay. Fakhfakh et al. (2009) and Arando et al. (2011) find the growth rates to be neither better nor worse. The worry that co-ops will not grow is based on the underlying concern that they will underinvest—perhaps because workers might prefer to siphon off the surplus into their personal wages instead of reinvesting, or perhaps because of short time horizons. Whatever the case, in practice there is no evidence that cooperatives under-invest (Dow, 2003, pp. 162–63). Bonin, Jones, & Putterman (1993) are conclusive about this: "No strong empirical support for the underinvestment hypothesis is found either in France or the UK" (p. 1311). They conclude that "the empirical literature contains no econometric support for this hypothesis" (1993, p. 1316). Recent studies confirm this (Arando et al., 2010; Fakhfakh et al., 2009). Indeed, in practice many co-ops overcome horizon problems by simply mandating a portion of surplus toward reinvestment (e.g., Burdín & Dean, 2009).

In terms of their ability to react to market changes, it is clear that co-ops do respond efficiently to broad changes in market demand: expanding in times of increasing demand and slowing in times of recession (e.g., Burdín & Dean, 2009; Mygind, 1987). Although as we will see below, co-ops tend to adjust to changes in demand in different ways (reducing wages or hours rather than laying people off). Indeed, Jossa and Cuomo argue that a co-op dominated economy would likely be economically *superior* in that it would have downturns that are less severe than capitalist ones. This is because when capitalist firms have downturns, they face wages that are quite rigid. Since workers' wages cannot be reduced they have to be fired altogether leading to some productive capacity remaining idle. Thus the familiar capitalist para-dox of recession: unemployment side-by-side empty factories, which is caused in part because wage rigidity leads to underutilization of capacity. But in a co-op economy, downturns mean that workers can choose to take pay cuts (an option that does not exist in typical capitalist firms), resulting in less unem-ployment and underutilization, and therefore a less severe recession (Jossa & Cuomo, 1997, pp. 283–285).

Next we might ask if cooperatives are efficient in the sense of being sus-tainable over the long term. If degeneration happens at all it is more likely due to organizational reasons than purely economic ones, such as hiring of nonmembers (e.g., the Plywood co-ops) or hiring members who are not com-mitted to workplace democracy (e.g., the Burley co-op in Oregon (Schoening, 2010)). Such forms of degeneration can generally be avoided with appropri-ate care and the implementation of rigorous democratic structures, though as Mondragon shows, economic pressure can lead to organizational degen-eration. According to Smith (2001), co-ops degenerate into capitalist firms only with "extreme rarity" (p. 28). The most important issue in this regard is whether co-ops can successfully compete over the long term. Here the evi-dence is clear: co-ops do not fail more often than comparable firms, rather they have robust survival rates (Bellas, 1972; Ben-Ner, 1988; Cornforth et al., 1988). Gregory Dow's excellent work is arguably the most authoritative synthesis of the literature. He ends his comprehensive study with the following: "The general conclusion...is that [co-ops] are not rare because they fail disproportionately often. Once created, they appear robust. Rather, they are rare because in absolute numbers they are created much less often than [capitalist firms]" (2003, p. 227).

Finally, it is clear that the efficiency of cooperatives cannot be written off as simply due to state subsidy. While co-ops (like capitalist firms) clearly perform better when supported, most states possess market environments that contain a complicated mix of supportive and hampering measures. For instance, co-ops often receive tax breaks but almost never receive institutional financial help in any way comparable to the gigantic banks and stock markets set up to aid capitalist firms. So while it may well be desirable to support co-ops more in the future, studies to date indicate that co-ops are robust and efficient despite the political-economic environment, not because of it.

The bottom line (pun intended) is that co-ops operate with levels of economic efficiency that are comparable to conventional firms; they are eminently viable kinds of businesses. Whatever efficiency losses they may suffer from the time that is required for participation, or the rigidities that come from the difficulties in firing bad workers, are balanced out by enhanced motivation and smoother coordination. Their rarity is not caused by any inherent inefficiency, or internal tendency to degenerate, but by contingent factors (such as structure and financing) which can in certain cases be decisively overcome—as early Mondragon and La Lega powerfully demonstrate. (We examine the reasons for the rarity of co-ops below.)

Of course, even if we can be relatively confident about cooperative efficiency on a small scale, this does not prove that an entire cooperative economy would be similarly efficient. We cannot know this for sure until we try. But what can we expect? A skeptic might argue that small co-ops can be efficient by attracting highly motivated people who are ideologically committed to the co-op model, but that economy-wide, co-ops would not work so well. I think such pessimism is unfounded. It is likely that worker co-ops possess a number of productivity advantages over conventional firms that stem from their motivational and coordination advantages: being one's own boss, having incentives to work hard because remuneration is directly tied to the firm's performance, mutual monitoring, being more involved in decision-making, having a more pleasant culture and therefore less turnover and absenteeism, and so on. Nothing about these factors relies on cooperatives being small and peripheral; logic suggests that they should be just as effective on a large scale as they are today.[30] Indeed, the indisputable economic vibrancy of places like Emilia Romagna (home of Parmesan cheese and Ferrari cars and one of the richest parts of Europe) where co-ops play a large role is compelling evidence of their large-scale potential. In Imola, for example, with a population of 100,000, approximately 50% of the people are stockholders in the area's 115 co-ops, and over 60% of the town's GDP comes from the co-ops (Restakis, 2010, p. 57).

Compiling the Social Evidence

It is interesting to note that the two main criticisms commonly leveled against co-ops are largely contradictory. The mainstream neoclassical view is that co-ops behave too differently from conventional firms, whereas the Marxist critique, on the other hand, is that they operate too similarly (i.e., degenerate to become indistinguishable from conventional firms). In fact, while competitive market pressure does provide a broad base of similarities between the two types of firm—in terms of concern about productivity and profitability, standardization of work, and establishment of pyramidal management—in various ways co-ops do consistently behave differently than conventional firms.

Co-ops do not generally aim for simple profit maximization. Indeed, it is unclear that they aim to maximize any one thing at all (Dow, 2003, p. 142). Most co-ops are interested in maximizing employment or job security in addition to profits, but this is not always the case (Burdín & Dean, 2012). Indeed, since co-op management is controlled by the workers collectively, it is unsurprising that there are a broader range of goals and priorities than a capitalist firm controlled by shareholders who are likely to share a uniform commitment to profit maximization (since that is why they bought shares in the first place). Most co-ops seem to have a broader notion of the bottom line, including profit, but also including various social concerns ranging from employment stability to community improvement. So the fact that co-ops are not single-mindedly profit-maximizing may make them less profitable than conventional firms in a narrow economic sense, but this "disadvantage" (if it is a disadvantage at all) may well be balanced out by the productivity advantages that tend to accrue to co-ops from reductions in antagonistic management.

One of the most important differences in co-op behavior is in regards to employment. This shows itself in two ways: co-ops have much greater job security than conventional firms, and they respond to downturns in more humane ways (Arando et al., 2010; Bartlett et al., 1992; Burdín & Dean, 2009; Fakhfakh et al., 2009; Pencavel & Craig, 1994; Pencavel, Pistaferri, & Schivardi, 2006). Indeed, Dow (2003) states that "one of the most robust empirical generalizations about LMFs [co-ops] is that they respond to negative demand shocks by maintaining employment, while restricting hours, wage rates, or both" (p. 198). In other words, co-ops deal with a downturn in ways that are egalitarian and collectively agreed upon. Instead of a capitalist management simply laying off workers to reduce costs, a cooperative structure allows workers to make shared sacrifices by collectively reducing hours or pay in a fair and equal manner. So in these respects, co-ops behave more progressively than conventional firms—economic rationality with a human face, as Morrison would say.

Likewise, there is wide consensus on the fact that co-ops allocate wages with much more equality than in capitalist firms (Arando et al., 2010; Arando et al., 2011; Bartlett et al., 1992; Berman, 1967). So it follows that a society largely composed of co-ops, other things being equal, would be significantly more equal too. Of course, by suppressing wage differentials co-ops may face difficulties acquiring scarce managerial talent; however, this problem is often overcome through a combination of educating managers from the internal workforce, modest wage incentives, and the moral incentives of working in a community of equals. While egalitarian collectives tend to operate with strict equality, many co-ops do allow some wage differentials (though rarely exceeding 3:1). But this differential is much more egalitarian than the comparative practices in social democratic countries (where the average CEO makes 15 times the average wage (Randoy & Nielsen, 2002) and is tiny compared to the American context, where the average CEO makes 300 times the average wage (*The Economist*, 2006); indeed in 2000 the gap was an extraordinary 531:1 (Bogle, 2008).[31]

Another important area of difference is in terms of relationship to the community. Although it is hard to precisely measure this, several points deserve mention. First, the practice of collective ownership serves to tie the co-op's assets to the community, as they cannot be sold off for speculative purposes.[32] More broadly, many co-ops (including Mondragon and La Lega) mandate a portion of their profits to go directly to the community for charities or social projects. Additionally, the fact that co-ops tend to maintain long-term, steady employment is clearly beneficial to the health of the community. Finally, since co-ops are controlled by workers who generally live in the community in which they work, there is less danger to the community from capital flight in the sense of the business leaving. This is an important point.

Normal firms, controlled by capital, will generally move wherever they can in order to maximize profit—sometimes responding to increased demand, sometimes simply to areas with fewer unions, fewer environmental protections, lower wages, lower taxes, and so on. This results in huge wealth for some, and abandoned communities, ghost towns, rust belts, and lower standards of living for others. Co-op practices are different. Since they are controlled by labor, co-ops will seek profits, but only in ways that benefit themselves as workers as well as community members. Instead of moving, co-ops tend to use capital instrumentally in order to achieve competitiveness *within the community*, through reinvesting in existing jobs, retooling, furthering education, and so on. Co-op business success thus provides all kinds of positive externalities that are otherwise lacking (e.g., stability, community reinvestment, etc.) In other words, the link that exists for co-ops between firm success and community benefit means that it is much truer for co-ops than capitalist firms to say that a rising tide lifts all boats. Of course, it is possible that this lack of mobility may reduce efficiency somewhat, but efficiency gains from capitalist mobility tend to concentrate unequally among the owners. As long as new co-ops are able to form in areas where demand is growing, this should not be a massive problem. From a societal perspective, whatever efficiency losses occur are likely to be outweighed by the social benefits of treating capital (as opposed to actual laboring human beings) as a production variable.

There are two other areas where there are good reasons to suspect that co-ops will produce socially superior outcomes than conventional firms: the environment and health (though since there is less hard evidence for these claims they must be taken a bit more speculatively). In terms of the environment, Booth (1995) has argued that cooperatives operate in ways that are more environmentally sensitive than capitalist firms. Although more investigation needs to be done on this question, it does stand to reason that workers, presumably, are less likely to pollute the community they have to live in than a comparable capitalist firm controlled by distant shareholders.

In terms of health, a specific reason that co-ops may be better is that low job control has been associated with ill health. For instance, Marmot et al. (1984) found that men with low job control had three times the 10-year risk of suffering coronary heart disease. Their follow-up study, examining over 10,000 people, confirmed these results and led them to conclude that "policies giving people a stronger say in decisions about their work or providing them with more variety in work tasks may contribute to better cardiovascular health" (Bosma et al., 1997, p. 564). This connection between low job control and ill health has also been corroborated by a number of other investigators (De Jonge, 1995; Sauter, Hurrell, & Cooper, 1989). A more general reason is that it is now well-known that inequality brings all kinds of health risks (Wilkinson & Pickett, 2010); this implies that a co-op dominated economy, with much less inequality, may well be healthier.

However, it is important to point out that there are certain areas where co-ops have not produced the social outcomes that proponents hoped for. First, co-ops have provided only weak and inconclusive evidence for the "spillover thesis" that participating at work will improve the civic virtue of people in their communities—making them better citizens, more eager to participate in politics, and less individualistic. In his extensive studies of American co-ops, Greenberg finds that the co-op workers were no more likely to vote in federal elections, though they were more likely to engage in local politics. Nor were they less classically liberal: they appeared to be just as "individualistic" as comparable workers (Greenberg, 1981). There is some evidence for a spillover effect but it is indirect. Sabatini et al. (2012), in the first study of its kind, find that co-ops produce more trust or "social capital" than other firms; and Putnam (1993) famously demonstrated that higher levels of social trust are associated with a stronger civic culture and engagement; so there does seem to be some evidence for a causal chain.

Second, co-ops do not always result in more pleasant jobs or enhanced job satisfaction. The fact is that much work is inherently tedious or dull, and so no amount of organizational transformation is likely to alter this fact. Clearly democratizing workplaces cannot magically transform work into play. So many co-ops have shop floor conditions that are not noticeably different than capitalist firms (Grunberg, Moore, & Greenberg, 1996). For instance, Greenberg (1986, p. 80) points out that work in all the plywood firms, co-op or otherwise, "is universally noisy, dirty, dangerous, monotonous, and relentless." This is partly due to the fact that competition and dominant technologies exert some pressure on the way that work needs to be organized, but even so, it is disappointing that a larger number of co-ops have not experimented more with different modes of work organization. Also, co-op workers often complain of substantial work stress, which likely accompanies the increased expectations and responsibilities that workers have in democratized firms (Arando et al., 2011; Rothschild & Whitt, 1986).

On the other hand, since co-op workers who experience shop-floor conditions firsthand are also the ones in control of management, the possibility of experimenting with shop-floor work organization remains much greater. Indeed, many co-ops do consciously strive to improve the quality of work, such as the Mondragon Bookstore in Winnipeg via balanced job complexes (Burrows, 2008). Indeed, there is evidence that work can be more pleasant in co-ops. For instance, Blumberg (1968) states that "there is hardly a study in the entire literature which fails to demonstrate that satisfaction in work is enhanced...from a genuine increase in workers' decision-making power" (p. 123). As mentioned previously, co-ops consistently have lower levels of quit rates and absenteeism (Bartlett et al., 1992), as well as less worker–manager antagonism (Greenberg, 1986). Even in large co-ops it is a consistent theme that members claim to prefer their workplace to the conventional alternative—usually pointing to some combination of the more egalitarian environment and the reduced antagonism and hierarchy so prevalent in conventional firms (though, of course, selection bias is possible) (e.g., Holmstrom, 1989). Additional evidence for the comparative pleasantness of work is that co-op managers consistently earn far less than they would elsewhere, yet nevertheless choose to remain.

So, overall, work satisfaction is only ambiguously related to workplace democracy. This can probably be explained by two factors. First, since work satisfaction is related not just to the objective conditions of the workplace but also to expectations of what work will be like, it is entirely possible for a co-op workplace to have somewhat better working conditions than conventional firms, but if there are also much higher expectations of what cooperative work should be like, overall job satisfaction might actually be lower. Second, it appears that participation at work—and the freedom of self-determination more generally—is not an easy breezy, obviously delightful kind of freedom. It can be both hard and stressful yet deeply rewarding at the same time.

Are Cooperative Workers Freer?

A central argument of this book is that a major advantage of workplace democracy is that it makes workers freer. So we must ask if the evidence backs this up.[33] Do workers in co-ops actually feel freer? The answer seems to be "yes," but with important caveats. Obviously how people subjectively feel about their work will vary immensely across workplaces and cultures. The experience of working in a six-person anarchist bike co-op in Toronto is very different from a 2,000-person industrial co-op in Italy. That said, the evidence points to several points. In general, it is clear that while co-ops are often successful at removing formal hierarchy at work, informal hierarchies often emerge, based primarily on bureaucracy and expertise which tend to dull the democratic freedoms.[34]

The main constraints on democratic freedom are the classic albatrosses of democratic practice: size and complexity (originally pointed out by Weber [1922] 1968 and Michels [1911] 1962). As the workplace grows in size, it becomes increasingly difficult for workers to directly participate in decision-making; participation inevitably passes into representation and bureaucracy starts to form. It is practically impossible to feel that you are self-determining in a large co-op if you never get to directly participate.

Feelings of self-determination, in other words, require participation at some level (though not every level). The second major constraint is that of complexity. Complexity tends to lead to informal hierarchies because dealing with complex issues requires specialization and the creation of managers and experts who acquire a monopoly over critical information and relevant knowledge. This makes them difficult for the rank-and-file to engage with and can undermine democracy as shop-floor workers feel obliged to simply go along with the advice of the experts. In particular the specialists who have access to information regarding changes in the market (e.g., new products, new manufacturing technologies, new competition) often manage to get their way much of the time (Holmstrom, 1989). So both size and complexity lead inexorably to a pyramid structure of governance in order to coordinate the whole. Such a pyramid may be harsh and capitalistic—with the top being unaccountable—or it may be parliamentarian and accountable to the bottom as in most co-ops, but regardless, all large firms will develop pyramid structures with bureaucrats and experts at the top, that if not circumvented in various ways will tend to create informal hierarchies, undermine participation, and ultimately undermine feelings of freedom and self-determination. It is important to recognize that these constraints are real; they flow from the realities of the institutions themselves and cannot be simply abolished or dismissed as the mere bagatelles of capitalism. Feasible radicalism needs to squarely recognize the ways in which these restraints undermine participation, otherwise it risks falling into the nonsensical utopianism of thinking that somehow the "associated producers" will one day be able to participate in every decision.[35]

Yet while these obstacles are consistent constraints on democratic practice, they can be largely mitigated, if not completely overcome, through sufficient dedication and the appropriate practices. The experience of successful co-ops points to two necessary things in this regard. First, workplace democracy requires solid parliamentary structures, by which I mean the establishment of a democratic constitution, regular General Assemblies, decision-making transparency, and availability of information. When these structures are operating well, they do provide an important sense of (negative) freedom: workers feel that managers are accountable to them, and that the gap between management and workers feels smaller and less intimidating than in conventional or unionized firms (Ammirato, 1996; Bradley & Gelb, 1983; Greenberg, 1986). Yet while these structures are clearly important, by themselves they constitute simply the shell or skeleton of a democratic body. For the workplace to be a living, breathing democracy—and for workers to feel free in the positive sense of self-determination—requires that the skeleton be fed with the oxygen and nutrition of participation. So, second, healthy workplace democracy requires rigorous practices of participation.

These practices in turn require at least two things.

(i) *The means for members to acquire the necessary skills and knowledge required to participate.* To this end democratic workplaces need to invest in education for its members in both technical matters (so that regular workers are better able to deliberate with experts) and cooperativist values (so that a participatory culture can flourish). Indeed, a democratic culture cannot simply be expected to grow by itself; what stands out at successful co-ops is an intense effort to foster and build it. This has been a constant feature at Mondragon, for instance, with its training programs, its Knowledge Group, and its own university. In Arizmendiarreta's words, "people do not normally become co-operators spontaneously, they have to be taught—the soil may be fertile but it has to be cultivated" (quoted in Morris, 1992, p. 9).

(ii) The second practice of participation required for healthy workplace democracy is *the opportunity for regular participation.* In large co-ops this requires open channels of communication and efforts to decentralize where possible in order to have semi-autonomous teams or working groups where direct participation can take place. For example, Irizar has developed a flat organizational structure based on work teams, with no bosses but with "shared leadership." Not only is this participation good from a democratic perspective, it has also proven to be important from an economic perspective, as it increases innovation, the transfer of ideas, and overall productivity (MacLeod & Reed, 2009).

So it is an important, if not particularly surprising, conclusion that in practice, democracy in the workplace (particularly in large co-ops) has many of the same strengths and weaknesses as it does in the state (although, of course, workplaces are much more numerous, so there is more room for experimentation). Co-op workers, like citizens, rarely describe themselves as being totally free or "in charge." Holmstrom (1989) poignantly describes how many co-op workers feel that managers make the crucial decisions, and that opportunities to actually participate are often few and far between. Such criticism will strike a familiar chord to most citizens in the West vis-à-vis their political democracy. But although few citizens today are overly ebullient about the quality of their democratic participation, even fewer would be willing to give it up for some kind of authoritarian or technocratic rule. Co-op workers feel similarly about workplace democracy. Although few feel that it is utopia, those who have it consistently do not want to give it up. On the contrary, participating often breeds the desire to participate more (Greenberg, 1986). Cornforth et al. (1998) concur, "We found that people did not want to give back control over their working lives once they had experienced it" (p. 111). People value the freedoms they have, even if they are not everything they had hoped for. This may be progress of an incremental sort, but it is progress nevertheless.

Summarizing the Evidence

Taking a step back, a useful way to think about the different ways that businesses can be governed is with respect to the degree of equality in management decision-making. From this perspective there are three broad families of firms: egalitarian collectives, worker co-ops, and capitalist firms. Clearly there is much variety and variation within these categories, but if we were to attempt a general assessment, what could we say? The evidence, I think, points to several basic conclusions. First, egalitarian collectives have little large-scale transformative potential. This is because their insistence on total equality in theory requires a high degree of leveling and homogeneity in practice, which keeps such organizations small and inefficient. Second, co-ops are in fact a kind of hybrid of egalitarian collectives and capitalist firms. They retain the formal equality and democratic aspirations of egalitarian co-ops, but structure themselves in a way that allows for a division of labor and a largeness of operational scale, characteristic of capitalist firms. The fact that co-ops are hybrids may make them unattractive to purists, but for those of us interested in feasible progressive politics, we can see that their hybrid structure is actually a strength, allowing cooperatives to operate with robust economic efficiency within a fundamentally democratic framework. Third, when compared to conventional capitalist firms, co-ops have a lot to recommend them. Importantly, they operate with comparable levels of economic efficiency to conventional firms. The standard perception of co-ops as inevitably small and bumbling organizations is a myth that should be disregarded; as examples like Mondragon and La Lega show, they can be large, complex, and immensely successful organizations. Fourth and finally, co-ops are not simply economically efficient; they are in many ways socially superior to conventional firms.

Obstacles to Co-op Formation

At this point we have reached a puzzle. If co-ops are roughly as economically efficient as capitalist firms (and arguably superior in certain social respects), then why are they so rare, usually making up less than 1% of most developed economies? Although there is no consensus on this question, several themes appear frequently in the literature.

First, probably the most basic obstacle to the formation of co-ops is what I call the "hiring bias," sometimes referred to as the "entrepreneurial problem" (Cornforth et al., 1988) or a public goods collective action problem (Schwartz, 2012). The problem is this: every single new firm (be it a single-person firm or a small partnership) must at some point decide how to grow. There are two basic options: either to hire an employee, in which case the firm becomes a conventional business, or, to bring in a new person as a partner to co-own and co-manage, in which case the firm can become a cooperative. Which is going to be more likely? For most people there is a strong bias toward hiring instead of forming a co-op. Hiring is much easier and less risky. It does not require an entrepreneur to make a long-term commitment to another person. An entrepreneur can simply hire an employee just like she might rent an office or some machinery. If it does not work out, it is not a big deal, she can just layoff the employee (the same way she might return unwanted rented machinery). Becoming co-owners with someone, on the other hand, is a massive commitment to sharing the firm's income, and doing so forever. Moreover, hiring an employee means that the entrepreneur retains sole control over the business development, whereas forming a co-op means that the entrepreneur is forced to share control and decision-making.[36]

This brings us to the second main obstacle that co-ops face—lack of financial support. All small firms need financing help to grow, but finance is particularly difficult for co-ops to acquire for several reasons. Co-ops cannot sell shares in the normal sense since that would compromise internal control[37] (indeed, the joint-stock company was invented precisely to serve this function of raising capital). And co-ops often find it hard to convince conventional banks to lend to them, partly out of discrimination against worker-ownership, partly out of ignorance about how co-ops function.[38]

These are the two most serious obstacles that co-ops face, though several other points deserve to be mentioned briefly.

A third obstacle is that some co-ops adopt unsustainable structures that tend to degenerate. One problem that we have seen is with "mule" firms.[39] Another common structural problem is not having procedures to guarantee sufficient reinvestment from revenues. An additional problem is the over-hiring of nonmembers, and a final problem is the ossification of democratic practices.

A fourth obstacle is a lack of cooperativist education, both among the general public, and especially among potential co-op workers. Cooperativist education is crucial, both in terms of the spreading the values of workplace democracy, as well as the requisite technical training.

Connected to this is the "familiarity effect" (Schwartz, 2012), which is that entrepreneurs are far more likely to start conventional firms than co-ops simply because they are much more familiar. It is easier to find out how to start them, easier to find models to emulate, easier to get advice about them, and so on.

A sixth obstacle is the difficulty in finding good compatible management. Some co-ops are ideologically hostile toward expert managers, and most offer smaller wages than they are likely to find elsewhere.

Taken together these obstacles explain why co-ops have lower birth rates than conventional firms, regardless of the fact that once they are set up they exhibit comparable longevity and economic efficiency.

Before moving on there is one final obstacle that needs to be mentioned, the issue of capital intensity. Industries with high levels of capital intensity (oil, steel, auto, pharmaceutical, etc.) are particularly difficult for co-ops to enter, since the always-prohibitive financing obstacles are here even more daunting. In chapter 2, I argued that these industries are unsuitable for traditional co-ops and are better suited for state ownership and co-management. Hence, we must address the question of whether co-management is economically viable.

Exploring this issue in depth is beyond our present scope, but a basic summary can be made. Co-management of state-owned firms is currently being experimented with in a number of important firms in Venezuela (Wilpert, 2007), and in Europe co-management of private firms has existed in some form for many years under the name of co-determination in Sweden, Denmark, Norway, Austria, and Luxemburg. But it is Germany that has gone the furthest. The German Co-determination Act of 1976 updated the legislation from several decades before, and provides worker representation on the supervisory board of all large firms: one-third of the representatives on the board for firms of 501–1,000 workers, and just under one-half for firms greater than 2,000 workers, with shareholders getting the other half (and the tie-breaker vote) (Dow, 2003, p. 86). The supervisory board elects the management board, which controls the firm's day-to-day operations. This system is now well established and enjoys widespread support and legitimacy in Germany, thus providing compelling evidence of the viability of co-management.

Although co-determination is clearly feasible—large German firms are among the most efficient in the world—it is not clear that it has resulted in the productivity gains that supporters hoped would stem from worker participation in management (George, 1993; Svenjar, 1982). A similar, and likely related disappointment, is that the degree to which co-determination has allowed for meaningful worker participation and empowerment seems ambiguous at best (Dow, 2003). So while the stability of co-determination in Germany provides compelling evidence of the viability of this form, there is clearly room for experimentation to improve its limitations.

Expanding Workplace Democracy

Last chapter we saw that workers are generally in too weak a position to easily bargain for workplace democracy. And, as we have just seen, there are also significant obstacles to creating new democratic workplaces. So what reforms should be pursued in order to help effect a transition to an economy characterized by significant workplace democracy?

Increasing the strength of workers to bargain for increased voice at work requires strengthening unions and increasing workers' ability to exit through an enhanced welfare system or, more profoundly, a basic income.

Expanding the presence of worker co-ops requires help along three axes: legal support, financial support, and educational support. Over the short term, the most important reforms include the following.

A sustainable legal framework is needed to prevent degeneration. This requires collective ownership (to prevent "mules"), provisions to mandate adequate investment levels, a policy of limiting the number of nonmembers, and so on.

The most useful reform in many instances would be that which increases the provision of finance. An arm's length co-ops bank is vital in this regard—partly to provide access to cheap credit and partly to provide financial expertise (à la Mondragon's Empresarial division of the CL) to help set up new co-ops. Beyond helping to set up co-op banks, the state could usefully help develop and legalize financial instruments suitable for co-ops to raise money on capital markets without having to cede control rights. Various suggestions for kinds of "cooperative bonds" of this sort have been put forward (McCain, 1977; Waldmann & Smith, 1999). Just as important, tax support is an immensely powerful tool for encouraging the spread of co-ops. For instance, in Venezuela in 1998 there were fewer than 800 co-ops. By 2007 it was estimated that there were over 30,000.[40] This exponential growth is almost entirely due to legislative changes under Chavez that allowed co-ops to pay less tax and access cheap credit.

In terms of educational support, an important initiative would be the promotion of cooperative business schools to educate students about the operation and management of cooperative firms. It is noteworthy that Mondragon started from humble beginnings as a school. Similarly in Venezuela efforts have been made to train students in cooperative business models and encourage them to start their own co-ops.[41]

Additionally, a league or network is vital to foster the spread of co-ops by providing a source of mutual aid in a capitalist sea. As S. Smith (2001) points out, "cooperatives are unlikely to be successful in a highly competitive environment without the roles played by higher level co-ops and networks" (p. 3). Networks provide a wide range of economic and political benefits. Economically, networks are vital in helping to reduce the "hiring bias," because they can facilitate like-minded people with similar ideological and entrepreneurial ideas finding each other and working together. Additional economic benefits of networking include: sharing risk through cross investment, so that workers' eggs are in many baskets; familiarizing regional workers, managers, bankers, and politicians with co-op practices; developing consortia to establish economies of scale; and providing examples of successful firms for others to emulate. Networking also provides important political benefits: a league provides increased leverage to lobby for political support; it helps to build a strong and vibrant political presence; and it helps maintain a culture of workplace democracy that prevents workers from feeling isolated and thus helps develop a new sense of the normality of workplace democracy. La Lega is a prime example of these benefits. Networking together in a league can provide a self-sustaining burst of energy as positive externalities reinforce each other, knowledge acquired in one place transfers over, an example here is emulated there, and so on. Lastly, networks like this are instrumental in building social movements to encourage broader changes toward economic democracy.

While reforms such as these are all important and eminently practical in the short to medium term, I want to propose two reforms of a more ambitious nature for the long term.

On the legal front, workers need a legal right to buy out their firm from the conventional owners.[42] This is the only thing that can really overcome the hiring bias inherent in present-day corporate market systems. The underlying idea being that employers should only be allowed to rent people's labor in the manner that one rents machines, *if* those same hired workers are legally entitled to turn around and buy in to become co-owners.

On the financial front, imagine a simple variant of the Swedish Meidner Plan,[43] which we might call an "Incremental Democratization Plan" (IDP). An IDP would require by law that every company set aside, say, 20% of its profits every year in the form of new shares into an internal fund controlled collectively by the firm's workers on a one-person one-vote basis. While workers would be able to use these shares to exert influence on the firm's operations they would not be permitted to sell the shares for personal enrichment. This would have two results. First, since the profits are not taxed, but are issued as new shares which stay in the company, the IDP would not drain corporate cash flow or reduce investment. Second, and more fundamentally, the plan would have a dramatic cumulative effect. Over time workers acquire more and more say over the firm's operations. They would be majority owners within roughly 35 years, and effective controllers much sooner (since effective control in corporations usually requires much less than 51% of ownership). This means that after a certain period, all workers would be in a position to contemplate buying out their firms and transforming them into worker co-ops. In other words, an IDP means that in a slow, nonviolent, and non-disruptive way, the entire economy would be radically altered, and worker co-ops could emerge as the dominant economic form. This would constitute nothing less than a peaceful non-revolutionary revolution.

Conclusion: Evaluating the Costs and Benefits

Democratization of workplaces would likely bring a number of costs. For interested individuals, starting a new co-op would require workers investing a sizable chunk of money, thus bringing certain financial risks. Most importantly, fostering workplace democracy (through increased bargaining power via welfare/basic income or through new co-ops via a co-op bank/tax breaks) requires public funds to pay for its expansion—funds that must be raised through additional taxation or diverted from existing social spending. Providing financial help for co-ops also brings with it the administrative costs of allocating money (and monitoring for fraud); so clearly a balance needs to be made between promoting co-ops but not in such a loose or unmonitored way as to open the door for fraud.[44]

On the other hand, when it works well, democratizing work brings with it a number of important benefits: the increased freedoms of protection and self-determination most obviously. We have also seen that co-ops bring clear benefits in terms of job security and wage equality (the latter of which is immensely important given current societal levels of inequality). Co-ops are also likely to provide a number of positive externalities to their community: they provide the regional stability that comes from long-term job security and long-term investment in an area (since they are more geographically rooted than conventional firms); they are also likely to be better for the environment and may well be beneficial for people's health.

How can we weigh these costs and benefits? Clearly the details of exactly how much money society should spend on fostering workplace democracy (versus other social needs) cannot be answered in the abstract, but depend on the most pressing needs of a particular polity at a particular time. As a left-wing Milton Friedman might say: there are no free freedoms. That said, the overall lesson is that co-ops are sufficiently superior to conventional firms that they deserve our support. They are important enough and successful enough to warrant ideological support from activists and material support from the state in order to expand this form of business. Co-ops are not perfect organizations. Their democratic structures can work poorly and be subverted by informal hierarchies, and they can be stressful and time-consuming even when they work well. Yet for all that, I hope to have demonstrated that their benefits are significant enough to warrant quite substantial public investment. Workplace democracy is worth it.

Part Two

The Market System

4   Democracy and the Market System

Markets make good servants but bad masters.[1]

Introduction

It has been said that the market is the most democratic of all institutions: an immense kind of voting machine where, as Ludwig von Mises puts it, "every penny is a ballot paper" (quoted in Ulrich, 2008, p. 182). The aim of this chapter is to explore the degree to which this is true. To what extent should democrats rely on the market for matters of economic allocation, and to what extent do we need to look to alternative institutions to achieve our goals? Two main arguments are advanced. The first is that a democratic economy requires a regulated market system. Neoliberal market systems are far from the democratic ideal; social democratic market systems are closer, but are still vulnerable to inherent market failures which inhibit real democracy. The second argument is that the market is not a natural or unitary thing—it can be shaped in fundamentally different ways, and in particular it can be shaped in ways that help foster democratic businesses.

The Market System as a Democratic Voting Machine

The last two chapters discussed democracy internally in businesses. But what should democrats desire of the broader economy—the myriad interactions of firms and consumers? Two clear values stand out. The first is that a good economy should provide, among other things, *consumer democracy*; in other words, it should provide the population with a roughly equal influence over what is produced. Second, a good economy should provide *citizen democracy*—in other words, it should provide the population with a roughly equal influence over how the economy develops over time. (Should there be increased oil extraction? Less deforestation? Promotion of green businesses? More highways or high-speed train systems? Larger suburbs or denser urban areas? Subsidies for local artists? Infrastructure for urban biking?) The central task for the pages that follow is to clarify what kind of economic system could accomplish these tasks.

The conventional answer, of course, is that the market is the appropriate tool for this. For instance, Paul Samuelson ([1948] 1992), in his classic economics text, described the market as a gigantic "voting machine," continually aggregating people's changing preferences into price information for others to respond to. And conservative economists have generally been even more forceful about this, arguing that the "free market," when not overly interfered with by the state, will be more-or-less democratic in both of these senses. They would not recognize a clear distinction between these two senses, reasoning that the market promotes "consumer sovereignty" by providing people with a say over what should be produced now, and thereby directs the economy to develop in ways to meet consumer preferences as they evolve (Friedman, [1962] 2002; Persky, 1993). The notion of consumer sovereignty is what underlies Adam Smith's famous idea that the reason the butcher, baker, and brewer provide their wares is because "the people" have demanded them for their supper. Indeed, Smith's homely example is a subtle evocation of market democracy—showing us how the market provides the regular goods desired by regular people. But, of course, the fact that the market provides "consumer sovereignty" does not at all mean that it provides "consumer democracy." Markets respond to money, and so if only a small subsection of the population possesses money, markets will respond only to them. "Consumer sovereignty" in a literal sense is nothing to celebrate; as a concept it is morally vacuous. It is only when consumers are recognized as equals, only when consumer sovereignty evolves into consumer democracy, that the concept acquires normative force.

That said, Smith's intuition of the democratic potential of markets is not entirely wrong. Markets *can* act in deeply democratic ways. Consider a simple, idealized market, such as a farmers' market, where strawberries, apples, oranges, and so on, are sold. How can the people choose which products they think society should produce, and in what proportion? In other words, how can the people exert a democratic say over economic production? The market, potentially, solves this problem in a deeply democratic way: if people simply buy what they desire, and if everyone has similar amounts of money, the demand for the various products would accurately reflect the population's desires. If the population prefers more apples than oranges, the sellers are led, as if by some invisible hand as Smith would say, to alter their production practices; some apple sellers would start growing oranges instead, supplying more of one thing and less of another, to reflect the consumers' changing preferences so that they don't go bankrupt. In this way the market forces sellers to be *accountable* to the consumers; poor services or bad products will be voted out, so to speak. This is why Schumpeter said that "there exists no more democratic institution than a market" (quoted in Jossa & Cuomo, 1997, p. 120). So given some crucial assumptions (equal dollar "votes," existence of competition, minimal externalities, etc.) the market *can* act to aggregate the preferences of the people in price information while simultaneously providing incentives for others to respond to this information. Thus the process indirectly causes production to occur according to the will of the demos. What could be more democratic than that?

Market Failures

So while the market does have democratic potential, critics have pointed to a number of problems with this idyllic image by highlighting the ways in which markets can fail (Samuelson & Nordhaus, [1948] 1992; Stiglitz, 2010). Of course, the recognition that markets *can* fail is very common; the degree to which they *do* fail is, of course, much more contentious. However, even conservative economists recognize that certain failures (such as monopolies) exist in many areas and diminish the efficiency of the market (Friedman, [1962] 2002).

Conventionally, economists discuss market failures in terms of Pareto inefficiencies (e.g., Stiglitz (2002b)). In other words, rectifying the failure can lead to more efficient results in the sense that someone can be made better off without making anyone worse off. I want to suggest that we think about market failures in a slightly different way—not just about Pareto optimality, but about limitations to economic democracy (in the senses of consumer and citizen democracy described above). In other words, an important way to think about market failures is in terms of the degree to which they prevent the market from providing citizens with a roughly equal influence over what is produced and how the economy should develop.

What is the advantage of thinking about market failures in this way? The answer is that market allocations can be efficient (in the narrow Pareto sense) without being particularly just (Hahnel, 2002). If A has $1,000,000 and B has $1, and it's not possible to increase B's wealth without affecting A, we have a situation that is "efficient" but not necessarily just. In addition to concerns about B's deprivation the democratic concern is that A is able to exert much more influence over the economy than B (since businesses are going to care much more about what A wants than what B wants). This is a problem because in a democratic society people should have a roughly equal say over what is produced, because no person's preferences should count as inherently more important than any others; to allow otherwise is to compromise the equal moral worth of individuals. If Adam Smith had not talked of butchers, bakers, and brewers, but about mansions and racehorses, the appeal of the market mechanism may well have been more qualified.

When I buy a strawberry I am not simply purchasing a commodity; I am also casting a vote for the production of strawberries. I am signaling a desire for society's scarce economic resources to be used in one way and not another. If, however, a millionaire comes to town announcing her plan to spend millions on raspberries, it's entirely possible that my strawberry grower will leave the business and take up raspberry growing. The millionaire's wealth has meant that society's scarce resources (in this case the labor and farmland) are being shifted to respond to her dollars, ignoring my preferences. Recognizing the unfairness of this does not mean that equal say over the market should trump every other goal. If achieving this kind of equality places additional costs on other people, as is standard in real life, the trade-offs must be weighed. The point is only that, other things being equal, we should desire more consumer democracy, not less. We should desire the market to respond to individuals as individuals, not as proxies for very different size bank accounts.

Let us look at six ways in which market systems can fail to act democratically.[2] Here we focus on neoliberal market systems; we consider social democratic market systems below.

The first and most obvious way in which market systems can fail to operate democratically is that consumers typically have very unequal amounts of dollar "votes." Markets respond to dollars, not people. This is why Pfizer, in 2000, developed no drugs for TB (which kills about 2 million poor people a year), but it developed eight new drugs for impotence and seven for balding—the maladies of the wealthy countries (Bakan, 2004, p. 49). Society's resources go into fancy cars, beauty products, and yachts, rather than affordable food or housing, simply because some have millions of dollar "votes" and some have very few. The extreme inequality that typifies neoliberal countries—where in the United States in 2007 the richest 5% possessed 61.2% of the nation's wealth (whereas the bottom 40% controlled only 0.2%)—creates a mockery of consumer democracy (Wolff, 2010, p. 44).

Second, monopolies undermine the market's democratic potential because they distort prices away from their true social costs and benefits. Monopolies do this by enabling sellers to keep prices artificially high, which means that the market will provide inaccurate price information for the population to "vote" on. Even worse, monopoly means that firms lose their accountability to consumers because consumers have no alternative choices. To get a sense of the degree to which monopoly undermines the democratic potential of market systems, it is instructive to recall that in 2008 the biggest 500 firms in the world controlled about 40% of the world's GDP (Foster, McChesney, & Jonna, 2011). Indeed, the authors argue that the existence of monopoly in the American economy is "greater today than it has ever been."

A third important market failure is that of externalities. Externalities are costs (or benefits) that are borne by people who are neither the buyers nor sellers of a transaction. Externalities are inherently undemocratic since by definition they mean that people are affected without having a say. The classic example is of a factory which emits toxic pollution into a nearby river. The resulting costs in terms of dead fish and sick humans are "externalities." Since the costs are externalized, the market price of the factory's products is distorted; it is not an accurate reflection of social costs, and so it gives people the wrong information on which they cast their dollar "votes." For example, a decade ago it was estimated that the true social cost of gasoline, taking into account the environmental costs of the pollution, would be about $15/gallon, compared to the market price of roughly $3/gallon (Hahnel, 2002). This means that people were (and still are) being led to "vote" for much more gasoline (and cars) than they would if the true social price were incorporated into the market price.[3] Externalities thus act to mislead the consumer about what she is voting for; the presence of externalities is like the presence of state-controlled media that consistently misrepresents the candidates' positions for an election. People can still vote, but they are misled about what exactly they are voting for. Externalities are a major issue because they can be extremely serious. Global warming, which has been called "the greatest example of market failure we have ever seen" (Stern, 2007, p. 1), is caused by externalities—the fact that many of our most important economic decisions in terms of industry, air travel, heating systems, and so on, ignore the true social cost of carbon emissions.

Fourth, public goods are those kind of goods (like national defense or sewers or highways) that once provided for some are very difficult to keep from others. Goods like this offer a strong incentive for people to "free ride"—to enjoy the good without paying for it, to use it without actually "voting" for it so to speak—which means that private businesses will not want to provide such goods and so the market will undersupply them irrespective of the population's desire for them.

Fifth, markets are often inadequate for making long-term investment decisions because market prices are determined by current supply and demand and so can be very inadequate for long-term planning. This is particularly so in cases where the supply is liable to change in a suddenly drastic or unpredictable way (for instance, as might happen when the population of a fish stock reaches a tipping point, such that all of a sudden positive feedbacks kick in and a smoothly declining stock suddenly collapses). In such cases, it is entirely likely that individuals "voting" with their dollars will end up with results that they do not actually desire, and may actually have acted differently if they had the relevant information that was not contained in the prices. This is why many of the people who happily continue to buy cheap cod for their fish and chips would also support tougher regulations on cod fishing to prevent the stocks from collapsing if they knew the broader ecological situation. But since such long-term information does not get transmitted through prices, the market is an inadequate mechanism for making such decisions.

Relatedly, since markets can only aggregate the preferences of current consumers, they are unable to factor in long-term consideration of future generations.[4] The interests of future generations (which presumably constitute much of the moral concern with environmental sustainability) cannot be aggregated by markets but must be planned for through public deliberation.

Sixth and finally, markets can fail to reflect collective choice. While prices reflect the aggregate of private preferences, it is important to realize that such an aggregate may be very different from what people think is best collectively, for society as a whole. For example, while individuals may privately buy plane tickets to fly back and forth across Europe, the same individuals may prefer that, collectively, people do not take such flights (and would support carbon taxes to reduce such flights). What an individual may think is good for me is often different from what the same person thinks is good for us.[5] In other words, voting with one's dollars on the basis of price reveals the aggregate will, but this is not necessarily the same as the collective will, which can only be gauged by actually asking people what they think (Sen, 1961). It is worth emphasizing that by "collective will" I am not referring to anything mysterious; there is no societal entity that has any existence or knowledge separate from the collection of real flesh-and-blood individuals. The point is simply the prosaic one that people often make different choices when they are considering what is best just for themselves versus what is best for themselves as part of a larger social group (including neighbors, community, or the society at large).

Could the Market System be a Democratic System?

Given these failures, it is natural to ask whether the market system could ever act in a truly democratic way. Are the barriers to consumer and citizen democracy barriers that could conceivably be overcome, or are they inherent in the very structure, the very DNA, of market systems themselves? To get some clarity on this question, let us clear aside the brambles of circumstance by talking initially in idealized abstract terms.[6]

First of all, what would be necessary to have a market system with genuine consumer democracy?[7] If we allow ourselves a utopian moment to think through the institutional requirements, we can see that genuine consumer democracy would require minimizing the first three market failures. Fundamentally, it would require rough material equality (and systems of taxation to redistribute much of the inequality generated through normal market processes) so that people had roughly equal "votes." Beyond this, consumer democracy would require that market prices be as close as possible to accurate reflections of social costs and benefits in order to give an accurate picture of what the population really wants. This means that monopolies would need to be restricted and major externalities would have to be dealt with (perhaps through regulation, taxation of negative ones, and subsidies for positive ones). If this were to be accomplished, then such a society would indeed resemble a generalized version of our idyllic fruit market. In such a case the market truly would be democratic—its production driven by the demands of the demos on an egalitarian basis.

Obviously such a society is very far removed from the actual market systems of today. But the crucial question is this: what is the nature of the barriers to achieving such consumer democracy? The important point is that it seems to me that *the barriers to achieving this are practical but not inherently institutional.* The barriers are very real ones of power, politics, class-interest, ideology, and so on, which although I do not want to downplay them at all, are, at root, contingent factors that are not inherent to the functioning of the market. If a population could be convinced of the need for redistributive taxation and reducing major monopolies and externalities, then such a population would find the market an excellent tool for providing consumer democracy. Recognizing this is crucial, because it allows us to see that the enemy of a democratic economy in this regard is not the market itself in any fundamental structural way, but the politics and power that shape the current unequal market systems in which we live. So unless one believes that market systems must inherently, always and everywhere, produce inequality and price distortions (which, as I will argue below, strikes me as an indefensibly ahistorical position), it should be apparent that the market can be a deeply democratic mechanism. Such an insight has important policy ramifications because it implies that market systems can be more or less democratic—the limits are those of political and ideological opposition, not institutional nature. The more we can reduce inequality and price distortions, the more the market will successfully provide consumer democracy.

What about the second dimension of market democracy—what would be necessary to establish a democratic economy in the sense of citizen democracy over economic development? In other words, what would be necessary for citizens to have a roughly equal say in deciding whether to promote, say, highways or high-speed trains, condominiums or social housing, casinos or bike lanes, suburbs or urban density? The market system is not an adequate mechanism for deciding such questions because decisions about economic development require collective decisions about priorities for the future. Decisions about developing suburbs or urban density (or about whether to subsidize green businesses or local artists) are inherently collective decisions about what kind of externalities matter enough to require public intervention—are the negative externalities from urban sprawl or pollution serious enough to warrant a tax, or the positive externalities from urban density or local culture worth the cost of a subsidy, and if so, how much? Decisions about transportation systems or housing development are questions about public investment—the market is inadequate for dealing with them because they involve public goods, collective decision-making, and long-term investment—all things at which we know the market often fails.

The barriers to achieving citizen democracy are: externalities, public goods, long-term investment, and collective decisions. But notice that unlike consumer democracy, where it is (at least theoretically) possible to overcome the relevant market failures so that the market delivers consumer democracy, it is *impossible* to fix these failures from within a market framework. This is because the market is an inherently individualistic and short-term preference-aggregating machine, so no amount of tweaking is going to allow such a machine to provide the means for collective deliberation. It is simply not possible to achieve citizen democracy through the market mechanism because the kind of decisions that are required for such democracy—decisions of a collective, future-oriented nature—are simply not amenable to individualistic market processes. These kinds of decisions require an altogether different kind of mechanism. Specifically, they require public institutions where popular representatives can discuss and deliberate about collective goals. In other words, even if we were able to achieve an egalitarian society with a high degree of consumer democracy, the market would still not be democratic in the sense of providing citizen democracy. The fundamental obstacles to citizen democracy are not practical or political per se; they are intrinsic to the institutional functioning of markets themselves.

So for issues of citizen democracy, the market is an inherently inappropriate kind of institution, whereas political institutions are inherently more appropriate. But this, of course, does not mean that political institutions, such as the familiar levels of government (municipal, regional, national), will be able to simply and unproblematically deliver these kinds of goods. The existence of market failures does not imply the nonexistence of government failures. It is undeniably true that political institutions face their own kinds of problems in providing democracy (from corruption to rent-seeking to bureaucratization to tyranny of the majority to tyranny of the eloquent, etc.) But in terms of citizen democracy, political institutions have much more promise than the market because they allow for collective, future-oriented decision-making in a way that markets cannot. A central goal of chapters 6 and 7 is, therefore, to investigate the kind of political institutions that have the most democratic potential in this regard (such as public banks and local level participatory budgeting).

What conclusions should we draw from this analysis? I think the basic lesson is that the evaluation of the democratic potential of market systems needs to be nuanced. Too often the discussion of the market raises undue passion, with evaluations ranging from adoration to vitriol. For instance, Blair Hoxby (1998) sees the market as "a means by which imperfect men may, in the long term, approximate the wisdom of God" (p. 188), whereas Michael Albert condemns it as "the single most horrendous and destructive creation of humanity in all of history" (quoted in Allard et al., 2010, p. 60). Such heat, it seems to me, is misplaced. I think we should take a more measured position: from a democratic perspective the market should be neither loved nor loathed.

Our analysis suggests that advocates of the "free market" are often too applauding of the democratic functioning of the market—particularly in neoliberal contexts where the market is very far from being democratic. On the other hand, socialists are often too eager to see the failures of particular markets as necessarily inherent in every market, and thus too hasty in rejecting the market system out of hand (Hodgson, 1999; Lerner, 1972). At a theoretical level at least I think we should conclude that market systems could potentially be good mechanisms for providing consumer democracy because they are good mechanisms for aggregating individual preferences. However, markets are not so promising for providing citizen democracy because they are not appropriate mechanisms for deliberating about collective, future-oriented preferences. Such decision-making requires public political institutions.

Social Democratic Attempts to Democratize the Market

In the real world, social democratic states, particularly the Nordic countries, are the ones that have gone furthest in the attempt to democratize their market systems. How have they done this?

Broadly speaking, social democratic states have managed to improve the levels of consumer democracy by reducing material inequality and correcting major price distortions by regulating certain externalities and restricting monopolies (the next chapter explores the details). Social democratic states have also managed to improve the levels of citizen democracy; the main mechanism for doing this has been state-directed public investment. The familiar idea is that citizens elect representatives to parliament, who then decide on the kinds of economic development they want to achieve; these goals are then implemented through public intervention in the economy—usually through regulation, taxation, subsidy, or direct public investment (Lindblom, 2001).

Unfortunately, social democratic market systems are still far from democratic. They have failed to achieve either consumer democracy or citizen democracy (though they are closer to both of these things than their neoliberal counterparts). The next several chapters build up this critique, but here it is useful to outline the argument. Social democracies fail to deliver consumer democracy because they retain substantial levels of material inequality, meaning certain people have many more "votes" than others. Even in Norway, one of the most egalitarian societies in the world, the richest 10% control 50.5% of the wealth (Davies et al., 2007). What stops the social democratic countries from reducing inequality further and thus actually achieving consumer democracy? After all, countries like Sweden had social democratic parties in power for 54 of the 60 years preceding 1991 (Pontusson, 1992). As we will discuss in chapter 6, the fundamental limits to achieving consumer democracy stem from the private control of finance and investment. Social democratic countries are limited in the degree to which they can redistribute wealth by the ability that private financiers and investors have to derail the economy. They have an effective "veto" over decisions of this nature, which means that democratizing the market in the sense of establishing real consumer democracy can only advance in step with the democratization of finance and investment.

Additionally, social democratic states fail to deliver genuine citizen democracy. The main mechanisms used by such societies to plan economic development are state regulation of the market and state-led investment. However, as I will argue in chapter 6, it is problematic that both of these things tend to happen at the highest levels of the central government, because it means that although they are formally accountable they fail to be meaningfully or substantively democratic. In social democratic societies the average person continues to possess very little influence over the economic development of her community. Again, this implies that democratizing the market in this sense of establishing real citizen democracy requires finding ways to decentralize and democratize public finance and investment institutions.

In sum, we have seen that the market system does indeed have democratic potential. Market systems are inherently voting machines, but they are only potentially democratic ones. Neoliberal market systems generally fail to function in a democratic way. Social democratic market systems are better, but they can still not be called genuinely democratic. A truly democratic market system would need to find ways to overcome the limits to consumer democracy imposed by private control of finance and investment (in order to be able to tax sufficiently to create a rough equality of "votes"). It would also require ways to deliver citizen democracy by establishing nonmarket public institutions that are decentralized enough to be meaningfully democratic. Exploring examples of such institutions is the task of chapters 6 and 7.

The Flexibility of Market Systems

Although markets have existed in some form since time immemorial, the "market system" is a fairly recent human invention. A market is simply a place where goods and services are exchanged for money—such as in village markets throughout history or farmers' markets today. The *market system*, however, refers to a political-legal structuring of the economy whereby the bulk of a society's economic activity is coordinated through buying and selling (Lindblom, 2001). In this section it will be argued that there is no unique kind of market system: markets can be embedded in very different institutions to produce a wide range of incentives and competitive practices. There are huge differences, for example, between the American neoliberal market system and the Swedish social democratic market system. Moreover, while both of these market systems can be categorized as "capitalist" in certain ways, it is entirely possible to have market systems that are socialist. There can be a market system where productive property is owned by the state (as existed in Yugoslavia under Tito). There can be a market system where the firms are co-ops, finance and investment are provided through democratic public institutions, and inequality is mitigated through taxes and transfers—such as the system of economic democracy advocated in this book. The important thing is to resist the automatic conflation of "markets" and "capitalism" because such thinking freezes our imagination and limits our possibilities.

Adam Smith ([1776] 2006) described the emergence of the market system as a natural outgrowth of humanity's "propensity to truck, barter, and exchange one thing for another" (p. 12). Today many conservatives, taking their cue from Smith, champion the idea of a "free market" (i.e., one that is unregulated and unaffected by the state). But the idea of a truly "free market" is conceptually confused. Karl Polanyi ([1944] 2001) famously described the ways in which despite the rhetoric of "free markets," actual market systems, since their beginnings in feudal Britain, have always been inherently political systems.[8] A market system is a system that has been built and constructed by political and legal means, and it is a system that inherently depends on the political-legal institutions of the state for its basic functioning.

This means that it is a mistake to think of the market system as something distinct from the state. In reality it is always embedded in the state; it is always institutionalized in various political-legal structures. The market system (a more accurate label would be the "market-state complex") is shaped by a large number of political-legal parameters. For example, the state determines the scope of what can and cannot be sold (e.g., usually not body parts, drugs, husbands or wives, votes, etc.), who is allowed to participate (e.g., minimum ages and foreign worker legislation), and sets key prices (taxes, interest rates, minimum wages). The state defines the basic laws of business: defining the rights and obligations of various market actors, determining property laws, and enforcing contracts. The state creates a whole host of legal regulations determining how businesses may or may not operate, from labor law to health and safety requirements. It determines how easy it is to declare bankruptcy, set up a corporation, or form a trade union. The state creates a whole set of business institutions and infrastructure to regulate exchange itself; for example, courts to deal with bankruptcies and frauds, central banks to be lenders of last resort, treasuries to protect the authenticity of the currency, police officers to enforce contracts, roads and telephone services to facilitate business operations, and so on. In all these ways it is apparent that the market system is deeply integrated into the political apparatus of the state. Indeed, even Friedrich Hayek, the free marketer par excellence, recognized that the question of state interference or not is a false alternative. The idea of laissez-faire, he recognized, is misleading because the state always acts (1944, p. 80). But even this way of putting it is slightly misleading because it is not a question of the state acting on a market distinct from itself, since the market is always institutionalized in various ways in the state. So, the fundamental question, as Polanyi ([1944] 2001) reminds us, is not "free market" or "intervention," but rather intervention "for whom" and "for what."

Talk of the "free market" is misleading because there is nothing natural about any particular market system. The market system is a political construction, which like every political construction can be shaped differently. Ultimately, given sufficient political will, each and every aspect of the market system is up for grabs. Indeed, the Polanyian insight is a fundamentally democratic one, because as soon as it is recognized that markets are always socially constructed, then the corresponding question becomes unavoidable: who should be empowered to construct it? (I would hope that any answer that is not "the people," or their representatives, in some kind of egalitarian arrangement, will be rejected as unacceptable.) Since nature is the antithesis of politics, to denaturalize the market—as Polanyi does to Smith—is to show that it is not formed of god or spirit or human essence but rather mere institutional clay. To denaturalize is to politicize; and that which is political can only be made with regards to the interests of some or the interests of all.

So from a democratic perspective, the question is this: how should we strive to shape the market differently (beyond the ways we have already discussed for consumer and citizen democracy)? While there are a number of areas of importance, I want to focus here on two dimensions that seem particularly germane: scale and fostering democratic businesses.

Structuring the Market System to Democratically Limit Its Scale

The ways in which the market is shaped constitute some of the most hotly contested political disputes. For instance, the determination of how income is distributed (vis-à-vis the scope of taxation and the ability to form unions), the determination of what kind of things are allowed to be bought/sold (e.g., marijuana or genetic material), and so on. However, there is one crucial aspect of the market system that is far too often ignored: its scale. The scale of an economy refers to its physical size relative to the containing ecosystem.[9] This is a crucial issue because it has tremendous ecological consequences.[10]

At the moment the question of the market's scale is largely politically abdicated. The issue has historically been a political black hole. It is not usually a clear part of political parties' public policy (except perhaps of some green parties); finance ministers are not beholden to anyone to balance growth with sustainability; extractive industries are rarely forced to produce public documents about the extent of their activities; and few institutional safeguards exist to measure the amount of throughput in core industries, much less to regulate it. This means that questions of scale are by-and-large left to private firms to produce as much or as little as they want. And since competitive pressure generally induces firms to grow as much as they can, this abdication of political decision-making over scale means that throughput will likely continue to grow on its deadly exponentially upwards course.[11] And since the question of scale is an inherently future-oriented collective issue, it is one intrinsically ill-suited to be left to market forces.

The scale of the economy must become a more normalized political issue. Just as it is common today to hear on the radio and read in the news debates about what the top tax rate should be, there likewise needs to be political debates about what the top levels of throughput should be. Governments can respond to the demos's wishes by increasing/decreasing taxes on extractive industries or placing caps on the legal limits of certain types of extraction. Imposing rigorous taxes or caps would cause price changes to ripple throughout the market, forcing consumers to take ecological ceilings into account.

From the perspective of economic democracy, the point is not that economic scale must be reduced. (Personally it seems to me that it must, as the drive for never-ending growth starts to look more and more like ecological suicide (Jackson, 2009)). The point is rather that it must be a societal question: figuring out how to balance the materialistic desire for more with the ecological need for less. Economic democracy cannot tell people what they should decide, but it can insist that they be empowered to decide. Without more established democratic procedures for this, the ongoing vacuum of accountability will inevitably continue, and issues of scale will continue to be abdicated to private businesses to ignore as they see fit.

Structuring the Market System to Promote Democratic Businesses

It is often argued that democratic business organizations (such as worker co-ops) are doomed because they cannot compete successfully in "the market." The story is a familiar one: co-ops operate differently from other firms, they do not simply maximize profits but strive for additional social goals (such as worker empowerment, job security, pay equity, etc.), and therefore make less profit than the cut-throat competition. Eventually they are forced to either change their structure or go bankrupt. This is usually referred to as the "degeneration thesis" (Gibson-Graham, 2003; Webb & Webb, 1907).

On this point Marxists have tended to be just as dismissive as neoliberals about the possibilities of alternative business practices within the so-called "free market" (Mellor, Hannah, & Stirling, 1988, chap. 3).[12] It is, however, a mistake to think that firms' actions are rigidly determined by the market system. In fact, firms are shaped by two general forces: external market competition as well as internal governance structure. Instead of thinking of market pressure as a constant underlying force, like gravity, it is more accurate to think of market pressures as emanating from a malleable market environment. We should conceive of the market system as a car race: the firms are the cars, the management is the driver, and the market is the kind of road (its shape, surface material, obstacles, pit stops, etc.). So if there are different kinds of cars competing, the kind that will win a race is, of course, partly determined by the driver and partly determined by which car is better suited for the particular road. We are not surprised that a tank beats an electric car on an off-road race, but, equally, no one should disagree with the proposition that the road could be changed (flattened, paved over, etc.) so that the electric car could win.

Democratizing the economy in the sense of restructuring the market system so that democratic businesses can flourish would require substantial changes—but there is nothing impossible about this. The market system is malleable. Indeed, when we look around the world today we see that there is in fact a wide range of institutional variety of market systems. The US market system functions very differently from the Swedish one (and both function very differently from China's).[13]

Consider a historical analogy. Those who hold to the degeneration thesis often argue that co-ops like Mondragon are doomed; they will ultimately be driven under through competition with multinational corporations in today's corporate market system. To see the problems with this way of thinking consider by analogy that we are in 19th-century Britain and examining the competition that occurs between a unionized, progressive factory and a corresponding "regular" profit-maximizing factory.

First, note that the institutional realities of this market system were substantially different from our own. There were no health or safety regulations. Parliament was generally reluctant to regulate the market, arguing that regulation would "infringe on personal liberty in...the free exercise of Industry, of Skill and of Talent" (cited in Kirby, 2003, p. 95). The workers in the unionized factory were in an extremely precarious position, constantly under threat from anti-combination laws which threatened fines and even jail time for union workers. In addition, most markets were systemically supported by child labor. Child labor would have made up about one-third of the workforce[14] in the regular factory, although the workers would have prevented such labor in the union factory.[15] There was no welfare system to speak of. Unemployed people were sometimes able to get minimal parish support. Others were jailed as vagrants or committed to workhouses. There were no minimum wages or limits to working hours (though the union factory would have done its best to insist on living wages and a ten-hour day).

Now think about the competition that occurs between these two firms. The unionized factory tries to establish living wages, a ten-hour day, basic health and safety conditions, and prevents children from working—the regular factory does none of this. So just as the critics say that Mondragon is doomed, they are likely to feel that the unionized factory is likewise condemned. And in a narrow sense, of course, this is true. The socially preferable union firm is likely to be driven under. But here is the point: in a broader sense there is absolutely nothing inevitable about the union firm's failure to compete (or that of Mondragon today). We know this with 100% certainty because the unionized firm that was a rarity in the market system of 19th-century Britain is actually the standard in many market systems today, whereas the "regular" firm of that era no longer exists—largely because it has been outlawed. Thus in a different market system we can see that entirely different kinds of firms succeed. By the same logic, there is absolutely nothing inevitable about the failure of co-ops like Mondragon. If the market system is altered sufficiently away from promoting profit-maximizing corporations toward promoting co-ops, then there is every reason to think that the firms that today appear fragile and rare can become the norm.

It is common to hear assertions that "the only kinds of firms that are viable are the ones that survive the competition," or that "such-and-such is impossible because markets won't allow it." The problem with statements like this is that they are inherently tautological. The kind of firms that survive are precisely the ones that are best suited to competition within that particular market system—but that says absolutely nothing about their possibilities in other market systems. As we pointed out earlier, it is misleading to think that there is such a thing as "the market" in any universal sense at all; all there is in fact are various *market-state complexes*, various ways in which the market is embedded in the state. And so those who talk about "market forces" or "market competition" or "what the market demands" in the abstract, divorced from a particular political-legal-historical context, are, quite literally, talking nonsense. There is no difference between "the market" and its political-legal institutionalization. The market *is* its political-legal institutionalization. Indeed, what else could it be? Whatever imperatives a particular market system in a particular time and place has flow from that political-legal structure. Recognizing this is crucial because it frees us from the constrictive thinking that there is only one possible market arrangement. It unleashes the freedom that many things (though, of course, not everything) are possible. And so there is no inherent reason why it should not be possible to alter the market system so that different types of businesses, particularly democratic ones, come to out-compete others and flourish throughout the economy.[16]

Promoting Cooperatives over Corporations

Conservatives tend to conceive of the market system as a natural environment, with no restrictions or advantages attached to any particular kind of firm. All firms can freely compete, and the ones that succeed are simply those that are most competitively efficient. For instance, Milton Friedman explicitly associates the market with the evolutionary process of natural selection: "the process of 'natural selection' [of firms]...summarizes appropriately the conditions for survival [in the marketplace]." Or in the words of the executive Vice-President of Ingersoll Rand Company, "the free-enterprise system—which is evolution in action—always improving—basically is a system of survival of the fittest" (both quotes from Block, 1996, p. 46).

There is an element of truth in this, but it is not quite the element that conservatives believe. The firms that survive in the market are not necessarily the "fittest"; rather, they are the ones that are best adapted to a particular market environment. It is the "adaptation" not the "strength" that is the element of truth in the nature metaphor. But beyond this, the metaphor of nature is misleading. Whereas the natural environment simply exists, the market environment is a human construct. It has been shaped very differently over the years, and operates very differently in different contexts.

In fact, contemporary market systems are not at all neutral with respect to the type of firm that predominates. Our contemporary market system should really be called a *corporate market system*, since it operates to foster and facilitate the corporate firm. (This is why a better metaphor for the market than nature is a race track because it is obvious that different tracks are advantageous for different racing cars.)

The key point is that corporate market systems, far from being neutral, represent massive and continual promotion and facilitation of corporate businesses over cooperative ones. As we saw last chapter, there are three main ways in which corporate market systems (such as the Anglo-American market systems) serve to foster undemocratic corporations. First, corporations have benefited from having a well-established, effective legal structure. Corporations have been given the legal right to hire workers who have no say in management, while workers lack the corresponding legal rights to buy out their firms.

Second, corporations have significant advantages in terms of raising finance. One reason for this is that the law endows corporations with rights of limited liability (Bowman, 1996). This allows unlimited numbers of people to combine their capital, remain anonymous, and do little actual work—yet all the while be sheltered from full financial responsibility. This means that corporate investors are legally provided with limited risk of loss but granted unlimited potential for gain. So limited liability greatly facilitates corporations' ability to acquire financial resources. Historically, limited liability proved to be an immensely significant innovation, as it allowed for massive capital accumulations to fund major projects—like national railways—that ignited the second industrial revolution and cemented corporations as the dominant form of business. Indeed, it is important to realize that the advantages that come from being able to legally incorporate (such as limited liability) are in essence permanent subsidies that corporations have received for 150 years. To get a sense of the magnitude of this support, recall that corporate income tax is a *voluntary* tax, since people are entirely free to form partnerships instead and not pay the tax—but then of course they would not get the corresponding legal privileges, such as limited liability, ability for shareholders to come and go easily, and so on. So the fact that American companies paid $278 billion in corporate income taxes in 2005 is evidence of the immense and ongoing value of state-provided legal incorporation (Baker, 2006).

In addition to limited liability, corporations have benefited from the existence of massive banking sectors geared toward them as well as extensive stock and bond markets. Cooperatives, on the other hand, have not been nearly so lucky. Although co-ops have limited liability too, it is not nearly as useful for them in terms of raising finance, since they cannot lure finance by offering to exchange it for ownership or control (Everett & Minkler, 1993). Co-ops have lacked an equivalent banking sector, as well as a cooperative version of a bond-market (allowing co-ops to raise funds by making interest payments without having to sacrifice workers' control)—since corporate market systems generally do not provide any of this.

Third, corporations benefit from a long history of societal investment into the training and educational services that inculcate millions of people with the ideology and the know-how of the corporate business form. Countries like Canada and the United States have public schools and technical colleges to train workers, business schools to train corporate managers, and consultancy firms to offer advice and strategic help. None of this exists for cooperatives. Far fewer societal resources go into training cooperative workers or managers in how to operate democratic businesses, or training consultants to advise them.

For all of these reasons, cooperatives, as alternative democratic businesses, have been forced to compete according to the dominant rules in an environment built to foster hierarchical firms. The deck has long been stacked against them. Cooperatives have had to survive the best they can in an inhospitable political-legal environment, like electric cars in a monster truck competition.

The opinion of democrats toward all of this should be clear: there is no good reason for a democratic society to go out of its way to foster undemocratic businesses. On the contrary, we should aim to shift away from the current corporate market systems toward a *cooperative market system* that fosters democratic businesses. The key ways in which this might be done were addressed last chapter—building sustainable legal structures, extending finan-cial support, investing in co-op education, and so on.

The fundamental point is that market systems are malleable things. They can and have been shaped in profoundly different ways and so there is no reason why they cannot be molded to serve democratic ends. Let us turn now to see some concrete examples of this shaping in practice.

5 Democratizing the Market System

Introduction

The last chapter argued that market systems have substantial democratic potential. They have the potential to act like democratic voting machines and the potential to be shaped in very different ways to promote different kinds of businesses. This chapter aims to substantiate these claims by examining the empirical extent to which this potential has actually been realized in various places. The first section shows how various states have been able to improve the consumer democracy of their markets (democratizing the market system in terms of increasing citizen democracy is discussed next chapter). The second section shows the feasibility of shaping market systems differently so that democratic businesses can flourish. In this section we also consider the important concern that globalization may pose a threat to economic democracy.

An important and recurring contrast will be made between the Liberal Market Economies (LMEs), meaning the United States, Canada, United Kingdom, Ireland, Australia, New Zealand, and the Social Market Economies (SMEs) of Western Europe, particularly the Nordic variety of Norway, Sweden, Finland, Denmark.[1] This contrast is useful, particularly in an era of market fundamentalism, in reminding us of the ever-present feasibility of shaping market systems in very different ways.

Democratizing the Market System by Improving Consumer Democracy

Last chapter we saw that market systems act like voting-machines, providing the population with a level of indirect say over what kinds of things are produced, through the act of voting with their dollars. Unfortunately, the democratic potential of contemporary market systems to provide real consumer democracy is usually undermined by deep material inequality and distorted by widespread monopolies and externalities. The market system is only able to act as a democratic voting-machine and provide actual consumer democracy once these things are minimized. So the question for us becomes: do we have real examples of states successfully doing this?

Reducing Monopolies and Externalities

It is nothing new for most states to attempt to make their markets more responsive and accountable to consumers by developing antitrust legislation in order to break up monopolies. In the United States this tradition stretches from attempts to regulate Rockefeller's Standard Oil to Bill Gates's Microsoft— the underlying rationale being that monopolies allow for a level of concentrated power such that firms can raise prices arbitrarily and ignore consumer preferences. After all, they know consumers have no alternative choices.

Less established or well known than antitrust legislation is legislation designed to deal with the price distortions that arise from major externalities. The basic remedy for dealing with externalities comes from the economist Arthur Pigou ([1920] 1960). The idea is that in order for prices to accurately reflect relative scarcity and demand (i.e., for prices to accurately reflect the number of "votes" each product has received), the cost of externalities needs to be included in the cost of doing business. For example, if a firm's production causes pollution as a byproduct, and that pollution imposes a cost of $1,000 on another entity, there needs to be a way to force the business to pay for this cost, to internalize the externality. Internalizing the costs means the business is required to pay the $1,000, some of which will get passed on to consumers as an increase in the price of the business's product. The price of the product will then reflect social cost more accurately, becoming a truer "ballot" with which citizens can vote.

There are two ways to internalize costs: a tax (commonly called a "Pigovian tax") or a cap-and-trade system. Most economists agree that these are largely equivalent from an economic point of view, though there are important practical differences between them. Considering the case of negative environmental externalities, a pollution tax means that firms know the cost of their emissions, but the government does not know how much total pollution will end up being emitted. On the other hand, with a cap-and-trade system, the amount of pollution is known in advance, but the firms' costs of emissions are unknown and liable to change (Krugman, 2010a).[2]

In terms of practical policy, major externalities are still mostly ignored, but where attempts are made to deal with them, cap-and-trade systems have become much more widely used than Pigovian taxes. The basic idea behind this approach is that the government sets a cap, or a limit, on emissions (hopefully on the basis of precautionary scientific data). This cap is then divided into quotas and allocated to individual firms. The method of allocation is extremely controversial. Quotas can simply be given to current emitters, a method which is obviously favored by business, and thereby make such a system easier to implement. Or they can be auctioned off, which raises revenue for the government but makes it much harder to achieve political consensus to implement. Either way, companies are only legally permitted to emit the amount of pollution that they have allowances for. But within this limit they are free to trade their quotas, to buy, sell, or bank them for future use. The advantage of this system (as opposed to standard command-and-control state regulations) is that it allows for flexibility, decentralized decision-making, and market incentives to change behavior. As the cap gets lowered it acts just like a tax on emissions. So firms have an incentive to lower their emissions, partly to avoid being heavily fined, partly in order to make money by selling the quotas they do not need. Thus the more a firm is able to innovate to reduce its emissions, the more of its quota it does not require and so can sell to others for profit. Firms thus acquire a direct incentive to change their own behavior. The inherent flexibility in such a system means that different companies are free to try to lower their emissions in different ways and at different speeds—which is much less damaging for businesses than having to conform to a one-size-fits-all directive passed from government. Over time the cap is steadily reduced, leading to lower and lower emissions. So the basic picture is that government sets the cap, but allows the market to determine the allocation of emissions within that cap.

Cap-and-trade systems are increasingly proposed as mechanisms for dealing with major externalities, including the biggest issue of all—global warming from carbon emissions. Advocates range from mainstream proponents of the Kyoto framework, to radical climate justice activists (cf. Hahnel, 2010a), though of course there is furious debate about the details. For our purposes, the central question is whether there is evidence that cap-and-trade programs can be successful in internalizing externalities, and, in the case of negative environmental externalities, actually protect the environment.

The Acid Rain Program (ARP) was initiated in the United States in 1990 under Title IV of the Clean Air Act, to deal with the effects of acid rain. It was the first large-scale cap-and-trade program ever initiated for pollution purposes (Joskow, Schmalensee, & Bailey, 1998). The program legislated a declining annual cap, aimed at reducing emissions to 50% of 1980 levels. Based on this declining cap, the Environmental Protection Agency (EPA) allocated each firm in the industry a number of "allowances" (i.e., permits to emit tons of sulfur dioxide) based on their historic production levels, plus bonus allowances under a number of provisions (Stavins, 1998). The allocations were given to firms, not sold (much to the chagrin of many environmentalists).[3] The allowances could be bought, sold, or banked. Since the cap established the overall level of sulfur emissions, the EPA did not have to specify exactly where or how reductions were made—allowing an important amount of flexibility. The system provided an incentive for firms to reduce their sulfur-dioxide emissions since they could make money by selling their allowances (thereby offsetting the cost of adapting their factories).

The ease of trading allowed an effective market to develop. Trading occurred via the EPA's online system, with trades processed in less than a day. Administration of the system required only one full-time employee. Furthermore, the system allowed firms to bank allowances for use in the future. This proved useful and contributed to the political success of the program since once firms built up a bank of unused allowances, they had a vested interest in maintaining the value of those credits and therefore in ensuring the continuation of the program (Napolitano et al., 2007).

The fact that the ARP used a market as opposed to state directives meant that different firms were able to adjust their practices in ways that made the most sense for their specific circumstances—by installing new smokestack "scrubbers" in some instances, or shifting to lower-sulfur coal in others, by reducing quickly, or buying more allowances and reducing more slowly. This is important because different types and ages of factories have very different reduction costs. Whereas it would have been extremely expensive for firms to comply to a one-size-fits-all government regulation (e.g., mandating the use of a specific kind of technology that every firm had to use), the cap-and-trade method allowed for substantial savings—estimated at over 50% compared to the costs of conforming to a uniform standard (Burtraw & Szambelan, 2009).

There is wide agreement that the sulfur cap-and-trade program has been successful. The system effectively put a price on sulfur emissions, preventing the associated costs from being externalized, and thus providing a less distorted price for the electricity generated by the coal-burning factories. This meant that consumers were able to "vote" on how much electricity they wanted based on prices reflecting truer social costs. The system has been an environmental success as well. By 2009, sulfur emissions had dropped to 5.7 million tons, well below the mandated cap of 8.95 million tons and down 67% from 1980 levels. Consequently, the amount of acidic sulfur returning to earth dropped by roughly 50% across the eastern United States (Malakoff, 2010). In many places, the local environment has recovered substantially, though further reductions will be necessary for full ecological recovery from the effects of acidification (Burtraw & Szambelan, 2009). The program was largely discontinued in 2010.

So while the ARP provides evidence that cap-and-trade systems can work well, there are several necessary cautions. Environmentally, the most important issue is whether the cap is set sufficiently low, on the basis of precautionary scientific evidence (not industry preference), and with sufficiently strong penalties for failing to meet one's quota.[4] Politically, there is intense controversy between selling quotas and giving them away. Giving them away provokes less industry opposition, but it also reduces revenues that governments might collect to invest in ecological restoration.[5] Economically, the quotas need to be allocated in a way that does not prevent new firms from entering the market, since it is often new firms that are leaders in innovation. Finally, there is an ethical issue, which is the same for all market systems: is it fair for wealthy participants to be able to buy more quotas and pollute more, simply because they are richer? This is a particularly thorny issue on the global level, where any satisfactory international cap-and-trade program would clearly have to have some mechanism for preventing rich countries from simply buying their way out of emission reductions, particularly since they caused most of the problem in the first place—one such mechanism is the Greenhouse Development Rights Framework.[6] There is no easy solution to this problem, but note that it is a critique not of cap-and-trade per se, but the market mechanism itself. Such a critique brings us back from the specific issue of cap-and-trade to the broader issue of market equality, to which we turn now.

Reducing Inequality

Probably the fundamental issue in terms of creating consumer democracy is the issue of wealth inequality. Even radical market abolitionists should agree that reforming the market so that the participants have roughly similar levels of wealth would make the system operate in a way that is much more democratic than at present. Markets in such a situation would be much more responsive and accountable to the preferences of the population as a whole. In particular, reducing inequality by bringing people out of poverty is a means of enfranchising the poor by giving them a vote in the market; and for marginalized people, indeed anyone who is not part of a co-op or credit union, their only direct source of power and say over the economy is through the money they spend in the market.

Although the radical Left has always been suspicious, if not outright hostile to markets, I think it cannot be denied that increasing material equality would have a profoundly salutary effect on the democratic nature of the market.[7] Of course, it is also true that wherever we have markets in practice we also have substantial inequality. The Right is often quick to praise the democracy of the market in theory while ignoring the plutocracy of its practice. But if we are willing to step beyond dogma, there is a serious question here: what are the concrete ways that inequality can be realistically but substantially reduced to render the market a fairer voting-machine?

The first point to make is that market societies can be hugely variable in terms of the amount of inequality they produce. Denmark and the United States are both market societies, but Denmark is one of the most equal market societies in the world, while the United States is among the most unequal.

Indeed, the Nordic countries are the most egalitarian market societies on the planet. The standard measure of inequality is the Gini coefficient, which represents the percentage of total income that would have to be redistributed in order to achieve perfect income equality. The Gini (post-tax-and-transfer) of the Nordic countries is 25.2; for continental SMEs it is 26.7, and for LMEs it is 33.0 (for Denmark it is 25.7 while for the United States it is 36.8). One can get a sense of the scale of these differences by realizing that the difference in inequality between the SMEs and LMEs today is similar to the difference in inequality that existed in the United States in 1979 (in the Keynesian era pre Volcker and Reagan) and the vastly higher levels that existed 20 years later after two decades of neoliberalism.[8]

How have the Nordic countries managed to reduce inequality to such an extent? Four institutional practices have been crucial.

(i) The first important feature for reducing inequality is the *tax and welfare system*. Nordic countries have high levels of progressive taxation. Total tax revenue in 2011 was 44.8% of GDP in the Nordic countries, compared to 29.4% in the LMEs.[9] This taxation funds a generous, universal welfare system. Social spending (i.e., spending on social assistance, unemployment insurance, family allowances, pensions, and social services, but excluding education) is a massive 25.6% of GDP in the Nordic countries (compared to 17% in the LMEs). While continental European SMEs spend similar amounts (24.8% of GDP) as the Nordic countries, they are generally less successful in reducing inequality. After taxes and transfers Nordic countries manage to reduce inequality by 32.9% compared to the continental countries 25.7%. In other words, the Nordic countries receive more bang (of inequality reduction) for their buck. Why is this so? Probably the most important difference between the Nordic countries and other social welfare states is in terms of how welfare is provided. Esping-Andersen (1990) points out that the Nordic welfare systems are characterized by *universalism* (i.e., providing a large range of public services for all), whereas the continental SMEs disperse benefits to specific targeted populations through means testing. In other words, the main difference between the Nordic and continental styles of welfare provision is that the former emphasizes universal, free-at-the-point-of-access services, while the latter focuses on targeted cash transfers. In order to see the extent of the free services provided, we can observe that in the Nordic countries 16% of the entire adult population is employed in welfare-related government positions (such as public health, education, welfare services, etc.)—meaning that the public sector is huge—while a smaller than average portion of social spending, 62.7%, goes to direct transfers. In the continental countries, by contrast, only 5% of the population is employed in welfare services (so it is a much smaller sector), but a much larger percentage of social spending (87.2%) goes toward cash transfers.[10] The bottom line is that Nordic style universalism has proven to be significantly better at reducing inequality than the continental style of targeted transfers (Esping-Andersen, 1990, pp. 146–53; Pontusson, 2005).

How successful overall is taxation and the welfare state at reducing inequality? The percentage of poor people (defined as those earning less than 40% of the median household income) who are brought out of poverty by the welfare system in the Nordic countries is 81.3%, compared to 69.9% in the LMEs, with the US system being the worst performer, bringing only 44.3% of poor people out of poverty. Perhaps the clearest way to measure inequality reduction is to measure the difference between market income (before taxes and transfers) and actual disposable income. Expressed as a Gini coefficient, the Nordic countries' taxes and transfers reduce inequality from 35.2 (market income) to 23.6 (disposable income), compared to a reduction from 41.8 to 32.4 in the LMEs. *This means that the Nordic countries achieve a 32.9% reduction of inequality through taxes and transfers* (compared to 25.7% for continental SMEs and 22.5% for LMEs). And these figures understate the real amount of redistribution that occurs because it ignores services, which are the core of the Nordic model. The evidence thus speaks for itself: Nordic welfare states have been able to achieve substantial reductions of inequality.

(ii) The second institutional mechanism for reducing inequality is unionization and collective bargaining. Probably the single most important source of inequality is wages, and probably the single most effective equalizer of wages is strong unions, particularly the presence of a system of coordinated collective bargaining.[11] It is an empirically robust generalization that wherever there are unions, there tends to be more wage equality (for evidence, see Austen-Smith 2008). Union density (i.e., the percentage of the employed labor force that is unionized) in the Nordic countries is 71% compared to only 26% in the LMEs (the United States is at 14% and Sweden is the highest at 79%). Moreover, collective bargaining covers 83% of the employed workforce in the Nordic countries, 75% in the continental SMEs, and only 36% in the LMEs.[12] The evidence shows that changes in union density are a pretty good predictor of wage inequality trends across the OECD. For instance, the decline in union density in the United States in the 1980s accounts for about 20% of the rise in wage inequality (Wallerstein, 2008, p. 252).

Nordic countries not only have strong unions and established institutions for coordinated collective bargaining, but they also have a solidaristic wage policy, which does a lot to further equalize wages. This policy aims to equalize pretax income by raising the wages of the lowest earners and limiting the earnings of the highest earners, thus reducing wage differences between firms in the same industry, between industries, between regions, and ultimately between occupations. By all accounts this policy has been extremely successful in compressing wages (Moene & Wallerstein, 2008; Pontusson, 2011).

(iii) The third crucial practice for reducing inequality is policies of full employment. The Nordic countries were very successful at achieving full employment from the 1950s to the 1980s (unemployment worsened in the 1990s and recovered somewhat in the 2000s). On the union side, full employment has always been a central goal. And having the capacity for coordinated wage bargaining facilitates this because it allows the unions to exercise a certain amount of wage-restraint in exchange for full employment.

On the government side, several policies have been very helpful in maximizing employment. Monetary policy and fiscal policy (i.e., keeping interest rates low and keeping government spending high), particularly in order to compensate for the business cycle, have been very useful in keeping employment high. The Nordic governments also undertake massive investments in public education. Public spending on all levels of education is 6.2% of GDP (compared to 4.8% in the LMEs). Additionally, the governments have been successful at creating employment for women—by 1983, 70% of working-age women in the Nordic countries were employed, compared to only 48.4% in the LMEs. This female participation in the labor force is encouraged by policies of generous parental leave insurance as well as expanded public child care, which make it easier for women to enter, and remain in, the workforce. A final important employment policy is that of Active Labor Market Policies (ALMPs). This was originally a feature of the Swedish state, which has since been emulated elsewhere. It involves policies for making it easier for unemployed people to find new work—by enrolling them in training programs to upgrade their skills, by offering relocation subsidies, or by employing them directly by the state. Government spending on ALMPs is 1.3% of GDP in the Nordic countries, versus only 0.5% in the LMEs.

(iv) The fourth and final institutional practice for reducing inequality is that of encouraging workplace democracy. As documented in chapter 3, worker co-ops tend to have much smaller wage differentials than conventional firms. Not only this, but co-ops allow the workforce to democratically control the level of income inequality, and hence change it if it is felt to be too egregious. Although the Nordic countries do not have large cooperative sectors, they

do have institutionalized worker participation in the form of co-determination. Worker representatives sit on the Boards of all large firms, and so have
transparent access to all of the firm's records and financial information, which
can mitigate some inequality through the increased bargaining power that it
provides to workers. Although workplace democracy has probably played less
of a role in reducing inequality in the Nordic countries than other factors, it
has likely played some role, and it could undoubtedly be much more influential in reducing inequality if workplace democracy (in the form of worker
co-ops) were to spread. It is useful to notice here the interconnections between
different areas of democratization: democratizing the workplace is also useful
for reducing inequality and hence democratizing the market. In this respect
democracy sustains democracy.

What can we conclude from all this? Principally, that the Nordic example
makes it undeniable that it is possible to have market systems with substantially reduced inequality—and therefore with substantially improved consumer democracy. Nordic systems provide a more equal number of votes to
different people and enfranchise the poor to be able to "vote" at all.

That said, it is commonly objected that the Nordic example is a bad model
because it is economically unsustainable. Don't Nordic countries embody the
worst of inflexibility and eurosclerosis? Hasn't their drive for equality fundamentally undermined growth and efficiency? Indeed, the idea that there is a
fundamental trade-off between equality and prosperity has been hugely influential. For instance Arthur Okun famously insisted on the inevitability of this
trade-off by maintaining that "we can't have our cake of market efficiency and
share it equally" (quoted in Pontusson, 2005, p. 4).

However, the Nordic example demonstrates that the assertion that one
must choose between equality and prosperity is, at least sometimes, completely wrong. In this case the evidence is clear: GDP per capita is virtually
the same in LMEs as SMEs, $29,483 versus $28,883 (that is $29,624 for Nordic
countries and $28,291 for the continental countries). And although the LMEs
grew slightly faster than the SMEs between 1980 and 2000, at 2.3% per year
compared to 1.9%, this superiority of the LMEs is almost entirely due to the
"Irish Miracle." If we exclude the fastest growing economy from each category
(Ireland and Norway), the average growth rate turns out to be exactly the
same for both: 1.8%. The conclusion that Pontusson (2005) draws is hard to
deny: "There is no consistent association whatsoever between economic afflu-
ence and the size of the welfare state" (p. 165).

So although overall prosperity in the Nordic countries is clearly comparable to the LMEs, one might still worry that their focus on equality undermines the capacity of the economy to create new jobs. Indeed, it is true that

during the 1990s unemployment was a serious issue for many European coun-tries—unemployment was substantially higher in the Nordic countries, while they were much slower at creating new jobs (with only 0.1% employment growth between 1990 and 2002, compared to 1.7% in the LMEs). However, this unemployment disparity largely (and shockingly) disappears when we take into account people who are unemployed because they are in prison. For thirteen European countries, average male unemployment in 1995 rises from 8.3% to 8.5% when prisoners are included in the unemployment num-bers. In the United States, the figure jumps from 5.6% to a stunning 7.5%. Indeed, Western and Beckett (1999) showed persuasively that a large part of the decline in male unemployment in the United States from 1983 to 1995 was actually due to the expansion in the prison population. It should go with-out saying that the Nordic costs of providing the unemployed with welfare are much less, in every sense of the word, than the costs of jailing them.

Furthermore, even though the notion of consistent unemployment in the Nordic countries remains a standard part of much North American discourse (particularly in the pages of the *Wall Street Journal*), the reality is that the situ-ation clearly changed after the 1990s. Indeed, even discounting the prison population, from 2000 to 2003 the unemployment average for Nordic coun-tries was virtually the same as that for LMEs (5.5% vs. 5.6%). Similarly, it is important to note that the common notion of "eurosclerosis" is largely a myth. European employment rates have consistently improved since 1997, overtaking American rates in 2008, as is illustrated in the graph (Figure 5.1), which shows prime-age employment—the percentage of adults aged 25–54 with jobs—for the 15 original members of the EU versus the United States (Krugman, 2010b).

So how is it that Nordic countries have been able to have both growth and equality? In a nutshell, I think the answer is that while equality may in cer-tain instances diminish incentives to work hard, that is only half the story, since economic growth requires not just incentives but also capabilities.[13] For instance, a child could be presented with maximal incentives (a $10 million gift or the threat of starvation), but neither of these incentives is going to make her a productive worker because she has such limited and undeveloped capa-bilities. Actual productivity requires the fostering of capabilities: investing in the child's future through education, care, protection, and so on. And the same is true with workers more generally. So whatever incentives may be lost from softening the rat race are compensated in the Nordic countries by the increased capabilities that come from society's investments into the population's welfare.

More precisely, Nordic countries have been able to create a number of complementary institutions that promote both growth and equality. First,

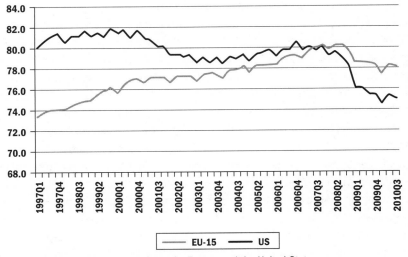

Figure 5.1 Prime-Age Employment Rates for Europe and the United States

coordinated collective bargaining allows for wage restraint, and thus for higher employment with less inflation (because without coordinated bargaining, if a union pushes up wages above productivity gains, the employers usually respond by simply raising prices, which therefore only benefits some workers at the expense of inflationary losses for others). Second, solidaristic bargaining not only increases equality of wages but it also indirectly benefits the efficiency of the economy. This is because wage-compression (raising wages of those at the bottom and lowering those at the top) squeezes the profits of less-efficient firms, driving them out of business while simultaneously restraining the wages of high-paid workers in more efficient firms, making them even more profitable and able to expand. This thus pushes the whole economy toward more efficiency. Third, large government spending on things like education, worker training, and women's ability to leave the home improves equality and enhances the capabilities and productivity of workers.[14] Fourth, worker participation schemes tend to increase equality as well as increase productivity (through increased motivation and coordination, as we saw earlier).

Taking a step back now, we can appreciate that it is indeed possible to substantially increase the amount of equality within market systems. The Nordic states provide a vital model of how a transition to consumer democracy could and should occur. Indeed, substantial reductions of inequality occurred in all Western countries during the "trentes glorieuses" following World War II. The high point of market equality came in the 1970s, particularly in the Nordic countries. Since then, however, inequality has become much worse in the LMEs and slightly worse in the Nordic countries as neoliberal ideology has become dominant (Immervoll & Richardson, 2011). There is no fundamental reason why we could not return to those 1970 levels—but looking beyond this it might be asked if this is as good as it gets. Is it possible to have more equality than the high point of 1970s social democracy within market systems?

The basic problem is that as the strength of workers and unions grows, workers gain higher wages, increased employment protection, and social security. These things act to reduce incentives for workers to work themselves to the bone and ultimately reduce profits. To an extent this can be offset by the increased productivity that comes from capacity-enhancing education, active labor market policies, female involvement, workplace participation, and so on, as the Nordic countries have been remarkably successful in doing. But at a certain point the increasing strength of working people starts to inevitably encroach on private profits and private power. From 1945 to the 1970s the strength and power of unions steadily grew, but it was, as G. D. H. Cole remarked in an earlier epoch, a largely negative kind of power—prohibiting what the employers could do. This created all kinds of difficulties for employers who complained (with some justice) that they could not run their firms the way they wanted and that smooth operations were increasingly being upset by antagonism and obstinacy (Bowles, Gordon, & Weisskopf, 1983). The move toward equalization cannot continue unabated within the parameters of a structurally unequal system. At a certain point in the 1970s, social democracy reached the limits of what was possible within a capitalist framework (Pontusson, 1992; Przeworski, 1985). At such a point, a fork in the road appears. Societies can either maintain private control over businesses and seek to reestablish private profits and power by sharpening incentives to work harder via increasing dependency (cutting wages, reducing welfare, dismantling unions, etc.), as was the chosen course in the United States and United Kingdom. Or, countries can start to replace private control of investment by public and cooperative control—in other words, by starting to democratize the economy. Either the power of the unions to impose restrictions is broken or the negative power of prohibition is transformed into a positive power of control. "Instead of having the brake in their hands, the Trade Unions... [must] assume control of the steering-wheel" (Cole, 1920, p. 20). In the late 1970s this was the choice between Thatcher and Reagan's neoliberalism, on the one side, versus Benn and Meidner's economic democracy, on the other.

In my view the wrong fork was taken. But with history as our guide, we can hopefully take a different route the next time we are presented with such an opportunity.

A basic lesson of the 1970s, therefore, is that social democracy can only take equality so far. In many ways Sweden was and still is the paradigmatic social democracy. Yet while it has achieved much more social equality than most other countries, it has not managed to comprehensively alleviate substantial poverty, wealth inequality, or worker powerlessness (Lister, 2009; Palme, 2006; Pred, 2000). This means that for anyone who thinks that this situation is good, but not good enough, the unavoidable implication is that social democratic goals are unlikely to be obtained through social democratic institutions. The level of equality that most social democrats desire is only likely to be achieved by moving beyond social democracy into economic democracy.

Shaping the Market System Differently

Shaping the Market System to Limit Scale

As environmental limits to growth become ever more pressing, the necessity for society to impose some limits on the scale of the economy becomes ever more necessary. No state has yet instituted rigorous comprehensive mechanisms for limiting the physical scale of their economy (such as broad limits or caps on environmentally sensitive industries that are set according to precautionary scientific data on the amount of throughput the environment can sustain). That said, there are some encouraging partial examples in particular fields. For instance, many states have instituted limits on the amount of fish that can be caught in order to prevent collapse of the fisheries, particularly since the UN's Food and Agriculture Organization has estimated that "75% of the world's fisheries are fully or overexploited" (Hilborn et al., 2003, p. 15.10).

Other important examples of limiting scale are experiments with caps in various cap-and-trade programs—for instance the program instituted for sulfur emissions in the United States. Although the "trade" aspect of this program has already been discussed, here the "cap" element is pertinent. The Clean Air Act amendments of 1990 created a sulfur trading program with annual declining caps. These caps were then divided into "allowances" for emissions for various firms. Compliance with the caps was ensured through systematic monitoring and substantial fines—if a firm emitted more sulfur dioxide than it had allowances for, it was penalized over $3,000 per ton and required to offset the excess the following year. This led to compliance rates of over 99% (Napolitano et al., 2007; Stavins, 1998). The caps were very successful at reducing emissions. By 2009, sulfur emissions had dropped to 5.7 million tons, well below the mandated cap of 8.95 million tons and down 67% from 1980 levels (Malakoff, 2010).[15]

Setting limits on scale is a hugely important parameter for societies to establish over their markets, and a key mechanism by which markets come to be embedded under societal control. Since markets clearly cannot set their own sustainable limits, left to themselves they will continue to deplete the oceans and poison the air. So while it is encouraging that caps are emerging in different sectors, transition to a democratic market society requires developing these examples in ways that expand and integrate them across the economy, particularly vis-à-vis fossil fuels.

Shaping the Market System to Foster Democratic Businesses

The most common argument made against economic democracy, by neoliberals and Marxists alike, is that democratic firms are unable to survive because of the way "the market" works. The argument is that competition in "the market" will inevitably lead to the dominance of the most profitable firm (for neoliberals this is the most "efficient" firm, while for Marxists it is the most "exploitative"). But in either case, the argument is undergirded by a vision of a free market, a realm of pure competition, ahistorical and unencumbered by any institutional specificity. So, for example, the argument goes that Mondragon will either survive by abandoning its co-op values, or it will remain true to its values and be driven bankrupt by more avaricious competitors.

There are two deep problems with this argument. The first is a straightforward empirical matter: even in the corporate market systems we are familiar with, co-ops are able to function about as well as profit-maximizing firms. This is essentially due to the productivity advantages that derive from a more empowered and less alienated workforce. However, the deeper and more fundamental problem with the critique has to do with the whole abstract conception of "the market." The last chapter challenged the conceptual idea that markets provide a level ground for competition. It was argued that market systems are never free of institutional specificity, but are always embedded in particular institutional arrangements that foster certain types of firms over others. Here I want to add that this is not simply a theoretical argument. In practice we can see that different market systems around the world have been constructed in very different ways leading to very different results.

The evidence for this is the institutional diversity that we can witness between market systems (Hall & Soskice, 2001). Consider, for example, the difference between the United States and Sweden. The American market system is a liberal market economy. Tax rates are low—accounting for 25% of GDP—resulting in a starved state. Public spending on social programs is only 14.6% of GDP, resulting in a minimal welfare system, below average social services, and paltry pension guarantees. The individualism of the system is also seen in the extremely low levels of collective bargaining—less than 15% of workers are unionized. Firms are governed by shareholders who see the company as their private property; workers tend to be seen as exchangeable inputs, often entering and leaving a variety of different workplaces during their working lives. When firms require external finance, it is often provided by the stock market, which arguably leads to an obsession with short-term profits in order to appease shareholders and ward off hostile takeovers. The American system is noted for its extreme wealth, with several hundred billionaires, as well as its massive racialized poverty and enormous jail population (Western & Beckett, 1999). The country is extremely unequal: its Gini coefficient is 36.8, worse than Russia; the welfare system brings only 44% of poor people out of poverty, so 12% of all households remain poor (i.e., living on a combined income of less than 40% of the median household income)—and even this does not include the substantial non-status population (about 10 million people), which is extremely marginalized and precarious; as mentioned earlier, the average CEO makes 300 times the typical worker (*Economist*, 2006).[16]

The Swedish market system operates significantly differently. It is a much more social and universalistic system. Taxes are much higher—accounting for 45% of GDP—funding a much more socially active state. Social spending is 27.5% of GDP, almost double the American amount, resulting in a much more robust public sector, with generous levels of welfare, universal services, and extensive training and educational programs. There are high levels of unionization (79% of workers) and a high degree of coordination in terms of collective bargaining. This facilitates a quasi-corporatist market system whereby the working class, through the large trade unions, is able to engage in regular rounds of collective bargaining. Firms are not governed purely by shareholders but partially by stakeholders. Although not quite as extensive as Germany, Sweden has had a system of co-determination since the 1970s, which allows unions to appoint two members to the Board of Directors of every joint stock company with more than 25 employees. Finance is traditionally arranged through banks as opposed to stock markets—which arguably engenders a longer-term perspective (Pollin, 1995). Active Labor Market Programs are relied on more than the threat of extreme poverty to get unemployed people back to work. Inequality is substantially lower: the Gini is 25.2; the welfare system brings 82% of poor people out of poverty, so only 3.8% of the population remain poor; and the average CEO makes 12 times that of employees.[17]

The point of this contrast is to highlight the fact that the institutional diversity of market systems is very real. Such contrasts are even starker vis-à-vis non-Western countries, such as Japan or China. It takes willful blindness to conflate all the existing varieties of market systems to "capitalism" *tout court*.

The institutional diversity of capitalism demonstrates that it is indeed possible to construct different kinds of market systems. So we can ask: what would a *cooperative market system* look like? In chapter 3 I argued for certain important features: cooperative financial institutions (such as co-op banks), tax support, educational infrastructure, a sensible legal framework, and so on. Yet this is not merely theoretical. Northern Italy provides a real-world glimpse of the beginnings of a cooperative market society in practice.

Perhaps the most developed example of a cooperative market economy is the region of Emilia Romagna in northern Italy, where 8,000 co-ops (of all kinds) account for about 40% of the region's GDP and 24% of the population works in or belongs to a cooperative.[18] Worker co-ops alone constitute 12.75% of GDP and dominate in many industries, including construction, agriculture, food processing, wine making, transport, retail, and machine production. Indeed, as mentioned in chapter 3, in the town of Imola (population 100,000) 50% of the adult population are stockholders in the area's 115 co-ops, and over 60% of the town's GDP comes from the co-ops (Ammirato, 1996, p. 2; Restakis, 2010, pp. 56–57). So Emilia Romagna shows that it is entirely possible for co-ops to play a central role in a vibrant and dynamic economy. Indeed, anyone who doubts the economic viability of cooperatives should ponder the fact that this particular region—the region with the highest density of co-ops in the world—is also one of the richest regions in all of Italy and indeed one of the most prosperous regions in all of Europe.

This has been accomplished by creating both internal and external support systems. Internally, co-ops have supported themselves through the establishment of networks and consortia that provide a web of mutual support, helping co-ops access credit, increase market share, problem solve, and so on. Externally, the market system has been shaped in important ways over the years so as to promote co-ops. The main features of this co-op-friendly market system include tax breaks (on co-op income that is invested in indivisible reserves); privileged access for co-ops to bid on public works contracts; financial support (e.g., the old National Institute of Cooperative Credit and the contemporary National Labour Bank); legal provisions that mandate a sustainable business structure (for instance, by requiring significant reinvestment of profits and forbidding sell-offs); and development funds for helping promote new co-ops (for instance, legislation from 1992 requiring that every co-op contribute 3% of its profits to a fund devoted to developing new co-ops and aiding worker takeovers of conventional firms). Together these things have started to alter the basic structure of the market system to allow co-ops to flourish. Emilia Romagna is thus an important model of how transition could be enacted toward a market system that fosters democratic firms.

Globalization

Globalization is often portrayed as a pall hanging over progressive aspirations. While shaping the market in democratic ways may have been possible in the past, hasn't globalization rendered national experiments with different types of market systems obsolete? Isn't globalization forcing different market systems to converge? Doesn't it undermine the prospects for economic democracy? These are important and controversial questions.

There are two main ways in which globalization could potentially undermine economic democracy: the first is that trade with the Global South produces a race to the bottom; the second is that the mobility of corporate capital drives down taxes thus making it harder for states to pay for economic democracy.[19] Let's look at these two areas in turn. Since no country has a robust system of economic democracy, we obviously cannot examine the effects of globalization directly. But we can look at the effects of globalization on the welfare state, which in many respects is a close cousin to economic democracy. So using the welfare state as kind of proxy for economic democracy allows us to evaluate the degree to which globalization does in fact constrain national policy.

A Race to the Bottom?

A standard argument is that international competition—particularly trade with the Global South—creates a "race to the bottom." The idea is that socially decent firms in the northern world, for instance, cooperatives or those that are unionized or environmentally conscious, will be driven under by competition from harsh, unregulated firms in places like China and India that employ workers in sweatshop conditions. This is the degeneration thesis again, this time applied to the global arena.

While this is a common perception, the evidence is actually quite mixed. In many ways, the image of low-cost goods from the Global South flooding the OECD is simply wrong. In the early 1960s OECD imports from non-OECD countries (excluding OPEC) accounted for 23% of trade. By 1994 (i.e., after several decades of globalization), southern imports actually accounted for less—representing 20% of imports (Garrett & Mitchell, 2001, p. 153). In other words, most trade in the Global North continues to happen between countries in the Global North. And even more importantly, an increasing bulk of economic activity nowadays is internal in localized services. Many kinds of businesses, from haircuts to dentists, provide inherently localized services and so are not threatened by global trade. Moreover, as our economies become more service-oriented, the threat of a race-to-the-bottom diminishes. Indeed, locally oriented economic activity is already estimated to represent 60% of the economy—and this is continually growing. In the words of Krugman, "although we talk a lot these days about globalization, about a world grown small, when you look at the economies of modern cities what you see is a process of localization: A steadily rising share of the work force produces services that are sold only within that same metropolitan area" (quoted in Alperovitz, 2005, p. 126).

Moreover, while sweatshops in the Global South may, through their grim working conditions, be able to keep labor costs very low, this creates harsh competition only in certain low-skill industries (such as clothing or low-tech assembly). In industries where production requires a skilled and knowledgeable labor force, it may well be that having a less-alienated workforce (such as may be achieved through cooperatives) is actually more productive than having to discipline a sweated one. This means that a race to the bottom may not be a general concern, but only an issue in certain industries.

But even in areas where it seems likely that odious competition will undermine decent domestic firms (such as unionized firms or co-ops), it is entirely possible to protect them. Tariffs are the basic protectionist mechanism that states have used for hundreds of years to protect themselves from competition that they saw as unfair or debilitating. Indeed, Ha-Joon Chang's (2002, 2007) groundbreaking research has brought to light the fact that tariffs have been substantially used by practically every developed country. Not only have tariffs been extremely widely used, but they have been a key ingredient in the development of many countries. Britain used extensive tariffs in the early years of its industrialization, up until the 1840s. Between 1816 and World War II, the United States, now the paragon of free trade, had one of the highest average tariff rates on manufacturing imports in the whole world. And from 1950 to 1970 Japan used similar, if more sophisticated, policies of tariffs to protect infant industries and develop its exporting capacity. Of course, once these countries achieved trade dominance, they were often quick to criticize the use of tariffs by other countries, in a hypocritical process that Chang (2002) refers to as "kicking away the ladder."[20]

This is not the place to engage in an in-depth analysis of the relative costs and benefits of tariffs. But even a cursory glance at recent history shows that tariffs need not be prohibitively costly—indeed, the most prosperous nations on the planet depended on them for their development. So it is instructive to note that even though protectionism is now unfashionable, tariffs and infant industry protection were used extensively in South-East Asia over the last 50 years and helped to spur some of the most dynamic economic growth in history.[21] This means that tariffs can be an important policy tool for countries to strategically protect themselves from the race to the bottom, foster development, and protect the kinds of firms they value.

Capital Mobility and Tax Competition

A second common argument is that globalization increases the mobility of corporate capital. This means that corporations find it easier to leave states with high tax rates (and/or engage in transfer pricing[22]). This creates tax competition as states feel obliged to cut their taxes in line with other states to attract corporate investment. The end result is that states will find it increasingly difficult to engage in independent fiscal policy as the continual downward pressure on corporate taxation makes it harder and harder to pay for the welfare state (or economic democracy).

While this argument is logically coherent, there are good reasons to be skeptical. Rodrik (1997) and Garrett and Mitchell (2001) have argued that globalization actually produces *increased* desire for higher taxes and more welfare in order for citizens to compensate themselves for the resultant insecurity. Additionally, countries with higher taxes also tend to have better public goods (such as government services and infrastructure), which make business more profitable and so can entice, rather than drive away, investment (Swank, 2002). Also, Pierson (1996) points out that retrenchment of the welfare state is politically difficult to carry out since it takes away concentrated benefits while providing only dispersed savings. Genschel (2005) has also shown that governments can adjust their tax systems to make them more globalization resistant. Finally, it is clear that regardless of globalization, many types of capital are largely immobile, and many types of firms may well desire to stay close to their home base. The bottom line is that corporations have complex incentives; by no means is the tax rate the sole factor on which they base their investment decisions.

What does the actual empirical evidence show? There are four basic points. (i) Everyone agrees that the statutory tax rates that corporations are legally obliged to pay have dropped significantly over the last several decades. According to Overesch and Rincke (2011, p. 2), in 1983, the mean statutory corporate tax rate of 13 Western European countries was 49.2%; as of 2008, the average rate had eroded to 27.2%. The statutory rate is important, since it is widely publicized and firms clearly pay attention to it. However, the statutory rate may not be a good measure for getting at the core of the issue because almost no business actually pays the full statutory rate (due to the multiple kinds of deductions and allowances that different countries offer). So the heart of the debate tends to focus on the effective tax rate that corporations are paying.[23] (ii) There is, however, considerable disagreement about whether effective tax rates are being driven down by globalization. Some scholars provide evidence that they are (Bretschger & Hettich, 2002; Genschel, 2005; Hansson & Olofsdotter, 2004; Hays, 2003; Overesch & Rincke, 2011; Winner, 2005). And some provide evidence that they are not (Basinger & Hallerberg, 2004; Dreher, 2006; Garrett, 1998; Garrett & Mitchell, 2001; Loretz, 2008; Plumper & Troeger, 2009; Swank, 2002). (iii) The bulk of the evidence shows that taxation is slowly being shifted from mobile capital to immobile labor in line with what tax competition would imply (Bretschger & Hettich, 2002; Genschel, 2005; Hays, 2003; Plumper & Troeger, 2009; Winner, 2005).[24] (iv) There is, however, overwhelming agreement that globalization has *not* reduced total public revenues (Bretschger & Hettich, 2002; Castles, 2007; Dreher, 2006; Dreher, Sturm, & Ursprung, 2008; Garrett, 1998; Garrett & Mitchell, 2001; Genschel, 2005; Immervoll & Richardson, 2011; Overesch & Rincke, 2011; Swank, 2002)

So, how should we interpret these points? I think that based on the current evidence the best interpretation is the following: capital mobility is indeed exerting some downward pressure on effective tax rates, which is being responded to by a slow shift of taxation away from mobile corporations and on to labor and other immobile factors. Yet since corporate taxation has never been the primary source of state revenue (in 2010 in the OECD, corporate tax accounted for an average of only 8.5% of total tax revenue (OECD, 2012a, p. 110)), and since total tax revenues have remained quite constant due to base-broadening, governments have retained just as much, if not more, total revenues overall.

From the perspective of economic democracy, the most important question is whether states still have fiscal autonomy. Can states today follow an independent fiscal path, for example, by raising taxes in order to pay for a transition to economic democracy? The answer is: absolutely. The evidence is clear and undeniable that overall tax revenues are larger now than during the earlier era of closed borders. Tax rates for the major industrial countries averaged 10% before World War I, around 30% in the 1960s (the era of the welfare state), and were 40% by the 2000s (Genschel, 2005, p. 55).[25] This means that not only does substantial fiscal room remain, but there is in fact more room for governments to fund the welfare state (or economic democracy) than in the 1960s or 1970s when no one doubted such a possibility existed.

And even if in the future it appears that capital mobility is starting to undermine total tax revenues, countries can always look to capital controls (which for a variety of reasons explored in the following chapters are an important component of economic democracy). Countries' tax systems can be particularly effective kinds of capital controls. Indeed, in the 1980s and 1990s, practically all the OECD countries revamped their tax systems to make them more globalization proof (clamping down on transfer pricing, tax havens, etc.) (Genschel, 2005).[26] All this points to the conclusion that it is political will, not the mobility of corporate capital, which is the real obstacle to economic democracy.

In sum, we can see that globalization does pose some challenges for countries wishing to move in the direction of economic democracy. Probably the most serious constraint is that odious competition risks undermining socially decent firms. But while all of the constraints are serious, they are not as debilitating as they are often thought to be. Odious competition is only a problem in certain specific industries and corporate mobility has not reduced countries' overall abilities to levy high taxes.

Overall, globalization is not nearly the implacable threat to economic democracy that it is often feared to be. Indeed, those who think that globalization inevitably undermines the prospects of economic democracy are also logically committed to the claim that globalization undermines the welfare state—since both require high government spending, both seek to promote socially decent kinds of businesses, and so on. Yet the welfare state is manifestly not being undermined. Or if it is, the deterioration is happening incredibly slowly. Moreover, a country wishing to deepen its welfare state (or pursue economic democracy) retains substantial fiscal room to maneuver and can acquire even more ability to do so through the implementation of things such as tariffs and capital controls. This is not to say that such protective measures would be costless, but that it is not at all obvious that the economic costs would outweigh both the economic benefits as well as the democratic benefits of a country having the political autonomy to independently direct its own future.

Conclusion

This chapter provided evidence to support the claim that it is possible to democratize the market system. Part of the difficulty with this endeavor is that no single place possesses all the elements of a robustly democratized market, meaning that examples are inevitably dispersed. Nevertheless, we can see the constitutive strands of a democratized market alive and well in various places. The sulfur cap-and-trade program and, particularly, the Nordic welfare states illustrate the possibilities of dealing with major externalities and reducing inequalities so as to improve the potential for consumer democracy. The example of northern Italy shows exciting glimpses of a new kind of cooperative market system that serves to foster democratic firms. Such examples are important because they not only confirm the possibility of democratizing the market; they also provide useful roadmaps for guiding transition.

We have seen that market systems have democratic potential. Social democratic states have been most successful in realizing this potential. But even here real economic democracy has proven elusive. Private control of finance and investment has acted as a barrier beyond which the egalitarian impetus of social democratic states has been unable to pass. This means that acquiring genuine market democracy—both in the sense of consumer democracy and citizen democracy over economic development—requires finding ways to transcend such limits. That is the task to which we now turn.

Part Three

Finance and Investment

6 Should Finance and Investment be Democratized?

Control over investment is the central political issue
under capitalism precisely because no other privately
made decisions have such a profound public impact.

(Przeworski, 1985, p. 218)

Since investment is the only guarantee of society's future, it
must be a subject of social deliberation.

(paraphrased from Cohen & Rogers, 1983, p. 161)

Introduction

Every society produces wealth, part of which is consumed, and part of which is invested for future consumption. The kinds of investments that are made play a defining role in shaping society's future. So those who control the financial and investment processes have significant control over the shaping of that future.

Any attempt to think through the possibility of reforming society must deal with the fact that when left-wing regimes have been democratically elected in the past, they have tended to get immediately battered and bruised by the economic fallout from those who control finance and investment. The attack from financiers and investors can be so strong that it forces the government to abandon their plans for reform—thus making a mockery of the people's sovereignty.

In 1981, François Mitterrand was elected in France promising "une rupture avec le capitalisme." Immediately financiers (institutional investors, short-term speculators, currency traders, bond traders, etc.) withdrew huge sums of money from the country—the capital flight measured $1 billion per day by inauguration. Massive speculation against the currency forced the country to devalue the franc again and again. At the same time, business owners led by the National Council of French Employers (CNPF) called for a hiring freeze and started to slow investment as their confidence in Mitterrand's ability (or desire) to protect their profits crumbled. Less than two years later, with inflation and unemployment skyrocketing, the government admitted defeat and reversed its socialist policies (Morray, 1997; Singer, 1988).

In 1999, Hugo Chavez was elected in Venezuela and radically shifted Venezuelan politics away from neoliberalism. He focused on social programs and expansive anti-poverty initiatives, providing education and healthcare, engaging with the indigenous population, and redistributing the nation's massive oil wealth. The response was immediate and predictable. Financiers engaged in large-scale capital flight—estimated at $26 billion from 1999 to 2001 (equivalent to roughly 12% of the country's entire GDP) (Parker, 2005). Yet even more devastating was the investment strike organized by the Venezuelan opposition and business elites. Businesses closed their doors, locked out workers, and the oil industry was shut down. The investment strike brought the economy crashing down—losing 24% of GDP in three months, close to great depression numbers.[1]

In tumultuous times like these, we see that those who control finance and investment possess significant power, perhaps even a veto, over government policy. Yet such power is apparent even in normal times. It is a daily occurrence to hear a business declare that its taxes must be cut in order for it to maintain investment and employment, or a politician to explain that environmental regulation is not possible because it will result in job loss. This is why Charles Lindblom (1982) famously said that the market in certain ways resembles a "prison," since democratic attempts to reform the system automatically trigger punishments in the form of unemployment or a sluggish economy. This imprisons democratic policy making within the limits of what will keep business happy. Indeed, a central theme of this book is that social democratic attempts to democratize the economy run into precisely these limits—the limits of the private control of finance and investment. This chapter and the next thus seek to explore ways in which we might break out of this prison and overcome such limits on our democracy.

The overarching argument of this chapter is that the current system of private control of finance and investment is undemocratic in the sense that it undermines popular sovereignty. There are two reasons for this. First, it keeps the population structurally dependent on, and hamstrung by, an unaccountable minority. And second, it deprives the public of an active democratic say (in the sense of providing meaningful involvement as well as broad control) in deciding how to allocate finance and investment, and thus how to form its own future. I argue for four kinds of fundamental reforms: democratizing finance through *capital controls* and *public community banks* and democratizing investment through the spread of *worker co-ops*, supplemented by *public investment rooted in local communities*.

Before beginning, it is useful to clarify several terms. From a democratic perspective, a central issue of finance and investment is the issue of "sovereignty." Sovereignty is commonly understood to refer to the ultimate political authority within a given territory (Philpott, 2009). For a country to be democratic, it must first of all be sovereign (it cannot be controlled by a foreign army or a secret cabal). But although a monarch can be sovereign, in a democracy, sovereignty must be vested, ultimately, in the people. In this chapter, sovereignty is assumed to mean popular sovereignty; in other words, sovereignty means that ultimate political authority to direct the country rests with the people or their elected representatives. Popular sovereignty does not imply any kind of mystical or transcendental unity of the people, but simply refers to the will of the majority of the population.

I understand sovereignty as having two main dimensions: first, a negative dimension, whereby sovereignty refers to not being dependent or under the control of another power; and, second, a positive dimension, where sovereignty means being able to actively self-determine.[2] This idea of self-determination is usefully broken down into two further dimensions: meaningful involvement at a local level and broad accountability at higher levels. Although the two dimensions of sovereignty are clearly bound up together, it is useful to keep them distinct because they often imply very different policies about reform. For instance, reforms to minimize dependence may do very little by themselves to augment self-determination.

What exactly is meant by finance and investment? Finance refers to the mobilization of savings to be used as credit to firms (or individuals or governments). Essentially it can be thought of as the lending of money. The main (non-government) sources of finance are banks, and stock and bond markets. Investment refers to the active spending of money by a firm (or individual or government) to increase or maintain its productive capacity—for example, purchasing buildings or office space, buying machines, or, critically, hiring new workers. So if a business wants to open a new office, it borrows money from the bank (or sells some shares on the stock market) to raise the necessary funds. The money that is raised I am calling "finance," whereas the actual spending of the money by the firm for the new office I am calling "investment." So, for instance, Bank of America *finances* Shell, which then *invests* in building an oil rig. This is a slightly, but not entirely, idiosyncratic use of the terms.[3] Often one hears the word "investment" being used to describe both of these spheres of action. However, it is useful to have a distinction because nowadays the two economic activities of mobilizing people's savings, and actually engaging in real production, are largely separate activities that tend to happen by different people in different places (Cui, 2000). If one prefers, "finance" and "investment" could be renamed "financial investment" and "real investment," though I refrain from this usage.

Financiers and investors represent the two sectors of the group of people usually called "capitalists." Financiers are essentially money-lenders (bankers, stock brokers, money managers, etc.). Generally their money comes from providing credit and receiving interest payments. Investors are essentially employers (business owners, managers, directors). Generally, their money comes from making profit. It is worth noting that in recent years, for the first time in history, the assets of financial corporations have surpassed those of non-financial corporations,[4] as finance has become increasingly central to contemporary capitalism.

Finance

From a democratic perspective, there are three main problems with the current financial system that we will examine in turn. The first is that private control of finance undermines popular sovereignty by restraining government policy. After making this argument, we will explore how capital controls might serve as a potential remedy. The second problem is that the system of private finance fails to provide the public with an active say over the direction of finance. It fails in other words to provide *citizen democracy*, since finance is not allocated in ways that represent popular preferences (especially if we think that each person's preferences should count the same); the allocations are not particularly accountable; nor are they particularly fair. The third problem is that the current financial system does very little to aid the survival of democratic workplaces. As we have seen, a crucial factor determining the sustainability of worker cooperatives is their ability to access finance on good terms. Insofar as the financial system facilitates this, it goes a long way to spreading democracy throughout the economy. I argue that these last two problems are better served by a system of Public Community Banks (PCBs) than the usual social democratic practices. I focus on capital controls and PCBs because they seem to me to be the most fundamentally important reforms for democratizing finance over the long term. The next chapter looks at a couple of other possibilities for democratizing finance—such as expanding credit unions and democratizing pension funds—that are important steps in the right direction and are more practical in the short term.

Financial Dependence and the Restriction of Government Policy

Economists typically conceptualize these issues in terms of the "trilemma" or "impossible trinity." Originally presented as a theoretical model for open economies by Mundell (1963) and Fleming (1962), the model now forms the basis of international political-economy since open economies have become the norm. The trilemma shows that of three presumed desirable goals—stable exchange rates, free mobility of capital, and autonomous monetary policy— it is only possible to have two of them. While the logic of the trilemma is indisputable, the standard characterization of it as a technical choice of complex economic variables obscures the degree to which there are fundamental questions of power and democratic freedom here. For example, there is wide agreement on the usefulness of having stable (if not totally fixed) currencies to maintain stable trade relations and stable purchasing power of the citizenry. The model makes it clear that to achieve this it is necessary to sacrifice either monetary policy or capital mobility. This is true enough, but what is presented as a technical economic choice glosses over the fact that what is really at issue here is that the ability for private financiers to move their capital at a whim directly contradicts the ability of a population to exercise democratic control over its economy. In what follows I suggest that we try to see under the technical trade-off to the social issues of power and freedom that lie just beneath the surface.

How does private control of finance restrain government policy? Consider what happens in a country when a new progressive government gets elected and begins to introduce policy changes aimed at increasing the well-being of the worst-off. Progressive governments typically initiate two kinds of overlapping policies: policies aimed at high if not full employment and policies aimed at promoting social justice.

Full employment is so central to progressive platforms because it is the most effective way to increase the wages and living conditions of the majority of the population. Moreover, the epochs of full employment have been the times when societal inequality has diminished the most—such as during the 1940s and 1950s in the United States (Goldin & Margo, 1992)—because this is when the incomes of the poorest increase most substantially. Yet not only is full employment useful for improving living standards and levels of equality; it is also vital for empowering workers to achieve workplace demands because of their stronger bargaining position. As Kalecki ([1943] 1990) famously argued, and as Bowles, Gordon, and Weisskopf (1990) and others empirically demonstrated, full employment softens the main disciplinary measure that employers have—the threat of the sack—and so enables workers to bargain more forcefully for improved workplace conditions, from increased holiday time to participation in managerial decision-making.

The standard policies for achieving full employment are monetary and fiscal stimulus. Monetary stimulus works by a Central Bank increasing the amount of money in the economy and so lowering short-term interest rates. Lower interest rates are expansionary because they make it easier for businesses to get loans to expand their business, hire new workers, and so on. Fiscal stimulus can work through tax cuts, or more commonly for progressive governments, through deficit spending.[5] Deficit spending simply means that the government borrows money from its own citizens (or foreigners) by selling government bonds and then spends this money in order to increase the overall level of demand in the economy to boost employment. Keynes famously said that it did not particularly matter what the government spent the money on—it could pay people to dig ditches then refill them—it was the spending that was important for reducing unemployment. But, of course, progressive governments should target such spending into socially useful projects (schools, hospitals, social housing, etc.).

The problem is that policies aimed at full employment almost always conflict with the desires of financiers because full employment tends to lead to inflation. Inflation (i.e., a general rise in prices) is the worst nightmare for financiers because it eats up the value of their money.[6] Of course, inflation is also a problem for those on fixed incomes—such as pensioners or students—but groups like this tend to be compensated in other ways by progressive government policy. Likewise, inflation is not usually a major problem for the majority of workers (at least not nearly as damaging as unemployment) provided the economy is growing and wages are increasing. This is why, for example, American workers have historically done much better under Democratic governments than Republican ones, since the progressive policies resulting in higher levels of employment have benefited them much more than the inflation hurt them (Bartels, 2004). It is only the richest segments of society (and those, like financiers, who earn their money through lending) that do worse in a situation of lower unemployment and higher inflation than the other way around. Indeed, the countries that have historically achieved the most rapid and significant improvements in overall standard of living and poverty reduction—such as South Korea during the 1960s and Venezuela in the 2000s—have done so with inflation levels near 20%, substantially higher than the now orthodox 2% (Chang, 2006; Weisbrot et al., 2009).[7]

While policies of monetary and fiscal stimulus were very helpful in maintaining full employment in the decades following World War II, they depended to a large extent on having relatively closed borders to capital. Most countries in this period used extensive capital controls to prevent money from fleeing the country. In other words, from the 1950s to the 1970s the combination of capital controls and left political success in elections meant that many developed countries, particularly in Western Europe, were able to insist on a compromise between workers wanting full employment and financiers wanting low inflation, that generally favored the workers. Things started to shift after the 1970s, with the elimination of capital controls by neoliberal governments who, increasingly seeing the world through the lenses of financiers, saw inflation as the central problem and unemployment as a voluntary choice rather than a severe economic problem (Mitchell & Muysken, 2008). Indeed, during the neoliberal era many Central Banks not only became independent of government but were forced to give up their dual mandate (of focusing on employment and inflation) in order to focus exclusively on inflation.

The increasingly open borders gave financiers enormous power to restrain government policy of full employment. Monetary stimulus became much harder to achieve because open borders to capital undermines governments' ability to use its control over interest rates to manage the economy (Scharpf, 1991). If a Central Bank lowers the interest rate, this can lead not to the desired effect of an expanding economy, but to outflows of capital as financiers seek higher interest rates elsewhere. This capital flight causes the currency to depreciate, which makes imports more expensive; and so if the country imports a significant number of goods, it can find itself with a lower standard of living and higher inflation.[8] This means that with open borders to capital, countries lose the possibility of maintaining the desirable combination of sovereignty over monetary policy with stable exchange rates. The loss of monetary sovereignty (with stable exchange rates) is a serious issue, because, as Keynes used to say, "the whole management of the domestic economy depends upon being free to have the appropriate rate of interest without reference to the rates prevailing elsewhere in the world" (quoted in Genschel, 2004, p. 5).

Likewise, fiscal stimulus through deficit financing becomes much harder.[9] The free mobility of capital makes it much harder to stimulate the economy this way because if bondholders become worried about the inflationary effects of potential government spending, they can sell their domestic bonds en masse. This mass selling of bonds will make interest rates rise, which makes it more expensive for governments to borrow the money necessary to pay for their promised policies (Glyn, 1995). The most famous example of this was during the Clinton years, when in 1992 the United States had debt interest costs of approximately $200 billion per year. Although Clinton was planning on increasing government spending (in line with his democratic mandate), the worry was that if bondholders were to react to the planned spending by selling bonds, and thereby sending interest rates up even one percentage point, the US deficit would increase by roughly $20 billion, effectively *doubling* the entire cost of the president's new programs (Sease & Mitchell, 1992).[10] It is this power of the so-called "bond vigilantes" that spurred American political strategist James Carville to say "I used to think that if there was reincarnation, I wanted to come back as the President or the Pope. But now I want to be the bond market: you can intimidate everyone" (*Economist*, 1995).

And although outright attacks by the "bond vigilantes" are quite rare, the evidence does seem to suggest that free mobility of capital poses at least a partial restraint on fiscal stimulus. The evidence shows that countries which engage in expansionary deficit spending over the long term, and so run persistent budget deficits, do indeed find it harder to borrow money on international markets than more austere countries (Garrett, 1998; Swank, 2002). While in the past countries could borrow money to pay for their programs based on their long-run expectations of growth, today global finance is so mobile, interconnected, and focused on maximum short-term profits that deviations from austerity are punished much more harshly.[11]

For similar reasons open borders make it harder for the government to implement social justice policies—such as higher taxes or regulating the financial sector or promoting public banks—because financiers can "veto" such policies by engaging in substantial capital flight. Capital flight refers to the act of financiers sending money outside of the country. Connected to capital flight is currency speculation (sometimes called "currency attack" if serious enough). This is when financiers speculate against the currency by selling the domestic currency and buying a foreign one. Financiers may do this partly for conscious political reasons of wishing to undermine government policy, but more often for straightforward economic reasons of self-interest, wishing to protect the value of their money which they expect to depreciate (due to inflation or higher taxes or more regulation).[12] Selling the currency makes it lose value. Others then see the depreciation and rush to join in the flight in order to protect the value of their money, leading to the currency falling even more, and often creating a self-fulfilling prophecy. So, if serious enough, capital flight and currency speculation can cause a currency to significantly depreciate—thus making the average citizen significantly poorer, because all their goods that come from abroad now cost more.[13] For example, if Mexico imports 50% of what it consumes, then a 40% devaluation (like the one that occurred during the massive capital flight of the Peso crisis of 1995) means a 20% across the board cut to standard of living. As Block (1996) points out, such capital flight can have devastating real-life impacts on people's lives, all because international financiers lose "confidence" in the profitability of a national market. The bottom line is that the system of private control of finance effectively narrows the range of feasible progressive government policy.

Capital Controls

The most basic tools for a population to reduce its vulnerability and protect itself from destabilizing capital flight or currency speculation are capital controls. Capital controls are regulations on how money can be brought in and taken out of a country. After World War II virtually every major country (the United States being the exception) used extensive capital controls in order to guide development, increase financial stability, and protect national sovereignty. In the 1980s and 1990s, however, capital controls were largely abandoned in the Northern world, due to the rise of neoliberal beliefs in the superiority of the free market and unfettered capital mobility.

The basic argument in favor of capital controls is that they are invaluable in protecting a country's democratic sovereignty (Block, 1992; Crotty & Epstein, 1996; Epstein, Grabel, & Jomo, 2005). First, to the extent that capital can leave the country, it can simply avoid democratic oversight. If people can send their capital to places like the Cayman Islands to avoid regulation or taxation, then democracy starts to lose its grip. Clearly democracy requires that all people within the borders of its jurisdiction be subject to the same rules and regulation. But capital mobility allows certain people—particularly the wealthy—to easily avoid the financial regulations that they dislike by sending capital across the borders (Shaxson, 2011). Second, free mobility of capital means that those who control large amounts of financial wealth can always threaten the government with leaving. And since finance is so integral to the continual functioning of the system such threats have real force. If financiers can credibly threaten to engage in capital flight against various government policies, then governments lose substantial autonomy to pursue their elected mandate. These are the two basic reasons why democracy and mobile capital threaten one another.

Capital controls reduce the force of capital flight and currency attack, and therefore serve to shift the balance of power between worker-oriented coalitions, on the one hand, and financial coalitions, on the other. This is why some progressive scholars have argued that capital controls are a vital ingredient for restoring a decent class compromise (Crotty & Epstein, 1996).

Objections to capital controls usually have a moral and a pragmatic dimension. On moral grounds, right-wing liberals and libertarians tend to object to the idea of the state interfering with one's personal control over one's own money. A journalist of the *Financial Times* described controls as "one of the most potent weapons of tyranny which can be used to imprison citizens in their own country" (Brittan, 1998). Likewise, Friedman ([1962] 2002) sees controls as a kind of financial repression and a terrible infringement on personal liberty. Such objections, it seems to me, are fallacious for the straightforward reason that a democracy can legitimately restrict all kinds of individual actions for the sake of other people's freedom. One's right to use private property is never absolute. One can own a car and paint it any color, but one cannot drive it any speed one chooses. One can own a knife and use it to cut any fruit one wishes, but one cannot use it as a weapon (except perhaps for self-defense). Property can be used freely at the individual's discretion only up to the point that it becomes a source of unfreedom for other people. So what is really at stake here is a disagreement about which kinds of freedoms are more important: the freedom for people to do what they want with their money or the freedom of a people to be able to enact its own laws and policies without being undermined by financiers. Both of these freedoms are important, so some kind of balance will inevitably be necessary. That said, it seems hard to argue that it is more important for multimillionaire financiers to be able to send millions of dollars to any country in the world instantaneously in order to speculate on slight deviations in interest rates than it is for a democracy to function according to the will of the majority. While one may reasonably object to specific controls as being too harsh or authoritarian[14] (just as one could object to overly harsh sentences for speeding), it is nonsensical to reject controls per se, since the freedoms they protect are often more important than the freedoms they restrain.

Probably the most common objection to capital controls rests on efficiency grounds. It is often argued that there is a trade-off between efficiency and prosperity, on the one hand, and state sovereignty, on the other. People in Western countries, it might be argued, have sensibly chosen to forfeit some of their democratic autonomy for more prosperity. Yet it is not at all clear that free mobility of capital really does lead to greater growth or prosperity, particularly when one factors into account the potentially massive economic costs of financial instability that comes hand-in-hand with mobile capital. The Asian crisis of the late 1990s and particularly the worldwide financial crises of 2008–2011 show the astronomical costs of financial instability and have led to renewed calls across the political spectrum for capital controls on purely economic grounds (Palley, 2009). The next chapter reviews the empirical evidence about this important question. But even if there is an economic cost to capital controls, it is not at all clear that such costs outweigh the political benefits of increased economic democracy. What is clear is that while many politicians are quick to denounce the cost of capital controls, most are unjustifiably silent as to the political and social costs of financial oligarchy.

Private Finance and Public Accountability

The central function of finance is to mobilize savings to be put to productive use: to match savers with investors and so fuel economic growth. In the Northern world, the main institutions for accomplishing this are banks and stock and bond markets. Banks provide finance through the provision of credit (loans, mortgages, credit cards, etc.), and stock or bond markets through the issuing of shares or bonds.

The most important thing to recognize about finance is that it is absolutely vital for contemporary economies to function. Many businesses require substantial money up front—to pay labor or purchase fixed capital (such as machinery or office space) and other inputs—before they can even begin to make money. Other companies require constant loans for their day-to-day operations (perhaps because they only make big sales once or twice per year). Finance can be thought of as the oil in a car engine—lubricating and facilitating the moving parts of the economy. Without it, the engine seizes up and can eventually break down.

In fact, finance is so important to today's economy that it is really a *public utility*—like a post office, water system, or an electricity grid. Society is dependent on it. If banks and stock markets stop providing finance, businesses go bankrupt, people lose their jobs, then their livelihoods. The 2008 financial crisis demonstrated this all too clearly—when the Lehman Brothers bank fell, followed swiftly by Washington Mutual in October 2008, it sparked a widespread credit freeze. The credit freeze provided a brutally clear illustration of the general public's dependence on finance—when the banks stopped lending money, businesses started collapsing and jobs were destroyed by the millions. The economy came scarily close to the edge of the abyss. This is the main reason that finance should be seen as a public service—it is so widely and generally needed for contemporary society to function smoothly. Moreover, the fact that finance is so crucially important for society means that having private banks creates perverse incentive problems (usually called "moral hazard"), whereby large private banks know that they will get bailed out if they fail. This encourages them to behave recklessly and take huge risks—since their wins will be privately enjoyed but their losses will be socialized (paid for by public taxpayers). So this is an additional rationale for public banks: if the public is forced to cover the risks of failure (as it always is), then it should also get the benefits of control (Buiter, 2008).

In the neoliberal context, financial decision-making is left almost entirely to the market. In North America and the United Kingdom, in particular, financiers increasingly control huge amounts of resources. The two largest banks in the United States—Citigroup and Bank of America—direct an enormous \$4 trillion in assets, about one-quarter of the country's entire GDP (Johnson & Kwak, 2010, p. 59). The immense centrality of the finance industry is a startling fact of the modern world. Indeed, in the United States in recent years over 30% of all profits were captured by the financial sector (Cameron, 2011). This is particularly striking when one recalls that the purpose of finance is entirely modest: simply to be an intermediary between savers and investors—to lubricate the gears. It is hard to believe that it is necessary for financial services to be so expensive for society—that it is necessary, for example, for Goldman Sachs to pay its employees an average of \$367,000 (Treanor & Wintour, 2012)—particularly when we recall that Western countries grew much faster in the decades after World War II than in recent years, even though postwar banks were much smaller, bankers made a more modest income, and finance as a whole was a much more staid affair.[15]

In neoliberal societies, financiers (either through banks or institutional investors) lend money to businesses on the basis of their expected profitability—with the underlying belief that profitability serves the public interest by reflecting popular demand. Unfortunately, due to common and widespread market failures, neoliberal financial systems provide what is essentially a public service with very unsatisfactory results for the actual public. A cursory glance around neoliberal societies shows many socially problematic projects receiving steady financing, while many socially useful projects get nothing. Banks are more likely to finance tobacco companies or tar sands than workers who want to start their own cooperative business. Private finance often goes to build strip malls and urban sprawl while ghost towns are left to decay. The casinos and condos never lack for financing, whereas affordable housing and accessible transport systems are invariably starved for funding.

Perhaps the most serious market failure in this regard is the number of poor communities left without adequate financing. In the United Kingdom, for example, 26% of people from the poorest quintile of society have been refused credit; many are thus forced to rely on the subprime credit market where annual percentage interest rates typically range from 100 to 400% (Collard & Kempson, 2005). Indeed, since finance is such a social necessity, a large part of the power of private financiers comes from their power to deny credit. In the middle of the 20th century, this power was potently illustrated by the example of redlining—the practice of banks discriminating against poor and racialized neighborhoods by refusing to offer mortgages to individuals or loans to businesses (Block, 1996). Redlining led to serious deprivation: community decay, a paralyzed housing market, urban abandonment, followed in turn by drugs, gangs, and other paraphernalia of hopelessness. While contemporary neoliberals are likely to agree that redlining as a form of racial discrimination is unacceptable, what is not widely recognized is that the system of private finance is, at root, a system of *institutional redlining*. The very raison d'être of private finance, after all, is to effectively discriminate against poor and risky clients—that is precisely how profit is maximized. Of course, neoliberals can argue that this kind of discriminatory profit-maximizing is justified, since it will, one day, lift all boats (and therefore it is all right for some communities to have to decay, since it represents merely a form of what Schumpeter ([1942] 1987) called the market's "creative destruction"). Nevertheless, redlining makes the issue clear: you can either say that it is acceptable for poor neighborhoods to be denied finance and left to decay, or you can say that this is not acceptable because finance is a public need and so should not be allocated solely according to profitability.[16]

This is all to say that the fundamental reason why the private market-based financial systems of neoliberal countries are problematic is because of the market failures that we identified last chapter. Private finance is not allocated in a way that respects consumer democracy because consumers have such different amounts of dollar "votes" (and prices are distorted by monopoly and externalities). Nor is it allocated in a way that respects citizen democracy because the market is not an appropriate mechanism for allowing the public to engage in collective, future-oriented decision-making in an egalitarian manner.

The Social Democratic Provision of Finance

While it is one thing to argue that the Anglo-American model of profit-driven "free market" financial allocation is deeply flawed, progressives risk arguing against straw men if they ignore the important position of social democrats. In what follows I want to contrast a social democratic perspective with an alternative view that what is actually needed is a deeper democratization of the financial system via the implementation of Public Community Banks.

Let's start by establishing some clarity about what democrats would want, ideally, from a financial system. Aside from providing protection from capital flight, a democratic financial system should aim to provide four basic things: (i) it would help firms to grow in response to consumer demand; (ii) it would allocate finance as an actual public service by responding to market failures (e.g., financing poor communities); (iii) it would provide citizen democracy (i.e., it would provide public financial institutions that are democratically accountable, so that citizens obtain a certain level of egalitarian voice in directing future economic development); and (iv) it would support the development of worker cooperatives. The first two criteria are necessary for finance to be democratic in the sense of consumer democracy. The third criterion is necessary for finance to provide citizen democracy. And the fourth is necessary for finance to foster workplace democracy.

How well do social democratic systems perform according to these criteria? In order to evaluate the social democratic system of finance I will contrast it with David Schweickart's prominent model of public banks (which I will then revise slightly to advocate a similar but slightly altered system of what I call Public Community Banks).

The standard social democratic position is that the market by itself is not an adequate mechanism for the allocation of finance and investment. Most social democrats recognize that the state must regulate the market to improve consumer democracy (so that the finance allocated by private financiers is more reflective of what the population, considered more equally, really wants). They also recognize that the market is an inherently inappropriate mechanism for providing citizen democracy and so the state must engage in a certain amount of direct investment itself to make the long-term or public investments that citizens collectively desire but cannot be adequately provided through the private market. A regulated market combined with state-led public investment—that, in a nutshell, is the social democratic approach (Lindblom, 2001; Rawls, 1971).

So how does social democracy perform in terms of our four criteria? In regulating the market, social democratic finance is allocated in a way that shows more regard for consumer democracy than the neoliberal countries; in other words it does (i) and (ii) slightly better because the market failures that make private profit (on which the allocation of finance is based) an unreliable proxy for popular preferences are somewhat mitigated. But the high levels of inequality, among other things, mean that there is still substantial room for improvement here. In terms of (iv), social democratic systems do not currently perform well in fostering the development of worker co-ops.

The third criterion is the most complicated. The problem is that the kind of public institution that social democracy relies on to provide citizen democracy is the central government, which is not well suited for the task. To see this, consider again the problem of citizen democracy. Should society promote green businesses and high-speed trains at a regional level? Should we subsidize community artists and bike lanes at a local level? No society (or rather, no democratic society) can rely purely on the market for such things; some kind of public institution that can allow future-oriented collective deliberation is necessary. For instance, the question of financing green businesses or local artists requires deciding whether the externalities involved (the negative ones of pollution or the positive ones of local culture) are important enough to warrant public intervention. In social democracies, if the state decides that they are, the usual method of dealing with such externalities is through pigovian taxes. The idea is that the central government calculates the cost (or benefit) of a common externality and offsets it by introducing a tax (or subsidy) (Krugman, 2010a). This "internalizes" the externality and corrects the price of the good, thus allowing private financiers to serve the public good by trying to maximize their own profit. In this vein Rawls (1971) argues that one of the tasks of government (via an "allocation branch") is "identifying and correcting, say by suitable taxes and subsidies...the more obvious departures from efficiency caused by the failure of prices to measure accurately social benefits and costs" (p. 276). Likewise, social democratic societies typically deal with questions of public goods, such as transportation systems, from trains to bike lanes, by having the state decide whether such goods are collectively important enough to warrant taxing the general population in order to provide them.

The main problem with this is institutional. The central government is an inadequate public institution to respond effectively to such market failures. This is because the central government is highly inaccessible to the average person affected by market failures; a single person in a 30-million-person country has essentially no influence in such matters, particularly since her vote is a sign of acceptance or rejection of the totality of the government's policies, her ability to express her like or dislike of a particular externality or public good is essentially nil. The broadness of government's responsibility makes it particularly unresponsive to popular opinion on specific economic policies like this. Moreover, since elected politicians have to make decisions on such a broad range of issues they cannot be expected to have particular expertise in dealing with the wide range of externalities and public goods that might exist. So the social democratic system of responding to market failures is too unaccountable because it provides no avenues for local involvement.

Another problem is that the basic tools that social democratic governments use to respond to market failures—such as pigovian taxes and direct investment—are very blunt and imprecise tools. Rectifying an externality by introducing a new tax affects the entire national economy in one blow. A pigovian tax may be suitable for dealing with a major economy-wide externality, but it is totally inappropriate for responding to the thousands of smaller, localized externalities that exist in every economy—such as poverty, homelessness, drug use, traffic congestion, pollution, unsafe streets, and the lack of bike

lanes, urban gardens, artistic studios, women's centers, social justice initiatives, etc.[17] Using national pigovian taxes for local externalities is like trying
to swat a fly with a wrecking ball. The inherent bluntness of pigovian taxes
is part of the reason why in practice we have seen that central governments
have been very slow and cumbersome at actually rectifying externalities. It
should give all social democrats cause to reflect when they consider that even
committed social democratic governments have only managed to implement
pigovian taxes (or analogous cap-and-trade systems) on a small handful of
externalities, such as sulfur and cigarettes. It would clearly be impossible to
try to deal with the multitude of local externalities by introducing hundreds
of different tax rates. Instead, a much superior method would be to establish
public financial institutions that can provide adjustable financial support, in
varying amounts, in rough proportion to the severity of each particular market failure they are trying to rectify. Since externalities are pervasive in nature
and varying in intensity, we need institutional mechanisms for dealing with
them that are specialized in focus and flexible in response.

To reiterate, social democracies attempt to provide citizen democracy
through the institution of the state. The state tries to fix major market failures
so that finance will be allocated more democratically; and state politicians
engage in deliberation about what kind of public investment is required. The
problem is that the state is not an ideal institution for this. The breadth of
its responsibilities means that citizens have extremely little accountability or
input into these matters; the state also lacks the necessary nimble tools for
dealing with numerous small-scale externalities (pigovian taxes/subsidies are
far too blunt). A more appropriate public institution would be one that is at
least somewhat more sensitive to local accountability, as well as having nim-
bler tools at its disposal—such as the ability to offer a variety of different loans
to respond to a multitude of local market failures.

A final problem with social democratic financing is that it is not geographically sensitive to the needs of diverse communities. In small, rural towns as
well as larger depressed areas and "rust belts," people's savings go into local
branches of large banks, which are then transferred into national pools of
capital, then sent around the world in search of the highest levels of profitability. The chances are that the bulk of the savings from such towns will not
be reinvested in the community from which they came; instead profit-seeking
finance often acts to suck capital out of such communities in search of higher
profits elsewhere (Gunn & Gunn, 1991). In other words, the geography of
financial allocation matters. While directing capital to areas of high profitability may benefit the people in those areas, social democratic systems have few
mechanisms in place to ensure fairness about returning capital to the areas

from which it comes. The familiar result is that some communities end up receiving much more financial support than others, year after year, making some communities flourish and leaving others to rust.

Schweickart's Model of Public Banks

One of the most prominent, and certainly one of the most thoughtful, investigations into the possibilities of democratizing finance comes from the work of David Schweickart (1996, 2011). Schweickart proposes an elaborate and detailed alternative to capitalism that he calls Economic Democracy, which is a form of worker-managed market socialism. For our purposes, it is useful to focus on one particular dimension of his model—the system of public banks.

In the most recent iteration of his model, Schweickart (2011) proposes the abolition of private banks and stock and bond markets to be replaced with a system of public banks. The state would allocate funds to the various regions in a fair manner (i.e., in proportion to the population of the region, so that every area receives the same relative amount of financial resources with which to develop their communities). Municipalities then allocate a portion of their funds toward public investment and a portion of their funds toward a number of local public banks. The public banks receive their funds based on "the size and number of firms serviced by the bank, and by the bank's success at making economically sound loans, creating employment, and satisfying other community-determined goals" (2011, p. 55). In other words, the banks are public, nonprofit institutions mandated to lend money according to three main criteria: (i) profitability, (ii) employment creation, and (iii) other municipal priorities (i.e., rectifying market failures, for example, by financing green firms). The public banks "compete" but not in the usual sense of profit maximization. Instead, the bankers at the different banks are remunerated according to how well they meet the threefold criteria set by the municipalities. (So the competition serves mainly as a source of comparison for a municipality to monitor in order to keep the banks honest.) In Schweickart's model, the bulk of private firms are worker cooperatives, so the public banks are well attuned to the particular needs of co-ops (perhaps having an Empresarial division similar to the one in original Mondragon's Caja Laboral). In sum, the democratically elected municipal governments do the economic planning, in the sense of deciding the broader social objectives to be met, and then public banks are used as tools to carry out and implement such objectives.[18]

What are the advantages of such a system? The first major advantage in comparison with social democracy is that a public banking system would allow finance to be allocated as a public utility (like a post office), which is necessary because it is such an essential service for society at large (it also thereby avoids moral hazard problems). Since public banks would be under the control of an elected municipality, they would allow communities to have a say (albeit a weak and indirect one) in the allocation of finance and thus in the economic development and self-determination of their communities. The public nature of the banks means that they do not need to allocate finance solely on the basis of profit and so are able to overcome market failures—for instance, such banks would be able to allocate funds to poor neighborhoods just as well as rich. In other words, public banks would be an effective response to the structural redlining of private finance. Relatedly, this system would be much more just in terms of allocating finance in a fair way. Instead of having funds flow to areas where, due of the vagaries of historical happenstance capital is the most profitable, funds flow equally to all areas according to the number of actual human beings living there—in a way that is thus geographically fair.

A second advantage is that public banks may well be more effective in responding to market failures than social democracies because banks not only have a staff dedicated to the issue, but they have more subtle tools at their disposal. Public banks can make financing decisions on a case-by-case basis, which allows them to be sensitive and selective in their response to externalities, for example, by providing loans to one green firm with a lot of potential but denying such loans to another green firm that is badly run. This allows for a much more fine-tuned allocation of finance than the social democratic method of blunt state-directed pigovian taxes/subsidies (for instance, instituting a state-wide subsidy for all green firms).

A third advantage, is that Schweickart's public banks are devoted to and specialized for the flourishing of cooperatives, so this system would be markedly better than social democracy at fostering workplace democracy.

Public Community Banks

Overall I think Schweickart's model has a lot to recommend it. But before defending it against the usual objections to public banks I want to offer one modification. The issue is that Schweickart's public banks, for all their advantages, still allow for only a very limited degree of accountability to the grassroots. As we will see in more detail next chapter, public banks tend not to be particularly sensitive or accountable to the grassroots since the only avenue for citizens to express their preferences about the direction of economic development of their community is through a vote for the central government (or, in Schweickart's case, the municipal government), which ultimately directs the banks. While this provides some accountability—and definitely more than the neoliberal norm—it is still very diluted. It would be better if banks had a more direct avenue for community members to voice their particular concerns, so that people who feel strongly about a particular aspect of their community development have an additional channel to have their voices heard (instead of simply waiting four years for an election when they can cast one vote in a million).[19]

To this end I would amend Schweickart's proposal so that the individual members of each public bank are entitled to elect an advisory committee that advises on the kind of social projects (i.e., the specific kind of market failures) that seem most pressing for that particular community. This means that municipal governments would plan the main parameters of bank lending by deciding on the relative priorities of profitability, employment creation, and other social (non-market) benefits. The function of the local advisory board would be to provide an avenue of local influence within these parameters particularly to help determine which of the multitude of market failures are the most pressing. In order to distinguish these kinds of banks from Schweickart's model, and to emphasize the added community accountability, I call them "Public Community Banks" (PCBs).

Now there are a number of reasonable questions that one might ask about such a financial system. First, would PCBs be inefficient? It is true that since the mandate of PCBs is broader than pure profit maximization they would generate less profit, but it is not clear that they would be less socially efficient overall. The whole point of having the banks be public is to allow them to serve objectives that are broader than profit, such as employment generation, geographical fairness, and the rectification of market failures. Likewise, PCBs may spur less innovation of profit-maximizing firms, but it is useful to recall that not all profit-focused innovation has been socially useful (indeed, over the last decade much of the "innovative" energies of financiers has gone toward the creation of new-fangled, extremely complicated debt instruments, like Collaterized Debt Obligations and Credit Default Swaps that played a large role in precipitating the subprime mortgage crises that crashed the real economy[20]). And just as importantly, PCBs may well spur more innovation in other areas; PCBs would be able to finance a much wider range of firms than only those which are thought likely to quickly turn a profit, and so could be more patient and long-term with their financing (since they are not controlled by shareholders demanding instant profits) and help to develop other socially innovative types of firms that are left out in the cold by the private banking sector.[21] Moreover, if at any time a municipality feels that its PCBs are stifling wealth creation by their focus on other concerns, the municipality can always reshift the balance of the banks' three criteria toward profit-making; but notice that while PCBs can shift in the direction of profitability if needed, private banks lack the same flexibility—they cannot shift in the direction of social lending and still survive as private banks.

A related question is whether having three criteria to think about would make it harder for bankers to make rational decisions. It is true that the specific criteria that PCBs would use to evaluate loan proposals would be inherently vaguer because it is impossible to compare apples (profitability of a project) with oranges (the employment potential of a project) with bananas (the social benefits of a project) with precise scientific objectivity. There is no easy answer to know whether it is better to finance a firm that will generate $1 million versus a firm that will generate $500,000 but twice as many jobs and half as much pollution. So while I grant that such decisions are inherently vaguer than just comparing profitability, I do not think that this makes them less rational or efficient. To ignore every factor other than profitability is to consider only one dimension of a multidimensional reality; it may be simpler, but it is hardly more rational. The one-eyed man may be less distracted by peripheral sights, but it seems strange to argue that he is anything other than more blind. So while I do not want to ignore the difficulties that come from having to try to weigh incommensurable criteria, vagueness does not mean impossibility. This kind of weighing is entirely possible and actually happens all the time, for instance, in the work of charitable foundations or social justice grant-giving bodies. Such organizations manage to give out grants year after year by devising protocols and guidelines for weighing concrete dollar costs with vaguer social benefits. Ultimately, it seems to me that the problem of vagueness is not a problem of PCBs per se; it is a reflection of the complexity of reality and the fact that different aspects of social life are all valuable even if their value cannot be easily compared.

The second major concern with public banks is whether they would be corrupt. For example, Jossa (2004) has argued that having multiple criteria may open the door to corruption, since it makes it easier for bankers to disguise nepotism under vague "social" criteria. "The efficiency parameter alone would be a precise criterion, one easily complied with and capable of ruling out discretion or arbitrary decisions. Conversely, a selection criterion based on the combination of... different parameters is not only difficult to define, but it leaves ample room for discretionary and/or arbitrary decisions" (p. 556). This is a good point. Public banks, like public institutions of all sorts, do indeed have the potential for corruption. In the real world it is quite common to see politicians who control the appointments of the top positions in public banks using their power to pressure public bankers to engage in corrupt lending to their friends and allies (e.g., see Khwaja & Mian, 2005). The task is to find ways of keeping the public bankers responsive to the will of the elected politicians (since this is how the banks are kept democratically accountable) while simultaneously reducing the bankers' dependence on any particular politician who may be corrupt.

PCBs should use several safeguards to reduce the risk of corruption. First, the banks should be operationally independent from the municipal government so that politicians have no direct involvement in the day-to-day loan dispersals. Of course, the banks' lending policy would not be independent from government, but the main priorities for lending should be laid out by the municipal government once every year or two in a transparent, public mandate or "performance contract" (just as some governments today do with their Central Banks). So while the government should be able to offer motivations of pay bonuses for successful banks, and threats of firing for unsuccessful bank heads, such rewards and punishments should likewise be issued publicly in a regular, periodic fashion to reduce the scope for arbitrary pressure. Second, the bulk of the bank staff should be public servants. So their job would be apolitical, and their salary contingent not on pleasing any particular political master but on professional conduct. Third, and most importantly, the PCBs should have regular transparent and independent audits.[22] Since the PCBs "compete" with other such banks, there is a fairly straightforward way to compare their performance to see if any particular lending practice is out of sync with the others and so requires special explanation or investigation. Fourth, PCBs would have a local advising committee with involvement and access to information of at least some of the banks activities, making it somewhat harder to hide corruption.

The third potential problem with PCBs is the worry of waste associated with soft budgets. Soft budgets mean that firms, even failing or unproductive ones, are continually bailed out by the authorities, wasting huge amounts of money, in order to avoid paying the political costs of unemployment—which was a source of significant problems in the USSR (Kornai, 1992). Is this a problem here? Would firms face soft budgets from PCBs?

It should be noted that it is definitely not the job of bankers in PCBs to support firms indefinitely. Some firms may produce consistent social benefits and so deserve consistent support, but others may fail to produce the benefits (economic or social) that their loans were contingent on and so should be cut off. Moreover, the PCBs cannot offer bottomless support, even if they wanted to, since they have limited funds to divide between a number of loan requests. And since PCBs act as financiers in a market system, it would be expected that some firms will go under—this is par for the course for market systems, since firms are kept accountable to consumers through the threat of bankruptcy. More generally, the basic mechanism to prevent PCBs from wasting funds is that they themselves are "competing" against other PCBs. In other words, PCBs themselves have hard budgets set by the municipality—they will not be funded *ad infinitum*, but only insofar as they fulfill their three-part mandate in a way that is at least as good as their competitors. The PCBs that fail to operate effectively should be shut down; indeed, it would perhaps be good policy for a certain number of new PCBs to be set up and the least effective ones closed down every couple of years to ensure continual, rejuvenated accountability in this regard. Likewise, public bankers should be paid more if they are less wasteful than their competitors. This does not guarantee that waste will not happen, but it does avoid some of the more perverse incentives that haunted the Soviet financial system.

In sum, a system of PCBs offers a number of advantages over social democratic modes of finance. It transforms finance into a public service, so that it can be allocated according to broad, inclusive social needs, in a stable, reliable manner. PCBs provide a more nimble and effective mechanism for responding to the diversity of market failures than the blunt pigovian tools used by social democracies. As public institutions, PCBs allow for some democratic accountability over the provision of finance, and, in particular, having advisory boards composed of local members helps to augment citizen democracy. PCBs are also likely to be far superior in their fostering of worker cooperatives. On the other hand, the inherent vagueness of the multiple criteria for loans may well lead to some allocational mistakes. Additionally, the vagueness may allow some scope for corruption or bribery—though I cannot see why this would be any worse than is the case now for social democratic government planners and private bankers. Such advantages seem to me to outweigh the risks, and so there is good reason to conclude that PCBs would represent important progress toward a democratic society. The next chapter discusses some ways that transition might occur to bring such a financial system closer to reality.

Investment

The remainder of this chapter focuses on how contemporary private investment works. We examine why it is a democratic concern and then investigate how it could be democratized in a way that provides meaningful participation at a local level within a framework of large-scale accountability.

Investment refers to the active purchasing of things so as to maintain or increase productive capacity (e.g., when firms upgrade their factories, buy more office space, or hire more workers). Slowing investment or "disinvesting" is the opposite—it involves reducing production and firing workers. In the normal course of a capitalist economy, profits → investment → jobs and increased profit. Chancellor Schmidt of Germany put it this way: profits today are investments tomorrow which are jobs the day after (quoted in Przeworski, 1985, p. 43). Business owners operate to make a profit. They will invest in the case that it seems likely that such investment will increase their profit. For investment to happen there needs to be, first and foremost, prior profit levels—this is the single most important factor determining investment levels (Bowles et al., 1990). In addition, business requires confidence—partly that the business environment is stable, as well as confidence that there will be demand for their products. So, for investment to happen—which is after all what society is interested in, the increased jobs and prosperity that result from investment—business has first of all to be profitable and confident.

The thing that is crucial to recognize is that we, society as a whole, are extremely dependent on the actions of investors because of what has been called the "privileged position of business" (Lindblom, 1977). Adam Przeworski (1985) describes the dilemma particularly well. Consider, he says, the perspective of a democratically elected left-wing government. The fundamental problem of which, and the main reason why progressive reform is consistently so hard to achieve, is the problem of investment. To see why this is so recall that left governments tend to get elected by a broad coalition of unionized workers, students, retirees, the unemployed, and others on a range of promises to increase wages and pensions, improve workplace and environmental regulations, and so on. However, these policy reforms inevitably bite into profit margins. So as soon as the government starts implementing its promises, private profits start falling (because, for example, business owners become forced to pay higher minimum wages, grant maternity leave, clean up their pollution, pay higher taxes, etc.). This reduces their incentive to invest (why would one go through the effort of investing if one were unlikely to profit from it?). If the government changes are drastic enough, and business confidence becomes seriously shaken, investment rates can plummet. Companies lay off their workers, cut back their activity, and stop buying products from other firms, which makes those downstream firms lay off workers too. So the amount of taxable revenue going to government starts to shrink, resulting in less money to fund the social programs that the government promised. Recall that there can only be social programs like welfare if there is sufficient investment and productive activity happening to tax to pay for it. Wealth has to be produced before it can be redistributed. So those who want welfare find that they have a direct interest in making sure production happens steadily. This means that, given private control of investment, even the most radical welfare-rights organizations, for all their anti-capitalist rhetoric, are still dependent on business proceeding basically as usual.

So with mass layoffs on one side, and deep cuts to social programs on the other, the average person may well conclude that she was better off under the former conservative government—at least then she had a job. If the investment crisis continues, the population comes face-to-face with a stark choice: be progressive and starve or reactionary and eat. The investment crisis swells into an economic crisis which fractures political coalitions, leaving left-wing governments facing a crumbling economy, mass unrest, and even a right-wing coup (Chile under Allende is a classic example of this).

This, then, is the paradox: the very capacity of left governments to intervene in the economy depends on the profits of the businesses which bear the intervention. Przeworski (1985) puts it this way, "This is the structural barrier which cannot be broken: the limit of any policy is that investment and thus profits must be protected in the long run" (p. 42). Another way to see this "paradox of investment dependence," as I call it, is to recognize that, on the one hand, employees and employers usually have opposing interests: lower wages = higher profits. On a deeper level, however, employees are dependent on their employers being happy, because if they are not, if profits are falling and confidence is shaken, then investment slows and everyone suffers. Employees thus find themselves in the paradoxical situation of having to care about the happiness of their bosses, and mitigate their own demands for improvements, because they are dependent on their employers continuing to invest. This means that what is good for the employer is usually bad for the employee, but, and this is the paradox, what is bad for the employer is usually worse for the employee. So the private control of investment means that workers find themselves in a structural straightjacket, unable to protest the inequities of their circumstances too vehemently without risking making themselves even worse off. This is what Lindblom (1982) meant when he called the market a "prison."

So in normal times, the stability and growth of the economy depend largely on the profit levels and the confidence of business owners who are making investment decisions. Profit-seeking private investment is the engine of economic growth. This means that government policy is ultimately constrained, and popular sovereignty ultimately undermined, to the extent that the government cannot risk overly undermining business profits or confidence. This is why governments, even progressive ones, find it so difficult to make important social justice advances, like redistributing wealth—because what would happen if they tried? Any attempt to engage in substantial redistribution would be less likely to generate actual equality as it would be to lead to investment slowdown and economic recession. As long as investment decisions remain predominantly in private hands, we would get collapse and depression far before we would get equality.

In tumultuous times, employers can use their control over investment as a weapon, usually called "capital strike" or "investment strike." If this is used collectively with other investors, it can serve as an effective veto over government policy. Investment strike means that businesses refuse to invest; they lay off workers, close factory gates, cancel orders from other companies, hoard money (or send it abroad), and thus bring the economy to a grinding halt. In practice, what often happens is that progressive governments find themselves hit with a deadly one-two combination of investment strike which causes a recession, forcing governments to borrow, followed by a financial strike (currency attack and lending freeze) which prevents the government from borrowing, leaving it in a desperate situation, such as the situation of France in the 1980s (Morray, 1997; Sachs et al., 1986; Singer, 1988) or Venezuela in the 2000s (Ellner, 2010; Weisbrot et al., 2009; Wilpert, 2007). Although the term "investment strike" implies a certain degree of conscious political activity on the part of investors, it is important to notice that precisely the same results occur when investors are not thinking politically at all and are just following the structural logic of their economic self-interest by cutting back investment because they think they will not make money. It is the structures more than the individual politics of a few rich men that is our main concern.

Investment and Democracy

Although investment has long been seen as a crucial structural issue of capitalism, it has rarely been recognized as a central issue for democracy itself. It might be objected that if you own a private business, the decision to invest or not is yours and yours alone—it is not a democratic concern. In chapter 2 I argued that workplace decisions, including investment decisions, should (with certain caveats) be accountable to the workers. In this chapter, the perspective is complementary but broader. The perspective is not the individual firm, but the society as a whole. Clearly investment decisions of individual firms affect the workers in those specific firms (and so they should have the right to a say). But also, the actions of investors, taken as a class, affect the society as a whole. So from a democratic perspective, the question is about the broad public or macro-effects of investment decisions on an economy-wide scale.

From this larger perspective, investment similar to finance, is currently undemocratic for two reasons.

(i) Society is critically dependent on the actions of a class of investors to maintain stable investment, which undermines the nation's sovereignty. A classic example is that of redistribution. For instance, many liberals following John Rawls think that a just society requires significant redistribution of wealth (see, e.g., Rawls, 2001, pp. 44, 51, 131, 135–39, 161); however, a society that attempts to redistribute would find itself hamstrung in that it is unable to do so without risking economic meltdown. The population's dependence thus undermines its sovereignty. The control that investors have over the economy represents significant social power because their decisions have massive public ramifications. Yet it is clearly undemocratic for such a powerful minority to be able to undermine popularly elected governmental policy—it makes a mockery of popular sovereignty.

(ii) There are basically no mechanisms by which regular people can have an active say over the direction of investment.[23] The future direction of society—which to a considerable extent is determined by current investment—is, for the most part, uncontrolled and unaccountable to the great majority of the population who are not private investors.

So how can investment be democratized (in the sense of reducing our dependence on a class of private investors and allowing for greater popular involvement and accountability)?

The social democratic position is now familiar. On the one hand, social democratic states strive to increase consumer democracy in the market so that private investment decisions respond more accurately to the population's desires. On the other hand, social democracies use the state to deliver a degree of citizen democracy by engaging in direct public investment. The problem with the first approach is that consumer democracy will remain a dream so long as there is such inequality in the number of dollar "votes" that different citizens have, and it is extremely difficult to improve this situation so long as private investors can "veto" any move to redistribute wealth. This means that it is necessary to start democratizing investment in order to achieve real consumer democracy: democratizing investment and democratizing the market thus go hand-in-hand. The problem with the second approach is the same as we saw earlier vis-à-vis finance: the state, particularly the central government, while allowing for some accountability, does not allow for meaningful democratic engagement in discussions about public investment at local levels.

This invites the question, how could public investment be organized in a more democratic manner? The basic answer, I believe, is that we need to spread worker cooperatives as well as build a public investment system with decentralized institutions that can be meaningfully democratic at local levels within a framework of higher-level democratic accountability. We need institutions for *participatory* citizen democracy embedded in larger structures of *representative* citizen democracy.

Cooperatives

The expansion of worker cooperatives throughout the economy is a crucial mechanism for expanding the number of people who can exert influence over investment decisions in a decentralized fashion. Since co-ops allow workers to direct investment themselves (at least indirectly through election of their Governing Council), the more an economy comes to be directed by self-managing workplaces, the greater the numbers of people who come to have some say over the broad contours of investment, at least as it pertains to their own firm.

Cooperatives also help to democratize investment by reducing societal vulnerability to capital strike. Co-ops are far less likely than standard businesses to go on investment strike in any way similar to that which occurred in Mitterrand's France or Chavez's Venezuela, since this would require co-op workers choosing to fire themselves. That said, cooperatives do not provide any general public control over investment: they are still essentially private organizations and so are not ideally suited to respond to market failures or provide avenues for citizen democracy.

Local Level Control over Investment: Participatory Budgeting

In a pioneering work on democratic theory, Josh Cohen and Joel Rogers (1983) made a case similar to the one here emphasizing the democratic importance of public investment. However, they (as well as other progressive democratic theorists) were quite vague about the institutional specifics of what a more democratic investment system might actually look like. Although public investment is not at all unusual—every social democratic country engages in it to a sizable extent—what is more unusual is the insistence here that for public investment to be meaningfully democratic it should be rooted at the local level as much as possible and democratized through active citizen participation. Most countries today have "public" investment that is largely dislocated from the actual public—a vote every four years is an extremely narrow avenue for citizens to express their investment preferences. The local level is the area where the least public investment is presently done, yet it is where the most democratic potential lies.

Imagine, instead, if the state were to devolve substantial funds to the cities or to neighborhood assemblies to democratically allocate investment. That way local people could engage in a meaningful way, deliberate about their investment priorities, and make decisions on an equal one-person one-vote basis. An important real-life model for this is participatory budgeting, the most famous example of which is from Porto Alegre, Brazil, where the state devolves tens of millions of dollars every year for the citizens themselves to decide to spend in a participatory fashion. The process started in 1989 and then spread to over one hundred municipalities across Brazil and has now spread to 1,200 cities across the world from Canada to India (The Worldwatch Institute, 2007, pp. 180–181). Residents in Porto Alegre meet in neighborhood assemblies to deliberate on spending priorities and elect delegates to implement these priorities. In many ways participatory budgeting has been a great success: there has been a flourishing of participation in local investment decisions with thousands of people participating every year, mostly through local neighborhood meetings to set investment priorities. Especially important is the fact that the process has involved the previously marginalized. A World Bank report describes how participatory budgeting has allowed low-income people to use the new democratic mechanisms to focus investment toward their social priorities, such as schools, public housing, sewage and water connections (Bhatnagar et al., 2003). This is thus a powerful example of a public institution responding to market failures, an example in other words of citizen democracy in action.

Public, locally controlled forms of democratic investment have much to recommend them in terms of augmenting popular sovereignty—both in the sense of protecting the citizens from the damage inflicted by investment strike, as well as in the active sense of empowering more and more people to take an active role in deciding investment decisions that will concretely affect their lives. It is at this level that serious numbers of people can be brought into the investment process, and thus where self-management and self-determination start to move from the realm of rhetoric to reality, with its empowerment as well as its messy imperfections, and so where democratic investment policies need to focus. The next chapter analyzes the example of participatory budgeting more closely to weigh its strengths and weaknesses compared to the contemporary systems of private control of investment.

Higher Level Control over Investment

In reflecting on the possibilities for democratizing finance and investment the primary focus of this chapter has been on the local level, the rationale being that this is the level at which democracy has the most grip, where participation can be the most meaningful and self-determination the most achievable. However, this focus should not be taken to imply that the local level is the only scale that matters. For democracy to be real requires not only meaningful participation at local levels but also accountability at higher levels (Dahl, 1994). As a rule of thumb it makes sense for public investment to happen at the scale that is appropriate for the issue in question. Participatory budgeting can happen at local levels, whereas higher-level investment requires other public bodies.

In particular, democratic accountability of investment at the highest national level is necessary for two kinds of issues: major geographically diverse market failures and macroeconomic Keynesian demand-management for full employment.

In terms of major market failures, consider the externalities associated with green businesses. It may well be sensible industrial policy for the government of Canada, for example, to help transform the area around Windsor (and the US government vis-à-vis Detroit) from a regular car-manufacturing zone into a green or electric car-manufacturing zone. Likewise it may be sensible environmental policy to try to replace the short-haul flights in southern Ontario with a system of high-speed trains. However, even if the population desired to institute such changes, they would require huge investments at levels which are likely to be far beyond the capacity of PCBs to respond to. What is required, therefore, is public investment by a body that operates at a sufficiently large geographical scale, is publically accountable, and technically expert. The options here range from a ministry of the central government (as is standard today) to a State Bank to a National Investment Fund. For example, it is possible to imagine a National Investment Fund that engages in occasional but major investment projects. It would rely on funding from the state and so would need to be transparent in its operations to prevent corruption. It could perhaps function like democratic Central Banks are supposed to function. In other words, it would function with a mandate that is set by government, but which actually engages in day-to-day work independently from the government to prevent any "politicking," so that it is goal dependent but instrument independent (Fischer, 1995).

The other high-level need is for the government to be able to pursue policies to manage aggregate demand in order to maintain high if not full employment. As we have seen, a major tool that governments require to achieve this is that of capital controls. Capital controls do not need to be used all the time, but it is very important for them to be "on the books," so to speak, so that they can be enacted quickly and effectively when they are required. Another

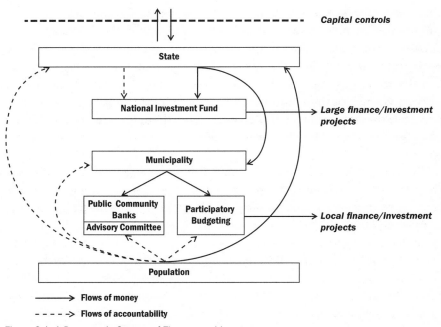

Figure 6.1 A Democratic System of Finance and Investment

tool that governments require for macroeconomic management is a Central Bank that will orchestrate monetary policy in line with fiscal policy and in line with the overall priorities of the government.[24] With both of these tools in the government's toolbox the state is in a much better position to be able to use the levers of fiscal and monetary policy to maintain aggregate demand at levels necessary for maintaining high employment.[25]

To sum up, we have seen that democratizing investment requires three main things. It requires the spread of cooperatives. It requires an increase in public investment, partly to reduce the population's dependence on private investors, partly to be able to respond adequately and democratically to market failures at a local and national level. Third, and most importantly, the majority of public investment should be reshifted from its current position at the top to the bottom, so that it can be filtered through meaningfully participatory structures.

Conclusion

At its most fundamental level, the essence of finance and investment is the relationship between the present and the future. Some people today must

choose how the economy should develop tomorrow. For democrats, it is obvious that such a vital task must involve popular accountability in some way.
But thinking through the precise institutions that might democratize finance
and investment is no easy task. So it is perhaps useful to take a step back to
envision how the parts that we have discussed might interact. Figure 6.1 thus
shows the respective flows of money and accountability of a democratic system of finance/investment. The basic point to appreciate is that general taxation provides funds which are then filtered back down through a number of
democratic institutions. In this way the population acquires some means for
democratically overseeing the allocation of finance and investment at various
levels, and thereby the development of their own society.

Three chapters ago we asked what exactly it would mean to have a democratized economy, above and beyond democratic workplaces. We are now in a
position to offer a fuller answer to that question.

In the negative sense, what is required is egalitarian protection from the
powerful decisions-makers. It is a common understanding in liberal societies
that citizens must have roughly equal political power or, in Rawls's words, "fair
value of the political liberties" (2001, p. 46). Yet the private control of finance
and investment undermines this basic equality. We in the West are not equal
in our fundamental rights of citizenship because private control of finance/
investment arrogates to a small minority the power to undermine and curtail
the sovereignty of the population. Another way to say this is that through
the contemporary workings of finance and investment, large inequalities in
property ownership come to be transmuted into deep political inequality.
And while the former inequality may be acceptable to some, no progressive
can accept the latter. Protecting ourselves and reducing democratic inequality thus requires the implementation of things like capital controls and public institutions for the allocation of finance/investment. This is necessary to
bring general accountability to economic power.

In a positive sense, a democratic economy needs to provide the institutional means for the citizenry to acquire a certain degree of active influence.
The two crucial components of this are consumer democracy and citizen
democracy. First, consumer democracy can come from the market, but only if
it is reformed to significantly reduce material inequality and price distortions
(stemming from monopoly and externalities). Such reforms, however, run
into stark barriers in social democratic countries because the extensive private
control of investment means that the population is unable to raise taxes high
enough to reduce the inequality of dollar "votes." Democratizing investment
is thus a prerequisite for democratizing the market. Second, citizen democracy requires that the populace acquire an egalitarian influence over economic

development. Yet due to the nature of market failures involved, this cannot be achieved through the market alone, but requires public institutions for collective, forward-looking deliberation. Social democratic institutions are not ideal for this for a variety of reasons. Better, but admittedly far from perfect, institutions would include Public Community Banks and Participatory Budgeting.

Such is a rough sketch of the institutions which would democratize the economy and thereby empower the citizenry, for the first time, to have an egalitarian say in the shaping of their collective future.

7 Finance and Investment Democracy in Practice

Capital Controls, Public Banks, and Participatory Budgeting

Introduction

If there is one lesson from the 2008 Great Recession that seems nearly incontrovertible, it is that contemporary international investors and financiers are among the most powerful people in the world. Presidents make way to them, parliaments kowtow to them, media reports their every move, and populations rightly fear them. When Lehman Brothers and Washington Mutual fell in 2008, other banks across the world quickly collapsed, yet the US government as well as other countries found incredible amounts of money—trillions of dollars—to bail out their banking systems (McNally, 2011). The necessity of keeping the banks solvent, and keeping credit flowing, was seen, correctly, as absolutely fundamental for the survival of the system itself. But the way of doing so was, of course, up for grabs. Fast forward two years, and the US banks, saved with public money, were privately flourishing once again, as Wall Street pay and bonuses broke record levels at $144 billion (Rappaport, Lucchetti, & Grocer, 2010), while their prior debts were socialized by forcing austerity on the population. In country after country, governments imposed austerity programs on their populations in order to save the banks.[1]

Although the financial crisis is not the main concern here, it focuses our attention on one particularly relevant aspect of the current banking systems across the West: their starkly undemocratic nature. While the last chapter argued that the current system of private finance and investment is deeply undemocratic, this chapter examines real-world examples of institutions that have been developed to overcome, at least partially, these democratic shortcomings—providing protection against a powerful elite, severing dependence, and establishing accountability so that the population attains increased voice and means to self-determine.

This chapter explores three main areas. In the first section we look at the efficacy of capital controls. The second section examines various institutions of democratic finance—public banks, credit unions, and Mondragon's bank the Caja Laboral. The third section looks at institutions of democratic investment—public investment at the state level and participatory budgeting at the local level. The final section inquires into the possibilities of transition toward these democratic structures. Overall, the central argument is that these democratic institutions, although not well known, are indeed practically feasible, and their implementation can lead to important democratic progress.

Capital Controls

Earlier the case was made that capital controls are crucial for democratizing the economy. They can enhance a population's sovereignty by reducing vulnerability to capital flight and allowing space for the government to pursue policies of full employment and social justice that are otherwise very hard to achieve. Controls are the fundamental mechanism for anchoring capital within a democratic jurisdiction, thereby limiting the degree to which financial wealth, through threat of flight, can transform itself into political power. Although controls are important for economic democracy, their importance is much broader than this—they should be of interest to all progressives because they are a vital ingredient for almost any kind of progressive economic reform. Any attempt to defy the current global market's logic of a race to the bottom— be it to defend the welfare state, extend environmental regulations, or engage in independent economic policy or endogenous development—is exceedingly difficult, particularly for smaller and poorer countries, if capital can simply leave on a whim for greener pastures.

Capital controls have a long history. In helping to construct the Bretton Woods system after World War II, Keynes strongly advocated them as a vital component of the new global economy. "Nothing is more certain," he said, "than that the movement of capital funds must be regulated" (quoted in Cohen, 2002, p. 104). In the postwar period almost every country followed his advice and used controls of some sort to guide their development and pursue independent policies. Indeed, capital controls were arguably a vital element of the development of many nations, including Japan, Korea, Sweden, and Germany (Crotty & Epstein, 1996). The East Asian tigers used controls extensively, helping them to achieve the fastest economic growth in human history (Chang, 2006; Stiglitz, 1996).

With the rise to dominance of neoliberalism, free trade and free mobility of capital became central to much of the economics profession. Capital controls were seen as anathema. Mainstream economists tended to dismiss controls on the grounds that they were impossible to effectively implement, they would inevitably lead to corruption and cronyism, and perhaps most importantly, that they would create inefficiencies and reduce economic growth. In 1997 the head of the IMF called for an amendment to its Articles of Agreement "to make the liberalization of international capital movements a central purpose of the Fund and to extend the Fund's jurisdiction to capital movements," thus making abolition of capital controls a basic condition of membership (Fischer, 1997, p. 11). The United States went so far as to make capital controls illegal in its various free trade agreements.

However, the mainstream faith in unrestrained mobility of capital has weakened drastically over the last 20 years. The first shock was the Asian crisis. In 1996, five Asian countries (South Korea, Indonesia, Malaysia, Thailand, and the Philippines) received net private capital inflows amounting to a massive $93 billion. A year later they experienced an estimated outflow of $12 billion—a turnaround, in other words, of $105 billion in a single year, an amount equivalent to more than 10% of the combined GDP of these economies (Rodrik, 1998, pp. 1–2). Not only were these unrestrained flows devastating to Asian economies, but it was hard to ignore the fact that the countries that recovered best from the crisis were precisely those that had used capital controls—such as China, India, and Malaysia. Increasingly, influential economists started to support controls in certain instances, arguing that financial markets were very particular types of markets, characterized by asymmetric information, herd behavior, and self-fulfilling panics. They argued therefore that controls were often useful for maintaining a country's monetary autonomy, preventing instability, and warding off financial crisis (Bhagwati, 1998; Kaminsky & Reinhart, 1999; Krugman, 1998; Magud & Reinhart, 2006; Rodrik, 1998; Stiglitz, 2002a).

The second shock to the faith in free capital mobility came from the Great Recession of 2008–2010. This led the World Bank to state that "In 1997–98, the words 'capital controls' were forbidden and stigmatized. Now the problem of capital is so systematic and huge globally, it has now become universally acceptable to have a certain type of temporary capital controls" (Porter, 2010). Indeed, even the IMF, in a remarkable about-face, declared in February 2010 that "there may be circumstances in which capital controls are a legitimate component of the policy response to surges in capital inflows" (Ostry et al., 2010, p. 15). The era of implacable hostility toward capital controls has come to an end.

In what follows I argue that the existing evidence supports the contention that capital controls are indeed feasible. They are not prohibitively damaging to a country's economic performance, and are ultimately an effective means for increasing national sovereignty.

Feasibility

While it is widely accepted that the present system of free mobility of capital risks undermining important aspects of national sovereignty, there is much controversy about whether capital controls are at all viable in the contemporary world. For instance, John Dryzek (1996) in his important work *Democracy in Capitalist Times*, recognized that capital mobility is "severely eroding the autonomy of states" (p. 82). Yet he suggested that controls can only work if they are negotiated on an international level involving the agreement of most major powers—a prospect which he sees as "highly improbable." The standard argument is that contemporary technology allows controls to be easily evaded, with evasion accelerating over time (Carvalho & Garcia, 2008; Edwards, 1999). Additionally, skeptics argue that controls will inevitably lead to black markets as people try to profit by evading them.

While there is indeed evidence of the difficulty of implementing controls (Magud & Reinhart, 2006), the bulk of the evidence shows that these arguments are overly pessimistic. Palley's (2009) evaluation of the existing literature is that the majority of the empirical evidence in fact indicates the practical feasibility of capital controls (Edwards & Rigobon, 2005; Epstein, 2005; Gregorio, Edwards, & Valdes, 2000; Yeyati, Schmukler, & Van Horen, 2008). Critics are right to point out that controls can sometimes be evaded—indeed, all regulations and forms of taxation are occasionally evaded—but that is hardly an argument against regulation per se. Controls appear to work best with strong macroeconomic fundamentals and require sufficient state capacity for comprehensive administration. Moreover, successful controls require nimble and dynamic application (i.e., closing loopholes, giving up on aspects of controls that are not working, etc.) (Epstein, Grabel, & Jomo, 2003; Valdés-Prieto & Soto, 1998). But when this is accomplished controls can indeed operate successfully over the long term (as Epstein et al. (2003) show with their case studies of China and Singapore). Indeed, Epstein et al. (2003) conclude their survey of numerous countries' experiences with capital controls by advising "*cautious optimism* regarding the ability of developing countries to pursue various capital management techniques" (p. 39).

What about Dryzek's argument about the need for multilateral implementation? Of course, global adoption, as Keynes wanted, would be most effective, but nevertheless it is noteworthy that there are examples of smaller countries effectively and unilaterally introducing controls (as the example below of Malaysia shows). In terms of feasibility, the key insight is that at the end of the day there is nothing fundamentally different between implementing capital controls and collecting taxes (Crotty & Epstein, 1996). Both can be evaded, both require a bureaucracy to enforce, but ultimately, both are fundamentally feasible. Likewise, the argument that advanced technology makes controls impossible is unconvincing. Does anyone think that new technologies make general taxation impossible? There is no reason why the state cannot use the same kinds of advanced techniques and technologies to regulate capital flows as financiers use to evade such regulation. Moreover, the most convincing argument about the feasibility of controls is that from the onset of the 2008 financial crisis, various countries started to unilaterally implement them, such as Brazil, Indonesia, South Korea, Taiwan, Thailand, and Iceland (Gallagher, 2010). When push comes to shove, and countries decide that controls are in their interest, the question of their feasibility in theory quickly evaporates in practice.

Economic Costs and Benefits

As mentioned earlier, neoclassical economists have long argued that the major problem with capital controls is that they bring substantial economic costs: they create inefficiencies and distortions, increase the cost of capital, raise barriers to investment, and ultimately slow growth (Edwards, 1999; Forbes, 2007; Prasad et al., 2003).[2] However, other economists have pointed out that controls bring a range of economic benefits. First, controls can stop too much money flowing in (which is dangerous because it can cause "Dutch disease" whereby currency appreciation undermines the competitiveness of a country's manufacturing sector). Second, controls can prevent large flows of money suddenly and abruptly leaving (which is dangerous because sharp currency depreciations reduce the standard of living); relatedly, without controls rich people are often more likely to send their money abroad in speculation than invest it at home. Third, controls can shift the composition of incoming investment by discouraging short-term speculation in favor of stable long-term investment (the kind that actually does promote economic growth). Fourth, controls provide the tools to fight recessions through the use of monetary policy (Krugman, 2009). And finally, controls can improve financial stability and help avert economic crises (Reinhart & Rogoff, 2009). This last issue is particularly important since the empirical record suggests that "banking and currency crises are closely linked in the aftermath of financial liberalization," the costs of which can be truly enormous (Kaminsky & Reinhart, 1999, p. 491).[3]

How can we weigh the economic costs against the benefits? Unfortunately, few studies attempt to weigh both. One exception is the study by Epstein et al. (2003) in which they conclude that the macroeconomic benefits of controls probably outweigh their microeconomic costs. Of particular significance is

Rodrik's well-known internationally comparative study, in which he finds *no evidence* that controls create significant costs. He does not mince his words: "There is no evidence in the data that countries without capital controls have grown faster, invested more, or experienced lower inflation" (1998, p. 8). Indeed, he finds that "capital controls are essentially uncorrelated with long-term economic performance once other determinants are controlled for" (1998, p. 9).

Even conservative economists who make strong theoretical predictions about the economic costs of capital controls have been unable to find substantive empirical support for their position that controls damage economic growth. For example, an IMF staff paper in 1995 reviewed the evidence from 61 countries and was forced to conclude that "no robust correlation is found between our measures of controls and economic growth" (Grilli & Milesi-Ferretti, 1995, p. 517). In 2003 the IMF published a particularly thorough analysis of the effects of controls, reviewing 17 recent studies. Their conclusion was that

> theoretical models have identified a number of channels through which international financial integration can promote economic growth in developing countries. A systematic examination of the evidence, however, suggests that it is difficult to establish a strong causal relationship. In other words, if financial integration has a positive effect on growth, there is as yet no clear and robust empirical proof that the effect is quantitatively significant. (Prasad et al., 2003, p. ix)

If even the IMF—the ideological apostle of free mobility of capital—cannot find "clear and robust" empirical evidence about the cost of controls, it must indeed be hard to find. Consider as well the more general fact that growth in Western Europe during the postwar period *with* capital controls was substantially higher (averaging 3.9% per year) than the same countries experienced in the subsequent neoliberal period *without* capital controls (averaging only 1.8% per year) (Baker, Epstein, & Pollin, 1998, p. 17). At the very least this correlation suggests again that capital controls are unlikely to be antithetical to growth. This means that while the debate about relative costs and benefits is an ongoing one, it seems reasonable to conclude that countries are not likely to find controls prohibitively costly. There is thus little reason to think that a country wishing to increase its sovereignty would only be able to do so by making enormous sacrifices in economic prosperity.

Political Costs and Benefits

Those on the Right have tended to argue that the main political cost associated with controls is that of rent-seeking (and the corruption it encourages)

(Krueger, 1974). The idea here is that the machinery of capital controls requires an extensive bureaucracy to oversee it. There is thus a temptation for bureaucrats to manipulate the controls to their own personal advantages. For example, Johnson and Mitton (2003) have argued that Malaysian controls created a screen for cronyism. On the other hand, those on the Left, while admitting the ever-present possibility of corruption, have tended to argue that if controls are implemented appropriately they can bring one overwhelming political benefit: increased democratic sovereignty (Crotty & Epstein, 1996). Indeed, there is substantial empirical evidence showing that capital controls can be effective in increasing a nation's sovereignty by providing protection from capital flight and currency attack, as well as providing room for independent economic policy. Beyond the studies cited above, Ma and McCauley (2008) and Hutchison et al. (2010) show the democratic efficacy of controls in this regard in China and India. Le Fort and Budnevich (1997), as well as the capital-controls pessimist Edwards (1999), concur in the case of Chile. Oatley (1999), in his study of 14 OECD countries between 1968 and 1994, found that capital controls were generally effective in allowing left governments to achieve increased policy autonomy.

In general, it seems to me that these political benefits outweigh the costs. That is not to say that rent-seeking and corruption are not real problems—they are. But they are problems that can be mitigated by transparency and accountability, as well as a professionalized civil service. As Palley (2009) says, "the neo-liberal concern with regulatory capture is real, but the answer should be promotion of effective governance rather than abandonment of this important policy tool" (p. 32). If government receded from every sphere of activity in which corruption was possible, there would be no government at all.

In order to demonstrate the feasibility of capital controls as a device for augmenting economic democracy (in the sense of protecting national sovereignty), it is useful to highlight a concrete example of successful controls in practice.

Malaysia

In May 1997, massive speculation against the Thai currency set off a financial crisis that quickly spread throughout Asia. In Malaysia, both domestic and international financiers quickly started selling their ringgits (the Malay currency) en masse and sending the money out of the country. This capital flight caused the currency to fall dramatically; domestic investment collapsed, the cost of credit skyrocketed, businesses started to falter, the economy slid into recession, and millions of people lost their jobs. In addition, financiers started massively speculating against the currency: they did this by borrowing ring-gits from offshore markets (mostly in Singapore) and using the money to pur-chase dollars, hoping the currency would depreciate further which would then allow them to buy back more ringgits than they started with, making money for nothing (even though such gambling was crashing the real economy in the process). This betting against the ringgit became a self-fulfilling proph-ecy as depreciation caused expectations of further depreciation, encouraging financial "herd behavior." More and more financiers rushed to join in and started selling their ringgits too, thus increasing even further the downward pressure on the currency (Kaplan & Rodrik, 2002).

The government, under Prime Minister Mahathir, sensibly wished to pur-sue expansionary policy to improve the economy, but found itself constrained by the free mobility of capital. Any attempt to expand the economy via the usual method of reducing interest rates to stimulate business investment was self-defeating, as reduced interest rates meant that even more capital would flee the country looking for higher rates elsewhere. The government thus found itself hamstrung, unable to pursue expansionary policies so long as financiers could freely move their money abroad and bet against the currency. The Malaysian government thus faced a stark choice: either to follow IMF advice to try to placate financiers by raising interest rates in order to stop the outflow of capital (which at the same time would cause the real economy to suffer even more) or break with the IMF and implement capital controls. And so, with fiery (and often bizarre) rhetoric,[4] Mahathir decided to forgo the loans the IMF was offering and chose instead to implement capital controls.

Capital controls were implemented in September 1998 (Kaplan & Rodrik, 2002). The controls were broad and comprehensive, with two essential com-ponents. First, was the mandatory repatriation of all offshore ringgits, which meant that ringgits could only be legally bought and sold in Malaysia through official channels at the new government-set fixed exchange rate. This pre-vented speculation against the currency and slowed depreciation. Second, controls on outflows were implemented so that foreign investors were not allowed to remove their money for a period of one year (though in February 1999 this ban was replaced with a system of graduated exit taxes, that decreased the longer money stayed in the country) (Dornbusch, 2001). This measure effectively ended capital flight and stopped short-term speculation while exempting long-term foreign direct investment.

The controls quelled the financial chaos and freed the government to engage in expansionary policies of lowering interest rates and introduc-ing an expansionary budget. It is noteworthy that, despite the worry of technical impossibility, there is broad agreement that the country had little trouble implementing the controls effectively (Edison & Reinhart, 2001; Kaminsky & Schmukler, 2000). Interest rates were successfully lowered and the controls succeeded in stopping an outflow of capital, thus protecting the fixed exchange rate (without a black market flourishing). Even the IMF reported only occasional circumvention of the controls—indicating that the government was successful in preventing widespread evasion (Kochhar et al., 1998).

So what were the costs and benefits of the controls? Rodrik and Kaplan argue that in comparing Malaysia with other Asian countries at a similar point in crisis, the results are clear and impressive.[5] The Malaysian economic recovery was faster, wages and employment did not suffer as much, the stock market did better, interest rates fell further, and inflation was lower (Kaplan & Rodrik, 2002, p. 7).[6] The controls thus proved to be immensely successful (Epstein, Grabel, & Jomo, 2005). Of course, they were not perfect. One important caveat is, as mentioned before, the possibility that controls created a screen for cronyism (Johnson & Mitton, 2003). Epstein et al. (2005) evaluate the controls in these words: "The most important cost of the 1998 controls was the political favoritism associated with their implementation. It is difficult, however, to estimate the economic costs of political favoritism.... Moreover, these costs (if quantified) must be weighed against the significant evidence of the macroeconomic benefits of the 1998 controls" (p. 29).

This example shows that capital controls can be successful not simply from an economic perspective, but from a democratic one as well. They restored relative autonomy by allowing the country to follow an independent monetary and fiscal policy. They allowed Malaysia to follow its own path, despite the wishes of the world's financiers and the IMF. The fact that a relatively small country like Malaysia could do this is powerful commentary on the efficacy and realism of controls. Of course it does not follow from this one example that controls can be implemented easily by every country, but it does show, I think, the importance of keeping capital controls in the government's toolbox should the need for them arise.

So considering the aforementioned evidence, what general conclusions can we state? The first is that capital controls are feasible to implement—which, of course, does not mean that such implementation is easy. States must have the capacity to administer and apply them nimbly and dynamically. Furthermore, capital controls must be transparent and accountably supervised in order to minimize the risk of corruption (Singh, 2000). But given these prerequisites, we can conclude that, with sufficient state capacity and political will, capital controls are feasible to implement, not prohibitively costly, and ultimately an effective mechanism for increasing sovereignty.

Democratic Finance

The last chapter argued that a good democratic financial system would fulfill four basic criteria: it would be responsive to consumer demand; it would operate as a public service; it would be democratically accountable; and it would support the development of worker cooperatives. Moreover, it was argued that these criteria could best be met by a system of Public Community Banks.

Unfortunately, Public Community Banks do not presently exist. But there are close approximations that let us get a sense of their viability. There are state-owned public banks; there are democratic credit unions; and there is Mondragon's Caja Laboral. So in what follows, we will briefly examine each of these types of institutions to try to gauge how successful they have actually been in democratizing finance. We will see that state banks hold the most potential for democratizing finance, while credit unions have somewhat less.

State-Owned Public Banks

State ownership of banks has been a common feature of many economies for many years. La Porta et al. (2002, p. 4) report that in 1970, 59% of the equity of the 10 largest banks in an average country was owned by the government, and still in 1995, 42% was state-owned. The fundamental concerns about public banks (which obviously extends to PCBs) are whether they are likely to be corrupt—serving as sources of personal gain for politicians and favoring clients or firms for narrow political reasons—and whether they are able to fulfill their social mission.[7] What does the evidence show?

In terms of the first issue, the current evidence suggests that indeed public banks can be a source of serious corruption. This has been substantiated by a number of scholars (Cole, 2009; Dinç, 2005; Khwaja & Mian, 2005; Sapienza, 2004). For instance, Khwaja and Mian (2005) find that public banks in Pakistan provide substantially preferential treatment to politically connected firms, where such firms borrow 45% more and have 50% higher default rates.

So while the potential for corruption in public banks is undeniable, two major caveats are in order. The first is that the major alternative—private banks—can be deeply corrupt too. There is evidence of substantial fraud in contemporary private banking (even in developed countries) (Francis, 2010). Moreover, the private banking system allows for significant waste through moral hazard. Private bankers, especially in large banks, know that they are too important to be allowed to fail and so take advantage of the situation by gambling recklessly in a "heads I win, tails you lose" situation. For example, Stanley O'Neal, the CEO of Merrill Lynch, pushed his firm heavily into mortgage-backed-securities in 2005 and 2006, which then disastrously crashed. Nevertheless, he still walked away with a severance package worth $162 million. The moral hazard that private banks face can be a source of absolutely massive waste, such as has occurred in the financial crisis. Indeed, according to the IMF the cleanup of the US banking system will probably cost close to $1.5 trillion (or 10% of GDP) in the long term (Johnson, 2009, p. 9). This kind of gambling and waste is hard to imagine in public banks. Johnson (2009) provides important insight into the levels of corruption that can exist in private banking systems due to the revolving door between banks and governments. Robert Rubin from Goldman Sachs was Treasury Secretary under Clinton (and then later chairman of Citigroup); Henry Paulson was CEO at Goldman before becoming Treasury secretary under Bush; John Snow, Paulson's predecessor, left the Treasury to become chairman of Cerberus Capital Management, a large private-equity firm where Vice President Dan Quayle was also an executive; Alan Greenspan, after leaving the Federal Reserve, became a consultant to Pimco, probably the largest player in international bond markets, and so on. This revolving door makes possible a great deal of corruption. For instance, when the financial crisis hit, the government stepped in to supervise the sales of Bear Stearns, Merrill Lynch, and Washington Mutual and provided massive subsidies and bailouts for Citigroup, AIG, and Bank of America. As Johnson (2009) points out, some of these deals may have been reasonable responses to the immediate situation. But it was never made clear to the public what combination of interests were actually being served, and how. "Treasury and the Fed did not act according to any publicly articulated principles, but just worked out a transaction and claimed it was the best that could be done under the circumstances. This was late-night, backroom dealing, pure and simple" (p. 7). This revolving door turns on its head the "political view" that public banks are more liable for corruption than private, since in a democratic setting opportunistic politicians may well actually prefer a private banking system to a public one. This is because the personal and political payoffs, the "rents" that can be extracted from private banks are likely to be far larger than those that could be extracted from public banks (Andrianova, Demetriades, & Shortland, 2010).

The second caveat is that public banks are not always corrupt. Corruption is of course possible, but it is by no means inevitable. It is important to note that there is much more corruption in public banks in developing countries than developed ones, likely because all public institutions in developing countries tend to have more significant problems with corruption. Dinç's (2005) analysis, which found significant corruption in public banks in developing countries, simultaneously failed to detect it in developed economies. Germany, for example, has had a long experience with public banks but few complaints of corruption. On the other hand, private German banks often give substantial donations to political parties, which is legal though ethically murky, whereas public banks are forbidden from doing so. In the rare cases where corruption in public banks has come to light, the democratic culture means that it usually ends in disgrace for the public banker and an end to her career (Andrianova et al., 2010).

What about the second major issue—are public banks, in practice, actually able to fulfill their social mission? There is indeed substantial evidence of public banks successfully fulfilling a social mandate broader than profit maximization. For instance, Stiglitz and Uy (1996) show how some of the East Asian countries used development banks in order to successfully channel finance to socially desirable areas. Hulme and Mosley (1996) provide detailed evidence of successful public or state-supported banking in poverty reduction in Bolivia, Indonesia, and India. Micco and Panizza (2005) likewise describe the success of certain Latin American development banks in privileging lending to various disadvantaged sectors of society.

So we see that there is evidence for both of these issues—public banks can be corrupt but they can also fulfill their social mission. India is a good example of this multifaceted reality. In 1969, then further in 1980, the Indian government nationalized the bulk of its banking system. The rationale for nationalization, codified in the 1968 Bank Nationalization Act, was that

> an institution such as the banking system which touches and should touch the lives of millions has to be inspired by a larger social purpose and has to subserve national priorities and objectives such as rapid growth in agriculture, small industry and exports, raising of employment levels, encouragement of new entrepreneurs and the development of the backward areas. For this purpose it is necessary for the Government to take direct responsibility for extension and diversification of the banking services and for the working of a substantial part of the banking system. (quoted in Cole, 2009, p. 222)

The banks were required to open branches in rural areas and to provide a portion of their credit to poor and marginalized people. Now it is clear that there was corruption in the public banks (Cole, 2009), as well as inefficiency (Arun & Turner, 2002; Hulme & Mosley, 1996). However, it is also clear that the banks were largely successful in their social mission. Indeed, India witnessed the largest rural branch expansion program ever seen: between 1969 and 1990, bank branches were opened in roughly 30,000 rural locations with no prior formal credit and savings institutions (Burgess & Pande, 2005). According to Burgess, Wong, and Pande (2005), this expansion of public banking can explain roughly half of the fall in rural poverty between 1961 and 2000. In addition, Burgess and Pande (2005) compared the period between 1977 and 1990, when the banks were public, to the subsequent period after the partial privatizations, in 1990. They found that rural bank expansion and poverty reduction were significantly greater in the public banking era than in the private one (since the private banks have been much less interested in operating in less profitable rural areas).

What should we take away from this example? I think the main lesson is that it is impressive that a public bank's social mission can be accomplished even despite significant corruption. And so it seems clear that if levels of corruption were reduced (as we know they can be), then the social mission of public banks would likely be accomplished that much more effectively.

So what can we conclude about the possibilities of public banking for democratizing finance? Overall the evidence shows that while corruption and rent-seeking require constant vigilance, it is indeed possible to have public banks which can operate with minimal corruption as well as fulfill non-market social objectives. In other words, there is no inherent reason to believe that an alternative banking system like that of PCBs could not work well.

Credit Unions

Credit unions emerged in Germany in the mid-19th century and slowly but surely spread across Europe and beyond. They were initially set up as a self-help response to the fact that poor people had no access to credit: banks would not lend to non-wealthy people, and money-lenders were notorious for their usury. Credit unions allowed poor people to pool their money in order to collectively access credit that would be unavailable to them as individuals. Over the years credit unions have developed as financial institutions that are collectively owned by their members and democratically controlled in a one-person one-vote manner. They are generally designed as not-for-profit organizations to serve a social purpose—that of providing the financing needs of their members in the local community—and therefore commonly receive tax exemptions.[8] For instance, credit unions in Saskatchewan initially focused on the stabilization of credit for low-income farmers. Over time they have come to focus mainly on small consumer loans and mortgages while continuing to support the community by investing in municipal bonds, sponsoring community events, funding various local anti-poverty initiatives, and so on (Purden, 1980).

Today credit unions exist all across the world, and although they are almost always smaller than the largest banks, they are far from negligible. Worldwide there are over 52,000 credit unions involving 188 million people in 100 countries (WOCCU, 2010). In Denmark they compose 15% of the market, in Germany 16%, in Italy 29%, in the Netherlands 40%, in Quebec 45%, and in the United States about 85 million Americans (approximately 33% of the population) are members (McKillop, 2005).

Since credit unions are not public institutions, they must be able to survive in the marketplace. This means that they always have to walk a tightrope in balancing their social and economic objectives. Although designed for fundamentally social purposes, they nevertheless have to make enough money to continue their operations. And while the aforementioned statistics provide compelling evidence of the economic viability of credit unions, the crucial question for us is whether they have been able to democratize finance in a meaningful way.

On the one hand, credit unions are democratically accountable to their members. Their one-member one-vote structure means that they are democratic oases in the contemporary desert of finance (Stanford, 1999). And there is evidence that this accountability does result in credit unions lending with somewhat broader criteria than traditional banks (Feinberg & Rahman, 2006; Thomas, Cryer, & Reed, 2008). For instance, there is evidence that credit unions are better than banks at providing the credit needs of the poor (though perhaps not the very poor) (Barham, Boucher, & Carter, 1996; Jones, 2008).

On the other hand, although credit unions are undeniably more accountable than private banks, it is important to remember than even the most democratic credit unions do not allow for much actual democratic engagement beyond a once-per-year vote for a board member. The biggest issue, however, is that as private organizations credit unions are severely constrained in their ability to respond to public needs (i.e., popular preferences that are not well served by the market). This is their fundamental democratic weakness. For instance, Mohanty (2006) points out that credit unions actually make a higher proportion of their home mortgages to richer people than comparable private banks (presumably so that they can afford to engage in slightly riskier social lending elsewhere). It is particularly problematic that, as Barham et al. (1996) show, credit unions are not able to lend to the very poorest people—those who may well need it the most—because extremely poor people are simply too risky for organizations who must make money to survive. More broadly, consider what happened when in 2011 there was a movement (associated with Occupy) to take money out of private banks and put it instead into credit unions (with the hope that this would increase democratic and publicly accountable lending).

As Henwood (2011) pointed out, the increased funds for credit unions only led them to transfer more savings to private banks and government bonds (where 42% of their overall assets were). Since they have to make money, they can only invest socially to the extent that such investment is financially sustainable, which is why such a large amount of their resources just sits in the vaults. From a democratic point of view, that is a very tight constraint.

It is useful to pause here for a moment to admit that this is one of the areas where the empirical evidence has forced me to re-evaluate my theoretical expectations. It has forced me to see that there is a conflict between democracy as *accountability to the grassroots* and democracy as *responding to the preferences of the public* (including responsiveness to popular preferences ignored by markets). To generalize, public banks tend to be worse at the first kind of democracy but better at the second. Credit unions, as smaller, member-led organizations, tend to be more accountable (at least to their own specific members) but less responsive to the public in general. I was initially more sympathetic to credit unions than public banks on the grounds that accountability seemed to me the most important democratic virtue; public banks are often technocratic and very removed from any grassroots accountability (Lipietz, 1988). But studying the actual operations of credit unions and public banks has caused me to re-evaluate this. I now think that while it is true that public banks are often removed from grassroots accountability, who cares? Few of us are dying to participate in such meetings in an intimate way or feel oppressed from being excluded. It seems to me much more important that democratic financial institutions be able to respond to the popular preferences of the public writ large than be somewhat more accountable to their own narrow membership. Helping to finance houses for the poor or green businesses, which public banks can do, is far more important than getting a vote every year for a credit union board member who, in any case, is invariably going to be much less able to provide this kind of lending.

This is why the PCB model that I have advocated is, most importantly, public; the addition of the advisory committees is an attempt to add the component of local accountability, which is the main strength of credit unions, to an institution that is fundamentally public.

The Caja Laboral

Up to this point the discussion has focused on the degree to which real-world financial institutions can be democratic in the senses of accountability and providing a public service. But recall that an additional important criterion for democratic financial institutions is an ability to foster democratic workplaces. To this end it is useful to mention the example of the Mondragon's Caja Laboral.

During the first 30 years or so of its operation, the CL had two primary functions.[9] First, it served to provide finance to the co-ops at below market rates. It funded the co-ops in need with the surplus attained from others, thus diversifying risk and putting the power of finance under the collective control of the co-ops. Second, its Empresarial division was dedicated to providing business and managerial advice, in particular with an eye to setting up new co-ops. For new co-ops to be set up, a group of workers approached the CL with their idea. Provided the workers' vision was of a firm that was a cooperative with appropriately rigorous democratic structures, the CL would help to carry out an in-depth feasibility study, which could take one to two years. If the project was thought feasible, the CL would bring in engineers to start planning construction of the new workplace, as well as provide the bulk of the initial financing. The co-op workers were expected to put up roughly 20% of the initial start-up capital (without which it was thought that projects might fail due to lack of commitment). A further 20% was available from a state loan at 3% interest, while the remainder was supplied by the CL. Beyond this, the CL provided management skills, seminars in cooperativist ideals, and even covered the new firm's losses for the first couple of years (which were expected to be paid back once the firm became profitable) (Campbell et al., 1977).

The CL was immensely successful in developing new co-ops and sustaining existing ones, to the point that it enabled Mondragon to become the largest cooperative business in the world. From our perspective, the Empresarial division—a division specifically tailored to helping co-ops develop—is the essential feature that needs to be emulated by other democratic financial institutions.

Let us take a step back now and review the conclusions we have reached. None of the financial institutions that we have reviewed satisfy all the criteria necessary for genuinely democratic financial institutions (responsiveness to popular demand, accountability, and support for co-ops). However, each of these criteria is fulfilled by at least one of the institutions examined. State banks are able to respond to popular (not just market) demand. Credit unions are accountable to their local membership. And the CL is supportive of co-ops. This is encouraging; it means that there is no obvious reason why the kinds of PCBs advocated in chapter 6 cannot be possible. There is no obvious reason why it would not be entirely feasible to combine the publicness of state banks with the accountability of credit unions (via an advisory committee) and the cooperative support of the CL into an overarching structure of Public Community Banks.

What would be necessary to get PCBs off the ground? Where public banks already exist, pressure could be exerted to have them extended (and ideally to incorporate advisory committees and Empresarial divisions into local branches). Where the political realities do not allow for this, activists could push for increased support for credit unions and other community development financial institutions (such as the Community Development Financial Institutions Fund in the United States, which already provides some public subsidy for community banking (Benjamin, Rubin, & Zielenbach, 2004)).

In the nearer term, PCBs could serve as an important supplement to private finance. This would mean that firms would have the choice about whether to try to obtain their finance in the usual ways—from banks, stock markets, or rich individuals—or from a PCB. This would bring about competition between private banks and PCBs—what would be the result of that? Some firms and clients would likely prefer to operate with PCBs—co-ops for sure, as well as other firms whose short-term profitability is questionable. But because private banks have such large resources and are therefore able to offer very competitive rates for loans to firms, it is possible that a divide would emerge between profitable firms preferring banks and less-profitable ones preferring PCBs. In a sense this is not a bad thing—after all, part of the point of PCBs is to provide finance to firms that are socially valuable even if they are not profitable. But it does mean that PCBs will not naturally outgrow private banks on the basis of monetary competition. For PCBs to make serious inroads into the banking sector they will need exogenous support, either by the state providing certain competitive advantages or shifting resources from private banks to public ones (e.g., through a kind of Meidner plan, as will be discussed shortly).

Over the long term, however, obtaining real financial democracy—overcoming dependency and increasing popular accountability—would require democratizing enough of the banking sector so as to actually serve the general public need of stable, regular financial provision. The more the sector is controlled by PCBs, the more the population acquires a say (on a per person not per dollar basis) over how its society should be developed. In the longer term, PCBs would ideally compose the entirety of the financial system—replacing the stock market and private banking system. While small private lending is unobjectionable, ultimately the main pillars of society's financial system cannot be private institutions, but must be public, accountable ones.

While this is clearly a long-term project, bank-based systems of finance are not at all unheard of (Gerschenkron, 1962). Japan, France, and Germany have all had them (Pollin, 1995). This shows that it is entirely possible to have fully functioning financial systems that are based around banks without having to rely on stock markets. So if we consider the fact that a bank-based financial system is possible, and the aforementioned argument that PCBs are a workable kind of bank, the provocative conclusion is that it may indeed be feasible to have a financial system based largely on PCBs.

Democratic Investment

Democratizing finance is about rendering accountable the channels through which capital flows to people and businesses. The next step in the production process, of course, is that of putting such finance to use in terms of actual concrete investment—building, expanding, repairing, developing, hiring—in a word, producing. We saw last chapter that the current system of investment is undemocratic in that it leaves the population dependent on private investment decisions. Investment strike (or "capital strike") can be devastating for a country and creates what I called the "paradox of investment dependence": that workers, and the population more generally, find their own well-being dependent on the prospering of the employers, because the employers can sink the ship that they are all on.

In addition to this dependence, the population has little active say or accountability over how investment is made, which is deeply problematic given that investment is the sine qua non of societal development. To a degree, investment can be democratized through the spread of co-ops, since this means that investment decisions are made more broadly accountable to workers in their firms. But, of course, this would not enfranchise those who are not working; nor would it provide scope for investment decisions that extend beyond a particular workplace. So what are the real institutional possibilities for what we have called "citizen democracy" (i.e., public and democratic control of investment)? For investment to be democratized, it first needs to be in public control. This can happen at different levels, and indeed needs to happen at different levels in order to be sensitive to the scale of different concerns. Public investment can, and already does, exist at the state level, especially for issues of broad societal concern. But additionally, public investment can exist at a local level, where the scope for meaningful democratic participation is greatest. So it is useful to consider public investment at both of these levels.

State-Level Public Investment

Market economies today are mixed economies. Every country in the West engages in substantial amounts of public spending. In 1870, government spending averaged only 10.7% of GDP, but by 2010 it was 33.8% (OECD, 2012a).[10]

The standard concern with public investment is that it risks crowding out private investment, thereby undermining successful firms. On a theoretical level, however, there is widespread disagreement about how serious this is. On the one hand, increasing public spending requires raising taxes or borrowing more (which can raise interest rates), both of which can discourage private investment. On the other hand, public spending (especially on infrastructure), can increase the marginal productivity of private capital, and thus crowds in private investment (Aschauer, 1989, p. 171). For instance, the more that government helps with the provision of healthy, educated people, roads, telephone lines, water, sewage, social stability (perhaps through a welfare system), and so on, the more private business will be able to profit from these investments.

Although a contentious area, there does not seem to be strong evidence for the crowding-out effect (Argimon, Gonzalez-Paramo, & Roldan, 1997). For instance, Aschauer (1989) finds both a real crowding-out and crowding-in effect of public spending, but concludes that "the net effect of a rise in public investment expenditure is likely to *raise private investment*" (p. 186; emphasis added). This is particularly the case for government investment in infrastructure. Likewise, neither Lindert (1996) nor Pontusson (2005) find evidence that, overall, countries with greater public spending have slower growth.

In previous chapters various reforms have been proposed that would require public spending. Workplace democracy requires public spending to foster new co-ops; citizen democracy requires public funding for PCBs as well as public investment (at the local and state level). Economic democracy is clearly not free. So is it possible to raise the necessary public funds to pay for it?

Social democratic countries already have significant levels of public spending. The average tax take in the Nordic countries in 2011 was 44.8% of GDP (OECD, 2012b). So an important goal for economic democrats should be to strive to increase this spending by 10% or so (to 55–60% of GDP). Spending at this level could go a substantial way toward fostering economic democracy in all its dimensions as well as marking a significant advance over social democracy.

Clearly there would be immense ideological opposition to spending at such levels, but for our purposes the more relevant question is whether such spending is institutionally viable. The major institutional limit to high levels of public spending is that of disincentives to work. Everyone agrees that at very high levels of taxes—near 100%—there would be little incentive to work, meaning that at a certain point higher tax rates actually result in less government revenue. In the economics literature, this issue centers on the so-called Laffer curve. A recent review of the research suggests that in the

United States the revenue-maximizing effective rate for income tax would be a massive 68.7%—nearly double the top rate of 35% that prevailed at the end of 2012 (Fieldhouse, 2013, p. 2). This suggests that there is nothing institutionally impossible about public spending at the levels suggested, even with the current cultural norms. Moreover, at the deepest level it is important to remember that limits to taxation are based on incentives and so are ultimately cultural in nature—they depend on broad societal norms about the relative weight of moral, reputational, and financial incentives to hard work (Cohen, 2001). During World War II, the United States was able to implement marginal income tax rates of 90% on the highest incomes (Quiggin, 2010), precisely because the cultural norms about moral incentives and public versus private benefit had radically shifted (albeit temporarily). This is not at all to imply that reaching public spending levels of 55–60% would be easy (it will not be) but to remind ourselves that the disincentives that underlie the Laffer curve, which are often treated as inviolable and given, are no more permanent or unmovable than any other cultural norm.

Local-Level Democratic Investment: Participatory Budgeting

Although it is rare to have investment funds allocated in a participatory manner, it is not utopian. Such practices do exist and often work quite well. In this section we examine one of the most prominent examples of local-level democratic investment: participatory budgeting in Porto Alegre.[11]

Participatory Budgeting (PB) was first implemented in Porto Alegre in 1989 after the leftist Partido dos Trabalhadores (PT) won the mayoral election. The precise process has ebbed and flowed somewhat over the years, but in general PB operates as follows: the city is divided into 16 districts, each of which deliberate on five key thematic areas: transport and traffic circulation; education, leisure, and culture; health and social welfare; economic development and taxation; and city organization and urban development (Souza, 2001). (Notice that it is no accident that these areas correspond closely to the market failures that limit citizen democracy which we identified in chapter 4). Each district has two rounds of large assemblies, one where officials explain the city's finances from the previous year and one where participants elect delegates to two bodies—the larger Fora of Delegates, which represents the grassroot and neighborhood associations,[12] and the smaller decision-making Participatory Budgeting Council. Between the assemblies, many more neighborhood meetings are organized so as to facilitate widespread participation. The main purpose of these meetings is to prioritize the type of desired public investment, which then forms the basis of the Council's plans. The Council (on the advice of delegates from the Fora) then meets every week to try to balance the investment priorities from the different parts of the city and develops an overall investment plan, which, when completed, is finally submitted to the municipal government for approval.[13]

Participation in PB has increased dramatically over the years, from 780 people in 1989 to an average of more than 35,000 for each of the years 2000–2003. In terms of demographics, the average participant is poorer and less educated than the citywide average; according to Wampler (2007), 78% of delegates are low-income (i.e., a household income of less than US$400 per month), 75% have less than a high school diploma, and 80% are involved in a community association of some sort (pp. 119, 109).

There is widespread agreement that PB has brought significant positive changes to Porto Alegre (Baiocchi, 2005; de Sousa Santos, 1998; Souza, 2001; Wampler, 2007). From 1996 to 2003, nearly US$400 million of new investment projects were implemented through PB; the projects ranged in size from small drainage systems and street paving to complex housing projects (Wampler, 2007, p. 106). It is important to note that the type of investment that has occurred is markedly different under PB than earlier eras. In terms of basic sanitation, for instance, in 1989, only 49% of the population was covered. By the end of 1996, 98% had water and 85% had sewage. De Sousa Santos reports that while all previous administrations combined had built 1,100 km of sewers, under PB, 900 km were built (1998, p. 485). Other common investment projects include roads, houses, and schools. Between 1989 and 1996, the number of students in school doubled and the number of schools quadrupled. Even the democratically recalcitrant IMF admitted that "the process of participatory budgeting has brought substantial changes in Porto Alegre" (Bhatnagar et al., 2003, p. 2).[14]

From our perspective, the chief virtue of PB is that it deepened the level of citizen democracy by providing a mechanism through which local people can influence investment priorities in an egalitarian manner. Compared to conventional market-led investment, PB has a number of advantages. First, it is much more egalitarian. It enfranchises the poor who are ignored by markets and provides much more equal influence than would happen if investment were guided by dollar "votes," which are distributed very unequally in Brazil, one of the most unequal countries in Latin America (Tornarolli, Cruces, & Gasparini, 2011). Second, PB reflects popular preferences for investment projects that would tend to be ignored by markets (such as goods with important positive externalities, like schools, and public goods, like roads or sewers). Third, PB allows for regular people to actively participate in the democratic process, which can contribute to a sense of empowerment and self-determination. After all, participation, as Saul Alinksy (1971) used to say, is the "heartbeat of the democratic way of life" (p. 123). Finally, PB provides a mechanism for collective deliberation about the future direction of the city's development; unlike the market which simply aggregates individual preferences, PB allows for deliberation, a mix of bargaining, cooperation, and contestation that creates a dynamic and developing sense of learning what other citizens require. In other words, it provides a forum for preferences to evolve through engagement with others. For instance, after deliberation has ended delegates have usually decided to allocate revenue weighted (at least in part) by poverty and infrastructure needs, so that poorer areas end up getting more than their proportional share. This would clearly not happen if investment was just left to the market and private preferences.

Democratic theorists often worry that participatory institutions such as PB will be undermined by unequal abilities to participate. One such problem, which we might call the "tyranny of the eloquent," is brought to light by the excellent work of Jane Mansbridge (1980), in which she documents the ways in which democracy can co-exist with severe inequalities between individiuals because of differences in the culture of participation. Since democracy is based on speech and deliberation, those who are skilled at these things will tend to dominate. Building on Mansbridge's work, I would submit that democracy tends to be biased toward the good persuaders: the powerful talkers (i.e., the articulate and charismatic); the knowledgeable (i.e., those who are educated, have been around for a long time and have all the relevant information); the extrovert (i.e., those who are loud, have more energy, emotionally thick skin, are sociable and enjoy meetings); the resourced (i.e., those who have the time and money to participate, do not have to look after children, etc.); and the authoritative (i.e., those who are seen as possessing authority by virtue of their identity).

However, while the tyranny of the eloquent is always a potential danger for democratic institutions, it does not seem to be a particularly serious issue here. In the course of his ethnography, Baiocchi (2005) does not find any evidence of systematic exclusion; indeed PB is highly inclusive, with very high levels of engagement of civil society organizations and a consensus that if the process is dominated by anyone, it is by the poor and less educated. (Although it is, of course, possible that within civil society organizations the leaders, who will likely become the PB delegates, are able to become leaders because they are more eloquent and knowledgeable than other members.) Wampler (2007) points out that government officials do play a role in providing technical information, but, at least in Porto Alegre, they do not dominate the process. PB encourages wide participation by offering training on how to run meetings, courses in law, management, and public finances, and free transportation and childcare for all citizens attending meetings (Latendresse, 2005, p. 289). Over the long term, fostering more egalitarian participation requires greater social equality, particularly universal access to a good education system. There is thus the possibility of a virtuous cycle here: as PB increases investment in public services, over the long term we can expect those kinds of investments to enrich PB.

So given the experience of Porto Alegre, should this kind of participatory budgeting be copied elsewhere?[15] I think that the answer is yes. Given the successes of PB in Porto Alegre, its emulation and expansion is a good idea. That said, the best scholarly investigations into PB remind us of the need for some caution in this regard. As Wampler (2007) powerfully demonstrates, PB was very successful in certain cities in Brazil—particularly Porto Alegre and Ipatinga. But it has not been successful everywhere. In certain cases it has achieved mixed results, and in other cases (such as in Blumenau and Rio Claro) it has been a clear failure—involving little delegation of actual authority and the implementation of only very few projects. So Wampler reminds us that PB cannot simply be cut and pasted into different contexts. Its success depends on several things: certain institutional factors, such as having a Mayor who is committed to delegating real power and having good, clear rules defining how the process works;[16] certain civil society factors, such as having sufficiently powerful civil society organizations that are willing to cooperate with the process but are also strong enough to contest it (so that they do not get co-opted);[17] and certain financial factors, in particular having sufficient resources to make popular participation worthwhile.[18]

Wampler's conclusion is apposite: "PB programs are not a universal, one-size-fits all solution to improving state performance, working toward social justice, empowering citizens, or deepening democracy....PB programs *do* have the potential to promote these positive attributes" and the results in Porto Alegre in particular have been "very encouraging," "but it has also been shown here that we should not necessarily expect such positive outcomes" in every city or in every circumstance (2007, pp. 280–81; emphasis added).

So we have seen that democratizing investment requires public control over investment at different levels. Higher levels of public investment allow for greater scope, while lower levels allow for more meaningful participation. At the state level, public spending already exists in sizable amounts, though it could be increased in many countries. However, the real key to democratizing investment is not simply an increase in the amount of money that the central government controls, but in reconceptualizing what state investment looks like, by redirecting larger and larger amounts of this money to locally controlled participatory bodies. This is where real participation can occur and where self-determination can be meaningful. The example of Porto Alegre suggests that there is enormous potential for this kind of local-level democratic investment. This is not to say that it can be simply cut and pasted into different contexts. Experimentation is clearly vital, but PB demonstrates that it is entirely possible to create decentralized, participatory institutions for local control over investment.

Transitions

This chapter has provided substantial evidence that democratizing banks and local investment is feasible. We have reasonable theories of what to do and various examples to concretely follow. But how do we get there? This is not the place to inquire about the political possibilities of transition in specific places—whether Canada will adopt participatory budgeting or whether the United States will expand its Community Development Financial Institutions Fund—but it is nevertheless important to ask about the institutional possibilities for profound transition.

In this regard it is useful to distinguish between short- and long-term reforms. The distinction is not only one of time but also of depth. Short-term reforms are ones that are immediately plausible and start from the institutions and structures that exist today, while long-term reforms, on the other hand, are ones that are more institutionally ambitious and actually challenge the very core structures. The aim is to show the continuity that bridges the short- and long-term visions. This division is useful because, in Ungerian fashion, it allows us to think ambitiously without sacrificing realism and to be realistic without abandoning imagination.

In the short term, several kinds of reform would be very useful. In terms of democratizing finance, the most obvious place to start is reforming the banking sector. The current financial crisis has made this obvious to practically everyone (Quiggin, 2010). Banks that are too big to fail should be seen as too big to exist. Governments should be more interventionist in their oversight of the financial sector—ensuring transparency and highly regulating, if not outlawing, excessively risky practices such as credit default swaps (Crotty, 2009; Johnson, 2009). Beyond the banks, the idea of a "Tobin Tax," initially suggested in 1972, is finally gaining ground. The Tobin Tax is a small tax on financial transactions. While it would be too small to discourage long-term investment, it would discourage very short-term speculative movements of capital, thereby reducing the danger that such movements of capital hold for autonomous monetary policy (Eichengreen, Tobin, & Wyplosz, 1995).[19] Indeed, there have been promising recent developments in this direction; at the time of writing there are plans to introduce a European-wide financial transaction tax (colloquially called a "Robin Hood tax"), starting in 2014.

However, the short-term measure with the most far-reaching potential is that of democratizing pension funds. Pension funds currently control gigantic amounts of wealth: US pension funds, for instance, held $7 trillion in assets in 2000 and owned about 24% of total equity—meaning that workers (understood broadly) own essentially a quarter of the entire economy through their funds (Blackburn, 2002, p. 102). So if pension fund legislation were relaxed to enable workers increased democratic say over how the funds are used, the possibilities would be enormous.[20] However, pension funds are currently controlled by trustees who are legally bound by "fiduciary responsibility," which means that they are obligated to aim for maximum returns and required to diversify the funds as much as possible. These legal requirements effectively prevent pension funds from being used for progressive purposes (a duty to maximize returns prevents social or ethical investing, and extreme diversification prevents obtaining sufficient equity to influence a company's policies or facilitate worker ownership).[21] If this legislation were relaxed, however, workers could gain a more active say in weighing and balancing the criteria by which they invest. Since their pensions represent the funds for their retirement, profitability will undoubtedly remain a key criterion, but there is no reason to think that it is the only criterion that workers care about—they may also value various social projects even if they have slightly lower rates of return (e.g., financing affordable housing, local infrastructure, etc., that involve positive externalities and so very real, even if non-market, value).

The tremendous size of pension funds makes them a source of enormous potential for furthering economic democracy. One possibility is that pension funds could be required to invest a portion of their funds into municipal bonds, which cities could then use for long-term investment in infrastructure, thus reducing the danger of capital strike. Another possibility is that pension funds could be required to deposit a portion of their funds into credit unions or even newly created PCBs, to capitalize them and help them grow, thus encouraging the growth of financial democracy.

In terms of democratizing investment, private investment could be regulated through a series of deterrents and incentives. In Pontusson's classic study of investment politics in Sweden, he argues that

it is at least conceivable that a reformist government committed to radical reforms could sustain an adequate rate of investment through a combination of carrots to stimulate private investment, sticks to discourage capital flight and hoarding of wealth, and perhaps a partial replacement of private investment by public investment. (Pontusson, 1992, p. 19)

We have already mentioned the "sticks to discourage capital flight," as well as the use of public investment, but the other main tool at a government's disposal to maintain an adequate investment rate is the tax system. One possibility is the shifting of taxation to consumption and away from corporate income so as not to discourage investment, for example, through a progressive Kaldor tax (Przeworski & Wallerstein, 1988; Unger, 2000).[22] Additionally, there could be tax penalties to companies for paying out large dividends, thus encouraging them to invest more. Furthermore, communities could raise the cost of investment strike by introducing plant-closing legislation: requiring notice, compensation, and severance pay (Schweickart, 1996). Complementary incentives could easily be envisioned, including tax breaks or subsidized credit to encourage investment.

What about the possibilities for long-term transition? The closest a country has come to fundamentally democratizing its system of finance and investment is the Meidner Plan, proposed by the Swedish government in the 1970s. Rudolf Meidner, Chief Economist of the largest Swedish union the LO, proposed that all firms with more than 50 workers should be obliged to create new shares worth 20% of their gross annual profit to be controlled in so-called "wage-earner funds" (Meidner, 1978). These funds would be controlled by the firms' internal workers until they reached a size of 20% of the firms' equity, at which point control rights would shift outside of the firm to be governed by regional public bodies controlled by the trade unions. These wage-earner funds would over time acquire more and more control over capital to direct toward public investment. It was estimated that firms making 10% profit per year would become majority worker-owned within 35 years. Thus the investment process would slowly and cumulatively become socialized.

The plan had a number of important strengths. The funds would not have expropriated presently existing wealth (instead they would dilute future control), thus somewhat calming the inevitable opposition to them. This is justifiable because while large amounts of private wealth may be justifiable, large amounts of private power that derive from such wealth is not. From a democratic perspective, the funds would have slowly reduced the power of unaccountable private investors and slowly increased democratic control over public investment. Additionally, since the funds would not remove any capital from the firms, and thus not subtract from internal cash flow, the plan would not hurt the firms' internal financing (Blackburn, 2002; Pontusson, 1987).

Most importantly, the cumulative nature of the plan allows for the gradual socialization of the economy. Bit by bit, private productive property would have become public and directed according to popular criteria. Unfortunately, the Meidner plan was ferociously attacked by business groups and ultimately abandoned by the socialist party.[23]

Although the Meidner plan was developed for a specific Swedish context (Pontusson & Kuruvilla, 1992), the core idea remains very powerful and replicable. Indeed, it does not require much of a stretch to imagine a Meidner-type plan, or what we earlier called an "Incremental Democratization Plan," to be adapted to the goals of economic democracy. Imagine for instance an IDP with two distinct streams—a *banking stream*, whereby profits from private banks are cumulatively placed under the control of newly established Public Community Banks,[24] and a second *business stream*, whereby profits from private firms are cumulatively placed under the control of a workers' trust, governed on the basis of one-worker one-vote, which could then serve as a basis for buying out the firms and transforming them into worker cooperatives (if the workers so desired). Thus over time, such a plan would gradually and fundamentally alter the economy, replacing private banks with PCBs and private firms with worker-owned co-ops. This would achieve at one stroke two fundamental goals of economic democracy: democratizing finance and democratizing workplaces. And such changes would be mutually reinforcing as the democratic banks would prove vital for helping the increasingly worker-owned workplaces transform into co-ops. Although such changes would be gradual, their cumulative effect would be massive.

While the specific details of the Swedish battle over the Meidner plan need not concern us here, there is a more general problem, which is that any attempt by a government to significantly socialize investment runs the risk of immediate capital flight and strike. This is why the short-term reforms identified above are so important: they provide the initial breathing room for a country to lay the groundwork for more major changes, without being threatening enough that they are likely to provoke hugely serious reactions from the holders of capital. It is also useful to remember that while there is always an immediate risk of capital flight and strike, over the medium-term if financiers and investors think that conditions are stable enough for them to make a profit, they will likely return home to continue investing, even if conditions are not as favorable to them as they once were. This is an important lesson of the Chavez regime in Venezuela. While elites were clearly unhappy with the new capital controls, government spending, nationalization of oil, and so on, business more-or-less went back to normal once they felt assured that they would not be expropriated and that economic conditions were stable enough to operate in profitably, even if less profitably than before (Weisbrot & Sandoval, 2007).

Conclusion

The proposals explored in this chapter—for capital controls, Public Community Banks, and local participatory investment—are the most radical proposals of this book. Although we can see examples of most of these things in action to a certain degree (with democratic finance being the least common), they remain exceptional and underdeveloped, though not entirely invisible. Malaysia shows us the practicality of capital controls. Credit unions, Mondragon's CL, and particularly public banks (such as India's) show us the possibility of creating PCBs. Participatory budgeting in Brazil demonstrates the possibility of local democratic investment. These examples not only illustrate the feasibility of increasing democratic control over finance and investment, they also illustrate real and concrete improvements from the status quo. Economic democracy can improve people's lives. Of course, for these changes to become robust the components need to grow, and become connected and integrated with one another. But even in their present nascent form, they allow us to glimpse a new world in the womb of the old.

———

We have now examined all the main elements of economic democracy, and so it is useful to take a step back in order to appreciate how the constituent parts are integrated and may actually sustain each other.

We have seen that workplace democracy could be increased by providing legislative and educational support, as well as by creating institutions to provide financial help and guidance, such as Public Community Banks. The expansion of worker co-ops would not only increase workplace democracy but would also increase investment democracy, as more workers acquire a say over investment decisions. It would also increase financial democracy to the extent that co-ops keep their savings in democratic banks or credit unions.

The market system could be democratized in the sense of providing consumer democracy by reducing inequality and price distortions so that the market becomes a more democratic voting-machine. Reducing inequality is not only useful for making the market function in a more democratic way, but it also promotes workplace democracy since reducing poverty means that more people can afford to buy out their firms or start new co-ops of their own. Additionally, shaping the market system through tax systems that benefit democratic businesses and using tariffs that prevent odious competition are not only useful for consolidating national democracy from global pressures but also for promoting workplace democracy (through the spread of co-ops).

Democratizing the market system in terms of citizen democracy requires financial and investment democracy. Financial democracy could be increased by capital controls and the spread of democratic financial institutions such as state banks or better yet, PCBs. PCBs would be useful not only for providing democratic accountability over the allocation of finance, but they would also promote worker co-ops (as the CL does for Mondragon).

Finally, investment democracy could be increased by the spread of co-ops as well as by increased public investment, particularly at the local level via participatory structures. Democratizing investment through increased public spending reduces the risk of investment strike, which means that taxes can be raised higher than in social democracies, which in turn allows for a greater reduction of inequality and thereby an increase in the democratic functioning of the market (as well as an increased ability to fund the expansion of workplace democracy via worker co-ops and financial democracy via PCBs).

Ultimately, economic democracy is both a goal and a direction of transition. It is a bridge that must be built brick by brick, pillar by pillar, to carry us from here to there. Yet even though the main pillars—workplace democracy, market democracy, finance and investment democracy—are important goals in their own right, we can see that they are also deeply interconnected and mutually sustaining. Democratic institutions in one place feed and foster those in another. This means that even though economic democracy is doubtless an ambitious project, it is also true that diverse actors and variegated movements, contributing to democratization in their own particular spheres, are likely supporting those of others they do not even know. As such, the grounds for comprehensive change in a democratic direction may not be quite as infertile as they often appear.

Conclusion
Toward a Feasible Socialism for the 21st Century

Introduction

Although economic democracy is primarily a set of reforms, it also embodies a vision of a future socialist society. This chapter, by way of conclusion, illustrates the main contours of what such a society might look like. Clearly this kind of speculative work requires careful vigilance in order to prevent it from falling into fantasy. One way to ensure this is to ask what might be possible within the lifetime of a young person considering these issues today (i.e., in the next 50 or so years). The point is not to build castles in the sand, but to try to paint a picture of society that is at once plausible enough to seem worth talking about yet inspiring enough to warrant the risk, energy, and commitment that building such a society would require.

One of the oldest debates on the Left is about whether models of future society are actually useful. On the one hand, it is clearly important to have enough humility to recognize that we cannot possibly envision the infinite complexities and multitude of dilemmas facing a future society.[1] The future falls inevitably within the penumbra of the present. Not to mention the obvious fact that different countries, with their particular histories and cultures, will unavoidably develop different types of institutions, even if they aim at broadly similar purposes. This means that any speculation must necessarily be of a high degree of generality and abstractness. But that does not make the attempt meaningless. Far from it. The most important reason to engage in this speculation is to concretize our vision of what exactly we are aiming for, so as to have a better idea of how we should direct our energy here and now. Having a vision to work toward is like having a north point on a compass—it orients our plans, projects, and strategies for reform. It gives coherence to our organizing and direction to our activism.

This conclusion presents an outline of a model of developed economic democracy in the form of market socialism. I describe the basic components of such a society in order to demonstrate its viability as well as its desirability. While this kind of analysis of large-scale economic alternatives is far from the norm in contemporary political debate, I end by arguing that it should be much more so.

Economic Democracy as Market Socialism

In the present context it is often difficult to imagine a radical break from that which currently exists. Yet imagining that nothing will radically change is even harder. As neoliberalism generates ever greater inequality in the form of riches for some and powerlessness for others, and as global warming makes current economic arrangements seem ever more impossible to continue, it is not unlikely that a number of governments around the world will start moving politically to the left. Although we have been talking about economic democracy as a set of reforms, it is more than just this, it is also a direction of reform. But if economic democracy is a direction of reform, where exactly does it point? It points toward the building up of possibilities for popular self-government of economic relations: building workplace democracy, democratizing the market, and increasing local control over finance and investment. Ultimately, if we carry the argument of the previous chapters to their logical conclusion, it points to a system of *market socialism*. Of course, such a system has nothing in common with the current Chinese regime, which is sometimes described in this way; rather it belongs to the school of thought that attempts to carve out a third way between capitalism and communism.[2] Theories of market socialism tend to fall into two camps—*public market socialism*, where firms are managed by a democratic state, which equally redistributes the profits to the population, and *self-managed market socialism*, where workers control their own firms and distribute the profits themselves (Weisskopf, 1993). Economic democracy falls into the second camp.

It is not inconceivable that within the next 50 years a number of countries will move substantially toward economic democracy. Countries in South America may move in this direction substantially sooner, with Venezuela, perhaps, already leading the way.[3] It is likely that the best chances for the success of market socialism will be in countries which experience a gradual accumulation of economic democracy over the years—expanding co-ops and public banks, and regulating the market in a democratic direction. Incrementalism is crucial because it builds up the democratic resources of a country, so that if and when the storm of opposition comes, the democratic institutions have a better chance of weathering it.[4]

Transition is impossible to predict with any accuracy, but in broad strokes one can imagine a variety of countries slowly building up various democratic components of their economies, perhaps propelled by legislation akin to the original Meidner plan, involving the slow but cumulative passing of control of business to workers, and private banks to PCBs. Over time, things like a Meidner plan, or a shaping of the market system so that co-ops outcompete private firms, could lead to a peaceful transition to economic democracy. Recall, for instance, an analogous transition that occurred in Swedish society from the 1930s to the 1970s in the building of the welfare state, which was just as deep and profound as it was peaceful and piecemeal.

Of course, it is possible, and perhaps more likely, that things will not be so orderly. Recall the case of Venezuela, where several years of democratic reforms transpired peacefully before finally reaching a tipping point where the opposition revolted, leading to massive capital flight, investment strike, and a coup. Not only did Chavez survive the coup (with massive popular support) but it led to the deepening and radicalizing of reforms, as the government initiated the Communal Councils and started explicitly calling for "21st century socialism." In a broadly similar way, it is possible to imagine a country peacefully moving toward economic democracy until it reaches a tipping point: perhaps welfare rates are increased, or a legislative proposal is put forward to increase the scope of the Meidner plan. Capitalists react en masse. Capital flight takes off; owners lock out workers; banks refuse to lend. Unemployment and inflation skyrocket, the economy starts to collapse. Yet instead of capitulating, the bulk of the citizens push back—riots break out, factories get occupied, elections get called, and a more radical left government is elected. Capital controls are implemented, Meidner-type reforms are sped up, the remaining privately owned small and medium-size firms pass into the hands of their workers, large firms are taken over by the state for co-management, private banks are put under public control, and the stock market is abolished. The wealthy are removed of their empires (but not of their homes). In addition to popular support, the depth of the previous reforms is crucial in providing a solid foundation for transition. The basic idea here is that given widespread co-ops and partial democratic investment, the capital flight and strike that leads to what Przeworski calls the "transition trough" is likely to be shallower and less destructive than otherwise (Wright, 2010, chap. 9).

In either case, peaceful and slow, or turbulent and quick, once the dust settles it is possible to ask what a society determined to enact full-blown economic democracy might actually look like. We can envision such a society based on the following core components.

(i) *Democratic workplaces.* Firms are run as worker cooperatives (except for those run by a single individual, or those of large capital-intensity or national importance, which are co-managed between worker representatives and state representatives).[5] The majority of the workforce of each co-op must be full members with equal rights to participate in the governance of the firm, elect managers, and receive a share of the profits. Temporary workers could be permitted, but after a probationary period they must enjoy full rights to become members should they wish to do so. Each firm is free to remunerate as it sees fit. While some firms may opt for strict equality, past experience with co-ops suggests that most firms would allow some inequality of wages to foster motivation, but not usually exceeding a ratio of highest paid to lowest of 3:1 (compared to contemporary rates of roughly 300:1 in the United States and at least 15:1 in the social democracies). Since firms are run as co-ops, the society has effectively abolished the segment of the capitalist class who are business owners. In other words, there is no longer a group of people who have the power to control workers based on the ownership of property. A guiding principle of a society like this is that control rights do not stem from ownership but from laboring, and are thus vested equally among working members.

(ii) *A democratized market system.* Co-ops and consumers interact with each other and are coordinated by way of a market system. This is the second component of the economy—a cooperative market system regulated by an interventionist state. The market system is regulated to improve consumer democracy by reducing inequality (as well as reducing the price distortions that arise from the market failures of externalities and monopolies). In addition, the market system as a whole is shaped to allow for public deliberation on economic scale and to promote the flourishing of democratic businesses.

(iii) *Democratic finance and investment.* Citizen democracy over economic development is protected by capital controls and promoted through public institutions that are both accountable and well-equipped to deal with market failures (such as externalities, public goods, etc.) These public institutions exist at different levels: accountable investment at the highest level is achieved through a National Investment Fund, while meaningful involvement occurs at the local level through Public Community Banks (ideal for dealing with local externalities) and participatory budgeting (ideal for dealing with local public goods). Public funds are allocated by the government to regions based on the share of their population; then municipalities direct funds to PCBs and PB. PB decides on local investment priorities and the PCBs disperse their funds as loans to co-ops (and individuals) on the basis of criteria decided by the elected municipal government. Each PCB has an advisory committee for local input and accountability, as well as a department devoted to co-ops—offering not just finance, but business advice, support, strategizing, and so on. Since investment is democratized and all the banks are run as democratic institutions there is no longer a group of people who have the power to make investment decisions, to direct capital and develop society, solely on the basis of their ownership of property—this segment of the capitalist class has likewise been abolished. The power to direct the economic development of society has evolved from a private privilege into a basic right of all citizens.[6]

So how would these components function in a day-to-day manner? The basic functioning of the economy would be straightforward and familiar: co-op firms would produce various goods and services to sell on the market. Firms would compete with each other to make profit, and consumers would buy what they desire in response to price signals. There would be substantial progressive taxation on income or consumption or some mix (up to, say, 60% or so of GDP) as well as extremely high taxes on inheritance (such as 99% for estates above a certain threshold). These taxes would fund the various public programs, such as high-quality universal education free at all levels, like Nordic countries do now, in addition to funding an extended welfare system, or, perhaps, a basic income. The size of the basic income would, of course, be dependent on what the society could afford, but hopefully it would constitute a living wage (which is within the reach of many developed countries today (Harvey, 2006)). In addition, these taxes would fund public investment at different scales. Funds for public investment would be divided between the national level, perhaps a regional level, with the bulk being reserved for the local level—split between PCBs and participatory budgeting. PCBs would loan their funds out to local co-ops, individuals, and community groups, thus recycling the nation's capital through democratic bodies. PCBs would compete with each other to provide better financial and social returns. Unsatisfactory ones would be closed down by the city and new ones opened. The practice of recycling investment up from general taxation then back down through democratic participatory structures is the mechanism by which the wealth that is the social heritage of the past becomes the social inheritance of the present.

Workers wishing to join an existing co-op apply in the usual fashion. Alternatively, workers can start a new co-op. There would be substantial support to do this. A group of workers can approach the co-op department of their local PCB with their idea. The PCB would perform a feasibility study and require a down payment from the workers (as the Caja Laboral used to do), and if the project is seen as feasible, financing and business advice will be provided. Clearly in a competitive market system like this certain firms will prosper and certain will fail. When co-ops go bankrupt, the workers can live off the basic income if they desire or try to find work elsewhere. Of course, there may well be structural unemployment in the economy (i.e., a mismatch between the demand for labor and the skills and location of workers looking for employment). In this case, economic democracy could follow the same strategy as Sweden does today (i.e., providing Active Labor Market Policies), which provide workers with opportunities to retrain and/or give subsidies for people to relocate to different areas. Economic democracy would be able to invest more into such programs than Sweden currently does because of the higher tax take.

In general, people will search for the jobs that appeal to them or choose to live off the basic income and devote themselves to other activities—art, music, activism, caregiving, parenting, and so on.[7] Since the basic income is unlikely to be very high, most people will likely choose to work. Basic economic incentives—to work, to move to a different job, or start a business—will come from two sources. People will retain an element of the material incentives that exist today, since hard work and innovation can provide individuals with a marginally greater income than others (though only marginal, since taxes and co-op business structures will prevent massive inequalities). Additionally, people will have moral incentives to work hard—such as the desire to excel, have high self-esteem, be respected by co-workers, obtain community status, and so on. Moral incentives are often sneered at and derided as ineffective, but they can provide enormous levels of motivation. Even in contemporary society—which champions self-interest above all else—we see that a huge amount of effort is galvanized by sources other than narrow profit maximization. Parents look after children out of an ethic of care; academics publish less for the money than the peer recognition; health practitioners study hard to be good at their job and perform a function that they see as valuable, and so on. A market socialist society based on democratic principles would almost certainly develop stronger cultural norms than exist presently about the importance of contributing to the community and working out of solidarity with the consumers (who are ultimately our neighbors and ourselves). This is not to say that such norms would entirely replace material incentives, but they could well complement them.

Taking a step back to visualize the interaction of the parts, there is no reason why such an economy could not function smoothly. Price signals would provide everyone in the economy with information about supply and demand. Workers would have incentives to find jobs. And businesses would have incentives to respond to consumers.

Furthermore the system would be stable, since there would be no inherent group or class of people with a vested interest in overthrowing it. Imagine, for instance, that a smart, self-interested individual does not wish to work in a co-op because he does not want to share his ideas or his profits. Imagine he wants to be a capitalist. There is no problem. He is perfectly free to start his own company, where he is king and hierarch, make all the decisions and keep all the money for himself (except for taxes). The only thing he is unable to do is to hire employees who are forever denied equal say, since the employees, after a probationary period, have a fundamental right to buy their employers out (with financial support from local PCBs); he is able to remain king only over himself. Such a person would have little reason to destabilize the system and even less ability to do so.[8]

It is worth pointing out that economic democracy is fully compatible with large-scale business and complex economic activities. While it is true that direct democratic participation (and feelings of empowerment through self-determination) can only occur effectively on a small scale, a central strength of economic democracy is the organizing of institutions in ways that operate at different levels and different scales simultaneously. Participation can happen to a certain degree in co-ops through decentralization of various tasks and delegation of various responsibilities. Yet nothing about the co-op structure requires them to be small or simple. Although co-ops are better able to retain their democratic character with less than, say, 500 workers, they can grow to be much larger than this, and incredibly complex, through spinning off departments as new co-ops and expanding through networking. Mondragon is a powerful example of this kind of network that is huge, complex, and yet allows for direct democracy at the base with representative democracy at the highest level. Moreover, economic democracy would likely retain some huge firms, such as oil or telecommunications companies, which make economic sense to keep large (for instance, because of natural monopolies). Such firms would ideally be co-managed. Additionally, direct participation can happen to a certain degree through the advisory committees of PCBs and more so through the local participatory budgeting process. Yet here too this system can very easily sit within broader systems of public investment occurring at the regional or national level. Although again, at this higher level the accountability comes from elected representatives, not direct participation. So nothing about economic democracy requires smallness or the lack of complexity; the system combines meaningful participation with large-scale effectiveness by nesting mechanisms for direct participation within larger structures of representative democracy.

Evaluating Economic Democracy

It seems to me that such a society would constitute a substantial advance over contemporary capitalism—both the neoliberal and the social democratic variants. Let's consider the harder case: how exactly is economic democracy better than social democracy?

One of the most simple and yet profound ideas in the history of democratic thought is the idea that people should have a say in decisions in rough proportion to the degree to which they are affected by them. Such a notion is usually referred to as the Principle of Affected Interests (PAI).[9] This idea has been, in many ways, the guiding light of this book, as I have attempted to work out a concrete vision of what it might mean for people to have a say in (admittedly rough) proportion to the degree that they are affected by economic decision-making. This PAI is the thread that ties together the different chapters: we analyzed the main manifestations of decision-making power in the economy and asked what it would mean for people affected by that power to have accountability. The PAI is the underlying reason, though not the only reason, why workers deserve a direct say in their workplaces (but consumers only indirect, since they are affected much less directly by internal workplace decisions); why certain workplaces of national importance need co-management (since different constituencies are differently affected), why consumers need a say over economic production (which can be acquired through a regulated market), and why citizens need a say over finance and investment decisions (which can be acquired through decentralized public bodies). In other words, one of the reasons why economic democracy represents an important advance over social democracy is that it fulfills the PAI to a much greater degree and is, therefore, a much more genuinely democratic society.

More specifically, this society would be significantly freer. First, there would be important increases in *social freedom* flowing from the institutionalization of democracy in those areas of society that exert major economic power. In particular, widespread workplace democracy constitutes a major advance from social democracy. For the first time in industrial history, workers would acquire formal equality at work—the right to elect their managers and influence the direction of their workplace with others who are peers and of equal status. There would no longer be structural inequality or institutionalized inferiority. Since co-ops tend to be freer, less demoralizing, and more pleasant places to work than capitalist firms, the fact that work occupies such a significant portion of people's time and energy means that we can expect the spread of co-ops to lead to substantial improvements in people's lives. Of course, this is not to say that worker co-ops are perfect institutions; we have seen that they can easily be marred by informal hierarchy stemming from the pressures of scale and complexity. But this should not disillusion us because we are not searching for perfection; we are searching for progress. Workplace democracy constitutes a wave of enfranchisement, similar in certain respects to the wave of female suffrage that occurred in many countries in the early 20th century. While acquiring the vote did not abolish all inequities between men and women, the formal equality that resulted nevertheless represented a fundamental improvement in women's freedom. Likewise, acquiring the vote at work will not abolish all inequities between workers and managers, but it represents fundamental progress all the same.

In addition, a society of this sort would possess increased social freedom from the increased accountability and self-determination that comes from having Public Community Banks, as well as being able to participate in local investment through PB. PCBs and PB are important mechanisms for enhancing the freedom of regular people to direct the development of their communities. Those who choose to engage and participate are able to, while those who choose not to are still afforded the democratic protections stemming from accountability.

Second, beyond the social freedom that democracy brings, this society would have much more *individual freedom*. Public services (like healthcare) and a strong safety net provide individual freedom in the sense of security. Public education and a basic income provide freedom in the sense of opportunity, by substantially increasing the scope of real choices that individuals have. Since economic democracy has public systems of investment, it is able to have taxes that are significantly higher than present social democracies. Clearly there are limits to taxation, but there is no reason why economic democracy could not have tax revenues a good 10% higher than the Nordic countries have ever achieved. This means that everything that social democracy does well—its partial provision of security and partial provision of opportunity—economic democracy could do better. More material equality and investment in education means that people's futures are more open and less constrained by the fluke of birth than in social democracies. Together with a stronger social safety net and increased investment in ALMPs, economic democracy would increase the scope of opportunities: individuals would face less compulsion to accept bad jobs, while enjoying more ability to find good ones. Furthermore, the existence of capital controls gives governments the tools to pursue full employment—thus allowing individuals to benefit from the increasing living standards and material security that this brings—which social democratic states find harder to achieve.

In addition, such a society would have rid itself of massive *inequality*. Incomes would be compressed by co-op remuneration standards as well as by high levels of taxation. Large inheritances would be taxed away. And wealth from capital ownership—such as dividends and interest payments which today transform the rich into the superrich—would no longer exist since the financial markets have been abolished. And just as the social democracies benefit more than neoliberal countries from the range of advantages that come from having increased equality—lower mental illness, homicides, obesity, and imprisonment rates, as well as higher life expectancy, children's educational performance, and social mobility (Wilkinson & Pickett, 2010)—we can expect these benefits to accrue even more substantially in economic democracy.

Beyond material equality, the democratization of finance and investment means that there is no longer a business class occupying a "privileged position" in society, which means that in this society citizens have roughly equal political freedom. This society therefore meets Rawls's criterion of being a just society, much more than social democracy, because it provides "fair value" of political freedom; in other words, all citizens have "roughly an equal chance of influencing the government's policy and of attaining positions of authority irrespective of their economic and social class" (Rawls, 2001, p. 46).

This society would also have the potential to be significantly better for the *environment*. Since co-op workers tend to live close to where they work, they are far less likely than far-flung capital owners to pursue economic goals which are detrimental to their local environment. But the main difference from social democracy is that economic democracy has more established mechanisms for setting limits on scale and dealing with large-scale environmental externalities. First, economic democracy is in a better position to limit the scale of the economy by taxing the extraction of basic materials and by setting caps on the use of various nonrenewable resources, since it would not face the same ferocious opposition from private energy companies that exists today. Using a rigorous system of caps and limits would allow the economy to continue growing in the sense of developing, without growing in the sense of increasing throughput.[10] Second, economic democracy would have a National Investment Fund to respond to major environmental externalities (e.g., by investing in large-scale mass transit systems or financing the conversion of car-producing regions to green tech companies).

In contemporary capitalism, rich countries are subject to the Huxleyesque paradox that in order to keep the economy functioning, citizens need to consume ever more (hence the inherent tension between the green movement and the labor movement (Jackson, 2009)). In the United States, for example, the average worker's productivity more than doubled between 1950 and 1990 and yet 100% of these gains were taken as increased wages for increased consumption, whereas 0% were taken as increased leisure (in fact Americans worked more hours in 1990 than they did 40 years earlier (Schor, 1991)). To encourage this, a relentless barrage of advertising and promotion of materialism is needed in order to inculcate the population with a desire for constant shopping. It is very difficult, under contemporary capitalism, to make the sensible trade-off of having less consumption for more leisure because capitalist firms prefer to hire fewer workers for more hours rather than more workers for fewer hours (since they usually have fixed overhead costs per worker from things like formal training, tacit knowledge of the workplace, etc., which makes it cheaper to hire fewer employees (Wright, 2010, p. 67)). In market socialism, however, the sensible choice for a rich society—to work less, produce and consume less (and so be more environmentally sustainable), while having more leisure—is much more structurally accessible because there is more democracy in workplaces, meaning individuals have broader options about personal work–leisure trade-offs. Instead of the typical position in both neoliberal and social democratic countries where worker productivity is rewarded every year or so with increased wages, in economic democracy workers would have the free choice to take productivity gains as more wages *or* as more time off. A democratic society is thus more able to adjust the tempo of its economy in line with the desired rhythms of people's lives, instead of working ever harder, like a hamster in a running wheel, for things no one really needs. "The trouble with the rat race" after all, "is that even if you win, you're still a rat."[11]

Notwithstanding all these advances, a market socialist society would likely retain similar levels of economic efficiency as social democracies do, since, broadly speaking, the basic source of efficiency in contemporary capitalist societies has very little to do with the existence of "capitalists" (i.e., the presence of a rich minority with power to control workplaces, finance, and investment) but rather stems from having markets comprised of decentralized firms which provide information and incentives for others to respond to. It is the existence of markets, not capitalism per se, that provide the basic grounds for allocational and innovative efficiency. And since market socialism maintains the market for allocation, while democratizing the sources of economic power, it retains the same bases of efficiency. Any loss of efficiency that workplaces might suffer from the absence of strict hierarchy is likely to be compensated for by the increased motivation and smoother coordination that comes from being one's own boss. Similarly, any incentive losses that might come from high societal taxes or the security of a basic income are likely to be more-or-less balanced by the increased productive capabilities that workers acquire from a society that invests heavily in them and in public infrastructure more generally.

That said, all of these advantages should not blind us to the fact that this society would be far from utopia. There would still be scarcity; people would not have the total freedom to "hunt in the morning, fish in the afternoon, rear cattle in the evening" (Marx & Engels, [1845] 1960), but would still need to do some work. Additionally, there would likely remain a range of troubles and injustices. For instance, the institutional changes we have talked about do nothing to address systemic issues of sexism, racism, or ableism. The new democratic structures would disproportionately benefit the most educated and articulate who can best take advantage of opportunities for democratic participation. Similarly, such structures are clearly not immune from informal hierarchy, meaning that without constant vigilance and experimentation, it is easy for informal practices of inequality (person A starting to monopolize this information or person B starting to monopolize access to those relationships, etc.) to sediment into rigid hierarchy. Finally, this society would face a range of similar external problems that social democracies face today, particularly those of global justice. If economic democracy occurs in a rich society, there are important questions to ask as to how this society should engage with an incredibly unequal world—what kind of obligations does it have toward helping to alleviate the poverty and debt of the Global South? For instance, Schweickart suggests that countries embracing economic democracy should also develop fair trade schemes to help alleviate global poverty.[12]

Yet these caveats notwithstanding, economic democracy would likely be a vastly improved society. A place where the values of *liberté, egalité, solidarité*, proudly articulated in France in 1789, would finally become more than simple decorations on European monuments and actually serve for the first time as a more-or-less (or rather, more-*than*-less) realistic description of the institutional basis of society.

Although economic democracy aims toward a socialist society that is also a market society, it is noteworthy that the conventional left-wing objections to market societies do not have much force here. There is, admittedly, still competition and greed, but these sentiments provide motivation to respond to economic information and are drained of their most pernicious consequences. There is no fear of extreme poverty or deprivation. No one suffers horribly from losing in the competition, and no one wins abundantly; there are neither beggars nor billionaires. Instead of a life-or-death struggle, competition in this society is more like an athletic race: serious, and with winners and losers, but hardly terrifying, since the winners gain no power, and the losers lose no dignity. In this society some people work hard out of noble goals (just as some do today), while some people work hard out of ugly goals, such as the desire to earn more than the person beside them to prove their superiority (just like today). But who cares? Earning more under economic democracy does not translate into more power or privilege. The crucial point is that in this society money has been depoliticized because it has been stripped of its ability to transform into power over people; it represents only consumption potential. The wealthiest person in society is able to consume more but is unable to acquire any power over anyone else. So the rich man under economic democracy is free to spend his time endlessly shining his coins in glee and self-aggrandizement, like the Businessman in *Le Petit Prince*, but his wealth grants him no power over his neighbors. So greed, under market socialism, is rendered a petty vice, instead of a social cancer.

Economic democracy is not a blueprint for a perfect order, but a direction of radical reform. Throughout this work a lot of attention has been focused on outlining possibilities for transition. The central motivation for this is the conviction that a vision of a better society is infinitely more persuasive when one can see how the institutions of today could, slowly but surely, develop toward institutions of the future. We do not need to be able to map each and every step of transition, but we do need to be able to conceive of a plausible trajectory of institutional change. This is a central strength of economic democracy: it does not require a revolutionary break in history to come into being; it could grow slowly and messily from the real institutions existing today. Recall that of its four constitutive components—co-ops, Public Community Banks, participatory investment, and a regulated market—*we already have real practical familiarity with all of them*. We have extensive knowledge of the market, solid empirical understanding of worker co-ops, a fair amount of experience with participatory investment in the form of participatory budgeting and communal councils. Democratic banks like PCBs are the least well explored, but even here we have real-world familiarity with close siblings, such as state-owned public banks and Mondragon's Caja Laboral. Economic democracy thus requires only the building up of the democratic tendencies already present in society, not a complete destruction and re-creation of society.

Such a society, it seems to me, is different enough to be worth fighting for, yet similar enough to what we know to be conceivably built from where we are today. It is concrete enough to be compelling, yet flexible enough to be adopted by activists in largely different circumstances, since there is no canonical program, only an insistence that economic power be recognized—in workplaces, financial and investment structures—and democratized where possible. The optimal methods for doing so are best left open for debate and experimentation.

Economic Alternatives and Hope for the Future

I want to bring this book to a close by suggesting that progressive people should be more engaged in thinking about systemic economic alternatives than is currently the norm. We need to spend more energy and effort conceptualizing alternatives to current forms of capitalism, including a questioning of social democracy. Such questioning should be at the very center of political debate and study, not at the margins where it presently resides. Indeed, I think there are at least three good reasons why the issue of political-economic alternatives deserves far more attention than it is presently getting.

(i) The first such reason is that there is currently insufficient recognition of the fact that the political values that most progressives now hold actually require for their realization economic institutions that go beyond familiar social democracy. For instance, some of the most widespread political value systems today fall within the broad traditions of such luminaries as J. S. Mill and John Rawls. Indeed, perhaps a majority of academics in the social sciences and humanities, as well as large numbers of regular people outside of academia, are broadly sympathetic to the core values underlying this kind of liberal egalitarianism. But what is often underappreciated is the degree to which these prevalent values imply economic alternatives that go beyond social democracy. This book has demonstrated numerous reasons for this: social democrats believe in the value of democracy for maintaining the freedoms of accountability and self-determination, yet many people in present society are compelled to be subservient in undemocratic workplaces; social democrats believe in the value of consumer democracy, yet material inequality and price distortions undermine any kind of egalitarian or fair say over what gets produced; social democrats believe in the value of citizen democracy and, more broadly, are committed to the ideal of political equality vis-à-vis societal development, yet the private control of finance and investment (the "privileged position" of business and financiers) undercuts this; social democrats believe in equal opportunity (and so require decent public services for all), yet raising sufficient funds to provide this is inherently constrained so long as the investment process remains largely in private hands. To a large degree, therefore, *social democratic values cannot be realized through social democratic institutions.*

Indeed, Mill and Rawls themselves point to such a conclusion. In Mill's words:

> The form of association, however, which if mankind continue to improve, must be expected in the end to predominate, is not that which can exist between a capitalist as chief, and work-people without a voice in the management, but the association of the labourers themselves on terms of equality, collectively owning the capital with which they carry on their operations, and working under managers elected and removable by themselves. ([1848] 1965, bk. IV, chap. 7)

Likewise, Rawls at the end of his career became much more explicit that his theory of justice—which is very widely accepted today—requires a move beyond social democracy. He says as clearly as could be that what justice actually requires is "an alternative to capitalism" (2001, p. 136). Such an alternative could take the shape of either a Property-Owning Democracy or a form of market socialism (2001, pp. 135–40)—both of which would be much more deeply egalitarian than present social democracy. Indeed, I suspect that Rawls would find very little to disagree with about economic democracy as it is described in these pages. So the point I wish to stress is there is little reason for contemporary scholars to shy away from thinking about economic alternatives when the leading lights are pushing us in precisely this direction.

(ii) The second reason to pay more attention to economic alternatives is that current economic arrangements are creating huge, systemic problems. The environment is one obvious area, where "the outer bound[s] of today's [political and economic] realism are still far shy of the inner bounds of scientific necessity" (Baer et al., 2008, p. 6). Inequality is another. Current levels of inequality in Russia, China, and the United States are actually worse than the levels that existed in Russia on the eve of the communist revolution a century ago (Nafziger & Lindert, 2012). In the United States, the top 1% controls 35% of the nation's wealth. The top 5% of households control over half of the wealth, and the top 10% control almost three-quarters of all wealth and over 80% of all financial assets. On the other hand, the bottom 40% of the population controls only 0.2% of all wealth (Blasi & Kruse, 2012; Wolff, 2010). This means that the contemporary United States is more unequal than the Roman Empire, where, during the height of its population (~150 c.e.), the top 1% controlled roughly 16% of total income (significantly less than the roughly 23% controlled by America's elite today) (Scheidel & Friesen, 2009). Perhaps most shocking of all, in 2007, the six heirs to the retail giant Walmart had the same net worth as the bottom 30% of all Americans (Allegretto, 2011). If we were to visualize individual income as being represented by people's height, so that an average income is an average height of 6-feet tall, then a third of the population would be less than 3-feet tall, the top 1% would be 35-feet tall, and the very wealthiest (those in *Forbes* magazine) would be a gargantuan 16 miles tall—three times higher than Mount Everest (Schweickart, 2011, pp. 90–93).

Inequality at such levels creates huge strains on the fabric of society. As Wilkinson and Pickett (2010) show, it corrodes social trust and brings a host of social ills, from crime to sickness. It provokes a never-ending rat race of working more to consume more in order to keep up with the Joneses, in an endless cycle that brings neither happiness (Layard, 2005), nor sustainability (Assadourian, 2010). Additionally, as Brian Barry (2005) points out in his furious final book, such high levels of inequality make a mockery of the cherished ideal of equal opportunity. And perhaps most worryingly, it concentrates power to such an extent that it threatens to undermine our very democracy—since how can democracy function between citizens who are supposed to be equals, in societies like ours where most people are tiny and a few are giants taller than mountains?

One of the fundamental reasons for caring about economic democracy in the first place is its potential for addressing much of this inequality in a systemic and systematic way. Of course, this is not to say that economic democracy has all the answers. The central thrust of economic democracy is to reduce the inequalities in economic decision-making; it is therefore mainly focused on the *social* or relational aspect of economic questions, which are mainly issues of production. But, of course, any comprehensive analysis of inequality would need to investigate the other side of the coin as well—the *individual* aspects of economic freedom (particularly in terms of issues around consumption). So, for instance, Ackerman and Alstott (2006) have critiqued investigations into economic democracy, like this one, on the grounds that things like workplace democracy do very little for the most marginalized people in society, such as the unemployed, caregivers, and the homeless. Their point is that it may well be that the biggest problem of contemporary capitalism is that of individual poverty, that is, the inability to consume (not issues of democracy per se). I have no quarrel with such a critique. Economic democracy is not meant to be a panacea and clearly cannot solve all of society's ills. As broad as it is, it is still only meant to deal with "half" of the issue—the issue of social inequality in economic decision-making. The issue of individual inequality, while clearly a complementary concern, must be worked out separately. So while I do not think that economic democracy possesses all the answers, I do think that the kind of broad, systemic analysis that it engages in is on the right track. The systemic nature of our problems makes it likely that the required changes will need to do more than simply tweak the edges of the system.

(iii) This brings us to the third reason why the question of economic alternatives deserves more attention: systemic problems require systemic solutions. Unfortunately, our culture has become largely pessimistic about the possibility of systemic political-economic alternatives. Although few people actually agree with Fukuyama (1992) that history is over, most people do find it hard to imagine a future that looks very different from the present, which, sadly, is not a very different conclusion. Toward the end of his life Richard Rorty argued that

> the most difficult task that faces us at the present time is finding a substitute for the communist utopia that Marx envisaged. Visions of that utopia stirred the imagination of half the world for more than a hundred years. Millions of honest and brave men and women died trying to bring it into existence. The collapse of communism has left us without any vision of comparable scope and power. Nobody now has doubts about the need

for market economies. But the unfairness produced by the operation of those markets is just as appalling as the Marxists said it was. Nobody, to my knowledge, has yet produced a plausible scenario in which this unfairness is gradually rectified, and in which social justice becomes possible on a global scale. (2006, pp. 378–79)

Slavoj Žižek, likewise, captures the prevailing mood perfectly when he says: "Thirty, forty years ago, we were still debating about what the future will be: communist, fascist, capitalist, whatever. Today, nobody even debates these issues. We all silently accept global capitalism is here to stay. On the other hand, we are obsessed with cosmic catastrophes: the whole life on earth disintegrating. . . . So the paradox is, that it's much easier to imagine the end of all life on earth than a much more modest . . . change in capitalism" (quoted in Taylor, 2005). This may well be true—that it is easier to envision nuclear holocaust or environmental catastrophe than deep changes to capitalism. But if this is so, it is a terrible thing to be true. It means that we, the people whom Howard Zinn called "the readers and writers of books" (1996, p. 628), have failed in our job of thinking through and constructing persuasive, poignant yet pragmatic visions of large-scale economic alternatives.

Part of the problem is pessimism, but another part is narrowness of focus. Those of us who work in the academy often find ourselves so focused on our niches that we instinctively react against any big picture thinking—and this is true whether we are engaged in political science, sociology, philosophy, geography, or elsewhere. We spend our time peering down our disciplinary microscope at the intricacies of the pebbles while the whole mountain is shaking. And when we are pushed (usually by activists outside academia) to come up with some broader ideas for alternatives, it is all too easy for us to fall back on the old trope of saying "anything more ambitious would be utopian." Roberto Unger captures the dilemma well when he says: "If I propose something distant, you may say: interesting but utopian. If I propose something close, you may answer: feasible but trivial. In contemporary efforts to think and talk programmatically, all proposals are made to seem either utopian or trivial" (2000, p. 29).

This is the paradoxical situation we find ourselves in today. A cultural pessimism and disciplinary narrowness have combined to create a mood of anti-utopianism masking itself as realism and a narrow-mindedness that is increasingly at odds with the breadth of contemporary problems. Of course, I am not advocating an embrace of utopianism in the sense of fantasizing about the future, devoid of attention to empirical and cultural realities, to the point where we allow ourselves to imagine, as Fourier once did, that the seas could be transformed into lemonade. But if any an age was in dire need of utopias, it is ours. The 19th century had its heavenly utopias of Fourier, Owen, Marx, and Bellamy. The 20th century had its nightmarish dystopias of *1984* and *Brave New World*. The 21st century needs to regain a hope in utopia—not the fixed and eternal utopia of the 19th century, but an open-ended, developing vision, expanding with our sensibilities of the scope of possibilities of human freedom. Not a candy floss utopia of heavenly paradise, but a *real utopia*, to use Erik Wright's (2010) wonderful phrase. A "real utopia" is a vision of institutions grounded in empirical reality that nevertheless contains radical emancipatory potential. A real utopia is sensitive to the material constraints, inevitable trade-offs, and inherent dilemmas that characterize social life; it is interdisciplinary and integrative, resisting the temptation to disappear down the rabbit holes of our intellectual disciplines; it is methodologically cautious and grounded, but normatively hopeful and aspiring.

Oscar Wilde (1891) said that "a map of the world that does not include Utopia is not worth even glancing at, for it leaves out the one country at which Humanity is always landing. And when Humanity lands there, it looks out, and, seeing a better country, sets sail. Progress is the realization of Utopias." That is right. We need to move away from any sense of shame in being utopian (at least in the "real utopian" sense). Rather, the shame is to retreat from the challenges of our times into our holes of comfort. The shame is for those of us privileged enough to spend our time thinking about political and social issues to shun the big questions, so that we are in fact doing little else than rearranging the deck chairs on a sinking titanic.

At its most basic level, the aspect of utopianism that we must not discard is the sense of hope—the hope that progress is possible. But progress does not fall from the sky; it can come from nowhere other than the tremendous effort of activists and intellectuals to think meticulously through alternative institutions and painstakingly build social movements to support them. Progress comes from activism (broadly understood) fueled on the energy of hope.

I cannot and would not claim that economic democracy is the only alternative worth considering. But as it is an attempt to seriously think through an aspect of real utopias, it is, I believe, a step in the right direction.

Conclusion

A decade into the 21st century the current neoliberal system seems strangely both invincible and doomed. The system has no clear competitors, and the world's elite (as well as a sizable portion of regular citizens) seem united in their conviction of the superiority of free markets and liberal politics bound together by the string of shallow political democracy.[13] Yet the extreme inequalities that exist in and between countries, and the increasing likelihood of environmental catastrophe from global warming, both undermine the apparent stability. The system seems at once unlikely to continue but unable to change course.

It is increasingly looking as though our societies have three broad possible futures. The first is to stay on the same path, driven by the inertia of the status quo, and the liberal faith in unregulated markets and avaricious people to regulate themselves, combined with the conservatism of those in power to hold onto their way of life, the blind indulgence of the middle classes, and the powerlessness of the poor to do anything about it. Unregulated global markets, mobile capital, and de-unionization create a race to the bottom destroying local safety nets and undermining social security. In the Global South, massive inequality and environmental destruction (from desertification in Africa to the sinking of large parts of Bangladesh) cause increased poverty and mass migration. In the Global North, the undermining of the welfare states combined with competition from the Global South causes islands of prosperity in seas of poverty. Both the first and third world develop gated communities and fenced off slums. Liberal values of freedom and equality continue to be preached while their material bases disintegrate more and more.

The second possibility is that environmental and social breakdown—combined with welfare state disintegration and mass immigration—lead to increasing xenophobia and social conflict, which expresses itself in a popular backlash against the status quo. The backlash is channeled by demagogues into anger at migrants and minorities and contempt for liberalism's individualism and free markets, thus bringing a desire for strong leadership and state security, culminating in authoritarianism and perhaps even fascism. The rise of the extreme Right across Europe is a particularly foreboding omen of this.

The third and most hopeful possibility is that environmental and social breakdown lead to a backlash which instead is channeled toward a radical deepening of democracy. The masses of people intimately affected by economic power demand increasing control over it. Instead of directing anger at each other, the backlash is directed at unaccountable power—multinational corporations, corrupt governments, bankers, and billionaires—demanding restitution in the form of enfranchisement: self-government in politics, self-management in economics, self-determination in general. Organs of self-management are developed throughout the economy so that the people are able to shape the market to serve the interests of the population at large: strict limits are put on the economy's scale, mass redistribution of wealth occurs, alongside transformation of firms from hierarchical corporations to democratic co-ops, and the democratization of the banks and decentralization of investment—all serving to empower those who have been previously excluded.

Of course, there is no way of knowing which of these broad possibilities is the most likely. All that we can do is start working toward the option that we would like to see. All we can do is start laying the groundwork for economic democracy so that people become better able to experiment with institutions they direct in order to further their own capacities and extend the means of controlling their own lives. All that we can do is struggle to bring this age-old aspiration of democracy—of equality and people power—a little closer to reality.

Notes

Introduction

1. The South African case is interesting since in certain respects the high hopes that the ANC inspired, about the power of political democratization to transform the country, have been disappointed. Although everyone would agree that political democracy has brought a range of vitally important improvements to the lives of the average person, it is also true that the hopes for social transformation have been undermined in many respects by the continuation of private economic power and massive economic inequality (Klein, 2007). Political democratization, in other words, has crashed headfirst into the wall of private economic power.

2. Based on Gates's 2013 wealth of roughly $67 billion, divided by the median personal income for American adults of roughly $30,000.

3. Of course, the economy is not the root of all inequalities. The institutional changes I discuss here do not directly address other systemic inequalities such as patriarchy, homophobia, racism, or ableism.

4. Throughout this book, the term "hierarchy" is understood to refer to an organization that formally institutionalizes inequality in its structure. Power and authority reside in a pyramidal structure or chain-of-command and are unaccountable to those below. The distinct levels or ranks of people acquire different material, moral, and/or cultural privileges. Examples include states (like apartheid South Africa, or contemporary Burma), traditional armies and militaries, and conventional capitalist firms. "Democracy" is understood to mean, by contrast, an organizational structure where ultimate authority resides in the collective membership in an egalitarian one-person one-vote manner. Those at the highest level are elected by and fundamentally accountable to those below. Examples include Western parliaments as well as cooperative firms. Democratic structures can range from representative and pyramidal to flat and participatory. Additionally, democratic structures can be tainted by "informal hierarchies," where informal relations of inequality exist despite the existence of formal equality, so that power and authority may be officially accountable but practically unaccountable. Most real-world democratic structures include instances of this, from patriarchy, to ableism, to the tyranny of the educated and eloquent.

5. Of course I do not mean to imply that the Left has produced no visions of alternatives in recent years; see, for example, the following visions of social democracy (Pontusson, 2011), democratic socialism (Roemer, 1994; Schweickart, 1996; Wright, 2010), Marxism (McNally, 2002), and anarchism (Albert, 2003).

Chapter 1

1. Equal formal decision-making means that decision-making authority rests, ultimately, on a one-person one-vote basis.
2. Historically, the social democratic movement emerged out of the programs of the socialist parties in Western Europe at the end of the 19th century. Over the 20th century much of the Marxian language was dropped and social democracy became largely indistinguishable from left liberalism (Sassoon, 1996).
3. In this respect Friedman perfectly echoes classical liberalism (cf. Bentham in Eccleshall, 1986, p. 139).
4. However, while Friedman says that in principle it is legitimate for the state to deal with externalities and counteract monopolies, he also argues that it is often (perhaps usually) the case that the cure is worse than the disease, in the sense that he believes state involvement will cause more harm (in terms of corruption, incompetence, inefficiency, etc.) than good. In this way he drastically circumscribes the need for state interventions in the market.
5. I am using the idea of "power over" in the basic sense that A has power over B to the extent that she can successfully get B to do something he would not otherwise do (Lukes, 2005, p. 16). See Lukes (2005) for a thorough discussion of other dimensions of power.
6. Although this perception is still widespread, it was never unanimous. For instance, Krouse and McPherson (1988) disagreed with the consensus by arguing that Rawls should be read as a kind of anti-capitalist, deeply critical of the welfare state. Indeed, in later life Rawls came to be much more explicitly radical, which I discuss below.
7. The primary goods are: (i) the basic rights and liberties, (ii) freedom of movement and free choice of occupation, (iii) powers and prerogatives of offices and positions of authority and responsibility, (iv) income and wealth, understood as all-purpose means to achieve a wide range of ends, (v) the social bases of self-respect (Rawls, 2001, pp. 58–59).
8. See chapter 3 for the supporting evidence for these claims.
9. In the literature this is sometimes referred to as "developmental" freedom (Macpherson, 1977). I prefer to talk of "self-determination" to avoid any suspicion of teleology—that freedom is about developing into something inherent or predetermined. In legal discourse "self-determination" refers to the ability of a state to exercise its sovereignty. Here the idea is applied more broadly to a variety of different associations, from small ones like workplaces to large ones like states.
10. See the fascinating work of Skinner (1998) and Pettit (1997) in reviving this tradition.
11. In the preface to the restated version of *A Theory of Justice* (1999), Rawls says that his lack of clarity on this point was a major problem with the initial work.
12. A Property-Owning Democracy is a system with widely dispersed ownership of property and capital, while liberal socialism is a system of market socialism (Rawls, 2001, Pt. IV). For an excellent discussion of Property-Owning Democracy, see O'Neill and Williamson (2012).

13. "We are not among those communists who are out to destroy personal liberty...we have no desire to exchange freedom for equality. We are convinced...that in no social order will personal freedom be so assured as in a society based upon communal ownership" (Marx and Engels, quoted in Eccleshall, 1986, p. 60). There is, of course, much debate about how exactly Marx understood freedom and emancipation—for penetrating analyses, see Lukes (1985) and Elster (1986).

14. Of course, this is not only a Marxist insight; see, for example, Lindblom (1977).

15. "Workers must not only strive for one and indivisible German republic, but also, within this republic, for the most decisive centralization of power in the hands of the state authority. They must not allow themselves to be misguided by the democratic talk of freedom for the communities, of self-government, etc." (Marx, [1850] 1978, p. 509).

16. This interpretation hinges mainly on two texts—the *Economic and Philosophical Manuscripts* ([1844] 1978), which Marx chose never to publish, and the *Civil War in France* ([1871] 1968), where Marx embraces the democratic Paris Commune in a way that struck his contemporaries as a radical change of perspective: "[the] general effect [of the Commune] was so striking that the Marxists themselves, who saw all their ideas upset by the uprising, found themselves compelled to take their hats off to it. They went even further, and proclaimed that its programme and purpose were their own....This was a truly farcical change of costume" (Michael Bakunin, 1973, p. 261). For further debate about this question, see Avineri (1968) for a view sympathetic to Marx and Nove (1991) for a critical one.

17. "Labour....obligatory for the whole country, compulsory for every worker, is the basis of socialism" (Trotsky quoted in Brinton, 1975, p. 64).

18. Again, "*Unquestioning submission* to a single will is absolutely necessary for the success of labour processes that are based on large-scale machine industry...today the Revolution demands, in the interests of socialism, that the masses *unquestioningly obey the single will* of the leaders of the labour process" (Lenin quoted in Brinton, 1975, p. 41, emphasis in original).

19. On this basis, G. D. H. Cole considered the "socialist" policies of the British Labour Party after World War II to be a failure partly because they failed to alter the major power relations in society (Dahl & Lindblom, [1953] 1976, p. 475).

20. Though not everyone shares this perspective (Albert, 2003; McNally, 1993).

21. Dual power refers to the creation of alternative or counter institutions alongside the dominant ones. While the term was initially used by Lenin ([1917] 1964), the idea has mainly resonated with anarchists and anti-authoritarian socialists as part of the attempt to build a new world in the shell of the old. Many anarchists now use the phrase interchangeably with that of "prefigurative politics."

22. For instance, David Held's *Models of Democracy*, which has become a standard text in the field, entirely passes over the contributions of anarchism (Held, 2006, p. 6).

23. Anarchists are sometimes caricatured as being against all authority. This is partly their own fault, due to overly general and passionate language. For instance, at one point Bakunin (1980) calls for "absolute rejection of every authority" (p. 76). In calmer moments, however, anarchists are, in general, not opposed to authority per se, but only to unaccountable authority. Bakunin illustrates this spirit when

he asks: "Does it follow that I reject all authority? Far from me such a thought. In the matter of boots, I refer to the authority of the bootmaker; concerning houses, canals, or railroads, I consult that of the architect or engineer....But I allow neither the bootmaker nor the architect nor the *savant* to impose his authority upon me" (quoted in Graham, 2005, p. 90). Anarchists have regularly made similar difficulties for themselves in their occasional condemnation of all power, or all organization. So care must be taken to separate their hyperbole (from which anarchists suffer more than most) from their practical proposals.

24. In Malatesta's words, "that aspiration towards unlimited freedom, if not tempered by love for mankind and by the desire that all should enjoy equal freedom, may well create rebels who, if they are strong enough, soon become exploiters and tyrants, but never anarchists" (quoted in Marshall, 2010, p. 38).

25. This characterization of Proudhon comes from James Guillaume (quoted in Mikhail Bakunin, 1980, p. 26).

26. I have translated these quotations from the French (Guérin, 1999, pp. 76 and 86).

27. In this respect anarchists are close cousins of participatory democrats. Participatory democracy is a tradition stretching from ancient Athens (James, 2005) to Rousseau ([1762] 1987), J. S. Mill ([1848] 1965), G. D. H. Cole (1920), Pateman (1970), Mansbridge (1980), and Bookchin ([1968] 2005), which emphasizes the importance of participation in political life for enhancing self-determination and spurring educational development.

Chapter 2

Portions of this chapter appeared previously in Malleson (2013a). Thanks to the editors of *Polity* for allowing the reproduction here.

1. These figures come from Wright (1997). However, his terminology is slightly different; what he refers to as the "extended managerial class" I am simply calling "professionals," and what he calls the "extended working class" I am calling "average workers." Of course, this tripartite division of the working population can be made much more fine-grained. For instance, Wright sometimes divides the class structure into three owning groups and nine working groups. But for our purposes such detail risks obscuring more than it would reveal.

2. For a calculation of a living wage, see James Lin and Jared Bernstein, "What We Need to Get By," *Economic Policy Institute* (2008). Welfare rates differ in each state—for some general information, see "Welfare Information," http://www.welfareinfo.org/payments/.

3. This management clause between the UAW and GM in 1990 is typical: "The right to hire; promote; discharge or discipline for cause; and to maintain discipline and efficiency of employees, is the sole responsibility of the Corporation except that Union members shall not be discriminated against as such. In addition, the products to be manufactured, the location of the plants, the schedules of the production, the methods, processes and means of understanding and solely and exclusively the responsibility of the Corporation" (Melman, 2001, p. 21).

4. What makes the average worker a "servant" is not simply that she follows orders, but that she is largely compelled to do so. To see this distinction, imagine a rich idiosyncratic person accepting a low-skill, low-autonomy job that she doesn't actually need, but wants to do for a lark. In such a case it would not be accurate to call this person a servant. This person retains her autonomy because she can leave at any time, and so we can be confident that she is performing the job's roles out of her own authentic desire.

5. The average American baby boomer had 11.3 jobs between the ages of 18–45 (5.5 of these between the ages of 18–24) (BLS, 2012). Nevertheless, with the exception of self-employment, it is likely that all of these jobs were for hierarchical firms.

6. Religious organizations might be a partial exception.

7. Kant defines "sapere aude" as the exhortation to "have the courage to use your own understanding" (Reiss, 1970). Mill expresses a similar hostility to subservience in *On Liberty* (1998).

8. Of course, different people will have different evaluations about what kind of work they enjoy or dislike, so balancing cannot be done with mathematical precision, but nevertheless there are often jobs that most people agree are unpleasant—washing the dishes, scrubbing the floors, taking out the trash, etc. An important advantage of democratic workplaces over conventional firms is that they allow for increased deliberation to identify the agreements that do exist in this regard, and then if the majority wishes, to implement some mechanism to share the benefits and burdens more equitably.

9. Co-ops with 50–75% members are in a grey area. It seems to me that these can be considered genuine co-ops only if the nonmembers can become members after a reasonable period. Of course, this numerical breakdown is only a rule-of-thumb. It is possible to imagine a co-op where 60% of the workers are nonmembers, but who nevertheless share in all the day-to-day decision-making in a one-person one-vote manner, and are only excluded from long-term strategic investment decision-making—this could still be a highly democratic workplace.

10. See, e.g., Van Parijs (1995). It is interesting to note here that basic income proposals, which are usually intended to increase individual freedom, complement proposals to increase workplace democracy; so this is an interesting instance where real utopian visions—of economic freedom and economic democracy—may well support each other.

11. In practice workplace democracy has rarely been successful without collective ownership due to the difficulties of establishing regular, secure financing in a capitalistic environment, as well as the difficulties in maintaining sufficient incentives without a material stake in the firm's ownership (Dow, 2003). For example, in the first 30 years of Mondragon's existence only three co-ops failed (out of more than a hundred). At least one of the failures was attributed to the fact that workers did not put up a large enough material stake in the firm, so it became an established requirement for workers to put up roughly 20% of the starting capital (Campbell et al., 1977; Morrison, 1997).

12. This is an important category as it made up (in 2000) about 15% of the American workforce, 21% of the Canadian, and 31% of the Swedish (Gomes, 2010, p. 3).

13. This was proposed by Tony Benn, Secretary of State for Industry, in Britain in the 1970s (Benn & Mullin, 1979). In chapter 4 we further discuss the issue of the degree to which consumers should have a say in economic decision-making.

14. Although there is a common prejudice against the idea that publicly owned firms can be efficient, there is much evidence to the contrary, from Renault in France to Singapore Airlines. Indeed, in today's fastest growing economy, China, state-owned enterprises account for 40% of national output (Chang, 2007; Cohen, 2010).

15. Just as in the United States, Western European countries have experimented with "worker participation" in various forms—some even have a system of co-determination for large firms. To the extent that these programs have actually increased workers' influence in firm decision-making they are praiseworthy, but none of them are meant to actually democratize work in the genuine sense of providing actual equal status or influence for workers. As we will see in the next chapter, co-determination has allowed workers increased access to information, but no ability to veto management plans, much less to actually elect or remove managers.

16. The first figure is derived from the number of worker co-ops existing in Sweden in the early 1990s (about 100) compared with the total number of private enterprises (about 55,000) (Johansson, 1997; Stryjan, 1990). For the second figure, 1.95%, of the 6.4% of the general adult population on assistance in 1987, received social assistance for 10 consecutive years (Andren & Gustafsson, 2004).

17. Likewise, regulations are blunt but often useful tools for the defense of workers' freedoms. But just like unions, their strength lies in their ability to defend and protect; they are largely inadequate in terms of fostering self-determination.

18. For workers to buy out their firms, even with state support, would require a financial commitment. It would likely require a significant degree of savings over a number of years, and since a worker's savings would have to be plowed back into the firm to gradually acquire ownership shares, she is potentially at risk by putting all her eggs (her job and her savings) in one basket. The lack of diversification means increased risk. So the normal risk-adverse worker may well prefer to continue working in an undemocratic firm. This is, of course, a choice she should be free to make. That said, successful co-op networks engage in substantial cross-investment precisely in order to reduce such risks.

19. Consider, for example, the massive campaign waged by the Swedish business class against the proposed plan for increasing economic democracy through wage-earner funds (Pontusson & Kuruvilla, 1992).

20. However, while the average American worker does want more influence at work, she does not currently share my perspective that workplace democracy is the answer. Indeed, the authors find that the vast majority (85%) of workers would prefer a firm "run jointly" by employees and management than one run "by employees alone" (10%) (Freeman & Rogers, 1999, p. 56). I suspect this has less to do with any actual antipathy toward co-ops than simply reflecting a lack of familiarity with them.

21. For empirical evidence that self-employment increases independence and work satisfaction, see Hundley (2001) and Benz and Frey (2008).

22. Although the language of "renting humans" sounds strange to our ears, this is precisely what is involved in the employment contract. Even Paul Samuelson, the

neoclassical economist par excellence, recognizes this: "Wages are the rentals paid for the use of a man's personal services for a day or a week or a year" (quoted in Ellerman, 1992, p. 95).

23. Whether expropriation is always unjust is a question that is beyond the scope of this chapter. At present it seems clear that large-scale expropriation of business property would be unacceptable to the vast majority of the population—thus making it undemocratic. Slow, incremental changes seem to me to have much more potential for actually improving the conditions of working people.

24. However, there is good reason to be skeptical of this. For example, Nobel prize winner Daniel Kahneman researched the performance of 25 well-paid wealth advisers over eight years and found that the consistency of their performance was nonexistent: "The results resembled what you would expect from a dice-rolling contest, not a game of skill" (Kahneman, 2011). Moreover, if remuneration was really due to expertise, it would be difficult to explain the explosion of high pay for CEOs in the United States (but not other countries) over the last several decades, since it is hard to believe that they have suddenly become more expert than all other American workers (or CEOs in other countries). A much more plausible explanation for their income is not their expertise but the use of stock options and other devices that have essentially allowed American CEOs to write their own paychecks (Baker, 2006; Chang, 2010).

Chapter 3

1. The intuitive idea here is that the more people employed means the more that the profits are shared out—so co-op members will have incentives to shrink their membership to get a bigger slice of the pie. Vanek and Robinson were quick to point out that even theoretically this argument makes little sense, as it would require co-operatives, which are organizations based on solidarity, to self-mutilate in order to make more money (Bonin & Putterman, 1987).

2. Although these are the most famous networks of worker cooperatives, such networks exist all over. For instance, one of the most well-known in the United States is the Evergreen cooperative network in Cleveland, Ohio. There are also cooperatives movements in South America—particularly in Venezuela (Malleson, 2010; Piñeiro, 2009) and Argentina (Vieta, 2010). Unfortunately, the empirical research into these cases is still preliminary.

3. This section is drawn from Malleson (2013b). Thanks to the publishers for permission to reproduce parts of it here.

4. The most critical account of Mondragon is Kasmir (1996), who makes a classical Marxist argument to the effect that Mondragon fosters middle-class values and undermines the larger working-class union movement without fundamentally challenging the worker–manager class divide.

5. For example, in 1985 the CL was offering loans to its member co-ops at a maximum rate of 13%, 8% for special sectors, and free of interest for very special cases, compared to the prevailing market rate of 18% (Ammirato, 1996, p. 48). From the 1990s, the CL's Empresarial division was moved to other institutional locations in

Mondragon, and the focus on creating new co-ops shifted to sustaining existing ones (Freundlich, 1998).

6. Originally, 10% of workers were allowed to be nonmembers, in order to ensure flexibility for things such as seasonal work, though, as we will see, this changed dramatically in later years.

7. For 30 years the internal ratio between the highest- and lowest-paid workers could not exceed 3:1. This has loosened in recent years to 6:1 (and 9:1 in a very few cases) (Flecha & Cruz, 2011).

8. Education is a foundational value. Indeed the co-ops grew out of schools set up by Arizmendiarrieta, who even went so far as to characterize cooperativism as "an educational movement that uses economic action" (quoted in Morrison, 1997, p. 15). This emphasis has continued. For instance, in recent years it has been reported that investment in continuous training in Mondragon represents 2.7% of the wage bill (compared with averages of 1.2% for Spanish firms and 1.6% in EU companies) (Arando et al., 2010, p. 36).

9. In the early years this investment was equivalent to roughly double a member's annual earnings (Dow, 2003, p. 59). Today it is roughly one year's earnings at the co-ops lowest pay rate, approximately 14,000 euros. Efforts are made to ensure that the membership fee is never an insurmountable barrier to membership. For instance, new members can often make this investment through wage deductions spread out over a period of five years (Arando et al., 2011, p. 7).

10. The Plywood co-ops were structured like normal corporations on the basis of individual-owned shares (the difference being that no shares were owned by outsiders) (Bellas, 1972; Berman, 1967). This meant that each member owned a share which gave him or her membership rights (to elect the management of the firm) as well as property rights (as owners of the firm's assets). The problem is that when these co-ops were successful, the value of the shares rose hugely. And since the firms were structured so that the shares gave both membership and property rights, expensive shares meant that membership itself became very exclusive. In this case, shares of the plywood co-ops went as high as $95,000 (often requiring $20,000 down-payment) (Ellerman, 1997). This meant that retiring workers could not find new members who could afford to purchase the shares; thus shares were sold to outsider speculators (in which case the firm degenerated quickly), or were not sold at all, and new employees were hired as nonmembers (in which case the firm degenerated slowly). This is why Vanek calls firms of this structure "mules"—they are hybrids of capitalistic individual-style ownership with cooperative practices, which due to their structure find themselves unable to reproduce another generation (Ellerman, 1984, p. 258).

11. In a Mondragon co-op, members have two analytically distinct sets of rights: membership rights (to governance) and property rights, which do not give individuals a claim to a portion of the assets (like in conventional firms) but give individuals a claim to a share of the post-tax profits. Should a co-op dissolve, the proceeds from the sale of its assets cannot go to co-op members but, according to Basque law, must stay in the regional co-op federation.

12. The bulk of these nonmembers (about 30,000 of them) are in Spain working for the Eroski retail chain. There are also about 12,000 nonmembers working in foreign affiliates, largely in the Global South (Arando et al., 2010).

13. An additional obstacle is the financial difficulty that many foreign workers face in making investments at anywhere near the same level that Basque members can make given the massive differences in relative purchasing power.

14. The General Council is the executive management of the entire Mondragon corporation. It is elected by the Governing Councils of the Groups and Divisions, which, in turn, have been elected by Governing Councils of individual cooperatives (Freundlich et al., 2009).

15. Although as we discuss below, this is starting to change with the attempt to cooperativize Eroski.

16. One note of caution in this regard is Morris (1992, p. 53), who claims that the co-ops may have been less efficient than some of their international, particularly Japanese, competitors. The most recent comparative empirical account, Arando et al. (2011), finds certain Mondragon co-ops to be more efficient than comparable conventional firms, and others to not be significantly different.

17. This has not substantially changed over the two periods. Currently the top salary for Mondragon managers is 6:1, although a few CEOs do earn up to 9:1. In the industrial group, which is the largest group in Mondragon, 67% of workers earn between the lowest rate and double that rate, while 30% earn up to 3.5 times the lowest rate, and only 3% earn between 3.5 and 6 times that rate (Flecha & Cruz, 2011).

18. See chapter 5 for a more thorough discussion of the ramifications of globalization for economic democracy.

19. It has been estimated that locally oriented economic activity makes up about 60% of total economic activity (in the United States)—and this is likely to increase as the importance of manufacturing in northern economies shrinks and the importance of services increases (Alperovitz, 2005, p. 126).

20. Of course, this is somewhat speculative since there is very little data (beyond the memories of present members) of what members thought of their workplaces during the 1960s and 1970s.

21. There is an important debate about whether Mondragon has really "degenerated" (Malleson, 2013b). I think that the current proportion of nonmembers means that, speaking in strict organizational terms, it has degenerated; nevertheless, such a label is arguably too pejorative given the efforts of generations of members who have achieved major cooperative victories in the face of extremely difficult circumstances. Especially since it may well be that the majority of Mondragon remains deeply committed to democratic ideals and is doing all that is possible to preserve them in adverse market conditions (indeed, I am sympathetic to such a perspective).

22. Chapters 4 and 5 develop this argument in more depth.

23. The International Cooperative Alliance, founded in 1895, represents co-ops world wide.

24. More recently, Maietta and Sena (2008) find similar evidence that Italian co-ops tend to be more efficient than conventional firms. However, the picture is not totally clear-cut; Jones (2007) is one of the few studies to find lower productivity among the co-ops.

25. For example, between 1945 and 1947, co-ops received only 0.83% of the total state funds provided to finance business (Ammirato, 1996, p. 83).

26. For instance, Bartlett et al. (1992, p. 113) report that government subsidy is respon-
    sible for an average of 5.6% of finance for the cooperatives, whereas it is responsible
    for 6.4% for private firms.

27. A similar critique is often made of Mondragon and other co-ops. Yet it is important
    to point out that low attendance at Assemblies is not necessarily a sign of demo-
    cratic decay. It may be the case that people are not attending because they are disil-
    lusioned and think participation is meaningless; but it may also be the case that the
    real participation happens elsewhere, in regular, smaller meetings leading up to the
    Assemblies. After all, an occasional, large Assembly is hardly the place for sustained
    deliberation; for large workplaces, it would be impossible for such Assemblies to be
    anything other than routine and symbolic. The crux of the issue is the quality of
    participation surrounding the Assemblies: whether there are meaningful opportu-
    nities for rank-and-file members to learn about the issues, for different positions to
    be heard, evaluated, deliberated, and then voted on.

28. There are very few studies that find the opposite—that co-ops are less productive
    than comparable firms—but such studies do exist (D. C. Jones, 2007; D. C. Jones &
    Backus, 1977).

29. For instance, Greenberg (1986) recounts how in one firm which used to be a co-op
    but was transformed into a conventional firm, the first thing the new manage-
    ment did was to quadruple the number of supervisors. In the words of the General
    Manager (who used to be a manager in the co-op): "We need more foremen because,
    in the old days, the shareholders supervised themselves....They cared for the
    machinery, kept their areas picked-up, helped break up production bottlenecks all
    by themselves. That's not true anymore...we've got to pretty much keep on them
    all of the time" (p. 44).

30. Indeed, there is strong indirect evidence for this in the case of shared capital-
    ism, i.e., firms that are not co-ops but directly tie workers' remuneration to the
    firm's performance (through profit-sharing or stock purchases, etc.). Almost half
    of American private sector employees participate in some form of shared capital-
    ism so it is much less marginal than co-ops. And even though these firms have
    weaker worker ownership and worker decision-making than co-ops, the largest
    empirical study to date (surveying over 40,000 workers in shared capitalist firms)
    still finds empirical support for significant productivity advantages (Freeman,
    Blasi, & Kruse, 2010).

31. In such a context as this, a CEO will make in a mere month's work the same amount
    as a worker will earn in 30 years—an entire career. Note also that these figures actu-
    ally understate the differences in inequality, since the statistics for conventional
    firms are comparing top to average, not top to bottom.

32. Bartlett et al. (1992) report that "cooperatives appear to have stronger links with
    the local economy: they are less export oriented, have higher shares of sales to
    local buyers, and are more likely to recruit unemployed labour than private firms"
    (p. 116).

33. The best way to grasp the subtle issues at play in the operation of democracy at
    work, the successes as well as the failures, is not through large-scale empirical stud-
    ies, which though eminently useful for other things lack the specificity and rich

detail that case studies offer. Some of the most insightful and nuanced of such case studies are Rothschild and Whitt (1986), Holmstrom (1989), Cheney (1999), Varman and Chakrabarti (2004), and Schoening (2010).

34. Another kind of informal hierarchy that often forms in democratic organizations is that of the tyranny of the eloquent. This will be discussed further in later chapters.

35. This kind of problematic utopianism is apparent in much of Marxism. See Marx and Engels ([1845] 1960) and Braverman (1974). For a powerful critique, see Nove (1991). See as well the Mandel/Nove debate (Mandel, 1986; Nove, 1987).

36. In technical language, the issue is that forming a co-op is a collective action problem in the form of a public good. Private actors do not have incentives to provide the good because the benefits of such provision cannot be privately appropriated (Schwartz, 2012).

37. In many jurisdictions, co-ops are legally allowed to sell shares, but they generally choose not to do so since bringing in "alien" capital undermines the democratic nature of the co-op by giving outside nonworker shareholders a say in the firm's decision-making.

38. Bowles and Gintis (1996) point out that co-ops will inevitably have higher financing costs because bankers have to deal with not just a single owner, but with many— which raises risk premiums.

39. See note 10.

40. Like everything about Venezuela, the numbers are hotly contested, so the figure cited here is a conservative estimate—about half the official state figure (Müller, 2007; Piñeiro, 2009). If this figure is accurate, it represents enormous cooperative growth.

41. According to Piñeiro (2005), the *Vuelvan Caras* Mission graduated 260,000 students in 2005 with training in various technical, managerial, citizenship, and cooperative studies. The students were encouraged to form cooperatives and nearly 70% did, resulting in 7,600 new cooperative businesses. (Although, again, numbers coming out of Venezuela should always be taken with a grain of salt.)

42. Perhaps on the model that once 50%-plus-1 of the workers indicate their desire for it, there is a legal right to a referendum amongst the workforce about whether to engage in a buyout.

43. The Meidner Plan was initially proposed by the Swedish Social Democratic Party in the late 1970s. I discuss it in more detail in chapter 6.

44. This has been a problem in Venezuela, where government exuberance to fund co-ops, particularly among marginalized people, has far exceeded any careful monitoring (not to mention any technical or entrepreneurial support in actually setting up successful businesses), resulting in tens of thousands of co-ops either failing rapidly or existing only on paper in order to avoid taxes (Müller, 2007; Piñeiro, 2009).

Chapter 4

1. This phrase has become widespread. Its origin is attributed to Beveridge's work on the welfare state (1948, p. 322).

2. This is not meant to be a comprehensive list of market failures. Important additional failures exist in terms of asymmetrical information (Stiglitz, 2002b), bubbles (Hahnel, 1999), and so on. The purpose of this list is to emphasize the failures that consistently undermine the market's democratic potential.

3. For instance, one recent study by Muller, Mendelsohn, and Nordhaus (2011) shows that even ignoring the costs of climate change, the externalized health costs of certain American industries (particularly coal-generated electricity) are actually greater than the entire value-added of these industries—meaning that market prices in these industries are allocating resources, and inducing consumers to make purchases, in an incredibly perverse manner.

4. For example, Baldacci et al. (2008) show that, internationally, an increase in education spending of 1% of GDP is associated with three more years of schooling and an average increase in the annual growth of GDP per capita of 1.4%. However, the full impact materializes only after 10–15 years, thus making long-term planning indispensable.

5. This was pointed out long ago by Rousseau who drew a distinction between the "general will" and the "will of all" (Rousseau, [1762] 1987). A similar idea is captured by Sen's (1961) "isolation paradox."

6. Joe Carens's fascinating work *Equality, Moral Incentives, and the Market* (1981) is an important investigation into these issues.

7. Although it is beyond the scope of this chapter, it is worth pointing out that another important mechanism for providing consumers with some accountability over production is via consumer cooperatives. Consumer co-ops, like Mountain Equipment Co-op in Canada, are businesses that are owned and controlled by the members who shop there. Particularly in the short term, consumer co-ops are one of the most promising routes to increase the amount of democratic and egalitarian oversight of consumers over business. Indeed, in a number of places, like North America, it is easier to envision a spread of consumer co-ops (perhaps galvanized by friendly tax breaks) than it is to envision an increase in consumer democracy through the market which would require significant redistribution of wealth.

8. Ellen Wood (1999) offers a penetrating analysis of the origin of capitalism. Although she differs from Polanyi in various respects she too highlights the importance of state involvement—particularly in terms of the importance of the enclosure movement.

9. More precisely, scale refers to "the physical volume of the throughput, the flow of matter-energy from the environment as low-entropy raw materials, and back to the environment as high-entropy wastes" (Daly, 1992, p. 186).

10. The increasingly clear scientific consensus is that without a 90% drop in our carbon emissions in the next couple of decades we will inevitably see a 2% rise in temperature, which is the critical tipping point at which many of our ecosystems may start to collapse. The interior of the Amazon Basin will become void of vegetation, two billion people will face water shortages, countries like Bangladesh will get flooded, de-housing millions and millions, and on and on (Monbiot, 2006).

11. The world currently extracts the equivalent of 112 Empire State Buildings from the earth every single day; 60 billion tons of resources are extracted annually. This is about 50% more than just 30 years ago and is growing all the time (Assadourian, 2010).

12. For instance, in standard Marxist fashion, Wood (1999) claims that "once the market is established as an economic 'discipline' or 'regulator'... even workers who own the means of production, individually or collectively, will be obliged to respond to the market's imperatives—to compete and accumulate, to let 'uncompetitive' enterprises and their workers go to the wall" (p. 119).

13. The next chapter examines this institutional variability more closely.

14. According to Tuttle, the proportion of the workforce under age 18 was close to 50% for the entire period 1835–50. According to Horrell and Humphries, more than 10% of 5–9 year-old children and more than 75% of 10–14 year-olds were in the labor force (for these statistics see Humphries, 2003).

15. The most influential legislation to reduce child labor were the Factory Acts of 1833, 1844, and 1874 (Humphries, 2010; Kirby, 2003).

16. Of course, an important issue today is that competition is structured not simply by a domestic market system, but by an international system as well. The next chapter discusses the implications of globalization for the prospects of economic democracy.

Chapter 5

1. Although there are many ways to characterize the varieties of capitalism, I follow here the distinction used by Pontusson (2005). SMEs are divided into Nordic and Continental, the latter of which includes Austria, Belgium, Germany, the Netherlands, and Switzerland.

2. Robin Hahnel (2010b) makes the case that progressives should theoretically prefer taxes over cap-and-trade programs, but that in practice it is much more likely to get progressive results from cap-and-trade programs. The reason for this is that if the issue is a cap, the relevant experts are the scientists (which is usually a good thing), whereas if the issue is a tax, the relevant experts are the economists (which is usually a bad thing from a progressive environmentally sensitive point of view).

3. There was a small annual auction for allowances—representing only 2–3% of quotas—which was designed to "jump-start" the market. The funds raised by the auction were given back to firms in proportion to their allowances (Joskow et al., 1998).

4. Some environmentalists have argued against the very idea of a cap-and-trade system on the basis that it is immoral to sell the rights to pollute (Goodin, 1994; Sandel, 1997). While it may be true that some kinds of pollution (such as coal) are so damaging to the environment that there is a case for an outright ban, other kinds of pollution, such as carbon dioxide, are not like this. We do not want to stop carbon emission absolutely—that would spell the end of industrial society—but to limit it to safe and sustainable amounts. Goodin (1994) is right, then, to argue that while we cannot allow the market to decide on what the caps should be (they must be chosen scientifically through non-market institutions), a cap-and-trade system may well be an effective policy enforcement mechanism once the caps are chosen elsewhere.

5. For example, the initial cap-and-trade program for certain New Zealand fisheries (called "individual transferable quotas") worked by giving private fishers a fixed

annual quota of the total fishing stock—essentially giving private interests a right to a part of the commons in perpetuity. This means that in order for the amount of overall fishing to decline the government itself has to purchase some of these quotas back from private fishers (Newell, Sanchirico, & Kerr, 2005).

6. The Greenhouse Development Rights (GDR) framework is a proposal for sharing the cost of dealing with global warming in a manner that is just and fair by taking into account a country's responsibility for causing global warming (its climate debt) as well as its capacity for fixing it (with the assumption that people below a poverty threshold have a primary right to development and so should have less obligation to reduce their emissions). The basic idea is that the GDR allows for a clear and logical calculation of every country's responsibility via a Responsibility Capacity Index, which can then serve as a basis for paying for climate costs or setting national caps (Baer et al., 2008).

7. It might be objected that market societies are never likely to achieve perfect equality, and so can never be truly democratic in the sense of every participant having precisely the same number of dollar-votes. Strictly speaking this is true, but it is also true that increasing equality would increase consumer democracy. The fact that we may never reach perfection should not prevent us from aiming for real improvement.

8. Unless otherwise stated, the statistics in this section are drawn from Pontusson's *Inequality and Prosperity* (2005).

9. OECD, 2012b. Statistics for Australia and Ireland are from 2010.

10. The contrast is most extreme between Sweden and the Netherlands. Sweden spends only 65% of its total social spending on transfers, whereas the Netherlands spent 98%. On the other hand, Sweden employs a massive 20% of adults in welfare-related government services, whereas the Netherlands employs only 4% (Pontusson, 2005, p. 147).

11. The Nordic countries used to have a distinctive system of corporatist centralized union bargaining. Over the last couple of decades, however, this has largely been decentralized and now more closely resembles the Continental countries. However, union membership has remained high in the Nordic countries and because of this they have retained a strong capacity to *coordinate* collective bargaining (Martin & Thelen, 2007; Pontusson, 2011).

12. This is why the decline in union density across Europe does not spell doom for the welfare state, since by all measures the levels of union coverage remain very high.

13. Chang makes this point with regard to development in his excellent work on the subject, *Bad Samaritans* (2007).

14. For example, public investment in education has meant that the Nordic countries not only have the highest mean scores in literacy rates in the OECD, but they also have the most compressed distribution of test scores (Pontusson, 2011, p. 97).

15. Unfortunately, not all caps have been successful. For example, Phase I of the European Union Emissions Trading Scheme totally failed to limit carbon emissions as the cap was actually higher than existing levels of emissions (Jones et al., 2007).

16. Statistics from this paragraph and the next are from Pontusson (2005) and the OECD (2012b).

17. For example, in 1999, the CEO of the Swedish telecommunication firm Ericsson made a total salary of $1.1 million while the CEO of Motorola, an American competitor, made $58.9 million (Randoy & Nielsen, 2002).

18. In addition, the region has been a world leader in the move toward providing social services through social co-ops, which are organizations that are state funded but democratically controlled in a decentralized manner by the workers and users of the services (Gonzales, 2010). In Bologna, 87% of the city's social services are now provided through municipal contracts with social co-ops (Restakis, 2010).

19. A third issue that appears in the literature is the idea that the mobility of financial capital makes it harder for states to engage in deficit financing. The idea is that globalization makes it easier for financiers to sell any particular country's debt and invest elsewhere, leading to increased risk premiums for states that engage in expansionary (and therefore potentially inflationary) policies (Garrett, 1998). Skeptics, however, find this unpersuasive, arguing that internationalization of capital markets makes deficit spending cheaper, rather than more expensive, because it gives governments access to a much larger pool of capital (Genschel, 2004).

20. While tariffs are still often used today, the establishment of various free trade regimes, such as the North American Free Trade Agreement, and the World Trade Organization makes it harder for countries to unilaterally impose them.

21. The development of the East-Asian countries—particularly Japan, South Korea, Taiwan, and Singapore—after World War II was the fastest economic transformation in history. These countries made extensive use of tariffs and other kinds of state instruments to guide their development and shelter their economies from global competition (Chang, 2006).

22. Transfer pricing is the practice of multinational companies using their subsidiaries in different countries to over or under charge each other so as to ensure that profits occur in the places with the lowest taxes. Notorious examples of transfer pricing include a US firm exporting bulldozers to itself for $528 apiece, and a Japanese firm importing tweezers from a subsidiary at $4,896 each (Chang, 2007).

23. Whereas the statutory rate is the legal amount that companies must pay, the effective rate is a measure of what they actually do pay. In Garrett and Mitchell's words, "the effective capital tax rate is calculated as the sum of households' capital income taxes, corporate income taxes, taxes on immovable property, and taxes on financial and capital transaction, divided by the total operating surplus of the economy (i.e., profits)" (2001, pp. 158–59).

24. However, there is no consensus on this (Hansson & Olofsdotter, 2004; Swank, 2002).

25. For the 34 nations of the OECD, total tax revenue went from 25.5% of GDP in 1965 to 35.1% in 2007—an increase of 38% (OECD, 2012a, pp. 96–100).

26. It is possible for governments to switch to a taxation model based not on the origin of corporate income but the destination of corporate products. This would allow for economic integration without a race to the bottom (Genschel & Schwarz, 2011).

Chapter 6

1. For a good analysis of the Venezuelan economy during the Chavez years, see Weisbrot (2009). Although these actions came close to toppling the government, Chavez was eventually able to renationalize oil, implement capital controls, and reassure private business that they would not be expropriated, resulting in substantial economic growth in the subsequent five years.

2. This distinction is similar to the famous distinction between positive and negative freedom (Berlin, 1969).

3. For instance, Sherman et al.'s well-known text follows this distinction (2008, p. 386). Although buying stock is usually called "investing," this is conceptually misleading because it conflates the providing of money with the actual spending of that money for real productive purposes. It is often the case that one can buy shares, without that act having any consequence whatsoever for the firm's actual productive capacity. This is why it should be called "finance" not "investment."

4. In Canada, this happened in 1990 (Stanford, 1999, p. 26).

5. For evidence of the effectiveness of fiscal stimulus during the Great Recession, see Romer (2011).

6. For example, say a banker lends $1,000 to X today. At this time that money can buy, e.g., one computer. At the end of the year, X pays back the $1,000 (plus an interest payment). However, if there has been substantial inflation the banker's $1,000 is now worth less (because the same computer now costs, say, $1,100). So in effect, inflation has made the banker poorer in real terms.

7. This is not to say that inflation is never a problem. Very high levels of inflation, so-called "hyperinflation" is disastrous because it makes it basically impossible for a market economy to function since the price signals, which are the basic data of such systems, become totally unreliable. However, the evidence shows that modest levels of inflation, below roughly 20%, do not pose serious problems for growth or employment (Bruno, 1995; Stiglitz, 1998). On the contrary, it is generally much better for the population as a whole to have lower unemployment with higher levels of inflation than the other way around (Hahnel, 2002).

8. Of course, currency depreciation can be expansionary because even though it makes imports more expensive it makes exports cheaper, and so boosts the competitiveness of local exporters. So with totally open borders monetary policy can still have an expansionary effect, but only through lowering the currency (and so only at the cost of currency depreciation and potential inflation).

9. Fiscal stimulus is still possible through tax cuts, but this is not usually compatible with the broader goals of progressive governments.

10. According to Bob Woodward (1995), Clinton is said to have responded to this news in a half-whisper: "You mean to tell me that the success of my program and my reelection hinges on the Federal Reserve and a bunch of fucking bond traders?" (p. 73).

11. However, a number of economists, such as Paul Krugman, have pointed out that while bond vigilantes can strike (making borrowing harder) it is unlikely that they could cause a country with its own currency (and debts denominated in that currency) to fall into recession. If bond vigilantes do strike in such countries, the result need not be a rise in interest rates (since these can be determined by the country's own monetary policy) but by a depreciation of the currency. This might be inflationary but it is also likely to expand, not contract, the economy as a depreciated currency helps exporters become more competitive (Krugman, 2012a, 2012b).

12. The fact that most financiers see their activities in terms of rational self-interest, not as politically motivated "attacking" of government policy, in no way changes

the real impact that they have. People who drive 100 km/hr through residential neighborhoods are not consciously attacking the safety of that community; they are acting in ways that are in some ways rational (getting from A to B as quickly as possible). But their potential impact on the community is still detrimental enough that such actions are legitimately restrained.

13. Currency attack is particularly dangerous for developing countries. If a small country's currency is attacked, the prices of local goods can become massively devalued; this allows foreign investors and speculators (usually from the Global North) to come in and buy everything at rock bottom prices, causing a shift of ownership and control from the Global South to Global North, and thereby threatening to undo many of the gains of the anti-imperialist era (Hahnel, 1999).

14. The old South Korean law threatening execution for breaching foreign exchange controls is a case in point (Chang, 2007, p. 14).

15. Financiers tend to justify their salaries on the basis that they are experts in managing risk, the results of which produce large benefits for the real economy. But, of course, given that these so-called expert risk-managers recently misjudged risk to such a colossal extent that they sunk half the world in recession, there are clearly valid questions to be asked about the real contribution of the financial sector (Haldane & Madouros, 2011).

16. Even the United States recognized the public nature of finance to some degree by making racial redlining illegal and instituting the Community Reinvestment Act of 1977, which required banks to apply the same lending criteria in all communities.

17. Such institutional problems are compounded by the realization that market failures are in fact not at all rare—they are pervasive. The mainstream view that externalities are rare is part of an "empty world" view of economics (Hahnel, 2011). Indeed the most celebrated proposition of welfare economics—that a competitive market economy will be socially efficient—is only valid when externalities are nonexistent. It is perhaps understandable that Adam Smith gave little thought to externalities living in a world of 800 million people, but in our contemporary world of 7 billion, it is incredibly unrealistic to think that our economic relations do not constantly affect other people. On the pervasiveness of externalities, see Arge and Hunt (1971).

18. Schweickart's system thus allocates finance and investment through a mixture of public planning and private markets. The basic picture is that each level of government decides on a portion of funds to invest in public goods, and a portion to pass down to the next level of government. At the municipal level, the funds are divided between public investment, allocated by the city, and public finance, allocated by the banks to private (mainly cooperative) firms. So although new investment is publicly controlled—which he estimates at about 10–15% of GDP (2011, p. 52), the bulk of regular economic activity is not state planned but controlled by private firms operating in a market.

19. While more accountability would be a good thing, this is not to say that financial institutions need to provide avenues for strong democratic participation (Barber, 1984). Banks are not like workplaces; we do not spend huge amounts of time in our banks, nor are we likely to feel unfree from being excluded from participating in

the nitty-gritty of loan dispersals. One's concern with a bank's financing decisions is less personal and acute than it is a broad and general interest in the community's future development. The different impacts of these associations on our lives imply different democratic requirements.

20. In 2009, Paul Volcker, former Chairman of the Federal Reserve, famously declared that "the only useful thing banks have invented in the last 20 years is the ATM" (Popik, 2010).

21. In terms of general efficiency, Block (1996) makes the additional point that private banks have incentives to economize on the information they collect. And since this information is the basis of loan allocation, this can be a big problem. Competition between private banks means that there is pressure to collect information more cheaply than one's competitors (so if a new bank starts doing something profitable, like saving money by spending less time discerning the credit-worthiness of people and just giving subprime mortgages far and wide, this creates significant pressure for other banks to follow suit—as actually happened, in recent years, with disastrous results). In public banks, on the other hand, there may well be stronger incentives to acquire reliable information.

22. Examples of how audits for both financial and social goals could function have been discussed by Schreiner (2002) and Woller (2006).

23. I say "basically no" because most states do provide some public investment (though this usually allows for only very limited input from regular people).

24. This is currently very difficult given that most Central Banks are, problematically, independent from government, and therefore from democratic accountability, in their policy setting (Stiglitz, 1998; Weisbrot, 2010).

25. As an alternative to relying on fiscal and monetary policy, some economists have proposed a jobs guarantee, whereby the government takes on the role of being the employer of last resort by offering minimum wage jobs to anyone who wants to work (e.g., Mitchell & Muysken, 2008).

Chapter 7

1. In the United Kingdom, nearly 500,000 public sector jobs were cut; in France, the retirement age was raised; in Greece, public pensions and bonuses were frozen while taxes were raised; in Spain, government workers faced a 5% pay cut while personal income taxes were increased; in Romania, government wages were cut 25% and pensions 15%, and so on (BBC, 2010).

2. The economic literature on the costs and benefits of capital controls is large and I cannot do justice to all its nuances here. For a good survey, see Epstein et al. (2003) and Palley (2009).

3. For instance, Indonesia after the Asian crisis, saw 20 million people join the ranks of the poor (Singh, 2000, p. 49). The costs of the 2008 financial-cum-economic crisis have yet to be calculated, but are sure to be astronomical. And now, just like then, the countries that are recovering best are ones that have used heterodox economic policy including capital controls, such as Iceland (Krugman, 2010b).

4. Mahathir is infamous for his inflammatory anti-Semitic rhetoric, blaming "the Jews" for conspiring against the Malaysian economy.

5. Dornbusch (2001) argues that it was unclear if controls made a difference since the region was recovering anyway. But as Kaplan and Rodrik (2002) point out, this misses the point since the situations of countries like South Korea and Malaysia were very different at the time of Malaysian controls. A meaningful comparison needs to measure the countries' respective performances from similar points of crisis.

6. In comparison with South Korea, Malaysia's reduction in GDP was less severe (9.9% compared to 15.1%). Malaysia's drop in manufacturing was 19.1% better; its drop in real wages was 10.8% better; and it had 18.5% less currency depreciation (Kaplan & Rodrik, 2002, p. 25). These results are particularly impressive given that by implementing controls, Malaysia missed the large capital injections from the IMF that countries like Korea and Thailand received.

7. The belief that public banks tend to promote corruption and political rent-seeking is usually referred to as the "political view" (see, e.g., Shleifer, 1998). The belief that public banks are able to operate with broader lending criteria than profit maximization is usually referred to as the "social view" (see, e.g., Atkinson & Stiglitz, 1980).

8. For instance, the original US legislation, which is standard for many countries, provides tax exemption to credit unions, which are defined as organizations with a central goal "to make more available to people of small means credit for provident purposes" (Ferguson & McKillop, 1997, p. 225).

9. This has changed since the 1990s, when part of Mondragon's reorganization involved moving the CL's Empresarial division to other institutional locations, and the focus on creating new co-ops shifted to sustaining existing ones (Freundlich, 1998).

10. For OECD countries in general, this is, on average, broken down as follows: about 52% of the public spending goes to subsidies and transfers (such as health, education, pensions, and welfare), 38% goes to public investment, and 10% goes to servicing government debt (Tanzi & Schuknecht, 2000, pp. 6–7).

11. Another important example of local-level investment is that of the Communal Councils in Venezuela (Irazábal & Foley, 2010). Communal Councils were launched in 2006 and have since become extremely popular. According to Pearson (2009), as of 2009 there were over 30,000 registered councils. The idea is that neighborhoods are free to form councils (usually involving 150–400 families), which can then apply for funding from the central government to engage in community investment projects that they have democratically decided upon. While there is still a lack of reliable research on their performance, they are a fascinating experiment that deserves future attention.

12. There used to be one delegate for every 10 participants. But since PB has grown so large over the years, the ratio of delegates to participants has evolved. If the assemblies have over 1,000 people attending, one delegate is selected per 80 people (Souza, 2001).

13. Although the municipal legislature is not legally bound to accept the participatory budget, in practice since the budget arrives from such a democratic process, it is accepted as a *fait accompli* (de Sousa Santos, 1998).

14. Likewise, Baiocchi (2005) points out that even some of the most vocal critics of PB agree that clientism has declined. For example, prior to PB, 41% of participants in Porto Alegre thought that it was necessary to rely on the direct intervention of

politicians to secure public goods; yet after experiencing PB, this had dropped to 26% (Wampler, 2007, p. 34).

15. In fact PB has spread quite remarkably. It was adopted in more than 250 Brazilian municipalities at some point between 1990 and 2004 (Wampler, 2007, p. 6), and also in hundreds of cities around the world, including Guelph in Canada and Chicago in the United States.

16. There is a dilemma about whether PB should become formally and legally institutionalized. On the one hand, the fact that PB has no formal legal recognition in Porto Alegre is a worry for some, since it means that its continued existence depends on the continual good will of the Mayor. On the other hand, some see the lack of a solid legal framework as an advantage, not a liability, because it allows for the rapid evolution and democratic experimentalism that is critical for creatively solving problems, and trying out new procedures, in a way that might well be impeded by formal statute.

17. In Baiocchi's (2005) memorable formulation, participants need to be both "militants and citizens."

18. For example, in Porto Alegre, resources for PB come partly from the central government, but also from the city's ability to raise taxes (the PT helped to pay for PB through a progressive income tax).

19. As the authors point out, the chief obstacle to implementing a Tobin Tax is the international coordination it would require. It would have to apply to all jurisdictions, since it it were imposed unilaterally in one country, the foreign exchange market would simply move offshore (Eichengreen et al., 1995, p. 165).

20. It is these possibilities which have stimulated debate over so-called "pension fund socialism" (Drucker, 1976; Simon, 1993).

21. It may be the case that this mainstream interpretation is actually more rigid than the actual case law. For example, in the British case, it has been argued that trustees are in fact legally permitted to consider a much broader range of issues that their beneficiaries may consider in their "best interest" than solely financial ones (Berry, 2011).

22. When consumption taxes are flat (i.e., everyone pays the same amount), which they usually are, they are regressive, because poorer people habitually spend a higher portion of their total income, so are taxed proportionally more. However, consumption taxes can be made to be just as progressive as income taxes—like Kaldor suggested—by taxing more expensive and luxury items at a higher rate.

23. While this defeat was unfortunate, it was in no way inevitable. In this particular case the socialists did a bad job of convincing the population of the benefits of the plan. Additionally, the fact that the proposal was for wage-earner funds to be controlled by the unions, instead of broader community representatives, made them unpopular (Pontusson & Kuruvilla, 1992).

24. Robin Blackburn (2010) proposes something similar to this.

Chapter 8

1. Consider that even a thinker of the stature of Murray Bookchin was able to start an essay on future "forms of freedom" by saying that "the problem of what social

forms will replace existing ones is basically a problem of the relations free *men* will establish between themselves" (Bookchin, [1968] 2005, p. 199; my emphasis). The fact that a thinker of Bookchin's intellect and sensitivity to hierarchy could be blind to the sexism in his language, as were most writers of the time, reminds us of the necessity for having humility ourselves in thinking about the future since we can never entirely escape the blind spots of our age.

2. Although Proudhon sometimes gestured in the direction of market socialism, it is usually historically associated more with Lange and Taylor (1938) from the period of the socialist calculation debates. The fall of the Soviet Union spurred a renewal of interest in market socialism, led by such theorists as Carens (1981), Miller (1989), Nove (1991), Bardhan and Roemer (1993), Roemer (1994), Schweickart (1996), and others.

3. Venezuela is a complex story. There is definite evidence of a move toward economic democracy—with expanding co-ops, communal councils controlling local investment, and a government at least formally committed to expanding workers' control and building socialism. However, there have also been countervailing tendencies, such as Chavez's authoritarian personality, the decline of co-management, and the ambiguity of the main political parties and the unions toward workplace democracy (Malleson, 2010). It is too early to speculate on the direction of the post-Chavez regime.

4. For a good discussion of the possibilities of transition to a socialist system, see Wright (2010).

5. Strategic firms as well as workplaces with broad social importance, such as schools, might experiment with extending co-management by including different proportions of internal workers, state representatives, and local community representatives. Various experiments would be needed to find successful ways to balance affected interests.

6. In terms of theories of market socialism, this model is probably closest to that of Schweickart (1996, 2002), from whom it takes considerable inspiration.

7. The most common objection to a basic income is that it means that some people will simply spend their time surfing, or in some other such activity, on the income that other people have generated. This objection is dealt with at length in Van Parijs (1995). The basic response is that most of society's wealth today is inherited wealth (i.e., from the labor of past generations), and so a basic income gives every individual a claim to a portion of that wealth to use as they see fit. While it is unlikely that a basic income (at the living wage level that it is currently envisioned) would lead to mass exodus from work, it is likely that various unpleasant jobs (such as trash collecting) would have to offer higher wages to attract workers—but this is hardly an undesirable result.

8. Moreover, there is, I think, a good case for allowing a capitalist niche sector—a kind of "capitalism between consenting adults," so to speak—as long as exit options are genuinely available for anyone who wants them (Schweickart, 2011, pp. 77–80). However, taking up this issue in depth is beyond the scope of the present work.

9. The PAI goes back at least to the Justinian code of the 6th century c.e., which states "*quod omnes tangit, ab omnibus approbetur*" (that which touches all should

be approved by all) (Watner, 2005). For contemporary discussions of the PAI, see Whelan (1983), Goodin (2007), and Fung (2013).

10. Of course, whether this potential is actualized depends on whether the majority of the population actually votes to restrain throughput growth in this way. There is nothing inevitable about that one way or the other. Clearly environmental sustainability requires a cultural shift just as much as an institutional one.

11. Attributed to Lily Tomlin in *People* Magazine, December 26, 1977.

12. He proposes a system of "socialist protectionism," which aims to protect domestic workers from low-wage competition while contributing positively to alleviating global poverty. To these ends he advocates that a "social tariff" be imposed on the imports of all goods coming from poor countries. This tariff would protect domestic workers from low-wage and/or environmentally unfriendly competition. At the same time all of the tariff proceeds would be rebated to the country of origin of the goods, particularly to those agencies most likely to help alleviate poverty—state agencies (where effective), unions, environmental groups, NGOs, etc. (Schweickart, 2002, p. 82).

13. In a worldwide poll, the majority of respondents in every country, except France, agreed with the statement that "the free market economy is the best system on which to base the future of the world" (WorldPublicOpinion.Org, 2006).

Bibliography

Ackerman, B., & Alstott, A. (2006). Why Stakeholding? In E. O. Wright (Ed.), *Redesigning Distribution: Basic Income and Stakeholder Grants as Alternative Cornerstones for a More Egalitarian Capitalism* (pp. 40–60). London: Verso.

Albert, M. (2003). *Parecon: Life after Capitalism*. London: Verso.

Albert, M., & Hahnel, R. (1991). *Looking Forward: Participatory Economics for the 21st Century*. Boston: South End Press.

Alchian, A., & Demsetz, H. (1972). Production, information costs, and economic organization. *The American Economic Review*, *62*(5), 777–95.

Alinsky, S. (1971). *Rules for Radicals*. New York: Vintage Books.

Allard, J., Davidson, C., & Matthaei, J. (Eds.). (2010). *Solidarity Economy: Building Alternatives for People and Planet*. Chicago: ChangeMaker Publications.

Allegretto, S. (2011). The few, the proud, and the very rich. *The Berkeley Blog*. Retrieved June 6, 2013, from http://blogs.berkeley.edu/2011/12/05/the-few-the-proud-the-very-rich/.

Alperovitz, G. (2005). *America beyond Capitalism: Reclaiming our Wealth, our Liberty, and our Democracy*. Hoboken, NJ: John Wiley & Sons.

Ammirato, P. (1996). *La Lega: The Making of a Successful Cooperative Network*. Aldershot: Dartmouth.

Andren, T., & Gustafsson, B. (2004). Patterns of social assistance receipt in Sweden. *International Journal of Social Welfare*, *13*(1), 55–68.

Andrianova, S., Demetriades, P., & Shortland, A. (2010). Is government ownership of banks really harmful to growth? (Discussion paper 987). Berlin: German Institute for Economic Research. Retrieved November 9, 2013, from http://hdl.handle.net/10419/36709.

Arando, S., Freundlich, F., Gago, M., Jones, D. C., & Kato, T. (2010). Assessing Mondragon: Stability and managed change in the face of globalization. William Davidson Institute Working Paper (1003), 1–47. Retrieved November, 9, 2013, from http://wdi.umich.edu/files/publications/workingpapers/wp1003.pdf.

Arando, S., Gago, M., Jones, D. C., & Kato, T. (2011). *Efficiency in employee-owned enterprises: An econometric case study of Mondragon*. IZA Discussion Paper (5711). Retrieved November, 9, 2013 from http://hdl.handle.net/10419/52071.

Archer, R. (1995). *Economic Democracy: The Politics of Feasible Socialism*. Oxford: Clarendon Press.

Arge, R. C., & Hunt, E. K. (1971). Environmental pollution, externalities, and conventional economic wisdom: A critique. *Boston College Environmental Affairs Law Review*, *1*, 266.

Argimon, I., Gonzalez-Paramo, J. M., & Roldan, J. M. (1997). Evidence of public spending crowding-out from a panel of OECD countries. *Applied Economics*, *29*(8), 1001–10.

Aristotle. (1998). *Politics* (C. D. C. Reeve, Trans.). Indianapolis: Hackett.

Arneson, R. (1993). Democratic Rights at National and Workplace Levels. In D. Copp, J. Hampton, & J. E. Roemer (Eds.), *The Idea of Democracy* (pp. 118–48). Cambridge: Cambridge University Press.

Arsdale, D. V., McCabe, M., Panayotakis, C., Sayres, S., Rehmann, J., & Wolff, R. (2012). Manifesto for economic democracy and ecological sanity. Retrieved October 29, 2013, from http://rdwolff.com/content/manifesto.

Arun, T., & Turner, J. (2002). Public sector banks in India: Rationale and prerequisites for reform. *Annals of Public and Cooperative Economics*, *73*(1), 89–109.

Aschauer, D. (1989). Does public capital crowd out private capital? *Journal of Monetary Economics*, *24*(2), 171–88.

Assadourian, E. (2010). The rise and fall of consumer cultures. *State of the World*, 2010, 3–20.

Atkinson, A. B., & Stiglitz, J. E. (1980). *Lectures on Public Economics*. London: McGraw-Hill Book Co.

Austen-Smith, D. (2008). Introduction. In D. Austen-Smith, J. A. Frieden, M. A. Golden, K. O. Moene, & A. Przeworski (Eds.), *Selected Works of Michael Wallerstein: The Political Economy of Inequality, Unions, and Social Democracy* (pp. 241–49). Cambridge: Cambridge University Press.

Avineri, S. (1968). *The Social and Political Thought of Karl Marx*. Cambridge: Cambridge University Press.

Azevedo, A., & Gitahy, L. (2010). The cooperative movement, self-management and competitiveness: The case of Mondragón Corporación Cooperativa. *WorkingUSA: The Journal of Labor and Society*, *13*(1), 5–29.

Baer, P., Athanasiou, T., Kartha, S., & Kemp-Benedict, E. (2008). *The Greenhouse Development Rights Framework: The Right to Development in a Climate Constrained World*. Berlin: Heinrich Böll Foundation, Christian Aid, EcoEquity, and the Stockholm Environment Institute.

Baiocchi, G. (2005). *Militants and Citizens: The Politics of Participatory Democracy in Porto Alegre*. Stanford, CA: Stanford University Press.

Bakan, J. (2004). *The Corporation*. Toronto: Penguin Canada.

Baker, D. (2006). *The Conservative Nanny State*. Washington, DC: Center for Economic and Policy Research.

Baker, D., Epstein, G., & Pollin, R. (Eds.). (1998). *Globalization and Progressive Economic Policy*. Cambridge: Cambridge University Press.

Bakunin, M. (1973). On Marx and Marxism. In A. Lehning (Ed.), *Michael Bakunin: Selected Writings* (pp. 232–70). London: Jonathan Cape.

Bakunin, M. (1980). *Bakunin on Anarchism*. Montreal: Black Rose Books.

Bakunin, M. ([1866] 1980). Revolutionary Catechism. In S. Dolgoff (Ed.), *Bakunin on Anarchism*. Montreal: Black Rose Books.

Baldacci, E., Clements, B., Gupta, S., & Cui, Q. (2008). Social spending, human capital, and growth in developing countries. *World Development*, *36*(8), 1317–41.

Barber, B. (1984). *Strong Democracy: Participatory Politics for a New Age*. Berkeley and Los Angeles: University of California Press.

Bardhan, P., & Roemer, J. (Eds.). (1993). *Market Socialism: The Current Debate*. New York: Oxford University Press.

Barham, B. L., Boucher, S., & Carter, M. R. (1996). Credit constraints, credit unions, and small-scale producers in Guatemala. *World Development, 24*(5), 793–806.

Barry, B. (2005). *Why Social Justice Matters.* Cambridge: Polity Press.

Bartels, L. M. (2004). Partisan politics and the US income distribution. Retrieved February 2, 2012, from http://www.russellsage.org/sites/all/files/u4/Bartels_Partisan Politics. pdf.

Bartlett, W., Cable, J., Estrin, S., Jones, D. C., & Smith, S. (1992). Labor-managed cooperatives and private firms in North Central Italy: An empirical comparison. *Industrial and Labor Relations Review, 46*(1), 103–18.

Basinger, S. J., & Hallerberg, M. (2004). Remodeling the competition for capital: How domestic politics erases the race to the bottom. *American Political Science Review, 98*(2), 261–76.

Bayo-Moriones, J. A., Galilea-Salvatierra, P. J., & De Cerio, J. M.-D. (2003). Participation, cooperatives and performance: An analysis of Spanish manufacturing firms. *Advances in the Economic Analysis of Participatory and Labor-Managed Firms, 7*, 31–56.

BBC. (2010). EU austerity drive country by country. Retrieved December 9, 2010, from http://www.bbc.co.uk/news/10162176.

Bellas, C. (1972). *Industrial Democracy and the Worker-Owned Firm: A Study of Twenty-One Plywood Companies in the Pacific Northwest.* New York: Praeger Publishers.

Ben-Ner, A. (1988). Comparative empirical observations on worker-owned and capitalist firms. *International Journal of Industrial Organization, 6*(1), 7–31.

Ben-Ner, A., & Jones, D. C. (1995). Employee participation, ownership, and productivity: A theoretical framework. *Industrial Relations: A Journal of Economy and Society, 34*(4), 532–54.

Benjamin, L., Rubin, J. S., & Zielenbach, S. (2004). Community development financial institutions: Current issues and future prospects. *Journal of Urban Affairs, 26*(2), 177–95.

Benn, T., & Mullin, C. (1979). *Arguments for Socialism.* London: Jonathan Cape.

Bentham, J. (1817). *Plan of Parliamentary Reform.* London: R. Hunter.

Bentham, J. ([1802] 1894). Principles of the Civil Code. In R. Hildreth (Ed.), *Theory of Legislation* (8th ed., 88–236). London: Kegan Paul.

Benz, M., & Frey, B. S. (2008). Being independent is a great thing: Subjective evaluations of self-employment and hierarchy. *Economica, 75*(298), 362–83.

Berkman, A. (1929). *What Is Communist Anarchism?* New York: The Vanguard Press.

Berle, A. A., & Means, G. C. ([1932] 1962). *The Modern Corporation and Private Property.* New York: Macmillan.

Berlin, I. (1969). *Four Essays on Liberty.* New York: Oxford University Press.

Berman, K. (1967). *Worker-Owned Plywood Companies: An Economic Analysis.* Pullman: Washington State University Press.

Bernstein, E. ([1899] 1993). *The Preconditions of Socialism* (H. Tudor, Trans.). Cambridge: Cambridge University Press.

Berry, C. (2011). *Protecting Our Best Interests: Rediscovering Fiduciary Obligation.* London: FairPensions.

Beveridge, W. (1948). *Voluntary Action.* London: George Allen & Unwin Ltd.

Beveridge, W. ([1942] 1969). *Social Insurance and Allied Services.* New York: Agathon Press.

Bhagwati, J. (1998). The capital myth: The difference between trade in widgets and dollars. *Foreign Affairs, 77*(3), 7–12.

Bhatnagar, D., Rathore, A., Torres, M. M., & Kanungo, P. (2003). Participatory budgeting in Brazil. *World Bank Report.* Retrieved October 29, 2013, from http://www-wds .worldbank.org/external/default/WDSContentServer/WDSP/IB/2009/11/03/000333 037_20091103015746/Rendered/PDF/514180WP0BR0Bu10Box342027B01PUBLIC1 .pdf.

Blackburn, R. (2002). *Banking on Death, or, Investing in Life: The History and Future of Pensions.* London: Verso.

Blackburn, R. (2010). For a public utility finance system. Retrieved September 19, 2011, from http://www.newleftproject.org/index.php/site/article_comments/for_a_public_ utility_finance_system.

Blasi, J., & Kruse, D. (2006). U.S. high-performance work practices at century's end. *Industrial Relations: A Journal of Economy and Society, 45*(4), 547–78.

Blasi, J., & Kruse, D. (2012). *Broad-Based Worker Ownership and Profit Sharing: Can These Ideas Work in the Entire Economy?* Paper presented at the International Association for the Economics of Participation.

Block, F. (1977). The ruling class does not rule: Notes on the Marxist theory of the state. *Socialist Revolution, 33*(6), 6–28.

Block, F. (1992). Capitalism without class power. *Politics & Society, 20,* 277–303.

Block, F. (1996). *The Vampire State.* New York: The New Press.

BLS. (2012). Number of jobs held, labor market activity, and earnings growth among the youngest baby boomers. Bureau of Labor Statistics (US Department of Labor) (Wednesday July 25). Retrieved November 9, 2013, from http://www.bls.gov/news. release/pdf/nlsoy.pdf.

Blumberg, P. (1968). *Industrial Democracy: The Sociology of Participation.* London: Constable.

Bobbio, N. (1987). *The Future of Democracy* (R. Griffin, Trans.). Cambridge: Polity Press.

Bogle, J. (2008). Reflections on CEO compensation. *The Academy of Management Perspectives* (formerly *The Academy of Management Executive) (AMP), 22*(2), 21–25.

Bonin, J. P., Jones, D. C., & Putterman, L. (1993). Theoretical and empirical studies of producer cooperatives: Will ever the twain meet? *Journal of Economic Literature, 31*(3), 1290–1320.

Bonin, J. P., & Putterman, L. (1987). *Economics of Cooperation and the Labor-Managed Economy.* Chur, Switzerland: Harwood Academic Publishers.

Bookchin, M. (1971). *Post-Scarcity Anarchism.* Berkeley, CA: Ramparts Press.

Bookchin, M. ([1968] 2005). The Forms of Freedom. In D. Roussopoulos & C. G. Benello (Eds.), *Participatory Democracy: Prospects for Democratizing Democracy* (pp. 199–217). Montreal: Black Rose Books.

Booth, D. E. (1995). Economic democracy as an environmental measure. *Ecological Economics, 12,* 225–36.

Bosma, H., Marmot, M. G., Hemingway, H., Nicholson, A. C., Brunner, E., & Stansfeld, S. A. (1997). Low job control and risk of coronary heart disease in Whitehall II (prospective cohort) study. *BMJ, 314*(7080), 558–65.

Bowles, S., & Gintis, H. (1986). *Democracy and Capitalism* London: Routledge & Kegan Paul.

Bowles, S., & Gintis, H. (1993). A Political and Economic Case for the Democratic Enterprise. In D. Copp, J. Hampton, & J. E. Roemer (Eds.), *The Idea of Democracy*. New York: Cambridge University Press, 375–399.

Bowles, S., & Gintis, H. (1996). The Distribution of Wealth and the Viability of the Democratic Firm. In U. Pagano & R. Rowthorn (Eds.), *Democracy and Efficiency in the Economic Enterprise* (pp. 82–97). London: Routledge.

Bowles, S., & Gintis, H. (1998). Efficient Redistribution: New Rules for Markets, States and Communities. In S. Bowles & H. Gintis (Eds.), *Recasting Egalitarianism: New Rules for Communities, States and Markets* (pp. 3–74). London: Verso.

Bowles, S., Gordon, D. M., & Weisskopf, T. E. (1983). *Beyond the Waste Land: A Democratic Alternative to Economic Decline*. Garden City, NY: Anchor Press/Doubleday.

Bowles, S., Gordon, D. M., & Weisskopf, T. E. (1990). *After the Waste Land: A Democratic Economics for the Year 2000*. Armonk, NY: M. E. Sharpe.

Bowman, S. R. (1996). *The Modern Corporation and American Political Thought*. University Park: The Pennsylvania State University Press.

Bradley, K., & Gelb, A. (1981). Motivation and control in the Mondragon experiment. *British Journal of Industrial Relations, 19*(2), 211–31.

Bradley, K., & Gelb, A. (1983). *Co-operation at Work: The Mondragon Experience*. London: Heinemann Educational.

Braverman, H. (1974). *Labor and Monopoly Capital: The Degradation of Work in the Twentieth Century*. New York: Monthly Review Press.

Bretschger, L., & Hettich, F. (2002). Globalisation, capital mobility and tax competition: Theory and evidence for OECD countries. *European Journal of Political Economy, 18*(4), 695–716.

Brinton, M. (1975). *The Bolsheviks & Workers' Control, 1917–1921*. Montreal: Black Rose Books.

Brinton, M. (2004). *For Workers' Power*. Oakland, CA: AK Press.

Brittan, S. (1998 October 1,). The control trap: Exchange controls do not tackle basic economic weaknesses, but like many 'temporary' measures, they tend to last. *Financial Times*, p. 22.

Bruno, M. (1995). Does inflation really lower growth? *Finance and Development, 32*(3), 35–38.

Buiter, W. (2008). The end of American capitalism as we knew it. Willem Buiter's Maverecon Retrieved October 29, 2013, from http://blogs.ft.com/maverecon/2008/09/the-end-of-american-capitalism-as-we-knew-it/#axzz2j8RvoplV.

Burdín, G., & Dean, A. (2009). New evidence on wages and employment in worker cooperatives compared with capitalist firms. *Journal of Comparative Economics, 37*(4), 517–33.

Burdín, G., & Dean, A. (2012). Revisiting the objectives of worker cooperatives: An empirical assessment. *Economic Systems, 36*, 158–71.

Burgess, R., & Pande, R. (2005). Do rural banks matter? Evidence from the Indian social banking experiment. *The American Economic Review, 95*(3), 780–95.

Burgess, R., Wong, G., & Pande, R. (2005). Banking for the poor: Evidence from India. *Journal of the European Economic Association, 3*(2/3), 268–78.

Burrows, P. (2008). Parecon and Workers' Self-Management: Reflections on Winnipeg's Mondragon Bookstore & Coffee House Collective. In C. Spannos (Ed.), *Real Utopia: Participatory Society for the 21st Century* (pp. 275–305). Oakland, CA: AK Press.

Burtraw, D., & Szambelan, S. (2009). US emissions trading markets for SO^2 and NO^x. Resources for the Future Discussion Paper (09–40). Retrieved November 9, 2013, from http://rff.org/RFF/Documents/RFF-DP-09-40.pdf.

Cable, J., & FitzRoy, F. (1980). Productive efficiency, incentives and employee participation: Some preliminary results for West Germany. *Kyklos, 33*(1), 100–121.

Cameron, D. (2011). It's time, nationalize the banks. Retrieved February 2, 2012, from http://rabble.ca/columnists/2011/10/its-time-nationalize-the-banks.

Campbell, A., Keen, C., Norman, G., & Oakeshott, R. (1977). *Worker-Owners: The Mondragon Achievement*. London: Anglo-German Foundation for the Study of Industrial Society.

Carens, J. H. (1981). *Equality, Moral Incentives, and the Market: An Essay in Utopian Politico-Economic Theory*. Chicago: University of Chicago Press.

Carnoy, M., & Shearer, D. (1980). *Economic Democracy: The Challenge of the 1980s*: Armonk, NY: ME Sharpe: distributed by Pantheon Books.

Carvalho, B. S. M., & Garcia, M. G. P. (2008). *Ineffective Controls on Capital Inflows under Sophisticated Financial Markets: Brazil in the Nineties*. Chicago: National Bureau of Economic Research, University of Chicago Press.

Castles, F. G. (2007). A Race to the Bottom? In C. Pierson & F. G. Castles (Eds.), *The Welfare State Reader* (2nd ed., pp. 226–44). Cambridge: Polity Press.

Castoriadis, C. (1974). *Workers' Councils and the Economics of a Self-Managed Society*. Philadelphia: Philadelphia Solidarity.

Chang, H.-J. (2002). *Kicking Away the Ladder: Development Strategy in Historical Perspective*. London: Anthem.

Chang, H.-J. (2006). *The East Asian Development Experience: The Miracle, the Crisis and the Future*. Penang, Malaysia: Third World Network.

Chang, H.-J. (2007). *Bad Samaritans: The Guilty Secrets of Rich Nations & the Threat to Global Prosperity*. London: Random House Business Books.

Chang, H.-J. (2010). *23 Things They Don't Tell You about Capitalism*. London: Allen Lane.

Cheney, G. (1999). *Values at Work: Employee Participation Meets Market Pressure at Mondragón*. Ithaca, NY: ILR/Cornell University Press.

Clark, B., & Gintis, H. (1978). Rawlsian justice and economic systems. *Philosophy and Public Affairs, 7*(4), 302–25.

Cohen, B. J. (2002). Capital Controls: Why Do Governments Hesitate? In L. E. Armijo (Ed.), *Debating the Global Financial Architecture* (pp. 93–117). New York: State University of New York Press.

Cohen, G. A. (1995). *Self-Ownership, Freedom, and Equality*. Cambridge: Cambridge University Press.

Cohen, J. (2001). Taking people as they are? *Philosophy & Public Affairs, 30*(4), 363–86.

Cohen, J., & Rogers, J. (1983). *On Democracy*. Harmondsworth: Penguin Books.

Cohen, P. (2010). Lessons from the nationalization nation: State-owned enterprises in France. *Dissent, 57*(1), 15–20.

Cole, G. D. H. (1920). *Guild Socialism Re-stated*. London: Leonard Parsons.

Cole, S. (2009). Fixing market failures or fixing elections? Agricultural credit in India. *American Economic Journal: Applied Economics*, *1*(1), 219–50.

Collard, S., & Kempson, E. (2005). *Affordable Credit: The Way Forward*. London: The Policy Press.

Commission on the Future of Worker–Management Relations Department of Labor (1995). Employee participation and labor–management cooperation in American workplaces. *Challenge*, *38*(5), 38–46.

Cornforth, C., Thomas, A., Lewis, J., & Spear, R. (1988). *Developing Successful Worker Co-operatives*. London: SAGE Publications.

Craig, B., & Pencavel, J. (1995). Participation and productivity: A comparison of worker cooperatives and conventional firms in the plywood industry. *Brookings Papers on Economic Activity. Microeconomics*, *1995*, 121–74.

Crotty, J. (2009). Structural causes of the global financial crisis: A critical assessment of the "new financial architecture." *Cambridge Journal of Economics*, *33*(4), 563–80.

Crotty, J., & Epstein, G. (1996). In defense of capital controls. *Socialist Register*, *32*, 118–49.

Cui, Z. (2000). An Appendix on Savings and Investment. In R. Unger (Ed.), *Democracy Realized* (pp. 279–88). London: Verso.

Dahl, R. (1985). *A Preface to Economic Democracy*. Berkeley and Los Angeles: University of California Press.

Dahl, R. (1994). A democratic dilemma: System effectiveness versus citizen participation. *Political Science Quarterly*, *109*(1), 23–34.

Dahl, R. (2000). *On Democracy*. New Haven, CT: Yale University Press.

Dahl, R., & Lindblom, C. E. ([1953] 1976). *Politics, Economics, and Welfare*. Chicago: The University of Chicago Press.

Daly, H. E. (1992). Allocation, distribution, and scale: Towards an economics that is efficient, just, and sustainable. *Ecological Economics*, *6*, 185–93.

Davies, J. B., Shorrocks, A., Sandstrom, S., Wolff, E. N. (2007). The world distribution of household wealth. UC Santa Cruz: Center for Global, International and Regional Studies. Retrieved October 29, 2013, from http://escholarship.org/uc/item/3jv048hx.

De Jonge, J. (1995). Job Autonomy, Well-Being, and Health: A Study among Dutch Health Care Workers. Unpublished Thesis, Rijksuniversiteit Limburg.

de Sousa Santos, B. (1998). Participatory budgeting in Porto Alegre: Toward a redistributive democracy. *Politics and Society*, *26*, 461–510.

Defourny, J. S. (1992). Comparative measures of technical efficiency for five hundred French workers' cooperatives. *Advances in the Economics of Participatory and Labor-Managed Firms*, *4*, 27–62.

Dinç, S. (2005). Politicians and banks: Political influences on government-owned banks in emerging markets. *Journal of Financial Economics*, *77*(2), 453–79.

Dolgoff, S. (Ed.). (1990). *The Anarchist Collectives*. Montreal: Black Rose Books.

Domar, E. (1966). The Soviet farm as a producer cooperative. *American Economic Review*, *56*(4), 743–57.

Dornbusch, R. (2001). Malaysia: Was it different? *NBER Working Papers* (8325). Retrieved November 9, 2013, from http://www.nber.org/papers/w8325.pdf.

Doucouliagos, C. (1995). Worker participation and productivity in labor-managed and participatory capitalist firms: A meta-analysis. *Industrial and Labor Relations Review*, *49*(1), 58–77.

Dow, G. (2003). *Governing the Firm: Workers' Control in Theory and Practice*. Cambridge: Cambridge University Press.

Dreher, A. (2006). The influence of globalization on taxes and social policy: An empirical analysis for OECD countries. *European Journal of Political Economy*, *22*(1), 179–201.

Dreher, A., Sturm, J.-E., & Ursprung, H. W. (2008). The impact of globalization on the composition of government expenditures: Evidence from panel data. *Public Choice*, *134*(3/4), 263–92.

Drèze, J. (1993). Self-Management and Economic Theory: Efficiency, Funding, and Employment. In P. Bardhan & J. Roemer (Eds.), *Market Socialism: The Current Debate* (pp. 253–65). New York: Oxford University Press.

Drucker, P. F. (1976). *The Unseen Revolution: How Pension Fund Socialism Came to America*. New York: Harper & Row.

Dryzek, J. S. (1996). *Democracy in Capitalist Times: Ideals, Limits, and Struggles*. Oxford: Oxford University Press.

Eccleshall, R. (1986). *British Liberalism: Liberal Thought from the 1640s to 1980s*. Harlow: Longman Group Ltd.

Economist. (1995). A survey of the world economy: Who's in the driving seat? *The Economist*, October 7–13.

Economist. (2006). The rich, the poor and the growing gap between them—Inequality in America. *The Economist*, June 17.

Edison, H., & Reinhart, C. (2001). Stopping hot money. *Journal of Development Economics*, *66*(2), 533–53.

Edwards, S. (1999). How effective are capital controls? *The Journal of Economic Perspectives*, *13*(4), 65–84.

Edwards, S., & Rigobon, R. (2005). Capital controls, exchange rate volatility and external vulnerability. *NBER Working Papers* (11434). Retrieved November 11, 2013, from http://www.nber.org/papers/w11434.

Eichengreen, B., Tobin, J., & Wyplosz, C. (1995). Two cases for sand in the wheels of international finance. *The Economic Journal*, *105*(428), 162–72.

Ellerman, D. (1984). Workers' Cooperatives: The Question of Legal Structure. In R. Jackall & H. M. Levin (Eds.), *Worker Cooperatives in America* (pp. 257–74). Berkeley and Los Angeles: University of California Press.

Ellerman, D. (1990). *The Democratic Worker-Owned Firm: A New Model for the East and West*. London: Unwin Hyman.

Ellerman, D. (1992). *Property and Contract in Economics: The Case for Economic Democracy*. Cambridge, MA: Blackwell.

Ellerman, D. (1997). The democratic firm. Retrieved October 29, 2013, from http://www.ellerman.org/Davids-Stuff/Books/demofirm.doc.

Ellner, S. (2010). Hugo Chavez's first decade in office: Breakthroughs and shortcomings. *Latin American Perspectives*, *37*(170), 77–96.

Elster, J. (1986). Self-realization in work and politics: The Marxist conception of the good life. *Social Philosophy and Policy*, *3*(2), 97–126.

Engels, F. ([1874] 1978). On Authority. In R. C. Tucker (Ed.), *The Marx-Engels Reader* (2nd ed., pp. 730–33). New York: W. W. Norton & Company.

Epstein, G. (Ed.). (2005). *Capital Management Techniques in Developing Countries*. Cheltenham: Edward Elgar.

Epstein, G., Grabel, I., & Jomo, K. S. (2003). Capital management techniques in developing countries: An assessment of experiences from the 1990's and lessons for the future. *Political Economy Research Institute, 56*, 1–49.

Epstein, G., Grabel, I., & Jomo, S. K. (2005). Capital Management Techniques in Developing Countries. In G. Epstein (Ed.), *Capital Flight and Capital Controls in Developing Countries* (pp. 301–33). Cheltenham: Edward Elgar.

Errasti, A. M., Heras, I., Bakaikoa, B., & Elgoibar, P. (2003). The internationalisation of cooperatives: The case of the Mondragon Cooperative Corporation. *Annals of Public and Cooperative Economics, 74*(4), 553–84.

Esping-Andersen, G. (1990). *The Three Worlds of Welfare Capitalism*. Cambridge: Polity Press.

Estlund, C. L. (2000). Working together: The workplace, civil society, and the law. *The Georgetown Law Journal, 89*(1), 1–96.

Estrin, S. (1989). Workers' Co-operatives: Their Merits and Their Limitations. In J. L. Grand & S. Estrin (Eds.), *Market Socialism* (pp. 165–92). Oxford: Clarendon Press.

Estrin, S., Jones, D. C., & Svejnar, J. (1987). The productivity effects of worker participation: Producer cooperatives in western economies. *Journal of Comparative Economics, 11*(1), 40–61.

Everett, M. J., & Minkler, A. P. (1993). Evolution and organisational choice in nineteenth-century Britain. *Cambridge Journal of Economics, 17*, 51–62.

Fakhfakh, F., Perotin, V., & Gago, M. (2009). Productivity, capital and labor in labor-managed and conventional firms. TEPP Working Paper (2011-8). Retrieved November 9, 2013, from http://www.tepp.eu/RePEc/files/Binder11_8.pdf.

Feinberg, R., & Rahman, A. (2006). Are credit unions just small banks? Determinants of loan rates in local consumer lending markets. *Eastern Economic Journal, 32*(4), 647.

Ferguson, C., & McKillop, D. (1997). *The Strategic Development of Credit Unions*. Chichester: John Wiley & Sons.

Fieldhouse, A. (2013). *A Review of the Economic Research on the Effects of Raising Ordinary Income Tax Rates*. Washington, DC: The Economic Policy Institute.

Fischer, S. (1995). Central-Bank independence revisited. *The American Economic Review, 85*(2), 201–6.

Fischer, S. (1997). Capital account liberalization and the role of the IMF. Paper presented at the Conference on Development of Securities Markets in Emerging Markets.

Flecha, R., & Cruz, I. S. (2011). Cooperation for economic success: The Mondragon case. *Analyse & Kritik, 1*, 157–70.

Fleming, J. (1962). Domestic financial policies under fixed and under floating exchange rates. *Staff Papers-International Monetary Fund, 9*(3), 369–80.

Forbes, K. J. (2007). The Microeconomic Evidence on Capital Controls: No Free Lunch. In S. Edwards (Ed.), *Capital Controls and Capital Flows in Emerging Economies: Policies, Practices and Consequences* (pp. 171–202). Chicago: University of Chicago Press.

Forcadell, F. J. (2005). Democracy, cooperation and business success: The case of Mondragon Corporacion Cooperativa. *Journal of Business Ethics, 56*(3), 255–74.

Forte, F., & Mantovani, M. (2009). Cooperatives' tax regimes, political orientation of governments and rent seeking. *Journal of Politics and Law, 2*(4), 44–57.

Foster, J. B., McChesney, R. W., & Jonna, R. J. (2011). Monopoly and competition in twenty-first century capitalism. *Monthly Review, 62*(11), 1–39.

Francis, L. (2010). Banking on robbery: The role of fraud in the financial crisis. *Casualty Actuarial Society E-Forum, 2*, 1–54.

Freeman, R., Blasi, J., & Kruse, D. (2010). Introduction. In D. L. Kruse, R. B. Freeman, & J. R. Blasi (Eds.), *Shared Capitalism at Work: Employee Ownership, Profit and Gain Sharing, and Broad-Based Stock Options* (pp. 1–40). Chicago: The University of Chicago Press.

Freeman, R., & Rogers, J. (1999). *What Workers Want.* Ithaca, NY: Cornell University Press.

Freeman, S. (2007). *Rawls.* London: Routledge.

Freundlich, F. (1998). The Mondragon Cooperative Corporation (MCC): An introduction. Retrieved March 13, 2013, from http://www.ownershipassociates.com/mcc-intro.shtm.

Freundlich, F., Grellier, H., & Altuna, R. (2009). Mondragon: Notes on history, scope and structure. *International Journal of Technology Management & Sustainable Development, 8*(1), 3–12.

Friedman, M. ([1962] 2002). *Capitalism and Freedom.* Chicago: University of Chicago Press.

Friedman, M., & Friedman, R. (1980). *Free to Choose: A Personal Statement.* New York: Harcourt Brace Jovanovich.

Fukuyama, F. (1992). *The End of History and the Last Man.* New York: Avon Books.

Fung, A. (2013). The Principle of Affected Interests and Inclusion in Democratic Governance (pp. 236–68). In J. Nagel & R. Smith (Eds.), *Representation: Elections and Beyond.* Philadelphia: University of Pennsylvania Press.

Furubotn, E., & Pejovich, S. (1970). Property rights and the behavior of the firm in a socialist state: The example of Yugoslavia. *Journal of Economics, 30*(3), 431–54.

Gallagher, K. (2010). Capital controls are prudent but not easy. Retrieved December 9, 2010, from http://blogs.ft.com/beyond-brics/2010/10/20/capitals-controls-are-prudent-but-not-easy/.

Gallie, W. B. (1955). Essentially contested concepts. *Proceedings of the Aristotelian Society, 56*, 167–98.

Garrett, G. (1998). Global markets and national politics: Collision course or virtuous circle? *International Organizations, 52*(4), 787–824.

Garrett, G., & Mitchell, D. (2001). Globalization, government spending and taxation in the OECD. *European Journal of Political Research, 39*(2), 145–77.

Gelderloos, P. (2004). What is democracy? Retrieved June 27, 2011, from http://theanarchistlibrary.org/HTML/Peter_Gelderloos__What_is_Democracy_.html.

Genschel, P. (2004). Globalization and the welfare state: A retrospective. *Journal of European Public Policy, 11*(4), 613–36.

Genschel, P. (2005). Globalization and the transformation of the tax state. *European Review, 13*(1), 53–71.

Genschel, P., & Schwarz, P. (2011). Tax competition: A literature review. *Socio-Economic Review, 9*(2), 339–70.

George, D. (1993). *Economic Democracy: The Political Economy of Self-Management and Participation.* London: Macmillan Press.

Gerschenkron, A. (1962). *Economic Backwardness in Historical Perspective: A Book of Essays.* Cambridge, MA: Belknap Press of Harvard University Press.

Gibson-Graham, J. K. (2003). Enabling ethical economies: Cooperativism and class. *Critical Sociology, 29*(2), 123–61.

Glyn, A. (1995). Social democracy and full employment. *New Left Review, I*(211), 33–55.

Goldin, C., & Margo, R. A. (1992). The great compression: The wage structure in the United States at mid-century. *The Quarterly Journal of Economics, 107*(1), 1–34.

Gomes, P. M. (2010). Fiscal policy and the labour market: The effects of public sector employment and wages. Discussion paper series, Forschungsinstitut zur Zukunft der Arbeit (5321). Retrieved November 9, 2013, from http://ssrn.com/abstract=1712628.

Gonzales, V. (2010). Italian social cooperatives and the development of civic capacity: A case of cooperative renewal? *Affinities: A Journal of Radical Theory, Culture, and Action, 4*(1).

Goodin, R. (1994). Selling environmental indulgences. *Kyklos, 47*(4), 573–96.

Goodin, R. (2007). Enfranchising all affected interests, and its alternatives. *Philosophy & Public Affairs, 35*(1), 40–68.

Gould, C. (1988). *Rethinking Democracy: Freedom and Social Cooperation in Politics, Economy, and Society.* Cambridge: Cambridge University Press.

Graham, R. (1989). The general idea of Proudhon's revolution. Retrieved June 27, 2011, from http://dwardmac.pitzer.edu/Anarchist_Archives/proudhon/grahamproudhon.html.

Graham, R. (Ed.). (2005). *Anarchism: A Documentary History of Libertarian Ideas* (Vol. 1). Montreal: Black Rose Books.

Greenberg, E. (1981). Industrial democracy and the democratic citizen. *The Journal of Politics, 43*(4), 963–81.

Greenberg, E. (1986). *Workplace Democracy: The Political Effects of Participation.* Ithaca, NY: Cornell University Press.

Gregorio, J. D., Edwards, S., & Valdes, R. (2000). Controls on capital inflows: Do they work? *NBER Working Papers* (7645). Retrieved November 9, 2013, from http://www.nber.org/papers/w7645.

Grilli, V., & Milesi-Ferretti, G. M. (1995). Economic effects and structural determinants of capital controls. *IMF Staff Papers, 42*(3), 517–51.

Grunberg, L., Moore, S., & Greenberg, E. (1996). The relationship of employee ownership and participation to workplace safety. *Economic and Industrial Democracy, 17*(2), 221.

Guérin, D. (Ed.). (1999). *Ni Dieu Ni Maître.* Paris: La Découverte.

Guin, U. L. (1974). *The Dispossessed.* New York: Harper & Row.

Gunn, C., & Gunn, H. D. (1991). *Reclaiming Capital: Democratic Initiatives and Community Development.* Ithaca, NY: Cornell University Press.

Hahnel, R. (1999). *Panic Rules!* Cambridge, MA: South End Press.

Hahnel, R. (2002). *The ABC's of Political Economy* London: Pluto Press.

Hahnel, R. (2010a). The ecological crisis and libertarian socialists. Retrieved October 29, 2013, from http://www.zcommunications.org/the-ecological-crisis-and-libertarian-socialists-by-robin-hahnel.

Hahnel, R. (2010b). Why cap and trade and not a carbon tax? Retrieved February 15, 2011, from http://www.zcommunications.org/why-cap-and-trade-and-not-a-carbon-tax-by-robin-hahnel.

Hahnel, R. (2011). *Green Economics: Confronting the Ecological Crisis*. Armonk, NY: M. E. Sharpe.

Haldane, A. G., & Madouros, V. (2011). What is the contribution of the financial sector? Retrieved October 29, 2013, from http://www.voxeu.org/index.php?q=node/7314.

Hall, P. A., & Soskice, D. (Eds.). (2001). *Varieties of Capitalism: The Institutional Foundations of Comparative Advantage*. Oxford: Oxford University Press.

Hansmann, H. (1996). *The Ownership of Enterprise*. Cambridge, MA: The Belknap Press of Harvard University Press.

Hansson, A., & Olofsdotter, K. (2004). Integration and tax competition: An empirical study for OECD countries. Retrieved November 9, 2013, from http://lup.lub.lu.se/luur/download?func=downloadFile&recordOId=1387128&fileOId=2061472.

Harvey, D. (2006). *Spaces of Global Capitalism: A Theory of Uneven Geographical Development*. London: Verso.

Harvey, P. (2006). The relative cost of a universal basic income and a negative income tax. *Basic Income Studies, 1*(2), 1–24.

Hayek, F. (1944). *The Road to Serfdom*. London: Routledge & Kegan Paul.

Hayek, F. (1960). *The Constitution of Liberty*. London: Routledge & K. Paul.

Hays, J. C. (2003). Globalization and capital taxation in consensus and majoritarian democracies. *World Politics, 56*(1), 79–113.

Held, D. (2006). *Models of Democracy* (3rd ed.). Cambridge: Polity Press.

Henwood, D. (2011). Moving money (revisited). *LBO News from Doug Henwood*. Retrieved October 29, 2013, from http://lbo-news.com/2011/11/08/moving-money-revisited/.

Hilborn, R., Branch, T., Ernst, B., Magnusson, A., Minte-Vera, C., Scheuerell, M., et al. (2003). State of the World's Fisheries. *Annual review of Environment and Resources, 28*(1), 359–99.

Hirst, P. (1994). *Associative Democracy*. Cambridge: Polity Press.

Hodgson, G. (1999). *Economics and Utopia*. London: Routledge.

Holmstrom, M. (1989). *Industrial Democracy in Italy*. Aldershot: Avebury.

Horvat, B. (1986). The theory of the worker-managed firm revisited. *Journal of Comparative Economics, 10*, 9–25.

Hoxby, B. (1998). The trade of truth advanced: Areopagitica, economic discourse, and libertarian reform. *Milton Studies, 36*, 177–202.

Hsieh, N.-h. (2005). Rawlsian justice and workplace republicanism. *Social Theory and Practice, 31*(1), 115–42.

Hulme, D., & Mosley, P. (1996). *Finance against Poverty* (Vol. 2). London: Routledge.

Hundley, G. (2001). Why and when are the self-employed more satisfied with their work? *Industrial Relations: A Journal of Economy and Society, 40*(2), 293–316.

Hutchison, M., Kendall, J., Pasricha, G., & Singh, N. (2010). Indian capital control liberalization: Evidence from NDF markets. *NIPFP Working Paper* (21771). Retrieved November 9, 2013, from http://mpra.ub.uni-muenchen.de/21771/1/MPRA_paper_21771.pdf.

Immervoll, H., & Richardson, L. (2011). Redistribution policy and inequality reduction in OECD countries: What has changed in two decades? Discussion Paper series, Forschungsinstitut zur Zukunft der Arbeit (6030). Retrieved November 9, 2013, from http://hdl.handle.net/10419/58948.

Irazábal, C., & Foley, J. (2010). Reflections on the Venezuelan transition from a capitalist representative to a socialist participatory democracy: What are planners to do? *Latin American Perspectives*, *37*(1), 97.

Jackson, T. (2009). *Prosperity without Growth: Economics for a Finite Planet*. London: Earthscan.

Jahoda, M. (1987). Unemployed Men at Work. In D. Fryer & P. Ullah (Eds.), *Unemployed People: Social and Psychological Perspectives* (pp. 1–73). Milton Keynes, England: Open University Press.

James, C. L. R. (2005). Every Cook Can Govern: A Study of Democracy in Ancient Greece. In D. Roussopoulos & C. G. Benello (Eds.), *Participatory Democracy: Prospects for Democratizing Democracy* (pp. 332–47). Montreal: Black Rose Books.

Jensen, M. C., & Meckling, W. H. (1979). Rights and production functions: An application to labor-managed firms and codetermination. *Journal of Business*, *52*(4), 469–506.

Johansson, D. (1997). The number and the size distribution of firms in Sweden and other European countries. Stockholm School of Economics. Retrieved November 9, 2013, from http://www.ratio.se/media/40918/the%20number%20and%20the%20size.pdf.

Johnson, S. (2009). The quiet coup. *The Atlantic*, May.

Johnson, S., & Kwak, J. (2010). *13 Bankers: The Wall Street Takeover and the Next Financial Meltdown*. Toronto: Random House.

Johnson, S., & Mitton, T. (2003). Cronyism and capital controls: Evidence from Malaysia. *Journal of Financial Economics*, *67*(2), 351–82.

Jones, B., Keen, M., Norregaard, J., & Strand, J. (2007). Climate Change: Economic Impact and Policy Responses. *World Economic Outlook: October 2007* (pp. 53–65). Washington, DC: International Monetary Fund.

Jones, D. (1985). The Cooperative Sector and Dualism in Command Economies: Theory and Evidence for the Case of Poland. In D. Jones & J. Svenjar (Eds.), *Advances in the Economics of Participatory and Self-Managed Firms* (Vol. 1, pp. 195–218). Greenwich, CT: JAI Press.

Jones, D. (2007). The productive efficiency of Italian producer cooperatives: Evidence from conventional and cooperative firms. *Advances in the Economic Analysis of Participatory and Labor-Managed Firms*, *10*, 3–28.

Jones, D., & Backus, D. K. (1977). British producer cooperatives in the footware industry: An empirical evaluation of the theory of financing. *The Economic Journal*, *87*(347), 488–510.

Jones, P. A. (2008). From tackling poverty to achieving financial inclusion: The changing role of British credit unions in low income communities. *Journal of Socio-Economics*, *37*(6), 2141–54.

Joskow, P., Schmalensee, R., & Bailey, E. (1998). The market for sulfur dioxide emissions. *American Economic Review*, *88*(4), 669–85.

Jossa, B. (2004). Schweickart and Economic Democracy. *Review of Radical Political Economics*, *36*(4), 546–61.

Jossa, B., & Cuomo, G. (1997). *The Economic Theory of Socialism and the Labour-Managed Firm*. Cheltenham: Edward Elgar.

Kahneman, D. (2011). Daniel Kahneman: How cognitive illusions blind us to reason. *The Observer*, October 30. Retrieved October 29, 2013, from http://www.guardian.co.uk/science/2011/oct/30/daniel-kahneman-cognitive-illusion-extract.

Kahneman, D., Krueger, A. B., Schkade, D. A., Schwarz, N., & Stone, A. A. (2004). A survey method for characterizing daily life experience: The day reconstruction method. *Science*, *306*(5702), 1776.

Kalecki, M. ([1943] 1990). Political Aspects of Full Employment. In J. Osiatynski (Ed.), *Collected Works of Michel Kalecki* (Vol. 1, pp. 347–356). Oxford: Oxford University Press.

Kaminsky, G., & Reinhart, C. (1999). The twin crises: The causes of banking and balance-of-payments problems. *American Economic Review*, *89*(3), 473–500.

Kaminsky, G., & Schmukler, S. (2000). Short-Lived or Long-Lasting? A New Look at the Effects of Capital Controls. In S. Collins & D. Rodrik (Eds.), *Brookings Trade Forum 2000* (pp. 125–166). Washington, DC: Brookings Institution.

Kaplan, E., & Rodrik, D. (2002). Did the Malaysian Capital Controls Work? In S. Edwards & J. Frankel (Eds.), *Preventing Currency Crises in Emerging Markets* (pp. 393–431). Chicago: University of Chicago Press.

Kasmir, S. (1996). *The Myth of Mondragon: Cooperatives, Politics, and Working-Class Life in a Basque Town*. Albany, NY: State University of New York Press.

Kautsky, K. (1888). *The Class Struggle*. Retrieved July 1, 2011, from http://www.marxists.org/archive/kautsky/1892/erfurt/index.htm.

Keynes, J. M. (1936). *The General Theory of Employment, Interest and Money*. London: Macmillan.

Khwaja, A. I., & Mian, A. (2005). Do lenders favor politically connected firms? Rent provision in an emerging financial market. *The Quarterly Journal of Economics*, *120*(4), 1371–1411.

Kirby, P. (2003). *Child Labour in Britain, 1750–1870*. Houndmills: Palgrave Macmillan.

Klein, N. (2007). *The Shock Doctrine*. New York: Metropolitan Books.

Kochhar, K., Johnston, B., Moore, M., Otker-Rober, I., Rogers, S., & Tzanninis, D. (1998). Malaysia, selected issues. *International Monetary Fund Staff Country Report*, *99*(86).

Kornai, J. (1992). *The Socialist System: The Political Economy of Communism*. Princeton, NJ: Princeton University Press.

Kropotkin, P. ([1912] 1974). *Fields, Factories, and Workshops*. London: Allen & Unwin.

Krouse, R., & McPherson, M. (1988). Capitalism, 'Property-Owning Democracy,' and the Welfare State. In A. Gutmann (Ed.), *Democracy and the Welfare State* (pp. 79–106). Princeton, NJ: Princeton University Press.

Krueger, A. O. (1974). The political economy of the rent-seeking society. *American Economic Review*, *64*, 291–303.

Krugman, P. (1998). Open letter to Mr. Mahathir. *Fortune*, September 28.

Krugman, P. (2009). *The Return of Depression Economics and the Crisis of 2008*. New York: W. W. Norton & Company.

Krugman, P. (2010a). Building a green economy. *The New York Times Magazine*, April 7. Retrieved October 29, 2013, from http://www.nytimes.com/2010/04/11/magazine/11Economy-t.html.

Krugman, P. (2010b). Lands of ice and ire. *The Conscience of a Liberal*. Retrieved September 19, 2011, from http://krugman.blogs.nytimes.com/2010/11/24/lands-of-ice-and-ire/.

Krugman, P. (2010c). Multidimensional Europe. *The Conscience of a Liberal*. Retrieved February 2, 2011, from http://krugman.blogs.nytimes.com/2011/01/26/multidimensional-europe/.

Krugman, P. (2011). Everyone has an ideology. *The Conscience of a Liberal*. Retrieved July 29, 2011, from http://krugman.blogs.nytimes.com/2011/04/13/everyone-has-an-ideology/.

Krugman, P. (2012a). Bond vigilantes and the power of three. *The Conscience of a Liberal*. Retrieved May 20, 2013, from http://krugman.blogs.nytimes.com/2012/12/24/bond-vigilantes-and-the-power-of-three/.

Krugman, P. (2012b). The simple analytics of invisible bond vigilantes. *The Conscience of a Liberal*. Retrieved May 20, 2013, from http://krugman.blogs.nytimes.com/2012/11/09/the-simple-analytics-of-invisible-bond-vigilantes-wonkish/.

Kruse, D., Freeman, R., & Blasi, J. (Eds.). (2010). *Shared Capitalism at Work: Employee Ownership, Profit and Gain Sharing, and Broad-Based Stock Options*. Chicago: The University of Chicago Press.

La Porta, R., Lopez-de-Silanes, F., & Shleifer, A. (2002). Government ownership of banks. *The Journal of Finance, 57*(1), 265–301.

Lafuente, J. L., & Freundlich, F. (2012). The Mondragon Cooperative experience: Humanity at work. Retrieved March 13, 2013, from http://www.managementexchange.com/story/mondragon-cooperative-experience-humanity-work.

Lange, O., & Taylor, F. (1938). *On the Economic Theory of Socialism*. Minneapolis: The University of Minnesota Press.

Latendresse, A. (2005). The Case of Porto Alegre: The Participatory Budget. In D. Roussopoulos & C. G. Benello (Eds.), *Participatory Democracy: Prospects for Democratizing Democracy* (pp. 287–91). Montreal: Black Rose Books.

Layard, R. (2005). *Happiness: Lessons from a New Science*. London: Allen Lane.

Le Fort, G., & Budnevich, C. (1997). Capital account regulations and macroeconomic policy: Two Latin American experiences. *International Monetary and Financial Issues for the 1990s, 8*, 37–58.

Lenin, V. I. ([1917] 1964). The Dual Power (I. Bernard, Trans.). *Lenin Collected Works* (Vol. 24, pp. 38–41). Moscow: Progress Publishers.

Lerner, A. P. (1972). The economics and politics of consumer sovereignty. *The American Economic Review, 62*(1/2), 258–66.

Levin, H. M. (1983). Raising Employment and Productivity with Producer Co-operatives. In P. Streeten & H. Maier (Eds.), *Human Resources, Employment and Development*. Volume 2: *Concepts, Measurement and Long-Run Perspective* (pp. 310–28). London: Macmillan.

Lewis, G., & Sloggett, A. (1998). Suicide, deprivation, and unemployment: Record linkage study. *BMJ, 317*(7168), 1283.

Lindblom, C. (1977). *Politics and Markets: The World's Political Economic Systems*. New York: Basic Books.

Lindblom, C. (1982). The market as prison. *Journal of Politics, 44*(2), 324–36.

Lindblom, C. (2001). *The Market System*. New Haven, CT: Yale University Press.

Lindert, P. (1996). What limits social spending? *Explorations in Economic History, 33*, 1–34.

Lipietz, A. (1988). The Limits of Bank Nationalization in France. In L. Harris, J. Coakley, M. Croasdale. & T. Evans (Eds.), *New Perspectives on the Financial System* (pp. 389–402). London: Croom Helm.

Lister, R. (2009). A Nordic nirvana? Gender, citizenship, and social justice in the Nordic welfare states. *Social Politics: International Studies in Gender, State & Society, 16*(2), 242–78.

Locke, J. ([1689] 1980). *Second Treatise of Government*. Indianapolis: Hackett Publishing.

Loretz, S. (2008). Corporate taxation in the OECD in a wider context. *Oxford Review of Economic Policy, 24*(4), 639–60.

Lukes, S. (1985). *Marxism and Morality*. Oxford: Clarendon Press.

Lukes, S. (2005). *Power: A Radical View* (2nd ed.). Basingstoke: Palgrave Macmillan.

Luxemburg, R. ([1900] 1986). *Reform or Revolution*. London: Militant Publications.

Luzarraga, J. M., & Irizar, I. (2012). La Estrategia de Multilocalización Internacional de la Corporación Mondragon. *Ekonomiaz: Revista vasca de economía*, (79), 114–45.

Ma, G., & McCauley, R. (2008). Efficacy of China's capital controls: Evidence from price and flow data. *Pacific Economic Review*, *13*(1), 104–23.

MacLeod, G., & Reed, D. (2009). Mondragon's Response to the Challenges of Globalization: A Multi-Localization Strategy. In D. Reed & J. J. McMurtry (Eds.), *Co-operatives in a Global Economy: The Challenges of Co-operation across Borders* (pp. 111–40). Newcastle upon Tyne: Cambridge Scholars Publishing.

Macpherson, C. B. (1977). *The Life and Times of Liberal Democracy*. Oxford: Oxford University Press.

Magud, N., & Reinhart, C. (2006). Capital controls: An evaluation. *NBER Working Papers* (11973). Retrieved November 9, 2013, from http://www.nber.org/papers/w11973.

Maietta, O. W., & Sena, V. (2008). Is competition really bad news for cooperatives? Some empirical evidence for Italian producers' cooperatives. *Journal of Productivity Analysis*, *29*(3), 221–33.

Maitland, I. (1989). Rights in the workplace: A Nozickian argument. *Journal of Business Ethics*, *8*(12), 951–54.

Malakoff, D. (2010). Taking the sting out of acid rain. *Science*, *330*(6006), 910–11.

Malleson, T. (2010). Cooperatives and the "Bolivarian Revolution" in Venezuela. *Affinities: A Journal of Radical Theory, Culture, and Action*, *4*(1).

Malleson, T. (2013a). Making the case for workplace democracy: Exit and voice as mechanisms of freedom in social life. *Polity*, *45*(4).

Malleson, T. (2013b). What does Mondragon teach us about workplace democracy? *Advances in the Economic Analysis of Participatory and Labor-Managed Firms*, *13*.

Mandel, E. (1975). Self-management: Dangers and possibilities. *International*, *2*(3), 3–9.

Mandel, E. (1986). In defence of socialist planning. *New Left Review*, *159*, 5–38.

Mansbridge, J. (1980). *Beyond Adversary Democracy*. New York: Basic Books.

Marmot, M. G., Shipley, M. J., & Rose, G. (1984). Inequalities in death—specific explanations of a general pattern? *The Lancet*, *323*(8384), 1003–6.

Marshall, P. (2010). *Demanding the Impossible: A History of Anarchism*. Oakland, CA: PM Press.

Martin, C. J., & Thelen, K. (2007). The state and coordinated capitalism: Contributions of the public sector to social solidarity in postindustrial societies. *World Politics*, *60*(1), 1–36.

Marx, K. (1873). Afterword to the Second German Edition of Capital (Vol. 1). Retrieved October 30, 2013, from http://www.marxists.org/archive/marx/works/1867-c1/p3.htm.

Marx, K. ([1844] 1978). Economic and Philosophic Manuscripts. In R. C. Tucker (Ed.), *The Marx-Engels Reader* (pp. 66–125). London: W. W. Norton & Company.

Marx, K. ([1850] 1978). Address to the Central Committee of the Communist League. In R. C. Tucker (Ed.), *The Marx-Engels Reader* (pp. 501–11). London: W. W. Norton & Company.

Marx, K. ([1867] 1933). *Capital* (E. & C. Paul, Trans.). London: Dent.

Marx, K. ([1871] 1968). *The Civil War in France*. In P. Publishers (Ed.), *Karl Marx and Frederick Engels: Selected Works* (pp. 271–309). London: Lawrence & Wishart Ltd.

Marx, K., & Engels, F. ([1845] 1960). *The German Ideology*. New York: International Publishers.

Marx, K., & Engels, F. ([1848] 1968). *The Communist Manifesto*. Harmondsworth, England: Penguin Books.

Mason, R. (1982). *Participatory and Workplace Democracy*. Carbondale: Southern Illinois University Press.

Mayer, R. (2001). Robert Dahl and the right to workplace democracy. *The Review of Politics, 63*(2), 221–47.

McCain, R. A. (1977). On the optimal financial environment for worker cooperatives. *Journal of Economics, 37*(3/4), 355–84.

McKillop, D. (2005). Financial cooperatives: Structure, conduct and performance. *Annals of Public and Cooperative Economics, 76*(3), 301–5.

McNally, D. (1993). *Against the Market: Political Economy, Market Socialism and the Marxist Critique*. London: Verso.

McNally, D. (2002). *Another World Is Possible: Globalization and Anti-capitalism*. Winnipeg: Arbeiter Ring Publishing.

McNally, D. (2011). *Global Slump: The Economics and Politics of Crisis and Resistance*. Oakland, CA: PM Press.

Meidner, R. (1978). *Employee Investment Funds: An Approach to Collective Capital Formation*. London: G. Allen & Unwin.

Mellor, M., Hannah, J., & Stirling, J. (1988). *Worker Cooperatives in Theory and Practice*. Milton Keynes, England: Open University Press.

Melman, S. (2001). *After Capitalism: From Managerialism to Workplace Democracy*. New York: Alfred A. Knopf.

Menzani, T., & Zamagni, V. (2010). Cooperative networks in the Italian economy. *Enterprise and Society, 11*(1), 98.

Micco, A., & Panizza, U. (2005). Public banks in Latin America. Paper presented at the Public Banks in Latin America: Myths and Reality, Washington, DC. Retrieved November 9, 2013, from http://cdi.mecon.gov.ar/biblio/doc/bid/sp/490.pdf.

Michels, R. ([1911] 1962). *Political Parties: A Sociological Study of the Oligarchical Tendencies of Modern Democracy* (E. & C. Paul, Trans.). New York: Free Press.

Mill, J. (1821). *Government*. London: Encyclopedia Britannica.

Mill, J. S. ([1848] 1965). *Principles of Political Economy*. Toronto: University of Toronto Press.

Mill, J. S. (1998). On Liberty. In J. Gray (Ed.), *On Liberty and Other Essays* (pp. 1–128). Oxford: Oxford University Press.

Miller, D. (1989). *Market, State, and Community: Theoretical Foundations of Market Socialism*. Oxford: Clarendon Press.

Mitchell, P. R., & Schoeffel, J. (Eds.). (2002). *Understanding Power: The Indispensable Chomsky*. New York: New Press.

Mitchell, W., & Muysken, J. (2008). *Full Employment Abandoned: Shifting Sands and Policy Failures*. Cheltenham: Edward Elgar.

Moene, K. O., & Wallerstein, M. (2008). How Social Democracy Worked: Labor-Market Institutions. In D. Austen-Smith, J. A. Frieden, M. A. Golden, K. O. Moene, & A. Przeworski (Eds.), *Selected Works of Michael Wallerstein: The Political Economy of Inequality, Unions, and Social Democracy* (pp. 378–408). Cambridge: Cambridge University Press.

Mohanty, S. (2006). Comparing credit unions with commercial banks: implications for public policy. *Journal of Commercial Banking and Finance, 5*(2), 97–113.

Monbiot, G. (2006). *Heat*. Toronto: Doubleday Canada.

Mondragon. (2011). *2011 Annual Report*. Mondragon, Spain. Retrieved November 9, 2013, from http://www.mondragon-corporation.com/ENG/Economic-Data/Yearly-Report.aspx.

Morray, J. P. (1997). *Grand Disillusion: Francois Mitterrand and the French Left*. Westport, CT: Greenwood.

Morris, D. (1992). *The Mondragon System: Cooperation at Work*. Washington, DC: Institute for Local Self-Reliance.

Morrison, R. (1997). *We Build the Road as We Travel*. Warner, NH: Essential Book Publishers.

Moye, A. M. (1993). Mondragon: Adapting co-operative structures to meet the demands of a changing environment. *Economic and Industrial Democracy, 14*(2), 251–76.

Müller, A. G. (2007). The big challenges of Venezuelan cooperativism today. Retrieved April 13, 2013, from http://venezuelanalysis.com/analysis/2531.

Muller, N. Z., Mendelsohn, R., & Nordhaus, W. (2011). Environmental accounting for pollution in the United States economy. *The American Economic Review, 101*(5), 1649–75.

Mundell, R. (1963). Capital mobility and stabilization policy under fixed and flexible exchange rates. *Canadian Journal of Economics and Political Science, 29*(4), 475–85.

Mygind, N. (1987). Are self-managed firms efficient? The experience of Danish fully and partly self-managed firms. *Advances in the Economics of Participatory and Labor-Managed Firms, 2*, 243–323.

Nafziger, S., & Lindert, P. H. (2012). Russian inequality on the eve of revolution. *NBER Working Papers* (18383). Retrieved November 9, 2013, from http://www.nber.org/papers/w18383.

Napolitano, S., Schreifels, J., Stevens, G., Witt, M., LaCount, M., Forte, R., et al. (2007). The US acid rain program: Key insights from the design, operation, and assessment of a cap-and-trade program. *The Electricity Journal, 20*(7), 47–58.

Newell, R., Sanchirico, J., & Kerr, S. (2005). Fishing quota markets. *Journal of Environmental Economics and Management, 49*(3), 437–62.

Nove, A. (1987). Markets and socialism: Comment. *New Left Review, 161*, 98–104.

Nove, A. (1991). *The Economics of Feasible Socialism* (2nd ed.). London: Harper Collins.

Nozick, R. (1974). *Anarchy, State, and Utopia*. Oxford: Blackwell.

O'Neill, M. (2008). Three Rawlsian routes towards economic democracy. *Revue de Philosophie Economique, 8*(2), 29–55.

O'Neill, M., & Williamson, T. (Eds.). (2012). *Property-Owning Democracy: Rawls and Beyond*. Chichester, England: Wiley-Blackwell.

Oatley, T. (1999). How constraining is capital mobility? The partisan hypothesis in an open economy. *American Journal of Political Science, 43*(4), 1003–27.

OECD (2012a). Tax revenue trends, 1965–2011, in OECD, *Revenue Statistics 2012*, OECD Publishing. Retrieved November 9, 2013, from http://www.oecd-ilibrary.org/taxation/revenue-statistics_19963726.

OECD. (2012b). Total tax revenue. Taxation: Key Tables from OECD, Retrieved October 28, 2013 from http://www.oecd-ilibrary.org/taxation/total-tax-revenue-2012_taxrev-table-2012-1-en.

Ostry, J., Ghosh, A., Habermeier, K., Chamon, M., Qureshi, M., & Reinhardt, D. (2010). *Capital Inflows: The Role of Controls*, IMF Staff Position Note: SPN/10/04. Washington, DC, International Monetary Fund.

Overesch, M., & Rincke, J. (2011). What drives corporate tax rates down? A reassessment of globalization, tax competition, and dynamic adjustment to shocks. *The Scandinavian Journal of Economics*, *113*(3), 579–602.

Palley, T. (2009). Rethinking the economics of capital mobility and capital controls. *Brazilian Journal of Political Economy*, *29*(3), 15–34.

Palme, J. (2006). Income distribution in Sweden. *The Japanese Journal of Social Security Policy*, *5*(1), 16–26.

Pannekoek, A. ([1936] 1970). *Workers' Councils*. Cambridge, MA: Root & Branch.

Parker, D. (2005). Chàvez and the search for an alternative to neoliberalism. *Latin American Perspectives*, *32*(141), 39–50.

Pateman, C. (1970). *Participation and Democratic Theory*. Cambridge: Cambridge University Press.

Pearson, T. (2009). Venezuela's reformed communal council law: when laws aren't just for lawyers and power is public. Retrieved October 30, 2013, from http://venezuelanalysis.com/analysis/4980.

Pencavel, J., & Craig, B. (1994). The empirical performance of orthodox models of the firm: Conventional firms and worker cooperatives. *Journal of Political Economy* *102*(4), 718–44.

Pencavel, J., Pistaferri, L., & Schivardi, F. (2006). Wages, employment, and capital in capitalist and worker-owned firms. IZA Discussion Paper (2188). Retrieved November 9, 2013, from http://papers.ssrn.com/sol3/papers.cfm?abstract_id=919920.

Persky, J. (1993). Retrospectives: Consumer sovereignty. *The Journal of Economic Perspectives*, *7*(1), 183–91.

Pettit, P. (1997). *Republicanism: A Theory of Freedom and Government*. Oxford: Clarendon.

Philpott, D. (2009). Sovereignty. *Stanford Encyclopedia of Philosophy*, Winter Edition. Retrieved October 30, 2013, from http://plato.stanford.edu/archives/win2009/entries/sovereignty.

Pierson, C. (1992). Democracy, markets and capital: Are there necessary economic limits to democracy? *Political Studies*, *40*, 83–98.

Pierson, P. (1996). The new politics of the welfare state. *World Politics*, *48*(2), 143–79.

Pigou, A. C. ([1920] 1960). *The Economics of Welfare*. London: Macmillan.

Piñeiro, C. (2005). The new cooperative movement in Venezuela's Bolivarian process. Retrieved October 30, 2013, from http://www.venezuelanalysis.com/analysis/1531.

Piñeiro, C. (2007). Workplace democracy and collective consciousness. *Monthly Review*, *59*(6), 27–40.

Piñeiro, C. (2009). Main challenges for cooperatives in Venezuela. *Critical Sociology*, *35*(6), 841–62.

Plumper, T., & Troeger, V. E. (2009). Why is there no race to the bottom in capital taxation? *International Studies Quarterly*, *53*(3), 761–86.

Polanyi, K. ([1944] 2001). *The Great Transformation*. Boston: Beacon Press.

Polletta, F. (2002). *Freedom Is an Endless Meeting: Democracy in American Social Movements*. Chicago: University of Chicago Press.

Pollin, R. (1995). Financial structures and egalitarian economic policy. Political Economy Research Institute (182), 26–61.

Pontusson, J. (1987). Radicalization and retreat in Swedish social democracy. *New Left Review*, *165*(9), 5–33.

Pontusson, J. (1992). *The Limits of Social Democracy: Investment Politics in Sweden*. Ithaca, NY: Cornell University Press.

Pontusson, J. (2005). *Inequality and Prosperity: Social Europe vs. Liberal America*. Ithaca, NY: Cornell University Press.

Pontusson, J. (2011). Once Again a Model: Nordic Social Democracy in a Globalized World. In J. Cronin, G. Ross, & J. Shoch (Eds.), *What's Left of the Left: Democrats and Social Democrats in Challenging Times* (pp. 89–115). Durham, NC: Duke University Press.

Pontusson, J., & Kuruvilla, S. (1992). Swedish wage-earner funds: An experiment in economic democracy. *Industrial and Labor Relations Review*, *45*(4), 779–91.

Popik, B. (2010). The Big Apple: "The only useful thing banks have invented in the last 20 years is the ATM." *The Big Apple*. Retrieved May 20, 2013, from http://www.barrypopik.com/index.php/new_york_city/entry/the_only_useful_thing_banks_have_invented_in_the_last_20_years_is_the_atm/.

Porter, B. (2010). World Bank says Asia may need capital controls to curb bubbles. Retrieved October 30, 2013, from http://www.bloomberg.com/news/2010-11-08/world-bank-says-asia-may-need-capital-controls-to-curb-fed-created-bubbles.html.

Prasad, E. S., Rogoff, K., Wei, S.-J., & Kose, M. A. (2003). *Effects of Financial Globalization on Developing Countries: Some Empirical Evidence* (Vol. 220). Washington, DC: International Monetary Fund.

Pred, A. (2000). *Even in Sweden: Racisms, Racialized Spaces, and the Popular Geographical Imagination*. Berkeley and Los Angeles: University of California Press.

Proudhon, P.-J. ([1847] 1888). *System of Economical Contradictions: Or, The Philosophy of Misery* (B. R. Tucker, Trans.). Boston: Benj. R. Tucker.

Przeworski, A. (1985). *Capitalism and Social Democracy*. Cambridge: Cambridge University Press.

Przeworski, A., & Wallerstein, M. (1988). Structural dependence of the state on capital. *The American Political Science Review*, *82*(1), 11–29.

Purden, C. (1980). *Agents for Change: Credit Unions in Saskatchewan*. Saskatoon: Credit Union Central.

Putnam, R. D., Leonardi, R., & Nanetti, R. Y. (1993). *Making Democracy Work: Civic Traditions in Modern Italy*. Princeton, NJ: Princeton University Press.

Quiggin, J. (2010). *Zombie Economics: How Dead Ideas Still Walk among Us*. Princeton, NJ: Princeton University Press.

Randoy, T., & Nielsen, J. (2002). Company performance, corporate governance, and CEO compensation in Norway and Sweden. *Journal of Management and Governance*, *6*, 57–81.

Rappaport, L., Lucchetti, A., & Grocer, S. (2010). Wall Street pay: A record $144 billion. Retrieved December 12, 2010, from http://online.wsj.com/article/SB1000142405274 8704518104575546542463746562.html.

Rawls, J. (1971). *A Theory of Justice*. Cambridge, MA: Harvard University Press.

Rawls, J. (1999). *A Theory of Justice: Revised Edition*. Cambridge, MA: Harvard University Press.

Rawls, J. (2001). *Justice as Fairness: A Restatement*. Cambridge, MA: Harvard University Press.

Reinhart, C. M., & Rogoff, K. S. (2009). *This Time Is Different: Eight Centuries of Financial Folly*. Princeton, NJ: Princeton University Press.

Reiss, H. (Ed.). (1970). *Kant's Political Writings*. Cambridge: Cambridge University Press.

Restakis, J. (2010). *Humanizing the Economy: Co-Operatives in the Age of Capital*. Gabriola Island, Canada New Society Publishers.

Richards, V. (Ed.). (1965). *Errico Malatesta: His Life and Ideas*. London: Freedom Press.

Rocker, R. ([1938] 1988). *Anarchism and Anarcho-Syndicalism*. London: Freedom Press.

Rodrik, D. (1997). *Has Globalization Gone Too Far?* Washington, DC: Institute for International Economics.

Rodrik, D. (1998). Who needs capital-account convertibility? Retrieved November 9, 2013, from http://www.hks.harvard.edu/fs/drodrik/Research%20papers/essay.PDF.

Roemer, J. (1994). *A Future for Socialism*. Cambridge, MA: Harvard University Press.

Rogers, S. (2011). Occupy protests around the world: Full list visualized. Retrieved February 20, 2012, from http://www.guardian.co.uk/news/datablog/2011/oct/17/occupy-protests-world-list-map.

Romer, C. D. (2011). What Do we know about the effects of fiscal policy? Separating evidence from ideology. Speech at Hamilton College. Retrieved November 9, 2013, from http://preview.hamilton.edu/documents/Romer%20lecture%20notes.pdf.

Rorty, R. (2006). Is philosophy relevant to applied ethics? Invited address to the Society of Business Ethics annual meeting, August 2005. *Business Ethics Quarterly*, *16*(3), 369–80.

Rosenblum, N. (1998). *Membership and Morals*. Princeton, NJ: Princeton University Press.

Rothbard, M. (1982). *The Ethics of Liberty*. Atlantic Highlands, NJ: Humanities Press.

Rothschild, J., & Whitt, J. A. (1986). *The Cooperative Workplace*. Cambridge: Cambridge University Press.

Rousseau, J.-J. ([1762] 1987). On the Social Contract (D. A. Cress, Trans.). In P. Gay (Ed.), *The Basic Political Writings of Jean-Jacques Rousseau* (pp. 141–227). Indianapolis: Hackett.

Sabatini, F., Modena, F., & Tortia, E. (2012). Do Cooperative Enterprises Create Social Trust? MPRA Paper (39814). Retrieved November 9, 2013, from http://mpra.ub.uni-muenchen.de/39814/1/Paper_Coop_and_trust-Full_manuscript_120703.pdf.

Sachs, J., Wyplosz, C., Buiter, W., Fels, G., & Menil, G. D. (1986). The economic consequences of President Mitterrand. *Economic Policy*, *1*(2), 262–322.

Samuelson, P. A., & Nordhaus, W. D. ([1948] 1992). *Economics* (14th ed.). New York: McGraw-Hill.

Sandel, M. (1997). It's immoral to buy the right to pollute. *New York Times*, December 17.

Sandel, M. (1998). *Liberalism and the Limits of Justice* (2nd ed.). Cambridge: Cambridge University Press.

Sapienza, P. (2004). The effects of government ownership on bank lending. *Journal of Financial Economics, 72*(2), 357–84.

Sassoon, D. (1996). *One Hundred Years of Socialism*. London: I. B. Tauris Publishers.

Sauter, S. L., Hurrell, J. J. J., & Cooper, C. L. (1989). *Job Control and Worker Health*. Chichester, England: John Wiley & Sons Inc.

SBA. (2010). *The Small Business Economy: A Report to the President*. Washington, DC: U.S. Small Business Administration, Office of Advocacy.

Scharpf, F. W. (1991). *Crisis and Choice in European Social Democracy*. Ithaca, NY: Cornell University Press.

Scheidel, W., & Friesen, S. J. (2009). The size of the economy and the distribution of income in the Roman Empire. *The Journal of Roman Studies, 99*, 61–91.

Schoening, J. (2010). The rise and fall of Burley Design Cooperative. *Oregon Historical Quarterly, 11*(3), 1–19.

Schor, J. B. (1991). *The Overworked American*. New York: Basic Books.

Schreiner, M. (2002). Aspects of outreach: A framework for discussion of the social benefits of microfinance. *Journal of International Development, 14*(5), 591–603.

Schumpeter, J. ([1942] 1987). *Capitalism, Socialism, and Democracy* (3rd ed.). London: Unwin.

Schwartz, J. (2012). Where did Mill go wrong? Why the capital-managed rather than the labor-managed enterprise is the predominant organizational form in market economies. *Ohio State Law Journal, 73*(2), 219–85.

Schweickart, D. (1996). *Against Capitalism*. Boulder, CO: Westview Press.

Schweickart, D. (2002). *After Capitalism*. Lanham, MD: Rowman & Littlefield.

Schweickart, D. (2011). *After Capitalism* (2nd ed.). Lanham, MD: Rowman & Littlefield.

Sease, D. R., & Mitchell, C. (1992). The vigilantes: World's bond buyers gain huge influence over U.S. financial plans. *Wall Street Journal*, November 6.

Sen, A. K. (1999). *Development as Freedom*. New York: Knopf.

Sen, A. K. (1961). On optimising the rate of saving. *The Economic Journal, 71*(283), 479–96.

Shaxson, N. (2011). *Treasure Islands: Tax Havens and the Men Who Stole the World*. London: The Bodley Head.

Sherman, H. J., Hunt, E. K., Nesiba, R. F., O'Hara, P. A., & Wiens-Tuers, B. (2008). *Economics: An Introduction to Traditional and Progressive Views* (7th ed.). Armonk, NY: M. E. Sharpe.

Shleifer, A. (1998). State versus private ownership. *The Journal of Economic Perspectives, 12*(4), 133–50.

Simon, H. A. (1951). A formal theory of the employment relationship. *Econometrica, 19*(3), 293–305.

Simon, W. H. (1993). The Prospects of Pension Fund Socialism. *Berkeley Journal of Employment and Labor Law, 14*, 251–274.

Singer, D. (1988). *Is Socialism Doomed? The Meaning of Mitterrand*. New York: Oxford University Press.

Singh, K. (2000). *Taming Global Finance: A Citizen's Guide*. London & New York: Zed Books.

Skinner, Q. (1998). *Liberty before Liberalism*. Cambridge: Cambridge University Press.

Smith, A. ([1776] 2006). *An Inquiry into the Nature and Causes of the Wealth of Nations*. Cirenchester, England The Echo Library.

Smith, S. (2001). *Blooming Together or Wilting Alone? Network Externalities and Mondragon and La Lega Co-operative Networks*. Helsinki: World Institute for Development Economics Research.

Sobel, R. (1993). Occupational involvement to political participation: An exploratory analysis. *Political Behavior, 15*(4), 339–53.

Sorensen, A., & McLanahan, S. (1987). Married women's economic dependency, 1940–1980. *American Journal of Sociology, 93*(3), 659–87.

Souza, C. (2001). Participatory budgeting in Brazilian cities: Limits and possibilities in building democratic institutions. *Environment and Urbanization, 13*(1), 159.

Stanford, J. (1999). *Paper Boom*. Ottawa: The Canadian Centre for Policy Alternatives.

Stavins, R. (1998). What can we learn from the grand policy experiment? Lessons from SO_2 allowance trading. *The Journal of Economic Perspectives, 12*(3), 69–88.

Stern, N. H. (2007). *The Economics of Climate Change: The Stern Review*. Cambridge: Cambridge University Press.

Stiglitz, J. (1993). Market Socialism and Neoclassical Economics. In P. Bardhan & J. Roemer (eds.), *Market Socialism* (pp. 21–41). New York: Oxford University Press.

Stiglitz, J. (1996). Some lessons from the East Asian Miracle. *The World Bank Research Observer, 11*(2), 151–77.

Stiglitz, J., & Uy, M. (1996). Financial markets, public policy, and the East Asian miracle. *The World Bank Research Observer, 11*(2), 249.

Stiglitz, J. (1998). Central banking in a democratic society. *De Economist, 146*(2), 199–26.

Stiglitz, J. (2002a). *Globalization and its Discontents*. London: Penguin.

Stiglitz, J. (2002b). Information and the change in the paradigm in economics. *The American Economic Review, 92*(3), 460–501.

Stiglitz, J. (2010). Government Failure vs. Market Failure: Principles of Regulation. In E. J. Balleisen & D. A. Moss (eds.), *Government and Markets: Toward a New Theory of Regulation* (pp. 13–51). Cambridge: Cambridge University Press.

Strauss, G. (2006). Worker participation—some under-considered issues. *Industrial Relations: A Journal of Economy and Society, 45*(4), 778–803.

Stryjan, Y. (1990). On ownership and membership. *Economic and Industrial Democracy, 11*(2), 217–47.

Svenjar, J. (1982). Codetermination and Productivity: Empirical Evidence from the Federal Republic of Germany. In D. C. Jones & J. Svenjar (Eds.), *Participator and Self-Managed Firms: Evaluating Economic Performance* (pp. 199–212). Lexington, MA: D. C. Heath.

Swank, D. (2002). *Global Capital, Political Institutions, and Policy Change in Developed Welfare States*. Cambridge: Cambridge University Press.

Tanzi, V., & Schuknecht, L. (2000). *Public Spending in the 20th Century: A Global Perspective*. Cambridge: Cambridge University Press.

Tawney, R. H. (1931). *Equality*. London: George Allen & Unwin Ltd.

Taylor, A. (Writer). (2005). Zizek! In L. Konner (Producer). Canada: Zeitgeist Films.

Taylor, M. P. (1999). Survival of the fittest? An analysis of self-employment duration in Britain. *The Economic Journal, 109*(454), 140–55.

Thomas, H., & Logan, C. (1982). *Mondragon: An Economic Analysis.* London: G. Allen & Unwin.

Thomas, R., Cryer, R., & Reed, N. (2008). "Straight from the horse's mouth": An empirical exploration of success in the Irish Credit Union Movement. *Journal of Social Welfare and Family Law, 30*(2), 107–16.

Thordarson, B. (1987). A comparison of worker-owned firms and conventionally owned firms in Sweden. *Advances in the Economics of Participatory and Self-Managed Firms, 2,* 225–42.

Tocqueville, A. de. ([1835] 1945). *Democracy in America.* New York: A. A. Knopf.

Tornarolli, L., Cruces, G., & Gasparini, L. (2011). Recent trends in income inequality in Latin America. *Economía, 11*(2), 147–90.

Treanor, J., & Wintour, P. (2012). Goldman Sachs enters £8bn "parallel pay universe". Retrieved February 2, 2012, from http://www.guardian.co.uk/business/2012/jan/18/goldman-sachs-pay-anger.

Ulrich, P. (2008). *Integrative Economic Ethics: Foundations of a Civilized Market Economy.* Cambridge: Cambridge University Press.

Unger, R. (2000). *Democracy Realized: The Progressive Alternative.* London: Verso.

Valdés-Prieto, S., & Soto, M. (1998). The effectiveness of capital controls: Theory and evidence from Chile. *Empirica, 25*(2), 133–64.

Van Parijs, P. (1995). *Real Freedom for All.* Oxford: Clarendon Press.

Vanek, J. (1970). *The General Theory of Labour-Managed Market Economies* Ithaca, NY: Cornell University Press.

Varman, R., & Chakrabarti, M. (2004). Contradictions of democracy in a workers' cooperative. *Organization Studies, 25*(2), 183–208.

Vieta, M. (2010). The social innovations of autogestion in Argentina's worker-recuperated enterprises. *Labor Studies Journal, 35*(3), 295.

Vincent, K. S. (1984). *Pierre-Joseph Proudhon and the Rise of French Republican Socialism.* Oxford: Oxford University Press.

Waldmann, R., & Smith, S. (1999). Investment and supply effects of industry-indexed bonds: The labor managed firm. *Economic Systems, 23*(3), 245.

Wallerstein, I. (1974). *The Modern World-System: Capitalist Agriculture and the Origins of the European World-Economy in the Sixteenth Century.* New York: Academic Press.

Wallerstein, M. (2008). Wage-Setting Institutions and Pay Inequality in Advanced Industrial Societies. In D. Austen-Smith, J. A. Frieden, M. A. Golden, K. O. Moene, & A. Przeworski (Eds.), *Selected Works of Michael Wallerstein: The Political Economy of Inequality, Unions, and Social Democracy* (pp. 250–84). Cambridge: Cambridge University Press.

Walzer, M. (1983). *Spheres of Justice.* New York: Basic Books.

Wampler, B. (2007). *Participatory Budgeting in Brazil.* University Park: The Pennsylvania State University Press.

Ward, B. (1958). The firm in Illyria: Market syndicalism. *American Economic Review, 48*(4), 566–89.

Ward, C. (1982). *Anarchy in Action* (2nd ed.). London: Freedom Press.

Ward, C. (2005). The Anarchist Contribution. In D. Roussopoulos & C. G. Benello (Eds.), *Participatory Democracy* (pp. 247–56). Montreal: Black Rose Books.

Warren, M. E. (2002). What can democratic participation mean today? *Political Theory, 30*(5), 677–701.

Watner, C. (2005). Quod omnes tangit: Consent theory in the radical libertarian tradition in the Middle Ages. *Journal of Libertarian Studies, 19*(2), 67–85.

Webb, S., & Webb, B. (1907). *The History of Trade Unionism*. London: Longmans, Green & Company.

Weber, M. ([1922] 1968). *Economy and Society*. London: Bedminster Press.

Weisbrot, M. (2010). Answer to the people, not greedy elites. *The Guardian*. Retrieved October 30, 2013, from http://www.guardian.co.uk/commentisfree/cifamerica/2010/feb/15/argentina-central-bank-independent.

Weisbrot, M., & Sandoval, L. (2007). The Venezuelan economy in the Chavez years. Washington, DC: Center for Economic and Policy Research. Retrieved November 9, 2013 from http://www.cepr.net/documents/publications/venezuela_2007_07.pdf.

Weisbrot, M., Ray, R., & Sandoval, L. (2009). The Chavez administration at 10 years: The economy and social indicators. Washington, DC: Center for Economic and Policy Research. Retrieved November 9, 2013, from http://www.cepr.net/documents/publications/venezuela-2009-02.pdf.

Weisskopf, T. E. (1993). A Demoratic Enterprise-Based Market Socialism. In P. K. Bardhan & J. E. Roemer (Eds.), *Market Socialism* (pp. 120–41). New York: Oxford University Press.

Western, B., & Beckett, K. (1999). How unregulated is the US labor market? The penal system as a labor market institution. *American Journal of Sociology, 104*(4), 1030–60.

Whelan, F. (1983). Prologue: Democratic Theory and the Boundary Problem. In J. R. Pennock & J. W. Chapman (Eds.), *Liberal Democracy*. New York: New York University Press.

Whyte, W. F., & Whyte, K. K. (1988). *Making Mondragon: The Growth and Dynamics of the Worker Cooperative Complex*. Ithaca, NY: ILR Press.

Wilde, O. (1891). The soul of man under socialism. Retrieved March 20, 2012, from http://www.marxists.org/reference/archive/wilde-oscar/soul-man/index.htm.

Wilkinson, R., & Pickett, K. (2010). *The Spirit Level: Why Equality Is Better for Everyone*. London: Penguin Books.

Wilpert, G. (2007). *Changing Venezuela by Taking Power*. London: Verso.

Winner, H. (2005). Has tax competition emerged in OECD countries? Evidence from panel data. *International Tax and Public Finance, 12*(5), 667–87.

WOCCU. (2010). International Credit Union System. Retrieved March 3, 2012, from http://www.woccu.org/memberserv/intlcusystem.

Wolff, E. (2010). Recent trends in household wealth in the United States: Rising debt and the middle-class squeeze—An update to 2007. *The Levy Economics Institute Working Paper Collection* (589), 1–58. Retrieved November 9, 2013, from http://www.econstor.eu/handle/10419/57025.

Wolff, R. P. (1977). *Understanding Rawls: A Reconstruction and Critique of a Theory of Justice*. Princeton, NJ: Princeton University Press.

Woller, G. (2006). Evaluating MFI's social performance: A measurement tool. *USAID microREPORT* (35). Retrieved November 9, 2013, from http://pdf.usaid.gov/pdf_docs/PDACG793.pdf.

Wood, E. M. (1999). *The Origin of Capitalism*. New York: Monthly Review Press.

Woodward, B. (1995). *The Agenda: Inside the Clinton White House*. New York: Simon & Schuster.

WorldPublicOpinion.Org. (2006). 20 nation poll finds strong global consensus: Support for free market system, but also more regulation of large companies. Retrieved May 5, 2011, from http://www.worldpublicopinion.org/pipa/articles/btglobalization-tradera/154.php?nid=&id=&pnt=154&lb=btgl.

The Worldwatch Institute. (2007). *State of the World 2007: Our Urban Future*. New York: W. W. Norton & Company.

Wright, E. O. (1997). *Class Counts: Comparative Studies in Class Analysis*. Cambridge: Cambridge University Press.

Wright, E. O. (2010). *Envisioning Real Utopias*. London: Verso.

Yeyati, E., Schmukler, S., & Van Horen, N. (2008). Crises, capital controls, and financial integration. *World Bank Policy Research Working Papers* (4770). Retrieved November 9, 2013, from http://papers.ssrn.com/sol3/papers.cfm?abstract_id=1297809.

Young, I. M. (1979). Self-determination as principle of justice. *The Philosophical Forum*, *11*(1), 30–46.

Zamagni, S., & Zamagni, V. (2010). *Cooperative Enterprise: Facing the Challenges of Globalization*. Cheltenham, England: Edward Elgar.

Zevi, A. (1982). The Performance of Italian Producer Cooperatives. In D. Jones & J. Svenjar (Eds.), *Participatory and Self-Managed Firms* (pp. 239–51). Lexington, MA: Lexington Books.

Zinn, H. (1996). *A People's History of the United States* (2nd ed.). New York: Longman.

Zipp, J. F., Luebke, P., & Landerman, R. (1984). The social bases of support for workplace democracy. *Sociological Perspectives*, *27*(4), 395–425.

Index

accountability, xii, xvi, 12, 139, 165, 183, 186, 204, 206, 230n7

Acid Rain Program, 114–115

Ackerman, Bruce, 213

Active Labor Market Policies, 119, 126, 202, 206

Albert, Michael, 101

Alchian, Armen, 28–29, 33

alienation, 16, 19

alimony, 38

Alinsky, Saul, 190

Allende, Salvador, 160

Alstott, Anne, 213

alternatives, xx, 213–215, 219n5

Ammirato, Piero, 66–67

anarchism, 19–23
  individualistic, 20
  social, 20–23
  vs. marxism, 20–21

Arando, Saioa, 73

Arge, R. C., 235n17

Aristotle, xi

Arizendiarrieta, José María, 56, 82

Arneson, Richard, 36

Aschauer, David Alan, 187

Asian crisis, 146, 171, 236n2

Auroux laws, 35

autogestion, 22, 35

Baiocchi, Gianpaolo, 190, 237n14, 238n17

Bakunin, Mikhail, 16, 20–21, 221n23

balanced job complexes, 40, 79

Baldacci, Emanuele, 230n4

banks, 126, 147–148, 178–179, 192, 235n19, 236n21, 237n7
  public, 147, 153–154, 178–181, 184, 196

See also Caja Laboral, central banks, Public Community Banks

Bardhan, Pranab, 239n2

Barham, Bradford, 182

Barry, Brian, 212

Bartlett, Will, 67, 228n26, 228n32

Basevi Law, 66

basic income. See guaranteed basic income

BDSM, 39

Beckett, Katherine, 121

Bellamy, Edward, 215

Benn, Tony, 35, 123

Bentham, Jeremy, 2, 12

Berle, Adolf, 27

Berlin, Isaiah, 13–14

Berlusconi, Silvio, 67

Bernstein, Eduard, 17

Beveridge, William, 7, 229n1

Blackburn, Robin, 238n24

Blasi, Joseph, 30

Block, Fred, 144, 236n21

Blumberg, Melvin, 79

bonds, 143–144, 147

bond vigilantes, 144, 234n11

Bonin, John, 74

Bookchin, Murray, 222n27, 238n1

Booth, Douglas, 78

Bowles, Samuel, 141, 229n38

Bradley, Keith, 60

Braverman, Harry, 229n35

Brazil, 59, 164, 173, 188–191, 196, 238n15

Brinton, Maurice, 17

Buchez, Phillipe, 28

Budnevich, Carlos, 175

Burdín, Gabriel, 73

Burgess, Robin, 181

Burley Cooperative, 74
business confidence, 159–160

Caja Laboral, 56–57, 62, 65, 153,
    183–184, 196–197, 202, 225n5
    See also Mondragon
Canada, 110, 112, 165, 230n7,
    234n4, 238n15
cap-and-trade, 113–116, 124–125, 231n2,
    231n4, 231n5, 232n15
capital
    controls, 140, 142–143, 145–147, 165,
        170–177, 206, 236n2, 237n5
    flight, 137–138, 144, 175, 195, 200
    intensity, 44
    mobility, 130–132, 233n19
    strike, 138, 161, 186, 193–195, 197
capitalist workplaces. *See* hierarchical
    workplaces
Carens, Joseph, 230n6, 239n2
Carville, James, 144
Castoriadis, Cornelius, 17
central banks, 104, 141, 143,
    165–166, 236n24
central planning, 18, 23
    See also state planning
CEO compensation, 51, 77, 126,
    178–179, 225n24, 227n17,
    228n31, 232n17
Chakrabarti, Manali, 229n33
Chang, Ha-Joon, 129,
Chavez, Hugo, 86, 138, 195, 200,
    233n1, 239n3
Cheney, George, 63, 229n33
child labor, 107, 231n14, 231n15
Chomsky, Noam, 20
citizen democracy, 93, 95, 98–103, 140,
    149–152, 158, 162–164, 167,
    186–189, 197, 201, 211
civic humanism, 13
civil liberties, xi
class, 16, 19, 145, 161–162, 201, 207,
    222n1, 225n4
classical liberalism. *See* neoliberalism
clientism, 238n14
Clinton, Bill, 234n10

clubs, 35–40
co-determination, 35, 85, 120,
    126, 224n15
    See also co-management
co-management, 44, 85, 239n5
    See also co-determination
Cohen, Josh, 163
Cole, G. D. H., 46, 123, 221n19, 222n27
collective action problem, 229n36
collective choice, 98, 100
communal councils, 200, 237n11,
    239n3, 237n11
Community Development Financial
    Institutions Fund, 185
Community Reinvestment Act, 235n16
consensus, 70
consortia, 66, 69, 87, 127
consumer democracy, 93–94, 96, 98–103,
    112–124, 133, 149–150, 162, 167,
    196, 201, 211, 230n7, 232n7
consumer sovereignty, 94
consumption tax, 238n22
contracts, 31–32
cooperatives
    consumer, 230n7
    social, 44, 233n18
    worker (*see* democratic workplaces)
cooperative bonds, 86
Cornforth, Chris, 82
corporations. *See* hierarchical workplaces
corporatism, 232n11
corruption, xvi, 156–157, 177, 178–181
credit default swaps, 192
credit freeze, 147
credit union, 181–184, 196, 237n8
cronyism, 177
Crotty, James, 19
crowding out, 187
Cuomo, Gaetano, 74
currency attack, 144, 234n12, 235n13.
    See also capital flight

Dahl, Robert, xxii, 7, 14, 28
daycare, 38
De Sousa Santos, Boaventura, 189
Dean, Andrés, 73

deficit spending, 142–144
democracy. *See* accountability, principle of affected interests, self-determination
democratic workplaces
  access to, 33–35, 39, 86–88, 196
  capital intensity of, 72, 85
  community relationship with, 62, 77–79, 228n32
  constraints on, 44, 80–81, 83–88
  definition of, 40–41
  degeneration of, 63–64, 74–76, 106–108, 125–126, 227n21
  desire for, 47–49
  discipline in, 55–56, 73
  education and training in, 82, 84, 86, 110, 226n8, 229n41
  efficiency or inefficiency of, in practice, 60–63, 67, 71, 72–76, 208, 227n16, 227n24, 228n29
  efficiency or inefficiency of, in theory, 55–56
  environmental impact of, 78, 88
  financing, 56–57, 65–67, 69, 84, 86, 110, 127, 183–184, 223n11, 224n18, 229n38
  fostering, 42–43, 196
  fraudulent, 88, 229n44
  global pressures on, 58–59, 62–64, 129, 227n19
  health impact of, 78, 88
  horizon problem of, 55, 74
  income equality or inequality in, 61, 68–69, 71, 77, 88, 119–120, 201, 227n17
  job satisfaction in, 62, 79–80
  job security in, 60–61, 63, 76–77, 88
  Marxist perspective on, 17–19, 62, 76, 106, 125, 225n4, 231n12
  membership requirements, 223n9
  monitoring in, 52, 58, 73, 75
  motivation, 71, 73
  networking in, 58, 65, 68–69, 86–87, 196
  participation in, 61–62, 69, 80–82
  potential for, 42
  prevalence of, 30

social councils in, 58, 63, 65
social democratic perspective on, 9–11, 44–46
state relation to, 39, 68–69, 75, 86, 227n25, 228n26
structure of, 57–58, 65–66, 69, 81–82, 84, 127, 223n11, 229n37, 226n10, 226n11
temporary workers in, 40, 51, 59, 200
trust in, 73
Demsetz, Harold, 28–29, 33
Denmark, 72, 85, 112, 117, 182
difference principle, the, 8–11, 14
Dinç, Serdar, 179
division of labor, 71
divorce, 37–38
Dornbusch, Rudiger, 237n5
Doucouliagos, Chris, 72
Dow, Gregory, 75–76
Dryzek, John, 172
dual power, 19, 221n21
Dutch disease, 173

ecology. *See* environment
economic growth, 106, 120
Edwards, Sebastian, 175
efficiency, 146, 155–156, 173–174, 208, 236n21
egalitarian collectives, 69–72, 83
Emilia Romagna, 76, 127–128
Engels, Friedrich, 15, 17
entrepreneurial problem, 83–84
environment, 98, 105–106, 113–116, 124–125, 207, 212
Environmental Protection Agency, 114–115
Epstein, Gerald, 19, 173, 236n2
equal opportunity, 212
Eroski, 59, 64
Esping-Andersen, Gøsta, 117
eurosclerosis, 121
Evergreen cooperative network, 225n2
exit vs. voice, 37–39
experts, 51–52, 81
expropriation, 51, 194–195, 225n23

externalities, 97, 99–100, 102, 113–116, 151–152, 165, 167, 189, 201, 207, 230n3

Fakhfakh, Fathi, 73
familiarity effect, 84
family, 37–38
feasible socialism, xxii, 198–217
feminism, 38, 49
feudalism, xv, 45, 50
finance, 139–158, 234n3
  neoliberal, 147–149
  private, 11–12, 102, 141–149
  social democratic, 149–153
financial crisis, 173
Fincooper, 66–67
Finland, 112
Firm. *See* democratic workplaces, egalitarian collectives, hierarchical workplaces
fiscal policy, 119, 143–144, 166, 177, 234n5, 234n9
Fleming, Marcus, 141
Fourier, Charles, 214–215
France, 35, 72, 74, 137–138, 161, 163, 185, 209, 224n14, 236n1, 240n13
free riding, 97
Freeman, Samuel, 15
Friedman, Milton, xix, 2–7, 33, 88, 108, 220n4
Friedman, Rose, 33
Fukuyama, Francis, 213
full employment, 119, 141–143, 165
Fung, Archon, 240n9
Furubotn, Eirik, 55

Garrett, Geoffrey, 130
Gates, Bill, xii
Gelb, Alan, 60
Gelderloos, Peter, 21
Genschel, Philipp, 130
Gini coefficient, 117, 126
Gintis, Herbert, 229n38
global justice, 209
global warming, 97, 114, 230n10, 232n6

globalization, 128–132, 227n19
Goldman Sachs, 148, 179
good life, the, 13–14, 40
Goodin, Robert, 240n9
Gordon, David, 141
Great Recession, 169, 171, 236n1
Greenberg, Edward, 79–80, 228n29
Greenhouse Development Rights framework, 116, 232n6
guaranteed basic income, 18, 42, 88, 202–203, 223n10, 239n7

Hahnel, Robin, 231n2
happiness, xvi, xxi, 35, 54, 212
Hayek, Friedrich, 2, 104
Held, David, 221n22
Henwood, Doug, 183
heteronomy, 41
hierarchical workplaces, 108–111
  education and training in, 110
  efficiency or inefficiency of, 52
  financing, 109
  freedom or unfreedom in, 6, 33
  power in, 31–33
  prevalence of, 30–31
hierarchy, xv, 41, 219n4
high performance workplaces, 31
hiring bias, 83, 87
Holmstrom, Mark, 82, 229n33
Hoxby, Blair, 101
Hulme, David, 180
Hunt, E. K., 235n17
Hutchison, Michael, 175

impossible trinity, 140
income inequality, 77, 96, 102, 126, 206, 212, 225n24, 232n17
Incremental Democratization Plan, 87, 195
India, 164, 171, 175, 180–181, 196
individual transferable quotas, 231n5
industrial democracy, 35
industrial policy, 165
inflation, 142, 234n6, 234n7
International Cooperative Alliance, 66, 227n23

International Monetary Fund, 171, 174, 176–177, 179, 189
investment, 139, 158–166, 234n3
  higher level, 164–166, 186–188
  local level, 163–164, 188–191
  long term, 97–98, 100, 173, 230n4
  private, 11–12, 102
  public, 102, 119, 150, 186–192, 194–197
  social democratic, 162
  strike, 138, 161, 186, 193–195, 197
Irizar, 59, 63, 82
iron law of oligarchy, xvi
Italy, 30, 44, 65–69, 72, 80, 127, 133, 182

Japan, 129, 170, 185, 227n16, 233nn21-22
job guarantee, 236n25
Johnson, Simon, 175, 179
Jones, Derek, 74, 227n24
Jossa, Bruno, 74, 156

Kahneman, Daniel, 225n24
Kaldor tax, 194, 238n22, 238n22
Kalecki, Michael, 141
Kant, Immanuel, 39
Kaplan, Ethan, 177, 237n5
Kasmir, Sharryn, 225n4
Kautsky, Karl, 15, 17
Keynes, John Maynard, 7, 142–143, 170, 172
Khwaja, Asim, 178
Kropotkin, Peter, 20
Krouse, Richard, 220n6
Krugman, Paul, 8, 129, 234n11
Kruse, Douglas, 30

La Porta, Rafael, 178
Laffer curve, 187–188
labor market, 29, 34, 123
Lange, Oskar, 239n2
Le Fort, Guillermo, 175
Le Guin, Ursula, 47
left liberalism. See social democracy
Lega Cooperatives, 65–69, 75, 77, 87
leisure, 207–208

Lenin, Vladimir Ilich Ulyanov, 15, 17
Levin, Henry M., 60
Liberal Market Economies, 112, 117–123, 126
liberal socialism. See market socialism
liberalism, 2–3, 7–15, 23, 220n2
  See also social democracy
libertarianism, 20, 145
limited liability, 109–110
Lindblom, Charles, xxii, 8, 11, 138, 160
Lindert, Peter, 187
living wage, 30, 107, 202, 222n2, 239n7
Locke, John, 2, 12
Logan, Chris, 60
Lukes, Steven, 15, 220n5

Ma, Guonan, 175
Mahathir, Mohamad, 236n4
Maietta, Ornella, 227n24
Maitland, Ian, 33
Malaysia, 175–177, 237n6
Malatesta, Errico, 20–21, 222n24
management clause, 31
Mandel, Ernest, 229n35
Mansbridge, Jane, xvi, 190, 222n27,
market socialism, 18, 153, 199–204, 239n2
market system, the, 103–104
market-state complex, 104, 108
markets
  and capitalism, 103
  and regulation, 107
  and the state, 104
  failures, 34, 95–98, 100, 148, 151, 153, 155, 165, 167, 201, 230n2, 235n17
  free, 103–104, 106, 240n13
  neoliberal views on, 3–5,
  scale of, 105–106, 124–125
  social democratic, 8–9, 101–103
  structure of, 64–65, 68, 104, 106–108, 125–128, 209
  varieties of, 103–105, 231n2
  Walrasian, 6
Marmot, Michael, 78
marriage, 37–39
Marx, Karl, xx, 15–16, 213, 215, 221n16

Marxism, 15–19, 106, 231n12
  anti-authoritarian, 17
  classical or orthodox, 17
materialism, 207
Mayer, Robert, 35
McCauley, Robert, 175
McPherson, Michael, 220n6
meaningful work, 34
Means, Gardiner, 27
Meidner Plan, 43, 87, 194–195, 200
Meidner, Rudolf, 123, 194
Mendelshohn, Robert, 230n3
methodology, xxii, 215
  See also radical realism, real utopias
Mian, Atif, 178
Micco, Alejandro, 180
Michels, Robert, xvi, 80
Mill, James, 2, 12
Mill, John Stuart, 15, 39, 211, 222n27
Miller, David, 239n2
Mises, Ludwig von, 93
Mitchell, Deborah, 130
Mitterrand, François, 137, 163
Mitton, Todd, 175
Mohanty, Sunil, 182
Mondragon, 10–11, 40, 46, 56–65, 75, 77,
  82, 86, 107–108, 184, 204
Mondragon Bookstore, 40, 79
monetary policy, 119, 141–143, 166, 173,
  177, 234n8
monopolies, 96–97, 99, 102, 113,
  167, 201
moral hazard, 147, 154, 178–179
moral incentives, 61, 71, 77, 188, 203
Morris, David, 227n16
Morrison, Roy, 77
Mosley, Paul, 180
Moye, A. M., 61
mules, 84, 86, 226n10
Muller, Nicholas, 230n3
Mundell, Robert, 141

National Investment Fund, 165, 201, 207
nationalization, 17, 44, 180, 195
neoliberalism, 2–7, 96–101, 103, 123,
  125, 143–149, 206, 208, 215

Netherlands, The, 182, 231n1, 232n10
Nordhaus, William, 230n3
Nordic countries, xxii, 5, 101–103, 112,
  117–123, 133, 187, 202, 206, 231n1,
  232n11, 232n14
Norway, 85, 102, 112, 120
Nove, Alec, xxii, 239n2
Nozick, Robert, 2
  See also libertarianism

Oatley, Thomas, 175
Occupy Wall Street protests, xvii, 28, 182
Okun, Arthur, 120
O'Neal, Stanley, 178
Ormaechea, José María, 60
Overesch, Michael, 130
Owen, Robert, 215

Palley, Thomas, 172, 175, 236n2
Pande, Rohini, 181
Panizza, Ugo, 180
Pannekoek, Anton, 17
paradox of investment dependence,
  160, 186
pareto optimality, 95
participation, 13–14, 61–62, 69, 80–82,
  190–191, 204, 228n27
participatory budgeting, 163–164,
  168, 188–191, 196, 201, 206,
  237nn12–16, 238n18
participatory democracy, 222n27
Partido dos Trabalhadores, 188
partnerships, 41, 60
Pateman, Carole, 28, 222n27
paternalism, 36
patriarchy, 37, 41, 219nn3–4
Pearson, Tamara, 237n11
Pejovich, Svetojar, 55
pension fund socialism, 238n20
pensions, xviii, 38, 117, 126, 140, 142,
  193, 236n1, 237n10
performance contract, 157
Pericles, 14
Pickett, Kate, 212
Pierson, Paul, 130
Pigou, Arthur, 113

Plato, 47, 52
plywood co-ops, 57, 65, 74, 79, 226n10
Polanyi, Karl, 103–104
political democracy, 11, 82, 207
Pontusson, Jonas, 120, 187, 193
poverty, 5, 116, 118, 124, 126, 142,
    151, 180–181, 196, 209, 213, 216,
    232n6, 240n12
power, xiv, 28–29, 31–33, 220n5
prefigurative politics, 221n21
primary goods, 8–10, 220n7
principle of affected interests, 205,
    239n9
prison, 121
private associations. *See* clubs
private property, 29, 126, 146, 195
private sphere, 35–40
privileged position of business, 11,
    159, 211
property rights, 31, 41, 49–51, 57, 65,
    226nn10–11
property-owning democracy, 15,
    212, 220n15
Proudhon, Pierre Joseph, 20, 239n2
Przeworski, Adam, 160, 200
Public Community Banks, 140, 150,
    154–158, 165, 168, 178, 183–185,
    195–197, 201–202, 206
public
  goods, 97, 100, 151, 189, 229n36
  sector, 43, 223n12, 224n14
  sphere, 37–40
  utilities, 147, 154
Putnam, Robert, 79
Putterman, Louis, 74

race to the bottom, 64, 77–78,
    128–130, 170
radical democracy, 16, 22
  See also anarchism
Radical Realism, xxii–xxiii
  See also Real Utopias
Rawls, John, 8–15, 35, 37, 151, 162, 167,
    207, 211–212
Reagan, Ronald, 117, 123
Real Utopias, 215, 223n10

redistribution, 51, 99, 102, 118, 160, 162,
    199, 216, 230n7
redlining, 148–149
regulation, 45–46, 64, 115, 150, 224n17
rent seeking, 101, 174–175, 179, 237n7
republicanism, 13
Rincke, Johannes, 130
Robin Hood tax, 193
Robinson, Joan, 225n1
Rocker, Rudolf, 20
Rodrik, Dani, 130, 174, 177, 237n5
Roemer, John, 239n2
Rogers, Joel, 163
Rorty, Richard, 213
Rothschild, Joyce, 70, 229n33
Rousseau, Jean-Jacques, 13–14,
    222n27, 230n5
rust belts, 152

Sabatini, Fabio, 79
Samuelson, Paul, 94
Schmidt, Helmut, 159
Schoening, Joel, 229n33
Schreiner, Mark, 236n22
Schumpeter, Joseph, 95, 149
Schweickart, David, 17, 150, 153–154,
    209, 235n18, 239n2, 239n6
self-determination, xii, xvi, xxi–xxii,
    12–14, 20, 31, 33, 40–42, 46–47, 49,
    51, 80–81, 88, 139, 154, 164–165,
    190, 192, 204, 206, 211, 216, 220n9,
    222n27, 224n17
self-employment, 31
Sen, Amartya, 230n5
Sena, Vania, 227n24
shared capitalism, 228n30
  See also worker participation
Smith, Adam, 2, 71, 94, 96
Smith, Stephen, 59, 74, 86
social capital, 79
social democracy, 7–15, 35, 211
  and the market, 8–9, 101–103
  limits to, 123–124 (*see also* citizen
    democracy)
  perspectives on workplaces,
    9–11, 44–46

social democracy (*Cont.*)
  perspectives on political
    democracy, 11–12
  compared to economic democracy, xxi,
    187, 204–210
  See also Nordic countries
Social Market Economies, 112,
    117–123, 231n1
social status, 30, 36, 38–39
socialism, 1, 16–17, 47
  anti-authoritarian, 17, 20-23 (*see also*
    anarchism)
  authoritarian, 17
  See also market socialism
socialist protectionism, 240n12
soft budgets, 157–158
South Africa, xi, 219n1
South Korea, 142, 170–171, 173, 233n2,
    235n14, 237nn5–6
sovereignty, 139, 143, 145, 164, 170,
    175, 178
Spain, 22, 56–65, 72–73, 226n12, 236n1
Spanish Civil War, 22
spillover thesis, 79
Stalin, Joseph, 17
state neutrality, 36, 39
state planning, 2, 17–18, 23, 97, 153,
    230n4, 235n18
Stiglitz, Joseph, 180
stock market, 75, 126, 139, 147, 185, 200
Students for a Democratic Society, 13
Sweden, 35, 44–45, 72, 85, 102, 112,
    118, 124–126, 170, 193, 202–203,
    224n16, 232n10

tariffs, 129–130, 196, 233n20,
    233n21, 240n12
Tawney, R. H., xvii
taxes, xvi, xxi–xxii, 4–5, 9, 18, 43,
    65–69, 75, 86–88, 99–106, 110,
    113–114, 117–119, 126–128, 130–
    132, 144–145, 151–154, 159, 167,
    172–173, 181, 187–188, 192–197,
    202–203, 206–208, 229n44, 231n2,
    233nn22–23, 233nn25–26, 237n8,
    238n19, 238n22

pigovian, 113, 151–152
Taylor, Fred, 239n2
Thatcher, Margaret, xix, 123
There Is No Alternative (TINA), xx
Thomas, Henk, 60
Tobin tax, 192–193, 238n19
Tocqueville, Alexis de, xii
trade-offs, xv, 24, 70–71, 96, 120, 141,
    146, 207–208, 215
transfer pricing, 233n22
transition, xviii–xix, 15, 86–88, 122–125,
    128, 131,133, 192–197, 199–200,
    210, 239n4
transition trough, 200
trilemma, 140
Trotsky, Leon, 17
Tucker, Benjamin, 20
tyranny of the eloquent, xvi, 190

unemployment, 30 , 120–122, 142
Unger, Roberto, 214
unions, 2, 4, 10, 31, 35, 42, 45–46, 58,
    69, 86, 104, 107–108, 118–119, 122–
    123, 126, 128–129, 159, 194, 222n3,
    232nn11–12, 238n23
utopia, xiii, xxii, 81, 208, 214–215
  See also Real Utopias
Uy, Marilou, 180

Van Parijs, Philipe, 223n10, 239n7
Vanek, Jaroslav, 225n1, 226n10
varieties of capitalism, 231n1
Varman, Rahul, 229n33
Venezuela, 49, 85–86, 138, 142, 161, 163,
    195, 199–200, 225n2, 229nn40–41,
    229n44, 233n1, 237n11, 239n3
voice, xxiii, 32, 34, 38, 48, 51, 86, 169
Volcker, Paul, 117, 236n20

Wall Street, 169
Walzer, Michael, 14, 28, 45
Wampler, Brian, 189–191
Ward, Benjamin, 55, 60
Ward, Colin, 52
Warren, Josiah, 20
Weber, Max, 80

Weisbrot, Mark, 233n1
Weisskopf, Thomas, 141
welfare systems, 8–9, 30, 117–118, 126, 132, 200, 232n10, 237n10
Western, Bruce, 121
Whelan, Frederick, 240n9
Whitt, J. A., 70, 229n33
Whyte, Kathleen King, 60
Whyte, William Foote, 60
Wilde, Oscar, xxii, 215
Wilkinson, Richard, 212
Woller, Gary, 236n22
Wong, Grace, 181
Wood, Ellen, 230n8, 231n12

Woodward, Bob, 234n10
workplaces. *See* egalitarian collectives, democratic workplaces, hierarchical workplaces
worker cooperatives. *See* democratic workplaces
worker participation, 30, 224n15
World Bank, 171
Wright, Erik Olin, xx, xxii, 18, 215, 222n1, 239n4

Zevi, Alberto, 73
Zinn, Howard, 214
Žižek, Slavoj, 214